Assessment of Culturally and Linguistically Diverse Students

THIRD EDITION

Socorro G. Herrera
Kansas State University

Robin Morales Cabral
Kansas State University

Kevin G. Murry
Kansas State University

Director and Publisher: Kevin M. Davis
Executive Portfolio Manager: Drew Bennett
Managing Content Producer: Megan Moffo
Content Producer (Team Lead): Faraz Sharique Ali
Content Producer: Deepali Malhotra
Portfolio Management Assistant: Michelle Hochberg
Executive Product Marketing Manager: Christopher Barry
Executive Field Marketing Manager: Krista Clark
Manufacturing Buyer: Deidra Skahill
Cover Design: Studio Montage
Cover Art: Rawpixel.com/Shutterstock
Editorial Production and Composition Services: Pearson CSC
Full-Service Project Management: Pearson CSC, Jean Acabal and Kabilan Selvakumar
Printer/Binder: LSC Communications / Willard DSC
Cover Printer: Phoenix Color
Text Font: Sabon LT Pro 10.25/12

Credits and acknowledgments borrowed from other sources and reproduced, with permission, in this textbook appear on appropriate page within text.

Library of Congress Cataloging-in-Publication Data

Names: Herrera, Socorro Guadalupe, author.
Title: Assessment of culturally and linguistically diverse students / Socorro
    G. Herrera, Kansas State University, Robin Morales Cabral, Kansas State
    University, Kevin G. Murry, Kansas State University.
Description: Third Edition. | New York : Pearson, [2020] | Includes
    bibliographical references and index.
Identifiers: LCCN 2018055570| ISBN 9780134800325 | ISBN 0-13-480032-X
Subjects: LCSH: Children of minorities--Education--United States--Evaluation.
    | Multicultural education--United States--Evaluation. | Linguistic
    minorities--Ability testing. | Educational tests and measurements. |
    Teachers--Training of--United States.
Classification: LCC LC3731 .H475 2019 | DDC 370.89--dc23 LC record available at
    https://lccn.loc.gov/2018055570

37 2023

Pearson

ISBN 10:   0-13-480032-X
ISBN 13: 978-0-13-480032-5

ABOUT THE AUTHORS

Dr. Socorro G. Herrera serves as Professor of Elementary Education at Kansas State University and directs the Center for Intercultural and Multilingual Advocacy (CIMA) in the College of Education. Certified in elementary education, bilingual education, and school counseling, Dr. Herrera's research focuses on literacy opportunities with culturally and linguistically diverse students, reading strategies, and teacher preparation for diversity in the classroom. She has authored several books including *Mastering ESL/EFL Methods: Differentiated Instruction for Culturally and Linguistically Diverse (CLD) Students* (2005, 2011, 2016), *Accelerating Literacy for Diverse Learners: Classroom Strategies That Integrate Social/Emotional Engagement and Academic Achievement, K–8* (2013, 2017), *Crossing the Vocabulary Bridge: Differentiated Strategies for Diverse Secondary Classrooms* (2011), *Biography-Driven Culturally Responsive Teaching* (2010, 2016), and *Teaching Reading to English Language Learners: Differentiated Literacies* (2010, 2015). Dr. Herrera has authored articles for numerous nationally known journals such as the *Bilingual Research Journal, Journal of Research in Education, Journal of Curriculum and Instruction, Journal of Latinos and Education,* and *Journal of Hispanic Higher Education.* In addition to her writing, Dr. Herrera conducts multistate and international professional development on issues of instruction and assessment with CLD students.

Dr. Robin Morales Cabral currently works as Instructor at the Center for Intercultural and Multilingual Advocacy (CIMA) in the College of Education at Kansas State University. She has a background in district-level administration, bilingual speech language pathology, special education (SPED), literacy, assessment, and intervention development for culturally and linguistically diverse (CLD) students. Dr. Cabral's research, teacher preparation efforts, and education consultant activities emphasize strengthening teacher, school, and district capacities to ensure CLD and SPED students' full access to an enriched core curriculum with appropriately individualized supports throughout their PreK–12 educational experiences.

Dr. Kevin G. Murry is Associate Professor of Curriculum and Instruction in the College of Education at Kansas State University and is Director of Research and Development for the Center for Intercultural and Multilingual Advocacy (CIMA). His scholarship has emphasized the professional development of K–16 teachers for the assets/needs of culturally and linguistically diverse (CLD) students. Dr. Murry's recent research and publications have emphasized teacher readiness for best practice with English learners, culturally responsive teaching and assessment practices, as well as the linguistic and cross-cultural dynamics of critically reflective and biography-driven teaching. In addition to his two textbooks in ESL/EFL, he has contributed book chapters for Erlbaum & Associates and Association of Teacher Educators (ATE)/Association for Childhood Education International (ACEI). His recent articles appear in the *Forum for International Research in Education, Journal of Curriculum and Instruction, Journal of Bilingual Education Research & Instruction,* and *Journal of Teaching and Learning.*

BRIEF CONTENTS

————■■■■■————

DETAILED CONTENTS

CHAPTER 3

Preinstructional Assessment: Re-Envisioning What Is Possible   47

CHAPTER 4

Assessment of Acculturation   76

CHAPTER **5**

CHAPTER **6**

CHAPTER 7

Data-Driven Problem-Solving Processes   215

CHAPTER 8

Special Education Issues in the Assessment of CLD Students   238

LETTER TO THE READER

Dear Reader,

We have been exceedingly fortunate to spend a great deal of time teaching in and collaborating with K-12 schools. There we are frequently reminded of the power that assessment has either to build the potential of the learner or to dehumanize and devalue what the learner brings to the classroom. Assessments are more than ever utilized to make program decisions about services to meet the needs of the learner. Often little attention is paid to the lens of assessment through which those needs are interpreted. Less attention is placed on what is happening in the classroom that might offer the teacher, instructional coach, administrator, and/or parent a more inclusive and balanced view of the learner's needs. Almost never are the student's inner strengths, from which he or she might build new skills and knowledge, the focus of truly authentic assessment.

As my colleagues and I have prepared the third edition of this text, we find that we are at a pivotal time to begin a new journey and re-envision how assessments are used to define the potential of the learner. We can choose to use what we learn from standardized assessments as a baseline for the programming and instruction that the learner will receive. However, we must proceed with caution, for the products of traditional assessments are merely point-in-time snapshots of the learner's growth to date. On the other hand, the best of assessments, as we embrace them, are dynamic processes that are best undertaken and maximized in real time. Decisions made solely on the outcomes of standardized assessments (often reviewed weeks or months after administration, and providing information gained through rather inauthentic means) too often become the longstanding basis for the labels that we pin on children and the ways that we circumscribe the possibilities for and the potential of each learner. Regrettably, this is especially and too often the case for our English learners.

As we approach assessment in today's schools, we encourage you—whatever your individual role in Education—to *begin with the learner*, not standardized assessments of that learner. Certainly, we all have many students, but we also have exceptionally powerful minds and hearts. It may take a few minutes with a student, it may take a few sessions over several days, it may take variety of communication avenues and/or student products to develop a more inclusive picture of this student and his or her unique voice. Yet, that more authentic, holistic, and humanistic understanding of the student is the location (the nexus) from which to reach, teach, bolster success, and celebrate with that learner.

Overwhelmingly quantitative, standardized, technocratic, and dehumanizing evaluation tools and methods have dominated Education for decades (many dating back to the incredible numbers of students generated by the baby boom and efforts to stratify that population). As a result, few regularly employed assessments first address what the learner already brings to the classroom. Today's student is much more likely to be viewed as "nontraditional," if we use a lens from the past. Many students speak a home language other than English, bring migrant or transnational experiences, and provide us with a glimpse into cultures that differ from our own. In short, the assumption of the so-called "standard" classroom or student population is no longer valid.

The increasingly diverse classrooms of today encompass a wealth of differential experiences, challenges, customs, survival skills, accomplishments, forms of knowledge, languages, cultures, and more that is rarely acknowledged, much less celebrated for its immense riches and used to advance learning. The single most important reason for this shortcoming is the body of unchallenged assumptions that we, as educators, have failed to reflect upon. Rather, we regularly embrace and act upon these assumptions in our perspectives and decisions regarding placement, programming, curricula, teaching, and assessment.

Consider, for example, the thousands of English learners who enter the educational system every year with incredible knowledge, experiences, and understandings. Yet our tendency in the United States is to operate from a *deficit perspective* that emphasizes not what the student already knows about language (an asset perspective) but what he or she doesn't know about the particularities of English. As a result, the student is typically assessed, in English, and often found lacking, rather than viewed as a gifted user of another language with the added benefit of some level of skill in English as a second (or third, or fourth, etc.) language. Accordingly, he or she often is taught English in very limiting ways – through curricula and instructional strategies that assume a *language deficit*. Not surprisingly, students in such scenarios frequently become further and further behind peers in the core content areas until they drop out, fail to graduate, or decide not to pursue their intended career goals.

As you read this text, we encourage you to do so with a mind *open to new ways* of thinking, assumption checking, teaching, and assessing. As a leap of faith toward operationalizing that perspective, if you currently teach or provide input on the teaching of a student, take time to write down the assumptions you have about him or her (don't worry, we all hold assumptions!). What assumptions do you have about the student's prior knowledge, experiences, skills, and capacities? As you read this book, find opportunities to talk to that student in ways that allow you to check the accuracy of your assumptions. Consider the multitude of questions you might have if the student knows a language other than English.

- Was the language learned communicatively, or did the student have formal instruction in it?
- How many years has the student used the language, and in what capacities?
- Is the language currently spoken at home? If so, by whom?
- Does the student know how structures in the language compare with those in English?
- In what ways has the student been encouraged to maximize cognates or other parallels between languages?

Based on your findings from such discussions, what assessments and tools might be most appropriate for this student, and for what purposes? In what ways might assessments be used to better inform her instruction and experiences with English language acquisition? This book will shed light on answers to such questions.

If you faithfully respond to our challenge, we believe that you will discover the merit and joy of a differential perspective on students, teaching, and assessment. Such experiences can illuminate the value of real-time, authentic and informal assessments to balance the assessment picture and inform instruction—not to stratify, but to ensure that all students are supported to achieve their full potential.

Best regards,

Socorro G. Herrera
Robin Morales Cabral
Kevin G. Murry

NEW TO THIS EDITION

It is with great excitement that we complete the third edition of *Assessment of Culturally and Linguistically Diverse Students*. Current policy and research in the field require us to pose questions about student learning and to document progress and achievement in systematic and creative ways. The new additions provide the reader with the most up-to-date research and strategies for effectively assessing culturally and linguistically diverse (CLD) students. Our focus in this new edition is on ensuring that readers have the necessary support to make theory-into-practice applications. We continue to highlight the CLD student biography and how it relates to decision making for assessment practices. At the same time, we have emphasized to an even greater extent how the theory and research that provides the foundation for best practices is brought to life within individual classrooms and through the collaborative efforts of teachers serving the unique students in their learning communities. Additional resources are provided to illustrate how teachers might develop activities and tools for both promoting and assessing CLD students' linguistic and academic growth.

New features specific to this completely revised edition include the following:

- Chapter 7 is a new chapter dedicated to data-driven problem-solving processes. Assessment and instruction with CLD students require educators to rethink assumptions about how assessment is used to inform practice. Educators are guided to use knowledge of students' biographies to gather assessment data, interpret assessment results, and support informed decisions about programming and student supports. Readers will benefit from this additional guidance on how to explore teaching and learning dynamics when CLD students struggle to succeed in their current learning settings.
- Teaching Tips provide readers with considerations for practice as they begin to formulate site-specific applications of key concepts.
- Activity Lesson Plans for easy-to-implement activities support readers to put conceptual learning into practice with K–12 students. Guidance regarding appropriate grade levels, materials needed, student behavior to observe, ways to differentiate instruction, and notes on timing of the activity during the school year are provided for each.
- Using assessment to inform instruction is a new focus of chapters dedicated to a specific type of assessment (Chapters 2–6). These chapter sections support readers to understand the practical implications of assessments and their results for daily instruction.
- New and updated research and features ensure readers have access to the latest being written and talked about in the education of CLD students. The updated features support readers' comprehension and retention of key concepts discussed.
- An expanded glossary provides an easy reference for definitions of all key concepts highlighted throughout chapters.

Through this third edition of *Assessment of Culturally and Linguistically Diverse Students*, we hope that educators across the nation will gain added confidence in their capacities to develop and use assessments that provide meaningful data, encourage student engagement, and ignite their passion for teaching and learning.

PREFACE

The trend toward increasing numbers of culturally and linguistically diverse (CLD) students in the classroom is not a new phenomenon. In border and coastal states such as Texas, California, New York, and Florida, this is a long-standing trend. What has changed is the intensity and scope of this trend, which now influences classroom, school, and district decision making and educational policy throughout the nation. This is not the first, nor is it likely to be the last, textbook to address assessment practices for diverse populations.

PURPOSE

If textbooks that address assessment practices for diverse students already exist, why is this text needed? Assessment texts have traditionally been organized around assessment types, practices, and protocols. However, we, the authors of this text, wanted the *student* to be the driving force behind the narrative and organization; therefore, we began with a critical examination of fundamental questions about appropriate assessment practices for CLD students.

This text is written from the perspective of a *differential lens on assessment* practices for CLD students. This perspective emphasizes the following fundamental questions:

- Who should be the focus of assessment?
- Where should assessment efforts be concentrated?
- What should be the key purposes of assessment?
- When should assessments be conducted?
- How are the findings of assessment best used to improve practices for, and academic achievement among, CLD students?

The discussions in this text are designed to guide PreK–12 classroom teachers as they successfully differentiate assessment practices for diverse student populations. However, essential to these conversations is an understanding that meeting the needs of students from diverse backgrounds requires a collaborative team effort. Reading and math specialists, special education teachers, school psychologists, and other educational specialists contribute valuable expertise and assessment data to decision making about these learners. The following

exploration explains how answers to the aforementioned questions have guided the design and organization of this text.

Who

The question of who should be the focus of assessment (and the content of this text) can be answered by recognizing the increasing numbers of students who bring to today's classroom a complex range of cross-cultural, language, and learning assets and needs. In many parts of the country, CLD student populations are radically changing from those whose needs were addressed years ago. Therefore, this text focuses on the assessment of CLD students. The changing nature of this student population, and the field's response in relation to teacher preparation and assessment practices, are the emphasis of discussion in Chapter 1.

Where

This text also assumes a differentiating approach to the question of where assessment efforts for CLD students should be concentrated. Traditionally, this question is answered according to either the range of (primarily formal) assessments available to school educators or assessment policy perspectives. Instead, this text aligns the emphases of assessment efforts with critical dimensions of the CLD student biography (Herrera & Murry, 2016). More specifically, this text devotes three chapters to core assessments that directly relate to the four critical dimensions of the CLD student biography: the sociocultural dimension (Chapter 4), the linguistic dimension (Chapter 5), and the cognitive and academic dimensions (Chapter 6). This alignment of assessments with the CLD student biography ensures that teachers and their instructional practices are better informed by data (Chapters 2–8) about each dimension of the student's life.

What

What should be the key purposes of assessments for CLD students? The purposes of classroom assessments for CLD students should first encompass the need to provide the classroom teacher with the critical information necessary to adapt and refine classroom instruction and related practices for increasingly diverse populations of students. If teachers are to prove successful with CLD students, they must determine more than what the student does not know. Today's teachers need to know what *assets* the CLD student brings to the learning environment.

Among such assets the CLD student may bring rich socialization experiences in another country or culture (Chapters 3 and 4); unexpected cross-cultural insights (Chapter 4); prior schooling, academic experiences, and cognitive skills (Chapters 3 and 6); strong first language knowledge and emergent capacities in a second language (Chapters 3 and 5); and real-world experiences that foster a diversity of perspective (Chapters 2). Thus, the purposes of assessments for CLD students are as much about informing teachers as they are related to the evaluation of learners.

When

The timing of appropriate classroom assessment practices for CLD students is the product of a teacher's reflection on student needs and assets, decisions about where to concentrate assessment efforts, and attention to the purposes of such assessments. Just as there are no recipes for successful instruction that work with all CLD student populations, there are few rules of timing for the implementation of assessments. Timing and sequence issues tend to vary according to types of assessments, including authentic versus standardized (Chapters 2–6), formative versus summative (Chapters 2 and 6), informal versus formal (Chapters 2–6), and norm-referenced versus criterion-referenced (Chapters 5 and 6).

Successful teachers reflect on their *informed* philosophies about appropriate assessment practices for CLD students (Chapters 2 and 3, as well as Chapters 7 and 8). Such teachers also collect and analyze data from formal and informal preassessments of students as well as ongoing assessments of growth (Chapters 3–8) to make decisions about which assessments and teaching practices are best for which purposes, given learners' individual needs.

How

Ultimately, reflective educators are concerned with the question of how the findings of assessments with CLD students are best used. From a best-practice perspective, assessment findings may be used for at least three critical purposes: student monitoring and motivation, instructional and assessment accommodations, and stakeholder reporting. Each of these purposes is addressed throughout the text in ways that are consistent with both the complexities of the CLD student biography and the teacher's challenges in differentiating assessment practices for increasingly diverse student populations.

1. *Student Monitoring and Motivation.* Valid and purposeful assessment findings may be used to:
   - Monitor student progress in level of acculturation, first and second language acquisition, and content-area learning (Chapters 4–8)
   - Identify and document incremental gains (Chapters 2–7)
   - Inform the provision of targeted interventions (Chapters 7 and 8)
   - Enhance student interest, engagement, and motivation (Chapters 1 and 2)
   - Enhance students' self-assessment and reflection on the quality and effectiveness of their learning efforts (Chapters 2 and 6)
2. *Instructional and Assessment Accommodations.* Valid and purposeful assessment findings may be used to:
   - Refine and improve future assessments (Chapters 2 and 7)
   - Adapt and tailor classroom instruction to accommodate CLD students' assets and needs (Chapters 2–8)
   - Inform the classroom teacher's personal understanding of CLD students' potential (Chapters 1–8)
   - Identify systemic adaptations or improvements to core instruction that increase CLD students' success (Chapter 7)
3. *Stakeholder Reporting.* Valid and purposeful assessment findings may be used to inform key stakeholders, including:
   - CLD students as self-monitoring learners (Chapters 2 and 6)
   - Parents, guardians, and family members of CLD students (Chapters 1, 2, 3, 7, and 8)
   - School and district administration (Chapters 2 and 7)
   - State or federal monitoring (or funding) agencies (Chapters 5, 6, and 8)

Recent educational reform initiatives have placed increased scrutiny on schools and school districts that educate CLD students. In some ways, the expectations of such measures, and the methods they recommend, fail to reflect the reality of today's increasingly diverse classrooms. In other ways, such measures remind us that the purposes of quality classroom assessment practices are numerous, multi-faceted, and sometimes intimidating. This text offers a way for educators to organize their perspectives and respond to these complexities as they seek to enhance their assessment practices with CLD students.

SPECIAL FEATURES

To enhance reader interest, accommodate different learning styles, and offer additional insights on topics covered, this text offers the following special features.

Chapter Outlines

By providing an outline near the beginning of each chapter, we have tried to afford our readers both an advance organizer and a fundamental understanding of the content of each chapter.

Chapter Learning Outcomes

It is our belief that learners should know the intended goals of a particular lesson (in this case, the chapter of the text) for them. Therefore, each chapter is introduced with a list of outcomes readers can expect to accomplish as a result of engaging with that chapter.

Key Concepts

This feature of the text is provided in all chapters and reminds the reader of the critical content discussed in that particular chapter. Related features at the end of each chapter, especially the Questions for Review and Reflection, help ensure that the reader's study of the chapter has emphasized these key theories and concepts.

Professional Conversations on Practice

This exceptional feature, included in every chapter, suggests topics for discussion and debate among pre- and in-service educators about critical issues that have been explored or detailed in the content of the associated chapter. The feature is designed to encourage critical thinking, reflection, articulation of new knowledge, and theory-into-practice applications.

Questions for Review and Reflection

This feature is part of each chapter of the book. The questions provide opportunities for self-assessment of content comprehension and readiness for applications to practice. The questions included in these features are applicable to educators at all levels, including preservice teachers, paraprofessionals, in-service teachers, staff specialists, and school administrators.

Text Boxes

Five types of text boxes are used throughout the text to reinforce, emphasize, or expand on chapter content.

- *Accommodative Assessment Practices.* These features offer the reader a glimpse of the bigger assessment picture and highlight ways in which key theories, concepts, and arguments from the narrative might be applied to professional practice with CLD students. These features are frequently structured as vignettes that identify and address assessment challenges related to the four dimensions of the student biography. They are provided in all textbook chapters except the introductory chapter.
- *Assessment Freeze Frame.* These enrichments offer the reader snapshots of key points from the chapter narrative. They are provided in every chapter.
- *Assessment in Action.* These features offer the reader detailed how-to information for adapting, refining, and developing accommodative assessments for CLD students. These features are provided in Chapters 2 through 6, which directly address types of assessments developed by PreK–12 classroom teachers.
- *Snapshot from Classroom Practice.* These teaching and learning enhancements offer the reader a greater level of detail surrounding theory-into-practice applications of key theories or concepts discussed. These features are provided in most textbook chapters.
- *Voices from the Field.* These features offer the reader an inside look at what practitioners from the field have to say about assessment for CLD students. They are provided in every chapter.

Figures and Tables

Every chapter of the text offers explanatory or illustrative figures or tables specifically designed to enhance the content of the chapter. Readers can capitalize on these features to understand more fully the concepts and research-based practices discussed in this book. These features also provide educators with quick-guide resources to easily reference key types of assessments used with CLD students.

Assessment Artifacts

Certain chapters also include Assessment Artifacts, which are special figures of interest to readers who already instruct or expect to teach CLD students. These figures are included in the core assessment chapters (Chapters 4, 5, and 6) of the text. The content of these chapters emphasizes differentiated assessments and practices for each of the four dimensions of the CLD student biography (discussed in Chapter 3), the sociocultural dimension (Chapter 4), the linguistic dimension (Chapter 5), and the cognitive and academic dimensions (Chapter 6). The feature also is included in Chapter 7, which guides readers to use data responsively to ensure that educational practices for CLD students are reflective of their needs and assets within each of these dimensions. Assessment artifacts are drawn from the actual field experiences of classroom teachers and typically highlight examples of assessments used with CLD students. Assessment artifacts are included to provide exemplars of teachers' creative resolutions of the many challenges involved in the development of equitable assessments for diverse student populations.

Appendices

The appendices provide teachers with Standards of Best Practice (Appendix A) as well as ready-to-use resources (Appendix B) for their assessment practices with CLD students.

- *Appendix A: Critical Standards Guiding Chapter Content.* As a model for professionalism in practice with diversity, this special addition aligns the content of all chapters of the text with the nationally recognized TESOL/CAEP standards (2010). The TESOL/CAEP teacher standards reflect professional consensus on standards for the quality teaching of P–12 CLD students. In addition, this feature provides teachers with a self-assessment framework as they progress through the text. Teachers can reflect on their own practices with CLD students and families, and determine the extent to which they meet each noted standard of professional practice. Thus, these features provide a road map to excellence as educators continually strive to improve their differentiated assessment practices with CLD students.
- *Appendix B: Resource List.* The resources in this section are drawn from chapter content that addresses the types of assessments developed by PreK–12 classroom teachers. It includes skills surveys as well as checklists and matrices/continua for classroom observation.

Glossary

This feature serves as an auxiliary resource for current readers and for applications of content to practice in the future. Particular attention has been given to key concepts from each chapter as well as those terms likely to seem unfamiliar to current and future educators who have had few educational experiences with CLD students.

References

Assembled in the American Psychological Association's bibliographic style, this feature documents the theory, research, and analyses that support the discussions, content, conclusions, and recommendations of the authors in *Assessment of Culturally and Linguistically Diverse Students*. The feature also serves as a resource for preservice and in-service educators of CLD students and those involved in teacher preparation.

ACKNOWLEDGMENTS

Assessment that does not highlight the accomplishments and further the potential of the student is like productive efficiency without a valuable product outcome. Similarly, the value of this text to the field and to the practitioners who find it useful will be a function of the accomplishments of those who contributed to it and who collaborated to maximize its potential. Therefore, the three of us wish to acknowledge the many contributions of others who have collaborated with us to make this text possible.

Pivotal to the rigor and quality of this edition have been the exceptional contributions of Melissa Holmes. Her academic perspectives, conscientiousness, and attention to detail are greatly appreciated. Her thoughtful contributions and expertise enhanced the purpose, content, organization, and authenticity of this new edition.

Shabina Kavimandan's contributions to this edition enriched the theory-into-practice, hands-on aspects of this edition. Her efforts were instrumental in bringing the theory to life, through her experience with what it means in schools to assess students' potential and value their growth. Her theoretical and practical perspectives and expertise have been pivotal and are appreciated.

We are grateful as well for the support of Joshua Snodgrass, Yifan Liao, and Graciela Berumen. The dedication and contributions of each of these individuals to support our literature review and development efforts were much appreciated.

We wish to acknowledge the significant people in our lives, Dawn Herrera Helphand, Kevin Herrera, Jesse and Isamari Davila, Esteban Cabral, and Dr. Nancy Kole, as well as our students, faculty, and staff, whose varied contributions from prior experience with (or as) CLD students in public schools and with diverse school practice have made this work possible. To these people, we each owe our heart and soul.

A number of classroom teachers who serve the differential learning and transition needs of CLD students have provided insights from their professional practices. These are greatly appreciated and have been included primarily in the Assessment Artifacts, Snapshot from Classroom Practice, and Voices from the Field features. The many experiences of these educators highlight the ways professional practice can effectively and mutually accommodate both the assets and needs of the CLD student.

Finally, we would like to thank the following reviewers for their comments on the manuscript: Yukari Amos, Central Washington University; Anthony Anderson, Nevada State College; Tatiana Cevallos, George Fox University; Lois Ann Knezek, University of North Texas; and Tatiana Sildus, Pittsburg State University.

CHAPTER 1

CLASSROOM ASSESSMENT AMIDST CULTURAL AND LINGUISTIC DIVERSITY

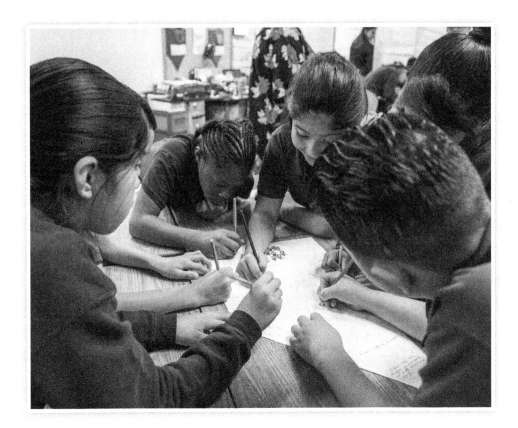

I have a student that has a very difficult time taking multiple-choice exams. But if I verbally give him the test, he has a much easier time completing the test. . . . I also have a student that is an incredible artist. I have asked her to take several vocabulary words and create pictures that portray these words, and I then ask her to explain the term and the picture. . . . If I fail to unveil [my students'] capabilities and strengths, then I am just . . . well, failing them, and shutting doors on a bright future. I do not want to be responsible for turning away from their right to a great education and having them leave my room feeling insignificant and discouraged. In concern for the ELL [English language learner or culturally and linguistically diverse (CLD)] student, my challenge is intensified!

Michael Berndt, Fourth Grade Teacher. Reprinted with permission.

Chapter Outline ■■■

Learning Outcomes ■■■

After reading this chapter, you should be able to:

- Explain the purpose of assessment from an asset-centered perspective.
- Detail U.S. trends in immigration and demographic changes that have an impact on families, communities, and schools.
- Explain challenges to teachers' readiness for student diversity.
- Hold informed conversations about ways educational reforms and related research have influenced shifts in thinking about assessment practices for CLD students.

■■■

LEARNING IS NATURAL

The focus of this text is on the assessment of learning in education. Specifically, it focuses on ways to authentically and accurately gauge the learning of culturally and linguistically diverse (CLD) students. Readers will find that the ideas presented in this text benefit every student, including those who may not perform well on formal tests as well as those who do.

Although exams and quizzes have long been part of school, the term "assessment" increasingly has become associated with large-scale, externally developed, technology-assisted products used to quantify student skills. The targeted skills are purported to reflect aspects of knowledge or capacities needed to be successful in school and society. The authors of this text agree that assessment is indeed essential to teaching and learning. We are less certain however that "universal," decontextualized skills are sufficient indicators of students' abilities to respond to, learn, and innovate within the rapidly changing world of *their* lives. How can we know what it is they will require?

To prepare students as learners, we first need to acknowledge learning as a natural human state. From the youngest child to individuals at each succeeding age and stage, we all observe, make connections, assess relevance, and adjust actions, knowledge, or skills to satisfy personal needs. These needs range from basic nutrition, safety, and shelter to the expansion of individual insight and creative endeavor. Prominent models of human need separate social/emotional and cognitive needs from those required for physical survival (e.g., Maslow, 1943, 1970); yet it is also important to consider how these types of needs intertwine. The achievement of basic needs frequently depends on social observations and interactions that start from day one.

Human beings are by nature *testers*, always probing and responding to their physical and emotional worlds. Babies notice and assess the feedback they get as a result of their babbled sounds or cries. Behaviors leading to satisfaction of needs (comfort, milk, smiles) are repeated. Adults may be equally new to such interactions, but they keep trying, adjusting, and learning what works, from their perspectives. Ongoing cycles of observation, (re)action, assessment, and adaptation ensue. The learning is reciprocal and at least somewhat generalizable to the next little or big person the individual meets.

We humans learn by interacting with our physical environment as well. Do babies crawl the same on carpeted floors as on steep, rocky terrain? Even with similar surface and opportunity, do all babies crawl at the same time, in the same way? Is it even essential to crawl in order to walk? How do babies figure out what works for them? Learning throughout our lives is based on cycles of self-awareness, assessment, and adjustment toward satisfaction of a need or drive. To that extent, we have been data-driven all along.

Differentiating between data that reflect human drive or potential and the more isolated metrics of component skills is the critical difference. Returning to our discussion of a developing baby, it is reasonable to conclude that symmetrical, coordinated crawling is positively associated with learning to walk. We might even consider it a "reliable" indicator that the skill of walking will develop. But just as often, the child who develops as a bottom-scooter, side-slider, or sit-to-stander also learns to walk, run, and climb to reach whatever it is he or she needs or desires.

Our goal as educators is to recognize that students come to us with uniquely individual drive and mechanisms to learn. These may look very different from what we assume works best for school, but it has been working *for them*. Our charge is to provide the spaces, means, and opportunities for each student to grow his or her competencies and passion to learn.

Learning comes naturally to teachers, too. While curricula tend to be prescribed, teachers with a "learning mindset" approach instruction as a powerful interactive space rather than as a method to cover material. The essential product is growth. Such teachers value individual differences and determine what students already know. They invite connections and conjecture to spur deeper interests, broader applications, and the development of personal learning tools. It will be *these* tools and resiliencies that best prepare students to successfully meet future individual and community needs.

> **assessment FREEZE FRAME 1.1**
>
> Our goal as educators is to recognize that students come to us with uniquely individual drive and mechanisms to learn.

More Than One Answer May Apply

The following problem was given to a classroom of urban middle school students from diverse cultural and linguistic backgrounds as part of a criterion-referenced classroom assessment (Glaser & Silver, 1994, p. 22).

Busy Bus Company Problem

Yvonne is trying to decide whether she should buy a weekly bus pass. On Monday, Wednesday, and Friday, she rides the bus to and from work. On Tuesday and Thursday, she rides the bus to work but gets a ride home with her friends. Should Yvonne buy a weekly bus pass based on the following fare information?

Busy Bus Company Fares
One Way: 1.00
Weekly Pass: 9.00

The classroom teacher was surprised to find that many of these CLD students concluded that Yvonne should purchase the weekly pass instead of paying the daily fare. The teacher considered the daily fare to be more economical.

Anxious to explore the reasoning behind students' decisions, the teacher decided to discuss the problem with the class. This discussion revealed surprising but reasonable applications of out-of-school knowledge and problem-solving strategies to this mathematical problem (Glaser & Silver, 1994). Basically, students who selected the weekly pass argued it was a better choice because it would allow several family members to use it, especially after work and in the evenings, but also on weekends. In effect, these insightful students had reasoned beyond the decontextualized statement of the problem to apply their background knowledge gained from urban living. They applied this knowledge in a way that demonstrated a cost-effective use of public transportation. The teacher became convinced that more than one correct answer existed for the problem. In fact, she concluded that future assessments should explore more thoroughly what CLD and other students knew and were able to do. That is, students needed opportunities not only to provide answers but also to explain their reasoning and their applications of knowledge gained.

This example illustrates several of the rewards and challenges of assessment discussions, adaptations, and teaching practices for CLD students. These students bring to the classroom background knowledge and experiences that are often different from those of other students yet powerfully connected to real-world challenges, dilemmas, and living. Unfortunately, traditional assessments may fail to capture the knowledge that CLD students bring to academic learning. Classroom teachers are often in the best position to create, adapt, and modify assessments and assessment practices appropriately for CLD students so that these measures reflect the authentic, real-world knowledge and abilities of these students. *Assessment*, in this sense, can be defined as a range of procedures used to gather information about what students or other individuals know and are able to demonstrate. It is this definition of assessment, centered on identifying and exploring student assets, that frames the content of this book.

Given the diversity of CLD learners' experiences and prior knowledge, it is not surprising that classroom teachers of increasing numbers of CLD students are searching for resources to help themselves create, adapt, and apply differentiated assessment practices appropriately. This text provides just such a resource, as well as a variety of useful guidelines for PreK–12 classroom teachers of CLD students. Among the sorts of questions this text addresses are those that surface among teachers as their numbers of CLD students increase on an annual and sometimes weekly basis. These teachers' questions often are similar to the following:

- How do I know that Jessie's difficulties with reading, language arts, and social studies do not indicate a disability?

- Thao has been in my class for 6 weeks. Why doesn't she respond to my questions during the lesson? Why doesn't she speak during group work? How can I evaluate what she comprehends and what she does not?
- I think that Marleny has already learned what we are studying in math right now. How do I find out what she learned while she was in El Salvador?
- We even used the Spanish version of the test! I know that Madai learned this material in Mexico. Why didn't she excel on this assessment?
- I know that my students from Bosnia are improving, but their 6- and 9-week tests don't show it. What's wrong?

The concern of such teachers is evident in their queries. Yet such questions also tend to illustrate why differentiated practices are critical to student (and teacher) success in today's classroom. What is so different about today's classroom that differentiation has become essential? Why is an understanding of our student populations necessary to interpret "standardized" results?

WHAT'S DIFFERENT ABOUT TODAY'S CLASSROOM?

One major and continuing change in today's public school classroom is the diversity of the student population. The fastest-growing and most heterogeneous group of students today is that which we refer to in this text as CLD students. In the literature of education, these students are sometimes referred to as minority or language minority students, English language learners (ELL), or limited English proficient (LEP) students.

We believe that the term *culturally and linguistically diverse* is the most inclusive and cross-culturally sensitive description of a student whose culture or language differs from that of the dominant culture. The use of this term and its associated acronym are increasingly prevalent in educational literature (e.g., California Department of Education, 2013; Gonzalez, Pagan, Wendell, & Love, 2011; New York State Education Department, 2002). CLD students are those who bring diverse cultural heritages and assets to the school (Baca & Cervantes, 1998; Escamilla, 1999; Herrera, 2010; Herrera & Murry, 2016; New American Economy, 2017). But because diversity does not imply a level playing field, the acronym CLD most appropriately and affirmatively describes students who will require classroom assessments and assessment practices that are appropriately differentiated for their biographies and their learning needs.

So who are these CLD students? Where did they come from? Like almost all Americans, the majority of CLD students are immigrants themselves or have familial ties to another country (Lurie, 1991; Cushner, McClelland, & Safford, 2012). Some are recently immigrated; others are second- or third-generation Americans. Others possess a rich Native American heritage. In 2015, children with at least one immigrant parent accounted for more than one quarter (26%) of the population of children in the United States under the age of 18 years (Zong & Batalova, 2017). Second-generation children, that is those who were born in the United States to at least one foreign-born parent, accounted for 88% (15.8 million) of all children with immigrant parents. The Pew Research Center has projected that, by 2050, more than one third of the nation's children below the age of 17 will be immigrants themselves or have at least one parent who is an immigrant (Maxwell, 2014). Therefore, it becomes increasingly valuable for classroom teachers to know something about immigration dynamics in the United States.

Immigrant CLD students and their family members, like immigrants of the past, come to this country for rational, valid, and compelling reasons. They not only contribute to the creativity and productivity of the nation, but they also want to learn English and become productive members of our society. A practical understanding of current trends among immigrant and other CLD students is often crucial to the teacher's appropriate preparation for a changing classroom. This is especially the case for the development and refinement of assessments that are valid and authentic for the populations of students taught.

The Next Generation of Students: America's Potential

Radically changing trends in birth rates, fertility rates, aging, and net immigration have resulted in the highest levels of classroom diversity witnessed in the United States in the past century. As illustrated in Figure 1.1, the number of immigrants, as a percentage of the U.S population is just beginning to approach that which resulted largely from European immigration in the late nineteenth century. Nevertheless, the same figure illustrates the rise in total immigrant numbers that has occurred steadily since about 1970. The slope of the curve projects rapidly increasing numbers of immigrant children will be entering U.S. schools for the foreseeable future.

Analysts and researchers at the Urban Institute, the Pew Charitable Trust, the National Immigration Forum, the Migration Policy Institute, and the Institute of Education Sciences continuously monitor the rapidly changing demographics associated with the increasing diversity and complexity of today's schools. The recent findings of these researchers indicate that classroom teachers of CLD students should monitor and adjust their professional practices, as necessary, to align with five major immigration trends. The first of these trends may be characterized as *key to productivity*.

According to the Pew Research Center (2017), immigrants are expected to drive future growth in the U.S. working-age population through at least 2035. As the Baby Boom generation transitions to retirement, immigrants and their children are expected to fill the gap between those retiring from, and those entering, the American workforce. They will do so by adding about 18 million people of working age between 2015 and 2035. Not surprisingly then, the CLD immigrant students of today are the youth upon which the country will depend to maintain high levels of productivity and competitiveness in a world economy. On the other hand, policies proposing

Figure 1.1 Number of Immigrants and Their Share of the Total U.S. Population, 1850–2015

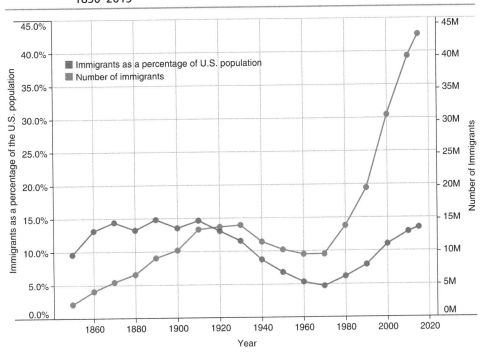

Source: Migration Policy Institute (MPI) tabulation of data from U.S. Census Bureau, 2010-2015 American Community Surveys (ACS), and 1970, 1990, and 2000 Decennial Census. All other data are from Campbell J. Gibson and Emily Lennon, "Historical Census Statistics on the Foreign-Born Population of the United States: 1850 to 1990" (Working Paper no. 29., U.S. Census Bureau, Washington, DC, 1999). Originally published on the Migration Policy Institute's Migration Data Hub. (www.migrationpolicy.org/programs/migration-data-hub)

Note: Retrieved August 3, 2017, from www.migrationpolicy.org/programs/data-hub/charts/immigrant-population-over-time

to limit or discourage immigration may impact this projection in a variety of ways (Costa, Cooper, & Shierholz, 2014; Edwards & Ortega, 2016; National Academies of Sciences, Engineering, and Medicine, 2017; New American Economy, 2017):

- Reduction in economic contribution and new business growth
- Insufficient labor force to meet needs of current small businesses, agriculture, and hospitality sectors
- Reduction of personnel and economic contributions by highly skilled, foreign-born laborers (doctors, specialists, engineers)
- Reduction in the jobs and pay for native-born workers that are associated with high-skilled immigration
- Inability to meet the growing demand for bilingual employees in all sectors of the economy

The second of these trends among CLD students and families is *dispersal to nontraditional receiving communities* (Pew Charitable Trusts, 2014). This trend reflects an ongoing diffusion of immigrant families to states not typically associated with high levels of student diversity. Recent immigration has shifted from traditional receiving states, such as California, Texas, and Florida, to 22 new growth states. Among the latest growth areas are states in the Southeast and the Pacific Northwest. New immigration also is offsetting significant population declines in the central states of the country (Pew Charitable Trusts, 2014; Zong & Batalova, 2017). This trend is especially important for schools and classroom teachers because schools and other institutions in these new receiving states are less apt to have the necessary infrastructures (e.g., bilingual teachers and paraprofessionals, adult English as a second language (ESL) programs, quality second language programming, and differential assessment instruments) in place to meet the needs of these families and their school-age children (Herrera & Murry, 2016).

A third trend among CLD students surrounds *ongoing language acquisition challenges*. In fact, the acquisition of academic English remains one of the major challenges for many first- and second-generation immigrant families and their children (Herrera, Kavimandan, Perez, & Wessels, 2017). The population of immigrants and U.S. natives who speak a language other than English at home has virtually tripled since 1980, when it was estimated at 23.1 million by the Migration Policy Institute (Batalova & Zong, 2016). These patterns suggest that increasing numbers of general education teachers will be called on to develop the capacities and skills necessary to differentiate their practices for students who are English learners.

A fourth trend in immigration surrounds the *changing home and family dynamics* for CLD students. In 2015, children living with at least one immigrant parent represented 26% of all children under age 18 in the United States (Zong & Batalova, 2016). The overwhelming majority (88% in 2015) of these children are U.S. citizens by birth. The number of children who are immigrants themselves has declined 22% since 2000. However, the number of children seeking asylum continues to increase (Mossaad, 2016). In 2015, the number of children from Guatemala, Honduras, and El Salvador seeking asylum increased by 112% from 2014 and 236% from 2013.

Although the nation is experiencing increasing economic growth since the end of the great recession in 2009, not all sectors of the postrecession economy are recovering well, and not all Americans in those sectors are satisfied with their job prospects, positions, or wages. Anti-immigrant sentiment remains high, especially toward unauthorized workers and settlers. There is increasing fear among many immigrant families—fear of exposure, reprisals, deportation, and more. Stress in immigrant families is compounded by isolation, as more parents reduce interactions with the larger community, including those that involve medical, safety, and school supports. The unfortunate irony is that the United States always has drawn momentum from the stories, tenacity, and dreams of those bold enough to pull up roots, undertake uncertainty, and cross land or sea to make the United States their home.

Children of unauthorized immigrants as a substantial percentage of K–12 students is a fifth and final trend in emergent immigration patterns. Recent estimates by the Migration Policy Institute indicate that children (under age 18) of unauthorized immigrants reflect approximately 7% of the total child population, and roughly 30% of all children of immigrants (Capps, Fix, & Zong, 2016). The majority (79%) of these children living with at least one unauthorized parent, however, are themselves U.S. citizens.

Although the citizen children of unauthorized parents are on an equal legal footing with all citizen children, their parents' unauthorized status affects them adversely in a variety of ways. Landale and colleagues (2011) report that unauthorized parents typically work in unstable, low-wage jobs that do not carry health benefits. As a result, CLD children of unauthorized parents are more likely to be poor than other immigrant children. Landale et al. further add that unauthorized parents often fail to take advantage of public benefit programs for which their children qualify because they fear deportation. These hardships may be intensified by unstable living arrangements and periods of separation from one or both parents.

A review of the research literature by the Migration Policy Institute (Capps, Fix, & Zong, 2016) provides similar findings, noting that that growing up with unauthorized immigrant parents exposes children to risk factors such as reduced frequency of preschool enrollment, reduced socioeconomic progress, higher rates of linguistic isolation, limited English proficiency, and poverty. Researchers currently know little about the family situations of children with unauthorized parents. As such, teachers and other educators should always guard against assumptions about these and any other CLD students.

---

assessment FREEZE FRAME 1.2

In 2015, children living with at least one immigrant parent represented 26% of all children under age 18 in the United States.

Implications for Unrecognized Student Assets

A recent report from the National Foundation for American Policy found that 83% of America's top high school science students in 2016 were the children of immigrants (Anderson, 2017). Many are children of parents on H-1B visas, which until recently enabled U.S. communities and business to staff unfilled medical and technical positions requiring needed expertise. Others are "Dreamers," achievers who have lived in the United States the majority of their lives. They consider this country their home, and its people their countrymen and women, but they first arrived in the United States in the company an undocumented parent.

We know that in our classrooms today, even more CLD innovators, scientists, and artists wiggle in their seats—neurons excited—making the unforeseen connections that may someday change the world. We need these students to be safe, in school, and fired up! Igniting those fires may hinge on our own abilities as teachers to see the embers. Sadly, many teachers never catch a glint. It is common for CLD students to be underrepresented in classes designed for those with high ability. In one district, identification for gifted programs increased 118% for Latinos and 74% for African Americans when universal cognitive screening was used rather than reliance on achievement or teacher perceptions of student ability. Yet when funds no longer supported use of that screener, representation of CLD and other "disadvantaged" students (e.g., females, low SES) fell back to previously reduced levels (Card & Giuliano, 2016).

The personal and financial cost of unrecognized student talent is huge. If our pool of students recognized as gifted is small and sifted by privilege, we lose the opportunity to be our national best. Finn and Wright (2015) address such failures on the part of our educational system to harness the possibilities that students bring to our classrooms, stating, "The problem is not that the United States lacks smart children; it's that such kids aren't getting the education they need to realize that potential" (p. 11).

Changing Classroom Demographics, PreK–12

With changing immigration trends come redefined classroom demographics, which by necessity require teachers at all levels to embrace adaptive practices and assessment approaches. These changing classroom demographics have been the subject of recent research and analyses (Headden, 2014; Herrera & Murry, 2016; Murry, Herrera, Miller, Fanning, Kavimandan, & Holmes, 2015; Wells, Fox, & Cordova-Cobo, 2016).

VOICES *from the* FIELD 1.2

Our community has changed tremendously over the past few years; therefore, my instructional and assessment practices must change to better assist the CLD students in my classroom. I teach in an ethnically and socially diverse district. I have a mixture of Asian, Black, White, Hispanic, Native American, and Central American students. I have students that range from lower-, middle-, and upper-class families. With such a diverse class, I have the opportunity to connect with the students on different levels. I understand that I must adjust my instruction as well as my teaching style to meet the needs of all students, regardless of their ethnic backgrounds and academic abilities. The strategies and skills I have learned throughout my ESL courses have helped me make the learning process productive, intriguing, and fair!

Melody Green, Middle School Teacher. Reprinted with permission.

Race/Ethnicity of CLD Students   By far the largest proportion of CLD students is Hispanic. These students represent 24% of all youth ages 5–17, and 78% of all English learners in the nation's public PreK–12 systems (Musu-Gillette, Robinson, McFarland, KewalRamani, Zhang, & Wilkinson-Flicker, 2016). Among others in this age group, 14% are Black, 5% are Asian, and about 4% are from mixed racial backgrounds. The proportion of White students in this age group is 53% (down from 62% in 2000).

Trends in the racial/ethnic composition of U.S. public schools are expected to continue well into the future (Landale et al., 2011; Passel, 2011). Among youth, the number of White school-age students will continue to decline, falling to about 40% of children by 2050. The number of Black children in classrooms will remain about the same (14% to 16%). By contrast, children of Hispanic origin will increase to more than one third of the school-age population. Also expected is an increase in the number of students who have ancestors in two or more racial and/or ethnic groups.

High Poverty Levels Among CLD Students   The percentage of children from low-income households, represented by the share qualifying for free and/or reduced-price school lunches, is significantly higher in schools with large numbers of CLD students (Cosentino de Cohen & Clewell, 2007). More than 30% of principals and 45% of teachers in these schools rank student health problems as serious or moderately serious. Notable aspects of these trends are especially exacerbated for immigrant CLD students. According to the Migration Policy Institute, 29.4 million children under age 18 in 2015 lived in low-income families—with incomes below 200% of the federal poverty threshold (this measure recognizes poverty as a lack of those goods and services commonly taken for granted by members of mainstream society) (Zong & Batalova, 2017). Of these children, 32% were children of immigrants.

Out of necessity, we as educators should always *check our assumptions* about our CLD and other students and their actual socioeconomic backgrounds through measures such as home visits and informal conversations. Children who do live in poverty tend to experience troublesome health and educational challenges, are more likely to experience parental divorce and live in single-parent families, and are more exposed to violent crime compared to children growing up in more affluent families (Mather, 2009). For many CLD students, poverty persists into adolescence and adulthood, and it is associated with greater risk of dropping out of school, becoming pregnant as an unmarried teen, and experiencing economic/employment difficulties (Ratcliffe & McKernan, 2012).

Research and analyses suggest other significant implications for increasing numbers of CLD students in poverty (Marzano, 2004; Mather, 2009; Skinner, Wight, Aratani, Cooper, & Thampi, 2010). Marzano (2004) has synthesized the findings of a comprehensive body of research to support arguments that poverty among students and families has negative influences on academic achievement. Based on his analyses, Marzano argues that students who are socialized at or near the poverty line are 70% less likely to pass an academic achievement test than their counterparts who do not experience poverty. Marzano demonstrates that poverty is associated with a variety of other factors detrimental to student success, including:

- An increase in home and family conflicts
- Decreased levels of self-esteem
- Family isolation
- Frequent and disruptive moves from one living unit to another
- Reduced exposure to language (especially academic language) interactions

Marzano's analyses also revealed a disconcertingly strong relationship between poverty and ethnicity. In 2013, 16% of all children under age 18 were living in poverty (Musu-Gillette et al., 2016). Among White children, only 9% were living in poverty during this time. This proportion stands in stark contrast to the 28% of Black children, 27% of Hispanic children, and 14% of Asian children who likewise were living in poverty. Fundamentally, these figures indicate that children of color differ considerably from White children in access to material resources during childhood and school-age years.

According to Marzano (2004), students of color are far more likely to enter school with disproportionately low levels of academic vocabulary and the kinds of background knowledge that have traditionally been valued in U.S. classrooms. Even more problematic, however, are the ways in which many educators currently assess the vocabulary knowledge and vocabulary-building processes these students *do* possess. Many of the assets that CLD students bring to the educational setting continue to be unexplored avenues to academic success.

Increasing Incidence of Secondary-Level CLD Students   CLD students who are foreign-born are more likely to be students in secondary rather than elementary schools (Mitchell, 2016). According to a recent analysis of U.S. census data, 35% of English learners in Grade 6–12 were born outside the United States, compared with 18% of PreK–Grade 5 English learners. (Note: As this analysis relied on data for children living with at least one parent, additional students might have been excluded.) This trend is practically a reversal of patterns typical among immigrant students since the late 1970s (Fix, Passel, & Ruiz-de-Velasco, 2004).

The sharp increases in the numbers of recently immigrated CLD students who are educated in secondary schools suggest noteworthy implications for classroom teachers. First, these students are far less likely to have received language-programming support services during their elementary school years. Consequently, they are less likely to demonstrate high levels of English language proficiency, especially the cognitive academic language proficiency (CALP) skills that promote success in content-area classrooms. A significant number of students immigrating at the secondary level have, by that time, experienced limited, interrupted, or disrupted formal education (Custodio & O'Loughlin, 2017). Students immigrating during the secondary years are less likely to take higher level coursework in high school than those arriving before age 12 (Arbeit, Staklis, & Horn, 2016).

Second, the incidence and history of language-programming services in secondary schools is typically more limited than that for elementary schools (Ruiz-de-Velasco & Fix, 2000). A recent study of public school districts indicates that only 3% of districts provided dual language programming, 8% provided bilingual instruction for English learners only, 47% provided sheltered English/content instruction, 61% provided push-in/pull-out ESL instruction, and 68% provided ESL instruction in scheduled class periods (Lewis & Gray, 2016). This study also indicated that districts utilized paraprofessional support by individuals who speak the student's native language (31% of districts) and individuals who do not speak the student's native language (33% of districts).

Third, secondary schools are less likely to have in place the necessary infrastructure and expertise, such as highly qualified content area teachers, that can deliver the differentiated programming, instructional, and assessment practices that CLD students require to be successful (Hopkins, Lowenhaupt, & Sweet, 2015). These include classroom routines to support self-directed learning, goal setting, and continuous monitoring with feedback to foster both collective and individual growth (Bondie & Zusho, 2017). Funding plays a key role, with Federal Title III funds historically having been allocated more regularly to elementary-level programs, instruction, and assessment.

Language Dynamics Among CLD Students   Today's public school classrooms are increasingly characterized by the native languages spoken by roughly 4.6 million English learners (Musu-Gillette et al., 2016). Sustained levels of immigration from nontraditional countries has increased the diversity of languages spoken. Today, CLD students speak more than 400 different languages (Goldenberg & Wagner, 2015). In five states, Spanish is not the most common first language; instead, German (Montana), Nepali (Vermont), Ilokano (Hawaii), Somali (Maine), and Yupik (Alaska) top the charts (Ruiz Soto, Hooker, & Batalova, 2015).

Among K–12 CLD students whose first language is not English, Hispanic students are more likely than other subgroups of this population to be characterized as LEP—youth who speak English with difficulty (Aud, Fox, & KewalRamani, 2010). LEP is a government-related designation. More and more CLD students who have been classified as LEP have lived in the United States for many years and are educated in schools in which the overwhelming majority of students are also classified as LEP. In fact, nearly 70% of the country's LEP students enroll in only 10% of elementary schools (Cosentino de Cohen & Clewell, 2007). More than half of all students classified as LEP are concentrated in schools where roughly one-third or more of their classmates are designated LEP. According to analyses from the Urban Institute (Cosentino de Cohen & Clewell, 2007), so-called high-LEP schools have more difficulty filling teaching vacancies, are more likely to employ teachers with emergency or provisional certifications, and have more new teachers than do schools with fewer LEP students.

Achievement Patterns for CLD Students   Academic achievement and progress will be major emphases of classroom-based instructional and assessment practices for CLD students tomorrow and for the foreseeable future. One reason for such emphases are ongoing patterns of low achievement demonstrated by CLD students on the National Assessment of Educational Progress (NAEP). Scores from 2013 indicate that the same patterns have persisted for the last 10 years (National Education Association, n.d.). English learners continue to demonstrate lower levels of proficiency in reading and math than their native English-speaking peers. For example, only 3% to 4% of English learners in eighth grade demonstrated proficiency in reading or math. English learners also have the lowest rate of high school graduation (61%) of all student subgroups.

Significant gaps also exist between White students and students of other races, though the gaps have narrowed some over the past 40 years (National Education Association, n.d.). For example, on the 2013 Grade 4 mathematics test, 34% of Black students performed below the basic level, compared with only 9% of White students. White students in fourth and eighth grade also significantly outperformed Black, Hispanic, and American Indian/Alaska Native students on both reading and math. In contrast, Asian/Pacific Islander students consistently outperformed their White peers, as well as peers from other racial and ethnic backgrounds. High school graduation rates also tell a troubling story, with disparities in rates among students of different races evident in the following numbers:

- American Indian students: 69.7%
- Black students: 70.7%
- Hispanic students: 75.2%
- White students: 86.6%

The need is greater than ever for effective classroom-based instructional and assessment practices that reflect the CLD student's culture, first and second language proficiencies, acculturation, and prior schooling experiences (both inside and outside the United States). These experiences are assets on which to build. Instructional models that recognize this power have been shown to promote students' positive socioemotional health (Herrera, 2016) and consistently result in higher achievement trends despite factors that otherwise signify risk (Thomas & Collier, 2002, 2012).

In a nutshell, schools are challenged to maintain high standards of educational quality in an era of educational reform and amidst an increasing scale and pace of changing student and family dynamics. To what extent do in-service teachers tend to demonstrate readiness for a rapidly changing classroom population? This question is the focus of the discussion that follows.

WHAT'S CHANGED ABOUT THE READINESS OF CLASSROOM TEACHERS FOR STUDENT DIVERSITY?

Although the federal government, many states, and some school districts are increasingly responsive to the changing demographics of the U.S. classroom, these efforts have often failed to match the pace of change (Briceno, 2008; Herrera & Murry, 2016; Ojalvo, 2010; Smyth, 2008). For example, in the years following implementation of the No Child Left Behind (NCLB) Act (2002), appropriation increased from $17.4 billion to $24.2 billion (Briceno, 2008). However, addressing the needs of low-income students and English learners to meet requirements of the law during that time amounted to $150 billion.

At the state level, 46 states provide differential funding to support English learners (Millard, 2015). There is great variability in the funding mechanisms (i.e., formula funding, categorical funding, or reimbursements). Among states that fund

English learners through the primary funding formula, three options are used: weights (ranging from 9.6% in Kentucky to 99% in Maryland), dollar amounts, and teacher allocations (Millard, 2015). Yet funding and the physical presence of teachers can only take us so far. These resources must be maximized to accelerate the language development and academic achievement of the learners who sit before us.

General education teachers are often the least prepared for changing CLD student demographics. Surveys and analyses of U.S. teachers by the National Staff Development Council (NSDC) are especially alarming (NSDC, 2009, 2010). In 2009, the NSDC found that more than 66% of teachers had *not received even one day of staff development specific to the assets and needs of CLD students* during the previous 3 years of teaching. In fact, although most CLD students are educated in general education classrooms for the greatest portion of the school day, the majority of teachers in these classrooms have had little or no professional development for meeting the differential needs of these learners (Cosentino de Cohen & Clewell, 2007).

In a recent study of 11 schools with large English learner populations (ranging from 35% to 90% of the total school enrollment), teachers' training related to the needs of English learners comprised an average of *less than 20%* of their total professional development hours (National Center for Education Evaluation and Regional Assistance, 2014). In addition, some states continue to allow general education teachers to test-out for ESL certification or endorsement with *no extra hours of staff development* particular to the needs of these students. The dire need for teachers trained to responsively educate this student population is evidenced by the fact that in 2016, 32 states indicated that they had an insufficient number of teachers for English learners (Sanchez, 2017).

Across the United States, English learners represent 9.3% of all public school K–12 students (National Center for Education Statistics, 2016). Research indicates that intensive, long-term professional development (49 or more hours per year) for teachers of these students has the potential to boost student achievement by more than 20 percentile points (Yoon, Duncan, Lee, Scarloss, & Shapley, 2007). Yet a 2010 topical analysis of professional learning opportunities for general education teachers found that teachers had fewer sustained professional learning opportunities than they had experienced 4 years prior (National Staff Development Council, 2010). Grade-level teachers were also about half as likely to report time for collaboration with colleagues (i.e., to solve complex education dilemmas of increasing classroom diversity) than they were eight years prior. With fewer opportunities for long-term professional development and collegial collaboration, teachers often are hard pressed to find, design, and innovate creative responses to the complexities of their diverse classrooms.

WHAT'S EVOLVED ABOUT ASSESSMENT PRACTICES FOR CLD STUDENTS?

From the standpoint of schoolwide achievement testing, this question could be answered, "Quite a lot!" . . . or, "Very little." Many states, districts, and educators experienced notable changes in practice and policy with the enactment of the No Child Left Behind Act (2002). NCLB was itself a reauthorization of the 1965 Elementary and Secondary Education Act (ESEA), which was designed to address inequities in education by providing additional funds for districts serving low-income students. In the decades that followed, it became apparent that despite improvements, educational outcomes varied. Personal stories and impersonal statistics revealed cohorts of students passed from grade to grade, and sometimes onto graduation, without acquisition of basic skills. NCLB was developed to raise district and state accountability for the education of all students regardless of demographic subgroup (e.g., socioeconomic, racial, exceptional, ELL). It was a call to action that "all means all."

Per NCLB, standardized testing at incremental grade levels held students, teachers, schools, districts, and states accountable for demonstrable and steadily increasing standards of performance. In some ways, this trend in assessment focused more proactive attention on CLD students' opportunities to learn, access to differentiated instruction, and meaningful schooling outcomes. Yet not all outcomes of this focus on quantitatively measured performance among students and on educator accountability have been positive. The focus, in some cases, became a major factor in the schoolwide firing of teachers and high levels of student frustration with recurrent testing (Crawford, 2004; Wolf, Herman, & Dietel, 2010).

In response to such concerns, ESEA was reauthorized in 2015 as the Every Student Succeeds Act (ESSA). ESSA was a bipartisan endeavor crafted to retain the spirit of ESEA but lessen the burdens and negative consequences of NCLB. Changes made also reflect acknowledgement that students may take multiple postsecondary paths to success. For example:

- Under NCLB, the federal government required states to stipulate standards for math, reading, and science. The goal was for all students, regardless of circumstance, to make the rates of gain needed to be on grade level by the year 2014. To avoid penalties for not making adequate yearly progress (AYP), some states actually lowered the standards required for each grade.
- Changes under ESSA encourage states to adopt challenging sets of standards in reading, math, and science. For each content area, three levels of achievement are described which align with varying (college, career, technical) requirements for postsecondary education. This allows individual student growth to be a recognized indicator and driver of achievement. Districts are also required to identify targets and improvement goals for areas outside of the curriculum (e.g., attendance) that are thought to positively impact academic and vocational success.

ESSA also allows states to afford districts increased latitude in test type, frequency, and administration of formal standardized assessments (including screeners). However, such tests continue to dominate the tools and vocabulary used in discussions of student growth (Martin, 2016). Therefore, despite the promise of new guidance, educators continue to work in climates (in)formed by assessment of achievement that has become increasingly standardized, norm referenced, and *high stakes*.

Among criticisms regarding these assessments and the consequences of building national educational reform initiatives around them are the negative effects these tests have on classroom climate, instructional practices, and classroom assessment routines. Ongoing analyses on such consequences (Abedi, 2004; Heubert, 2009; Wolf et al., 2010; Martin, 2016) have variously concluded that these standardized, norm-referenced, high-stakes tests:

- Prompt teachers to narrow the curriculum taught in classrooms
- Encourage so-called teaching to the test
- Divert classroom instruction to an emphasis on low-level content and basic skills
- Push students out of the system
- Increase redundancy of instruction
- Result in short- and long-term underestimation of student potential

Indeed, the frequency of assessment and penalties for insufficient gain have led many schools on paths that reduce instructional power, without providing quality information on student growth. Structures intending to be responsive (e.g., RTI, MTSS) can become overly prescriptive, with an emphasis on filling "*holes*" rather than on fostering learning *prowess*. Shifting from data- to asset-driven models is discussed further in Chapter 7.

The negative consequences of high-stakes, formal assessments have been especially recurrent for English learners. Under both NCLB and ESSA, this population of students must perform on two types of accountability assessments: English language proficiency testing, and assessments in reading/language arts, math, and science (Abedi, 2004; Wolf et al., 2010). Given the sheer quantity of assessments required to be taken, underperformance for the subgroup is not necessarily an unexpected outcome (Abedi, 2009).

An emergent body of evidence also indicates that standardized formal assessments and assessment milieus used to measure academic growth among this subgroup of students are often invalid or unreliable at several levels (Abedi, 2004; Cosentino de Cohen & Clewell, 2007; Wolf et al., 2010). Dr. Jamal Abedi (2004, 2009), a research partner of the National Center for Research on Evaluation, Standards, and Student Testing at the University of California at Davis, is perhaps the foremost researcher in the nation on this topic. His longitudinal research on high-stakes formal assessments for English learners has found, among other indicators, the following disconcerting issues of validity, reliability, and generalizability:

- *Strong confounding of language and performance:* Students of this subgroup exhibit substantially lower performance than other general education students in areas involving a strong understanding of academic English. That is, subgroup students may possess the content knowledge but may not have the academic English language proficiency to understand the language structure of the formal assessment tools.
- *Substantially lower baseline scores:* Low proficiency in academic English often means that the baseline scores of subgroup students are substantially lower than those of the larger student body. Therefore, the groups are not comparable. The expectation for these students to reach grade level at the same rate as native English-speaking peers is often referred to as trying to "catch a moving train."
- *Heterogeneity in the subgroup population:* States and districts do not consistently classify students whose first language is not English. As a result, the population tested as belonging to the subgroup may be far more heterogeneous than anticipated. With greater levels of heterogeneity, or difference, larger samples of students are needed to provide statistically reliable results. In other words, results about "subgroup performance" often tell us little about what students actually know or need, or how to respond effectively.

For these reasons, Abedi (2009) reports that the formal assessment of CLD students is a much more complex conundrum than was anticipated. Olah (n.d.) agrees, noting that states have rarely checked to see that student performance on English language proficiency exams correlates with performance on the reading portion of statewide exams. She argues that such comparisons could provide valuable information about the language proficiency needed for school achievement. As a result of such critiques of assessment practices in schools, the emphasis of best-practice literature related to the assessment of CLD students is on finding alternatives to these and similar types of tests (Mathews & Kostelis, 2009; Mueller, 2011; Neil, 2010; Soltero-Gonzalez, Escamilla, & Hopewell, 2012).

Of growing value for teachers of CLD students (and relevance under ESSA) are issues and dynamics of teacher-created, formal assessments. These tests, tools, and measures are at the other extreme of the formal assessment continuum. Chapter 6 explores fundamental issues of formal assessment for classroom teachers. Among the key topics and issues are formative and summative assessment, baseline data, rubrics, and criterion-referenced instruments.

The trend toward more authentic assessment practices for CLD and other students tends to emphasize classroom-based assessments in more inclusive areas such as level of acculturation (Chapter 4), language proficiency (Chapter 5), and content-area learning (Chapter 6). Informal assessments that are directly related to classroom practices and instruction—referred to as *authentic assessments* (Chapter 2)—often are essential to the trustworthy assessment of incremental gains in language proficiency and content knowledge among CLD students. The identification of these gains—and the sharing of them with learners—can provide students with powerful motivation and promote student-driven learning.

This text has been designed specifically as a resource for classroom teachers of CLD students (PreK–12). The chapters to follow reflect the latest trends in appropriate and authentic assessment for the differential needs and assets that CLD students bring to the classroom. This book not only examines what is novel about differentiated practices, but also offers background information, details on assessments used in today's classrooms, examples of assessment in practice, and an exploration of how teachers can use assessment results to increase their teaching effectiveness for CLD students.

SUMMARY

This chapter explored how learning, from infancy to adulthood, results from cycles of stimulus/observation, response, assessment, and adaptation as we strive to satisfy our needs and achieve our goals. In this sense, we are data-driven from our earliest days. To effectively meet the needs of CLD students, we must remember that their learning processes are contextualized within their life experiences. Accommodating our assessment practices to support CLD students to reach their full potential requires us to view assessment first and foremost as a process of identifying assets—what students know and are able to do.

Today's classrooms are different in many ways from those of the more recent past. However, the increasing diversity present in 21st-century schools reminds us of the wealth of heritages, cultural traditions, and languages that have been an ever-present reality in our nation's history. Particular trends in U.S. immigration and changes in demographics accentuate conversations about challenges that schools systems and classroom teachers face in their current efforts to provide all students with a high-quality education. The underlying message remains the same: by learning more about our students' backgrounds (e.g., cultures, language proficiencies, acculturation, prior schooling experiences) and the knowledge and skills they bring, we become better equipped to plan, deliver, and assess instruction in ways that advance learning for everyone—including ourselves.

Many resources can support our collective efforts to address the differential needs and assets of CLD students. Adequate funding facilitates the development and implementation of programs and services for English learners. General education teachers especially are in need of opportunities for long-term professional development that targets the needs of this complex student population. Collegial collaboration also is pivotal to the development of innovative, site-specific solutions to dilemmas of daily practice.

Over time, increasing emphasis has been placed on accountability for CLD students' learning. Unfortunately, even the best of intentions can have unintended negative consequences. The outcomes of recent educational reforms (e.g., ESEA, NCLB, ESSA) suggest that overreliance on formal, high-stakes tests can leave both students and teachers disenfranchised and far from achieving the learning goals and expectations we espouse to hold for all students. A demand for more authentic measures of CLD student progress and learning has resulted.

KEY CONCEPTS

Assessment

Culturally and linguistically diverse (CLD) students

Nontraditional receiving communities

PROFESSIONAL CONVERSATIONS ON PRACTICE

1. Discuss assessment in terms of identifying and building on students' assets. What are at least two implications of such a mindset for teachers' classroom practices?

2. Defend the use of the term culturally and linguistically diverse (CLD) student versus alternative terms, including *minority student* and *LEP student*. Why is

it important to consider such distinctions in serving the needs of CLD students and families?

3. Reflect on factors that might account for current achievement patterns of English learners. What growth areas might you identify for your own setting of professional practice?

QUESTIONS FOR REVIEW AND REFLECTION

1. How might the descriptors *natural*, *individual*, and *data-driven* be used to characterize all learning?

2. In what ways are classroom teachers in the best position to appropriately create, adapt, modify, and accommodate classroom assessments for CLD students?

3. What are five major trends in immigration discussed in this chapter?

4. What is a nontraditional receiving community? What should teachers know about such communities in relation to classroom diversity and assessment?

5. What are at least three ways that poverty serves to "stack the deck" against students and their academic achievement? Describe one way teachers can promote the academic success of students who are socioeconomically disadvantaged.

6. What are at least three patterns that have tended to accompany recent increases in the number of secondary-level CLD students?

7. What group of CLD students is more likely than others to be identified as LEP? What school factors may contribute to the challenges faced by students identified as LEP?

8. What factors discussed in this chapter hinder teachers' readiness for effective practice with CLD students?

9. What are at least five problematic consequences of an increasing emphasis on standardized, norm-referenced high-stakes tests in recent educational reform initiatives?

10. What are at least three issues that add to the complexity of formally assessing CLD students using high-stakes assessments?

CHAPTER 2

AUTHENTIC ASSESSMENT

It is important to have authentic assessment when assessing ESL [CLD] students. Authentic assessment allows teachers to be able to look at the results and know that they truly represent where the students are, at that time. We all know that assessments can often offer different struggles when it comes to ESL [CLD] students. Often students can struggle on some assessments just because of the way the question is asked. Authentic assessments allow teachers to not test the students over language, but test them over content to make it an accurate assessment. Teachers can use authentic assessment in a variety of ways to benefit future learning in the classroom.

Rick Malone, High School Mathematics Teacher

Learning Outcomes

After reading this chapter, you should be able to:

- Justify use of alternative and authentic assessments in today's classrooms.
- Hold informed conversations with administrators, colleagues, and parents about issues of reliability and validity in assessment.
- Explore CLD student learning using multiple types of authentic assessment.
- Create authentic assessment tools to document learning gains.

INTRODUCTION

One of the primary purposes of this text is to explore the range of ways for gathering and interpreting information about culturally and linguistically diverse (CLD) student learning to inform instruction. For years, standardized and teacher-made tests (e.g., multiple choice, fill-in-the-blank) have dominated our views and practices about measuring student learning. These tests typically require memorization and do little to encourage students' independent thinking. The assessments fail to demonstrate whether or not the students are able to process the new information to produce clear understanding of the material covered. The results of such assessments have not always yielded information useful to classroom teachers for creating instructional accommodations for CLD students. Although the data generated by traditional tests are certainly helpful in comparing students, programs, and schools on quantitative bases, what the data actually mean for each individual student is often much more obscure and tells us little about language and academic growth.

The ability of an assessment tool or strategy to measure incremental gains is especially critical for CLD students, who often are struggling to simultaneously acculturate to new living and school environments, acquire a second and unfamiliar language, and perform according to grade-level standards in the content areas. Not surprisingly, there is increasing recognition that alternative forms of assessment are essential to best practices. Especially needed are assessments that are authentic, that are process- as well as product-focused, and that are capable of measuring incremental gains. Such assessments are the focus of this chapter.

Many classroom teachers are seeking or have already developed their own forms of assessment that provide more usable information about how well their students are learning what is actually being taught in class. These instruments are sometimes referred to as *alternative assessments* because they can supplement formal assessments and may also help refine or enhance current assessment practices. Because alternative assessments usually represent nontraditional or accommodated approaches to measuring student learning, they are often considered more authentic than the formal assessments they replace; however, not all alternative assessments can be characterized as authentic.

For example, one teacher may provide CLD students with a closed set of responses in a multiple-choice format as an alternative to an open set fill-in-the-blank format. Although such a format may increase the students' abilities to recognize targeted responses, it does not increase the authenticity of the assessment for measuring acquired knowledge and skills. Conversely, a teacher across town may feel that such a multiple-choice format is constraining for CLD students and alternatively provide an open set format to allow for a broader range of potentially appropriate responses. In this case, the alternative design may in fact be considered more authentic if it elicits and credits the students for both on- and off-curricula responses that demonstrate understanding of the desired content.

As is evident from these examples, the terms *alternative assessment* and *authentic assessment* are not strictly synonymous. However, the many common reasons for using alternative and/or authentic assessment approaches leads to overlapping references that can confound our understanding of such means of assessment. Because well-designed alternative assessments are also more authentic and may be used additionally as well as alternatively, we simply refer to these as *authentic* assessments throughout the remainder of this text.

Although the literature of assessment has employed a variety of criteria to define *authentic assessment,* such definitions tend to share certain commonalities (Cooper, 1999; Crawford & Impara, 2001; Diaz-Rico & Weed, 2006; Hancock, 1994; Linn & Miller, 2005). Among these commonalities, authentic assessments:

- Are generally developed directly from classroom instruction, group work, and related classroom activities and provide an alternative to traditional assessments
- Can be considered valid and reliable in that they genuinely and consistently assess a student's classroom performance
- Facilitate the student's participation in evaluation processes
- Include measurements and evaluations relevant to both the teacher and the student
- Emphasize real-world problems, tasks, or applications that are relevant to the student and his or her community.

Figure 2.1   Authentic Assessment Embedded Throughout the Lesson

Ms. Kerr began her English lesson by providing the eighth-grade students with an opportunity to record initial thoughts about the target concept. In this case, the focus of the lesson was verb moods. Students from each class used sticky notes to document different forms of verbs that came to mind. These ideas allowed Ms. Kerr to preassess students' background knowledge and provided her with a springboard into the lesson.

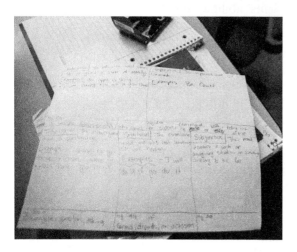

As students worked with the curricular material, they used a tool to document their new learning and personal thoughts about each of the new vocabulary terms (indicative, imperative, interrogative, conditional, and subjunctive verb moods). For each, they wrote the meaning of the term, an example of that form of verb, and their personal ideas. These individual connections increased the relevance of the material and promoted comprehension and retention. While students collaborated with peers to share ideas and worked individually to record information, Ms. Kerr was provided with a wealth of formative assessment data.

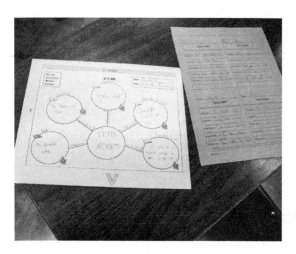

Ms. Kerr provided students with a U-C-ME graphic organizer (Herrera, Kavimandan, & Holmes, 2011) to support their self-monitoring and evaluation of what they had learned during the lesson. This tool served as a bridge to the more typical, curriculum-bound post-instructional assessment, which required learners to write sentences using verbs in each of the moods. Given the scaffolding they had been afforded through Ms. Kerr's use of authentic assessment throughout the lesson, students were able to approach this final assessment with confidence.

Across the nation, many classroom teachers already have embraced authentic assessment techniques as useful for gathering information that helps them plan, adapt, and individualize instruction. These techniques may prove even more valuable for CLD students because, with careful planning and implementation, teachers can avoid a number of cultural or linguistic biases inherent in traditional assessments.

When assessing CLD students, it is particularly important to design tasks that help us distinguish what we are in fact actually testing (e.g., language, content knowledge, acculturation). We must also assess CLD students in ways that allow them to demonstrate how they understand, access, and apply their knowledge in novel or real-life contexts. Use of authentic assessments need not be restricted to add-on or follow-up components of a lesson. They can often be embedded within the actual context of instruction. Figure 2.1 illustrates how authentic assessments can be integrated in instruction throughout the course of a lesson.

Authentic assessments identify and build on student strengths such as language, prior experiences, interests, and funds of knowledge (Moll, Armanti, Neff, & Gonzalez, 1992) to facilitate learning. They typically invite CLD students to become much more engaged, emphasizing student-constructed (rather than prescribed or regurgitated) responses. Student involvement in the assessment process facilitates learning by increasing motivation and ownership and lowering anxiety levels

---

SNAPSHOT from _CLASSROOM PRACTICE_   `2.1`

In this picture, 2nd graders in Ms. Wilhite's class are writing about the topic of _weather_. Ms. Wilhite first had students document their initial connections to the key vocabulary using words (in their native language or in English) and pictures. Then throughout the lesson, as the vocabulary words were read in context, Ms. Wilhite had students discuss word meanings with peers and record new learning on the same tool. This process allowed students to confirm/disconfirm their original associations and document new understandings that would support their writing at the end of the lesson. Strategies such as this enable Ms. Wilhite to authentically assess students' background knowledge, their evolving understandings and perspectives, and ultimately their comprehension of the lesson's vocabulary and content.

Stephanie Wilhite

VOICES *from the* FIELD 2.1

When teachers use observations as forms of assessments and allow students to bring their own schema to each vocabulary word, it helps teachers identify any misconceptions that may need to be addressed during instruction. When the teacher continues to observe and question as the students work in groups to show connections between the words, the assessment process becomes part of the instruction. This allows us as teachers to consider the following: Are the students able to read the words correctly? Are their connections making sense? Are all students participating? If a student is not participating, why? Does he or she need more opportunities exploring the words? Maybe more visuals or manipulatives need to be used. So, in a way, the assessments that are happening during instruction help us with the instruction process.

Mika Rutherford, Kindergarten Teacher

---

assessment FREEZE FRAME 2.1

Authentic assessments identify and build on student strengths such as language, prior experiences, interests, and funds of knowledge to facilitate learning.

(Chappuis & Stiggins, 2002; Sajedi, 2014). Authentic assessments center on strategies and activities that challenge students and encourage them to integrate knowledge and skills. Well-designed authentic assessments promote higher-order thinking and self-evaluation as students monitor their growth and progress. Because we create and employ authentic assessment to sample what students can actually do as well as what they know, most assessments, regardless of format, include a focus on individual growth and learning over time.

RELIABILITY AND VALIDITY OF AUTHENTIC ASSESSMENTS

When creating authentic assessments, it is important to keep in mind:

- *Why* they are used
- *What* information can be obtained from them
- *How* can this information help improve instruction and learning

As with other forms of measurement, we judge authentic assessments by their reliability and validity as indicators of student learning.

Reliability is best understood as the power of an assessment to gather consistent evidence of skills, regardless of the examiner, time, place, or other variables related to its administration. Reliable tests are also those that prove sensitive to measuring the incremental changes that reflect growth and improvement in the areas being assessed (Stiggins & Chappuis, 2017). This is a critical feature when assessments are used to inform instruction rather than merely provide baseline or end-term indices of achievement. The reliability of an assessment can be compromised or threatened by numerous factors. The presence of distracters (internal such as hunger and anxiety, or external such as ambient noise) can affect the performance of a student or group of students in ways that render those results less reliable or representative than if the assessment had occurred under different conditions.

An important measure of reliability is *inter-rater reliability*. This is the degree to which a student's product or performance is rated the same by different raters or evaluators. Ensuring inter-rater reliability is especially important for authentic assessments, which generally lack the discrete point scales of more objective forms of assessment such as multiple-choice and true/false tests. Inter-rater reliability for authentic assessments is often achieved through well-defined criteria and training for teachers and students in how to rate works according to specified criteria. This practice helps enhance rater reliability, and the resulting focus on key criteria sharpens the teacher's attention to those skills during teaching and learning activities.

> **assessment FREEZE FRAME 2.2**
>
> *Reliability* is best understood as the power of an assessment to gather consistent evidence of skills, regardless of the examiner, time, place, or other variables of its administration.

Validity refers to the ability of an assessment, process, or product to measure the knowledge or skills it is intended to measure. Teachers of CLD students are particularly concerned with *content validity*, which is the extent to which the assessment tasks and items represent the domain of knowledge and skills to be measured (especially regarding the most critical content). For example, we might question the content validity of a test that purports to measure only computational skills but includes problems such as the following:

> The players on Morgan's baseball team take turns bringing water bottles for their teammates. Last week, Tyler brought 12 bottles, and one player was absent. The coach decided to save the extra bottles and just have Morgan bring the remaining number needed the following week. How many bottles does Morgan need to bring next week so there are just enough for each player on the field?

Teachers should consider the level of knowledge and skills needed to answer this question, as well as language cues a CLD student might misinterpret. Although seemingly simple, this problem requires much more of students than basic computational skills. The question also requires:

- Knowledge of baseball (number of players on the field and on a team)
- An understanding that water bottles come in individual sizes
- The cultural assumption that bottles are not shared
- The linguistic savvy to understand that *just enough* implies exactly the right amount (a one-to-one correspondence), whereas *enough* may signify at least enough for everyone, but more may be fine

Much cultural knowledge is implicit in questions of this sort. An astute teacher may notice such content bias right away or, as often happens, only later begin to wonder why certain groups of students have greater difficulty than others with specific assessment items or formats. Because the goal of assessment is to provide information about student learning related to specific content, assessments must be meaningful indicators of whether—and how—that learning occurs.

Another area of assessment validity is *construct validity*, which deals with the question: How well do the skills required for the test items reflect the student's targeted knowledge bases and competencies in that area? For example, a science assessment that focuses on student recognition of target vocabulary in print may fail to sample (and therefore inform

> **assessment FREEZE FRAME 2.3**
>
> Teachers of CLD students are particularly concerned with *content validity*, which is the extent to which the assessment tasks and items represent the domain of knowledge and skills to be measured (especially regarding the most critical content).

instruction about) the deeper levels of understanding intended by the curriculum. It is important to continually calibrate the purposes of assessment (what we intend to measure) with the outcomes obtained by the tools, and the manner they are used. If the constructs of a given assessment are not well defined, the results will not adequately reflect students' skills in those areas. It is crucial that we consider validity and reliability when choosing and administering all forms of assessment, including those considered authentic, to ensure that they are consistently measuring what they are supposed to measure.

TYPES OF AUTHENTIC ASSESSMENT

We can authentically tap into our CLD students' formative (along-the-way) learning processes and summative (endpoint) grasp of curricular material through many different forms of authentic assessment (see Chapter 6 for in-depth discussion of formative and summative assessment). Many types of authentic assessment are popular for the ease with which teachers can adjust them for their own class of diverse learners. Authentic assessments include experiments, projects, observations, interviews, and student narratives. However, these are only a sample of the many ways academic skills can be assessed relative to their uses in the real world. Although a variety of authentic assessments are suitable for use with all students in the classroom, the following discussion explores some of the types most useful with CLD students. Many of these authentic assessments can be adapted for multiple purposes and for almost any content area.

Performance-Based Assessments

If we think of assessments as snapshots of student learning in time, *performance-based assessment (PBAs)* provide a longer exposure with a panoramic lens, or real-time video. PBAs typically involve the "actual doing of a task" (Linn & Miller, 2005, p. 7). This type of authentic assessment prompts higher-order thinking and integration of skills. PBAs encompass a variety of ways to observe and monitor student learning over various spans of time and involve much more authentic applications than do traditional paper-and-pencil tests.

Grade-level teachers who use PBAs generally embrace the idea that knowledge is constructed during learning—that students *discover* knowledge for themselves rather than *receive* knowledge from the teacher. Applying this *constructivist perspective* to learning and assessment facilitates how students take in information as well as how they store and retrieve this information and apply new thinking to novel situations. Some educators think of constructivist learning as teaching students to scuba dive rather than water ski. Because water skiers are able to stay upright and cover a relatively large amount of territory, their skills are easier to see and may, at first glance, be more impressive. Unfortunately, this ability to skim the surface does not speak to what lies underneath and does not guarantee the necessary skills to swim in deep or unfamiliar waters.

By contrast, scuba divers intentionally learn to investigate more deeply and propel themselves to areas of further interest. This can result in far greater knowledge at ever-deeper levels, as well as an ongoing desire and ability to continue the learning process. As with scuba diving, much of the learning that takes place in constructivist contexts occurs at these deeper levels and may be neither obvious on the surface nor measurable by traditional means. PBAs are designed to create situations that tap into the depth as well as the breadth of student learning. Instead of asking students to reiterate static facts or volumes of superficial content, PBAs allow students to demonstrate how deeply they understand and can navigate the waters of novel concepts, as well as the degree to which they can make new discoveries through self-directed learning.

It is relatively common for classroom teachers to acknowledge hands-on activities, such as PBAs, as appropriate and beneficial for young children. However, these activities are equally powerful for older students. For example, science applications facilitate content instruction and assessment because they generally lend themselves to students' storage of information both as procedural memory (information on the steps or sequences involved in a process) and as declarative memory (factual information about the science content). Figure 2.2 provides an example of a science-related PBA.

Because PBAs help to scaffold student learning naturally and sequentially, they are particularly appropriate for CLD students, who may have little prior exposure to the information, language, or process involved. Teachers can encourage CLD students to create their own personalized scaffolds to document their learning as they engage in PBAs. Learners can use the resulting tools to help answer questions that appear on more traditional assessments.

Figure 2.2   Science PBA

Preparation of a Dry Mount Microscope Slide

This performance-based assessment is designed to document the student's ability to independently prepare a dry mount microscope slide.

The following materials must be among those available to the student:

- Microscope with which the student has familiarity
- Slides
- Cover slips
- Object to be examined

The following steps are considered essential elements of this procedure. Circle each as it is completed by the student. Add observational notes as desired.

1. Place slide on a flat surface.
2. Lay specimen on top of slide.
3. Attend to thickness of specimen (does student seek thinnest sample?).
4. Place cover slip slowly on top of specimen.

If a student has been exposed to the creation of and rationale for both wet and dry slides, this PBA can be modified to require the student to determine and execute the appropriate procedure for one or more objects or organisms.

In this picture, Ms. Melton is seen at the end of the lesson assessing a group of 6th-grade students on their understanding of the characteristics of prisms. The students are working with different shapes that represent a prism and explaining their characteristics. By doing such types of performance-based assessments, a teacher is able to help students discover knowledge for themselves.

Lisa Melton

Portfolios

Ms. Carpenter was a 1st-grade teacher who once believed that her instructional time was best spent directly teaching to curricular goals. She would follow up her lessons with quick, objective quizzes to assess student mastery of content. However, the addition to her class of students who spoke English as a second language inspired her to adopt a host of new teaching and assessment practices. A case in point was how she altered her methods to incorporate the portfolio assessment of language arts objectives related to story skills.

Ms. Carpenter began by leading her class in discussions of books she read aloud, in terms of the main characters, setting, possible solutions, and so forth. Together they discovered and discussed the essential components of a "good story" and formulated a simple class rubric (see Figure 2.3) for judging future story-time selections. Over the next few weeks, Ms. Carpenter intentionally chose stories she knew would be rated either exemplary or poor, according to the class criteria. Such exercises built the students' skills in applying the criteria and reinforced their understanding of the usefulness of the criteria. These skills would be needed when students later assessed their own story-writing efforts.

Figure 2.3   Story Rubric

STORY ELEMENTS

	The Main Character?	The Setting?	The Problem?	The Solution?	Score (add here)
Does this story describe . . .	Yes = 2 A little = 1 No = 0	Yes = 2 A little = 1 No = 0	Yes = 2 A little = 1 No = 0	Yes = 2 A little = 1 No = 0	

One day, after a particularly disappointing selection, Ms. Carpenter guided the group in revising the lower scoring elements of the story. As she wrote the new version on poster paper, she also modeled the use of rebus cue drawings (e.g., I was riding my 🚲 and a 🚗 drove by.) for words that were unfamiliar or hard to spell.

The next day, students were anxious to write their own original stories. Although all the students were excited about this, Ms. Carpenter's experience told her that many students would not know where or how to start. As she reviewed the story elements featured in the rubric, she focused first on the importance of setting. To demonstrate the vital importance of the setting to a story, Ms. Carpenter told all the students to line up and, with digital camera in hand, she led them on a walk around the school building and grounds. As they talked about different settings, Ms. Carpenter took photos of students in settings they had chosen. Once they returned to class and printed these photos, the students took turns talking about the various settings in which each classmate appeared (e.g., "James is on the bench in front of the school," "Ana is under the big slide near the swings").

Ms. Carpenter hoped these visuals would trigger experiences and memories students could use as scaffolds for writing their first stories. These stories were drafted with an emphasis on content, so Ms. Carpenter encouraged students to use invented spellings and rebus pictures for words they could not spell. Students would search for these words in the dictionary and correct them later.

She then recorded students as they read their short stories aloud in groups. No one interrupted the readings with comments. When the recording was replayed, however, group partners listened for and commented on the simple elements of the story rubric that the class had devised earlier. Group members also attended to key curricular objectives and practiced the important skills of explaining and supporting their opinions.

The primary purpose of the recordings was to document students' developing narrative skills. However, the recordings also documented other parameters of language acquisition such as vocabulary, word order, sentence length, and pronunciation. Because all students were allowed to use rebus pictures for words they could not spell, vocabulary gaps were less of an issue. Students could still demonstrate their knowledge of the concept of setting. At this point, the students were able to add the written story (to be revised later) and the recorded narrative to their portfolios. Both would be strong benchmarks by which to measure future progress. Ms. Carpenter then planned an extension of the lesson to build on this new learning and stimulate students' imaginative thinking skills.

As she carried out the photo-taking activity with her class the following year, Ms. Carpenter remembered observing a CLD student who was not following directions—and yet she *loved* what he was doing. This year she deliberately incorporated that student's "detour into fun" as an extension of the lesson. After writing and recording their first stories, the students cut themselves out of the photos they took during the "setting" exercise. Then came the really fun part. Students were encouraged to place the picture of themselves anywhere and any way (such as upside down) on a blank piece of drawing paper. This step served as the launch point for their creating an entirely new setting and story for their main character. It also helped Ms. Carpenter focus on the next element of the rubric (the problem). She always marveled at how these new stories reflected the students' interests, background experiences, and creativity.

For example, Joel (who was swinging on the monkey bars in his original setting) was suddenly transported to a locale in which he hung precariously from the lower lip of a *Tyrannosaurus rex*. Tuyen, no longer poised at the water fountain, was now bending over to smell the abundant flowers in her grandmother's garden. Ms.

Carpenter noticed how the stories that evolved from this activity were more personal and animated than those elicited by her typical story starters. The students were eager to share these new stories with peers. When the drawings were finished, they were laminated and added to each student's portfolio.

Throughout the year, students had other opportunities to practice and build narrative skills, such as reporting the news (e.g., family, community, world) and retelling events or stories from different perspectives (e.g., the perspective of one of their favorite action figures). As the year progressed and Ms. Carpenter conferenced with students about their portfolio entries, she was amazed at how often students commented that their earlier stories could have been better. Some students even contrasted them to more recent selections. For instance, Magda said, "That story didn't have a very good ending. This one has a better problem and solution. I tell you more about my characters now, too." By the end of the year, Ms. Carpenter felt that she, her students, and their parents had a much better grasp of student progress than they ever could have gained through traditional indicators of achievement.

Portfolio in various forms have been in use for some time. However, early versions often amounted to undifferentiated compilations of student work, sometimes judged merely by overall heftiness or mass. Although portfolios were appreciated as indicators of student (and teacher) effort, many parents felt that this abundance of academic memorabilia provided little information about the actual progress of their children in school. Following are tips for moving away from simply collecting student work and toward a systematic collection of documents/artifacts that exemplify socioemotional, linguistic, and academic growth.

Teaching Tips:

- Create an oral language rubric for informal observation of language production three times a year.
- Create a checklist to document the learner's ability to take risks when working in groups.
- Gather writing samples for each grading period.
- Video the student two or three times each grading period sharing information orally (Simple computer applications for recording speech samples enable creation of powerful audio portfolios of students' developing oral or narrative skills.)

These are but a few suggestions for systematically collecting informal and authentic artifacts produced by the learner that move assessment to a new level.

Portfolios also can include:

- Samples of student work that illustrate either mastery or progress
- The sequential planning, process reflections, and product outcomes of a project
- Some indication of how the student rated him- or herself on the samples, processes, or products included
- Student justification and insight regarding the work included

The criteria for judging portfolio pieces should reflect outcomes that align with curricular standards. In many cases, school districts align these standards with relevant state and/or national benchmarks.

Portfolio assessments are beneficial for CLD students because they offer learners the opportunity to share in their own words what they have gained. Portfolios provide a safe space for students to communicate with the teacher and showcase their work. The tangible proof that they are learning, growing, and contributing is especially motivating for CLD students. Having students create a portfolio sends the message not only that their ideas and thoughts matter, but that regardless of their language proficiency, they can demonstrate their knowledge. The final portfolio serves as a treasure trove of artifacts students can look back on and be proud of.

E-portfolios offer the distinct advantage of increasing accessibility of the portfolio with peers, parents, and other educators. With such access comes opportunities for individuals who are influential to the student to provide additional feedback. The exchange of ideas made possible through electronic sharing can benefit students and the larger learning community. E-portfolios have been shown to positively affect students' literacy and metacognition (Nicolaidou, 2013).

In summary, portfolio assessments have the power to authentically connect classroom instruction and the assessment of its impact on students. They are *alternative assessments* in the sense that:

- They incorporate both teacher and student perspectives on learning and the assessment of learning.
- They offer a longitudinal perspective on academic and language development.
- They measure incremental gains in knowledge, skills, and proficiencies.

Portfolio assessments are *authentic assessments* in that:

- They derive directly from classroom activities.
- They effectively assess student performance.
- They reflect in-process adaptations to instructional methods and assessment.
- They assess learning in a way that is relevant to and motivating for the student.

Self-Assessment and Peer Assessment

Student *self-assessment* can be an extremely valuable tool for learning as well as measurement. When CLD students are engaged in assessing their own work, they more thoroughly and purposefully understand the criteria for high-quality products and performance—and experience greater motivation for meeting those criteria (Sajedi, 2014). Rather than simply attempting to produce work that will satisfy the teacher, students involved in effective self-assessment work toward a positive vision of the instructional goals. This vision is enhanced and authenticated by their own perspectives and interpretations. In addition, many teachers report notable improvements in students' ability to regulate their own behaviors related to time and task management.

Figure 2.4 depicts a self-assessment rubric that can be used to supplement a content scoring rubric. This rubric requires students to assess not only their overall achievement but also the *effort* they actually put into the task. Students' completed self-assessment rubrics then support teacher–student conversations about the task outcomes.

Figure 2.4   Effort and Achievement Comparison Rubric

Name: _____   Date: _____

Assignment/Project: _____

Effort & Achievement Comparison Rubric	
Effort	**Achievement**
5 = I put maximum effort into this task. I stretched myself to complete this task despite its difficulty. I approached task difficulties as challenges to be overcome. I built new capacities as a result of confronting these challenges. 4 = I put exceptional effort into this task. I stretched myself to complete this task despite its difficulty. I approached task difficulties as challenges to be overcome. 3 = I put moderate effort into this task. I stretched myself to complete this task despite its difficulty. I approached task difficulties as challenges to be overcome. 2 = I put average effort into this task. I stretched myself to complete this task despite its difficulty. 1 = I put limited effort into this task.	5 = I exceeded the objectives of this task. 4 = I met all of the objectives of this task. 3 = I met most of the objectives of this task. 2 = I met at least half of the objectives of this task. 1 = I met less than half of the objectives of this task.
Scale: 5 = Excellent, 4 = Outstanding, 3 = Good, 2 = Improvement Needed, 1 = Unacceptable	

Teaching Tips:

Use student self-assessment results in the following ways:

- Identify patterns of low interest or low self-confidence in the learner
- Discuss why the task was low effort (or what served to motivate high effort)
- Support the learner in setting goals to improve in the area he or she feels least confident
- Create a plan of action to be successful in the future.

Peer-assessment is equally beneficial because it provides students with additional opportunities to identify and evaluate targeted skills related to established criteria. Peer assessment requires students to consider how examples of other students' work meet the criteria. Such comparisons enable students to discern outstanding elements of their own *and* their classmates' performances and products, as well as those components in need of improvement. This type of critical consideration often prompts students to refine their concept of a quality product.

Another advantage of peer assessment is that many students are more apt to engage in dialogue with and accept criticism from peers than from teachers, and they are more likely to do so using language that is uniquely comprehensible to them. This is particularly important for CLD students, for whom peers who share the same native language may more effectively mediate and clarify the concepts of instruction.

Peers: Our Learning Lifelines

Grade Level: 3–6

Materials:

- Students' lesson-based writing samples
- Copies of the Learning Lifeline template (one per student)

Directions:

- Explain to students that oftentimes we arrive at our best learning by collaborating with others. Share with students that now they will be working with a partner to reflect on and continue to learn from their written work.
- Place students in pairs and give each student a copy of the template.
- Model for the whole class how to complete the top portion of the template.
- Provide students with time to read their partners' writing and complete the "I statement" prompts.
- Then ask partners to take turns to share feedback/questions and to have the peer-authors respond and ask their own questions.
- Next, have partners document questions for you that they are unable to answer for themselves using the resources available. Also encourage them to share comments about the peer-assessment process with you.
- Have partners discuss what they learned from each other.
- Encourage each pair to share with the class at least one thing they learned from the process.

Observing Students:

As students work individually to read their partners' writing and evaluate it using the "I statement" prompts, observe CLD students and take time to talk with them about their observations to support understanding. Note patterns in students' comments and questions about their peers' writing. These observations can serve to inform subsequent instruction. Also make notes about recurring questions/comments directed to you, the teacher, so that you can begin to address them within the context of the lesson. Continue to circulate around the room, attending to what students write in their summaries. Use insights gleaned to highlight assets of the learning community.

Differentiating Instruction:

- For English learners who need additional language support, consider having students read aloud their peer's writing, with the author listening and available to clarify vocabulary/meaning as needed. Then students proceed with the activity according to directions.
- Jot down notes about aspects of the peer-assessment process that challenge individual students (e.g., finding evidence of objective attainment within a peer's writing, responding well to criticism, offering constructive feedback, finding value in another's perspective). These notes can inform subsequent decisions about which peers to pair together, which skills to target for continued development, and which tasks might need additional scaffolding.

Additional Notes:

This activity can be repeated as often as desired throughout the academic school year.

Learning Lifeline Template

Content Area: ⬜ Writing   ⬜ Reading   ⬜ Science   ⬜ Math

⬜ Other Content Area _____

(Peer 1 Name) _____

I like the way (Peer 2 Name) _____ ⬜ thought out, ⬜ reasoned, ⬜ worked, ⬜ explored, ⬜ documented, ⬜ visualized, ⬜ described, _____ (another word you could use to give your peer feedback) _____ (e.g., problem, challenge, assignment).

I can tell that you (Peer 2) understood the objective(s) by:
1.
2.
3.

I have questions about:
1.
2.
3.

What questions do you (Peer 2) have?
1.
2.
3.

Questions and comments **we** (Peer 1 and Peer 2) have for the teacher.
1.
2.
3.

A summary of what we learned from each other:

VOICES *from the* FIELD 2.2

When students are allowed to assess their own work and that of their peers, they are able to develop a level of cultural awareness and commitment. Such assessment practices help to foster intellectual self-confidence and social self-confidence. This is definitely something we need to consider so our students have the self-esteem they need to succeed in society.

Darla Fisher, Middle School, Information Technology Teacher

Interview-Based Assessment

Mrs. Bontrager had always felt that the bilingual paraprofessional, Mrs. Silva, shared more common experiences with and could therefore better relate to the Spanish-speaking CLD students in her 4th-grade class. Over time, Mrs. Silva assumed a more and more significant role in their instruction while Mrs. Bontrager concentrated her efforts on the native English speakers. This seemed to be a reasonable approach given that Mrs. Silva, a Puerto Rican–born New Yorker, was able to communicate with the students in their native language.

Mrs. Bontrager felt confident that, because of this shared language, Mrs. Silva's instruction would foster the students' engagement in a farm simulation that the class conducted. She eagerly anticipated listening to the students' accounts of choices they had made during postproject interviews. However, she got a big surprise when she interviewed Abel. He began with a wonderful explanation for his group's decision to raise cattle instead of sheep. Abel stated, "Sheeps eat the whole grass and it might not grow back. But cows eat just the top, and it keeps growing so you've always got food for them."

Mrs. Bontrager was impressed and, thinking Abel would credit Mrs. Silva or the school library as sources, asked how his group had learned this important piece of information. "We already knew it," Abel replied. "My uncle has cows in Mexico, and Hector's seen sheeps eat grass 'til it's all gone. Mrs. Silva told us sheeps might be better 'cause you can make a sweater, but we decided that doesn't matter because if there's nothing left for them to eat, they die." Of course, this made perfect sense to Mrs. Bontrager, who grew up on a farm.

Suddenly, Mrs. Bontrager felt a sense of loss for what her CLD students could have gained, or for the deeper levels of application they could have achieved, had she been a more active mentor. After all, Abel, Hector, Rosa, and several others were farm kids, just as she had been. Imagine what could have happened if their knowledge had surfaced and been valued as a resource to enrich cooperative groups of mixed-language students.

Mrs. Bontrager decided to continue to use summative interviews but also resolved to conduct a *pre*project interview that would allow her to discover the knowledge and skills her students already possessed. This interview strategy would also provide an opportunity to talk about what students were learning as the lesson moved along. Mrs. Bontrager concluded that both she and the students had missed valuable opportunities.

This scenario vividly illustrates the assessment value of informal interviews with CLD students. Interview discussions often provide the classroom teacher with invaluable insights about the CLD students' prior knowledge and experiences, cultural backgrounds, language use at home, level of adjustment to a new culture and school, academic history, interests, beliefs, and more. Perhaps one of the greatest potential outcomes of this approach is that it often results in teachers and students having a deeper sense of mutual endeavor.

Interviews can vary from casual to highly structured. Whether through informal conversation or a more detailed interview process, teacher–student interviews are an efficient way of gathering pertinent authentic assessment information. The teacher can then use this data to adapt instruction appropriately for the students' benefit. For example, a math teacher may realize that particular students enjoy cooking. She may find that connecting mixed fractions to measurement conversion during a lesson on baking greatly facilitates comprehension of the math concept.

Informal interviews are a long-standing aspect of professional practice for many classroom teachers. However, most teachers do not consider them a valid form of assessment. This is unfortunate because interviews can be an accurate and effective means of obtaining data crucial to accommodative instruction for CLD students. As tools to evaluate and advance learning, interviews provide a forum in which teachers and students feel free to discuss preexisting ideas, learned information, desired information, and feelings or reflections related to the learning process. Although interviews need not (and probably should not) be highly uniform in nature, Stiggins and Chappuis, (2017) recommend that teachers develop targeted questions in advance, allow ample time for full discussion, and conclude each interview with a summary of noted learnings and future objectives.

Play-Based Assessment

One often-overlooked source of valuable information on student knowledge and skills is *play-based assessment*. Such assessments are especially suitable for evaluating young children and English learners of any age. Children as young as preschool age are often able to use toys or "pretend" objects in ways that signify an understanding of their actual use and function in the real world. Such representational play is a fundamental precursor to comprehending the similar nature of oral and written words. Other ways to promote literacy instruction and assessment during play, as described by Roskos and Christie (2002), include:

- Creating literacy-rich play settings (housekeeping centers with shopping lists, newspapers, magazines, and cookbooks, in addition to the typical pots, pans, and ironing board)
- Encouraging children to play-act roles and scenarios that require literacy activities (ticket pads for police officers, waiters, and waitresses; prescription pads for doctors; small, dry-erase boards or chalkboards for teachers)
- Promoting social interaction and including literacy-related challenges during play

For English learners, providing props, tools, and opportunity allows them to demonstrate procedural or conceptual knowledge they would not otherwise be able to demonstrate on written or verbal tests. An example of this is the CLD student who cannot verbally explain or understand the words for concepts of relative weight, size, or amount (e.g., *heavy, light, equal, more,* or *less*) but who is amazingly skillful in a game that calls for adding or subtracting just the right number of plastic beans to counterweight a classmate's wooden pegs so that neither pile on

SNAPSHOT from *CLASSROOM PRACTICE* 2.3

During their science unit, Mr. Pride provided students in pairs with a set of cards with concepts written on them. Students were then asked to take turns informally sharing their knowledge of the concepts. As students shared, Mr. Pride circulated around the room and listened to the kinds of things discussed. These connections allowed him to make instructional conversations more relevant to his learners.

Jeremy Pride

the balance falls to the floor. Although this student definitely possesses conceptual knowledge of weight, amount, and equivalence, he would fail almost any traditional test that exclusively examines the acquisition of words we use to describe this knowledge, rather than evidence of the knowledge itself.

Astute teachers at higher grade levels tap into the power of play by having students role-play or dramatize events and concepts from history, literature, or even the sciences. After all, who wouldn't want to be a germ-fighting white corpuscle? Other highly engaging forms of role-play, such as teacher- or technology-facilitated simulations, can provide alternative ways for CLD students to demonstrate acquired skills and concepts. Whatever the format of the particular assessment, reflective teachers observe and value student play as evidence of who these students are, what they know, and how they learn. Such teachers then use this information to construct more responsive instructional contexts.

Cooperative Group Assessment

Mr. Martinez told his sophomore biology students that their new reflection journals would enable him to understand what they were really learning from their group projects. He also planned to rely on their journals to document where students were struggling so that he could reteach material in a different way that might enhance their understanding. He showed his students some exemplary journal samples, as well as a rubric, so they would clearly understand his expectations for this new responsibility. After the next group project, Mr. Martinez's students used their journals to reflect on their individual learning. In these journals, the students:

- Provided written or pictorial demonstrations of how they understood the material presented during the project
- Noted questions, concerns, or misunderstandings for follow-up with the group or Mr. Martinez
- Logged new learning and continued to revise as needed

- Cited related commentary and information from outside resources
- Described and reflected on their own contributions to the process and progress of the group
- Detailed personal feelings, thoughts, hypotheses, and conclusions, even if different from the group's consensus

Because maintaining scientific logs was an identified objective for this course, Mr. Martinez gave students direct feedback on the grammar and organization of their written notes. More importantly, the information available in these journals provided him with a wealth of ongoing (formative) insights about how his students comprehended the subject material. He found the process of discovering *how* his students understood the material—as well as what in their lives they connected it to—much more interesting and helpful to his teaching than the previously used project checklists that simply indicated groups' completion of various project tasks.

In this example, Mr. Martinez used *cooperative group assessment* to advance the teaching, learning, and assessment process. The Western perspective on what constitutes success places priority on individual effort and achievement. This is particularly evident in sports and entertainment in which individual success frequently commands more attention than the accomplishments of collaborative (e.g., team) endeavors. In fact, people in the United States are more often inclined to identify and empathize with the "stars" in activities—even activities that require ensembles or teams. Similarly, educational institutions are most apt to grade, rank, and reward students based primarily on measures of individual achievement.

Schools and educators, however, are increasingly recognizing that many students are better able to demonstrate their genuine skills, knowledge, and proficiencies through cooperative learning and assessment activities. This reality is not surprising when we consider how most children learn the noncurricular, and potentially more critical, lessons of life. In everyday situations across many cultures, children have been taught to work cooperatively and collectively (as a family, extended family, community, or tribe) and to reflect on what they have learned from life's daily "lessons." This experiential, hands-on, real-world education features the most authentic assessment system possible—surviving the continuous challenges of life itself! There is great power and potential in drawing on those natural patterns of cooperative behavior to design and conduct effective learning and assessment environments.

Planning for cooperative group assessment requires us to consider both group rewards and individual accountability. Teachers sometimes have difficulty discerning individual student learning and contributions when projects and activities are carried out collectively. In this section's example, Mr. Martinez, a high school science teacher, overcame this problem by having students create reflection journals to document individual progress.

Teaching Tips:

Additional suggestions to promote individual accountability include:

- Provide students with a tool for documenting individual thinking and learning throughout the lesson (e.g., initial connections to the topic, new understandings gained, writing that demonstrates what was learned)
- Build in opportunities for students to discuss critical questions or key concepts with a partner (within the same group). Listen for individual understanding of the content and document with anecdotal notes.

- Track individual contributions to handwritten compilations of student thought by having each student use a different color of utensil.

Peer assessment also can be effectively used within the context of cooperative groups to enhance each student's experience with and interpretation of processes and products. As with other forms of authentic assessment, the group's understanding of outcome criteria will guide the creation of these products. Opportunities for ongoing refinement enable the group to improve the quality of both their processes and products.

Dialogue Journals and Scaffolded Essays

Teachers can gather valuable information about student learning through carefully accommodated and scaffolded assignments. CLD students in particular are often better able to demonstrate learning through tasks that incorporate supportive structures than through all-or-none applications. Because one goal of authentic assessment is to find out what students *can do* with what they know, focusing on what they *cannot do* is often of limited value. Fortunately, some of the most salient information about student learning is readily available to teachers who purposefully observe and read student responses to instruction.

> **assessment FREEZE FRAME 2.4**
>
> Because one goal of authentic assessment is to find out what students *can do* with what they know, focusing on what they *cannot do* is often of limited value.

Dialogue journals constitute one tool that classroom teachers can use to meld assessment with accommodative teaching. Although they may take many forms, dialogue journals provide a safe space for students to use written language in an ongoing dialogue with the teacher about events, thoughts, feelings, stories, and more (Denne-Bolton, 2013; Stillman, Anderson, & Struthers, 2014). The teacher often responds to the content of the interaction by intentionally modeling grammar, spelling, or vocabulary that would improve the student's communications, though the primary focus is on meaning. When CLD students are genuinely engaged in conversation with someone else, they are more highly motivated to communicate effectively.

Dialogue journals can be used prior to instruction on a topic to provide CLD students with an opportunity to gather their thoughts and engage in initial communication about the topic. This early engagement with the topic supports English learners' subsequent participation in classroom discussions (Denne-Bolton, 2013). Likewise, by having students journal after the lesson, teachers prompt students to reflect more deeply on what was learned and ensure that all students, even those who are shy and reluctant to participate in class, have an additional chance to share what they learned.

Another example of accommodated teaching as a means of assessment is the *scaffolded essay*. With this type of authentic assessment, a more complex essay question is reduced to a variety of prompts that require only short answers. This accommodation ensures that students are being assessed on their knowledge of content-area material and not on their capacity to answer the question in the essay format (Fisher & Frey, 2014). If the teacher wants to ascertain what a developing English learner knows about a given subject, a scaffolded essay often is an excellent option.

If the purpose of the assessment is purely to gauge the student's ability to construct an essay, a scaffolded essay might also be used to help determine whether the student can do so with accommodations. Figure 2.5 depicts a scaffolded essay question that

---

Figure 2.5   Scaffolded Essay

Essay Question: Who do you think was the most important president of the United States? Why?

1. Who do you think was the most important president?

(e.g., I think _____ (name of person) was the most important president of the United States.)

2. Why do you think he was the most important president?

(e.g., I think _____ (name of person) was the most important president because _____.)

3. What other characteristics made this person a great leader?

(e.g., _____ (name of person) was also very knowledgeable about _____ _____ and skilled at _____.)

4. How do you know this?

(e.g., I learned these facts about _____ (name of person) by reading the book _____ written by _____.)

5. What else did you learn about this president?

(e.g., I was surprised to learn _____.)

6. Summarize or restate what you have learned or believe about the topic.

(e.g., In summary, _____ (name of person) was a very good leader whose ability to _____ and _____ made him my choice for the most important president of the United States.)

could be used with a history class. As with all assessments, the teacher first must decide what a given tool will assess before implementing and drawing conclusions from it.

In general, authentic assessment approaches, such as dialogue journals and scaffolded essays, benefit teachers and students because these assessment tools:

- Provide more precise information about the student's learning and skills than traditional assessments
- Support identification of the levels and types of scaffolding needed for students to demonstrate what they know or can do
- Embed assessment within an instructional process that helps students acquire targeted skills
- Increase students' awareness of how scaffolds can facilitate their learning

Although they may not be aware of it, many classroom teachers already incorporate authentic assessment into their accommodated instruction for CLD students. Continual daily assessment helps teachers know when to modify instruction and when to strengthen (or reduce) supports or scaffolds to keep students challenged, engaged, and learning.

ACCOMMODATIVE ASSESSMENT PRACTICES 2.1

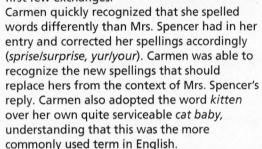

In the following example, Mrs. Spencer, a 5th-grade teacher, assessed Carmen's writing and scaffolded her response to it, maintaining an encouraging, enthusiastic, and nurturing perspective that focused on the content of Carmen's journal entries.

Carmen [first entry of the week]: *Last nite my dad came home with a big sprise. He say close yur eyes and then he say open them. Ther was a cat baby under his chert. I can wate to go home and play with the cat baby.*

Mrs. Spencer: *What a surprise! What did you think when Dad said, "Close your eyes"? Were you happy there was a kitten under his shirt? I used to have a gray kitten named Tom. What color is your kitten? I can't wait to hear more about your new kitten.*

Carmen [next day's entry]: *When my Dad said close your eyes I thot the surprise was candy. I like the kitten better than candy. It's a gril and hes white all over. I tol my Dad about your kitten and he said he used to have a gray cat to.*

Mrs. Spencer was pleased by the insights she gained from these first few exchanges. Carmen quickly recognized that she spelled words differently than Mrs. Spencer had in her entry and corrected her spellings accordingly (*sprise/surprise, yur/your*). Carmen was able to recognize the new spellings that should replace hers from the context of Mrs. Spencer's reply. Carmen also adopted the word *kitten* over her own quite serviceable *cat baby*, understanding that this was the more commonly used term in English.

Through her authentic assessment of Carmen's writing, Mrs. Spencer was able to identify areas for growth and scaffold subsequent writing. Her indirect corrections were more effective than simply using a red pencil to mark Carmen's errors. Mrs. Spencer's feedback with modeling apprentices Carmen to English vocabulary and spelling. At the same time, it prioritizes relationship building and self-expression. ■

SNAPSHOT from *CLASSROOM PRACTICE*   2.4

In this picture, Ms. Rinne gave her group of 6th-grade students the option of working on a scaffolded essay on the topic of area and perimeter at the end of the lesson. This kind of assessment allowed students to focus on the content rather than on the mechanics of the language. It also provided students with an opportunity to apply what they had learned authentically.

Jennifer Rinne

USING AUTHENTIC ASSESSMENT TO INFORM INSTRUCTION

One of the most common reasons that teachers express hesitancy about using authentic assessments is that the assessments rarely provide information in the numerical format traditionally associated with tests. This has left intuitive and reflective teachers in the awkward position of recognizing that traditional tests often fail to measure actual student achievement, yet feeling somehow unprofessional—or even guilty—about switching to more authentic measures given the current test-driven environment in which they teach. Multiple tools can support teachers' efforts to utilize authentic assessments in their classrooms and still summarize learning in ways that address issues of scoring. Among these tools are rubrics and checklists.

Rubrics

Rubrics are frequent components of performance-based assessment but are also valuable in other contexts. Students can become quite proficient with rubrics at almost any developmental level. For example, even preschool-age children can match the face they have drawn with a rubric that depicts a list of faces (i.e., faces with eyes only; eyes and mouth; eyes, nose, and mouth; and eyes, nose, mouth, and ears). When an "eyes only" drawing earns a smaller sticker than an "eyes, nose, mouth, and ears" drawing, young learners quickly begin to adapt their work.

In the upper grades, teachers can either provide students with examples of work on which to model their efforts or help them select appropriate examples for themselves. Discussion about how to identify key attributes of these examples increases the likelihood that students will attend to these attributes when creating their own products. When used as self-assessment tools, rubrics guide student compilations of ongoing work (such as portfolios described in this chapter) or help students prepare for more summative events (such as written or oral presentations).

Involving CLD students in rubric creation is particularly worthwhile because the ensuing discussion typically provides multiple opportunities to focus on the key features of the targeted criteria and helps build content-area vocabulary. When creating rubrics or other sets of criteria for authentic assessments, teachers must be clear about the skills being targeted. Even though the activity might afford opportunities to measure other skills, a narrower focus helps students thoroughly attend to the target skills. For example, the rubric developed in Ms. Carpenter's class (see Figure 2.3) was designed to focus on grade-level narrative skills. However, the resulting voice recordings and written products also provided a wealth of information and evidence about student growth in other areas, such as spelling, vocabulary, sentence structure, and pronunciation. Although it would be beneficial for Ms. Carpenter to make notes on these additional areas of student progress, such skills would not be included in the rubric.

When creating a rubric, the first step is to determine the desired outcome. In a given content area, what do you want your students to be able to do? This step requires familiarity with the academic standards to which the curriculum is aligned. Some secondary teachers may choose additional outcomes that reflect skills relevant to potential employers or institutions of higher education. Figure 2.6 illustrates a simple rubric designed for a secondary-level social studies project.

Figure 2.6   Rubric for 6th-Grade Social Studies Project

	Beginning 1	Developing 2	Accomplished 3	Exemplary 4	Score
Evidence Supported Zoning Decision	Student presents few concepts and details related to the assigned situation.	One or more relevant concepts are presented, but the position is lacking in supportive detail or relation to the financial, environmental, and sociological impact at the local, state, national, or global level.	A decision is presented and supported based on evidence of the impact of one to two factors (financial, environmental, sociological) at one or more levels (local, state, national, global).	A well-stated and supported decision based on evidence of the financial, environmental, and sociological impact of each option at two or more levels (local, state, national, global) is presented.	
Collaboration	Final work product (written/oral report, role-play, model/data representation, etc.) reflects little evidence of peer/community collaboration or consideration.	Final work product (written/oral report, role-play, model/data representation, etc.) reflects and/or describes collaboration with or consideration of another individual (class or community).	Final work product (written/oral report, role-play, model/data representation, etc.) reflects and/or describes collaboration with or consideration of multiple individuals (class or community).	Final work product (written/oral report, role-play, model/data representation, etc.) reflects and/or describes collaboration with or consideration of individuals from class and community.	

(See Assessment in Action 2.1 to explore how this rubric was designed to target a specified curricular standard.)

Bear in mind that the behaviors or skills you choose as features of an assessment should be measurable. For example, although "pays attention in class" is an important objective, it is comparatively difficult to measure because some students may appear to be attentive when they actually aren't, and vice versa. In this case, the teacher may want to identify a more quantifiable behavior associated with paying attention, such as "responds appropriately when called on" or "follows directions in class." When CLD students are involved, it is important to ensure that their ability to demonstrate the identified skill is not compromised by their level of English language proficiency.

Checklists

Authentic assessments can also take the form of *checklists* as a means of teacher, peer, or self-evaluation. Although the format of these assessments varies, the instruments themselves can be developed the same way as rubrics, starting with the identification of skills, knowledge, and competencies necessary to perform tasks associated with the activity. Once those skills and competencies are clearly defined, a series of questions or statements can describe varying levels of product development. For instance, an assessment checklist of skills related to synthesis of nonfiction text might include the following:

_____ Selected character of interest from California's history

_____ Found three sources of information on this person (list follows)

_____ Highlighted or noted the most important points from each source

_____ Developed a chronological outline of the subject's life

ASSESSMENT IN ACTION 2.1

Let's explore a specific curricular example, such as the way a teacher might create a rubric to address the following 6th-grade social studies standard:

Economics Standard: *The student uses a working knowledge and understanding of major economic concepts, issues, and systems of the United States and other nations, and applies decision-making skills as a consumer, producer, saver, investor, and citizen in the interdependent world.*

Step 1: State the desired outcome.

Mr. Bryant is a 6th-grade teacher of a class in which about 50 percent of the students are English learners. In targeting the economics standard, he focused on the need for students to understand basic principles of market forces. Based on this target knowledge, he stated the desired outcome as follows:

The student will demonstrate an understanding of how the scarcity of resources requires communities and nations to make choices about goods and services (e.g., what food to eat, where to locate food, how to use land).

Step 2: Develop or identify within your current classroom practices a task that will create opportunities for students to demonstrate the target skill.

Mr. Bryant decided to do a simulation that required students to weigh the economic, environmental, and sociological impacts of either preserving a specific area of forested land for recreational use or converting it to commercial use. He chose their town for the setting and selected a wooded tract of land just beyond the school's outermost attendance zone. The students were required to examine the issue from a variety of perspectives and to rely on multiple resources to determine whether this piece of land should remain natural (for recreational use) or be developed commercially as a site for a discount superstore. Although Mr. Bryant recognized there might be disadvantages to portraying a fictitious development opportunity, he hoped local relevance would increase student interest, motivation, access to authentic resources, and opportunities to learn more about the politics and priorities of their own community. As a result, students would be compelled to construct their own meaning and apply the targeted skills in a real-world context.

Step 3: Determine what a high-quality performance on this task might look like. Later, you can revise this vision to reflect the highest-quality responses or products actually produced. A new rubric usually remains a draft, pending its proven capacity to describe and guide student work accurately.

Because half of his students are culturally and linguistically diverse, Mr. Bryant decided they would be allowed to present their final decisions and defend their choices by means of any format that met the rubric criteria of providing "a well-stated and supported decision based on evidence of the financial, environmental, and sociological impact of each option at two or more levels (local, state, national, global)." Whether students chose to demonstrate their knowledge through a written report, an oral presentation, a graphic display (e.g., local polling results on the issue), an object representation (e.g., a model or diorama), a drama (e.g., a re-creation of a city hall meeting or a news exposé), or any other appropriate means, they were required to support their decisions by addressing each element in the criteria to meet the highest rating on the rubric.

Step 4: Complete the rubric by describing the requirements that must be met to attain each quantified level of performance.

Once the target level was operationally defined, Mr. Bryant described the elements that had to be present at each successive level of performance. He continued until all levels of the rubric criteria had been detailed and quantified in a way that could describe almost any type of product or outcome. The lowest levels of achievement included descriptors of unmet criteria such as "student presents few concepts and details related to the assigned situation" or "little evidence of peer collaboration or discussion." Figure 2.6 provides the final rubric that Mr. Bryant used with his class. In the end, the pragmatic value of a rubric depends not only on how much time and detail goes into its development but also (as with all forms of assessment) the degree to which the information is used to improve teaching and learning for each individual student.

This checklist might be used solely for the activity, or it can be included in a student's portfolio along with other components of teacher and student assessment.

Using a checklist to identify steps to task completion helps students recognize and monitor their own progress toward a goal. Students soon understand that each level of the task is built on the knowledge gained at previous steps. Authentic assessment tools of this sort help students recognize their own areas of difficulty and encourage them to seek assistance with specific challenges. Creating such a checklist also requires the teacher to analyze tasks in ways that enhance his or her awareness of subskills with which the CLD student may need additional supports or accommodations.

SUMMARY

In classrooms, CLD students are expected to use their language skills, cognitive resources, and academic knowledge to listen, read, comprehend, synthesize, analyze, compare, contrast, relate, articulate, write, evaluate, and more. Yet attaining these capacities is a long-term process, the success of which cannot be adequately measured through traditional, standardized, or even norm-referenced student assessments. For teachers of culturally and linguistically diverse populations, the best pathway for documenting language and academic growth during the lesson and across time is to compliment more formal forms of assessment with authentic assessment of learning.

As teachers it is easy to feel defeated when our students are not reaching the benchmarks set forth by states or districts. Yet it is important to remember that such benchmarks oftentimes are determined by those who know little about the complexity of our students' needs. Moreover, the very tools and processes used to assess our CLD students' growth and achievement can suffer from significant threats to reliability and validity, making results difficult to interpret. Using authentic assessments provides teachers, parents, and stakeholders with the necessary evidence and documentation to defend student growth.

In this chapter, we explored multiple types of authentic assessments readily available to classroom teachers. From performance-based assessments to dialogue journals and scaffolded essays, authentic assessments afford educators opportunities to explore the depth of student knowledge. Rather than requiring students to demonstrate learning in ways that fit our preconceived notions or personal preferences for how best to express ideas and structure responses, authentic assessments present a wide playing field for students to demonstrate what they know and can do. When used strategically, authentic assessments provide teachers with windows into students' thinking, which enables us to accommodate our instruction to meet the needs of each unique learner.

In today's age of accountability, teachers understandably are concerned with how they might document the language and academic gains made evident through authentic assessment practices. Rubrics and checklists serve as two highly adaptable means of systematically monitoring and recording student outcomes. Such tools not only inform our grading and subsequent planning and instruction, but they also support students to develop metacognitive capacities for monitoring and evaluating their own learning.

KEY CONCEPTS

Alternative assessments
Authentic assessments
Checklists
Construct validity
Constructivist perspective
Content validity
Cooperative group assessment

Dialogue journals
Inter-rater reliability
Interview-based assessment
Peer assessment
Performance-based
   assessments (PBAs)
Play-based assessment

Portfolio
Reliability
Rubrics
Scaffolded essays
Self-assessment
Validity

PROFESSIONAL CONVERSATIONS ON PRACTICE

1. Explain the use of authentic assessments with CLD students. What sorts of information do such assessments gather that traditional assessments do not?

2. Explore how performance-based assessments may draw on the prior experiences and knowledge that CLD students bring to the classroom in ways that traditional assessments may not.

3. Discuss the advantages of self-assessment for CLD students. How might self-assessments play a role in the portfolio-based assessment of CLD students?

QUESTIONS FOR REVIEW AND REFLECTION

1. What reasons account for the increasing popularity of alternative and authentic assessments with teachers of CLD students? Describe at least two.

2. What are key characteristics of authentic assessments? List at least four.

3. What is the difference between reliability and validity in relation to assessment? Explain.

4. How might you design a portfolio assessment to ensure documentation of CLD students' socioemotional, linguistic, and academic growth? List at least four data sources you would include.

5. What are at least two advantages of peer assessment for CLD students?

6. What types of information might be collected through the use of interviews? List at least three.

7. What is play-based assessment, and why is it useful in the authentic assessment of CLD students?

8. How can teachers design cooperative group assessments to facilitate both individual and group accountability?

9. What are the benefits of dialogue journals and scaffolded essays in the authentic assessment of CLD students? List at least three.

10. Compare and contrast rubrics and checklists. List at least two similarities and at least one difference.

CHAPTER 3

PREINSTRUCTIONAL ASSESSMENT: RE-ENVISIONING WHAT IS POSSIBLE

To help students respond to our efforts, teachers must first acknowledge students as persons, legitimize their knowledge and experiences, and engage with them personally and intellectually. In doing so, educators recognize students as whole people and show them that they are valued, thereby relaying a message of hope.

Louie Rodriguez, "Yo Mister!"

Chapter Outline

Formal and Informal Preassessment

History/Herstory: What the CLD Student Brings to the Classroom
   Biopsychosocial History of the CLD Student
   Education History of the CLD Student
   Language History of the CLD Student
   Keepers of Students' Stories: Parents, Caregivers, and Families

Preassessment in Lesson Delivery

Summary

Objectives

After reading this chapter, you should be able to:

- Hold informed conversations with administrators, colleagues, and parents about implications of formal and informal preassessments for highlighting students' needs and assets.

- Use preassessment tools and strategies to develop a holistic understanding of each CLD student.

- Implement and advocate for assessment practices that maximize students' native languages and background knowledge.

Teachers' documentation of student potential is essential to teaching and learning. Most of our work, as teachers, tends to focus on formative assessment to inform our in-the-moment decision making, or postinstructional assessment to assign a grade. Often absent is preinstructional assessment that occurs before the lesson to assess what is known by the student.

As the term suggests, preinstructional assessment is student assessment that occurs *before* instruction. Preinstructional assessment, generally referred to as *preassessment*, is essential for effectively teaching diverse students in today's schools. Making decisions on formal and informal preassessments, including when and how to use them, is critical to creating a positive and productive community of learners, both for the individual and the collective community.

Students need the classroom to be a space where they are equal contributors to the learning process. Insightful teachers effectively use a combination of formal and informal assessment tools to gather baseline information, explore background knowledge, and inform their holistic understanding of each learner. Only with a solid understanding of the knowledge, language, skills, and experiences that learners bring to a lesson is a teacher able to orchestrate learning processes effectively during the lesson. Accordingly, this chapter discusses both formal and informal ways to preassess CLD students.

FORMAL AND INFORMAL PREASSESSEMENT

Educational preassessments can take many forms and can be used for a variety of purposes. Currently in the spotlight are the types of tests used to meet federal or state accountability mandates. These high-stakes tests are typically formal and generate numerical data used to compare students, schools, and districts regarding specific areas of student achievement. Such standardized assessments are usually administered to all students under similar conditions (although assessment accommodations may be possible for some CLD and special education students). Data from formal tests not only serve to measure learning to date, but also commonly provide an index of preinstructional skills and knowledge for the coming year.

Unfortunately, teachers who rely exclusively on the results of high-stakes tests for preassessment information often receive an incomplete, if not misleading, picture of what each student actually knows and is capable of demonstrating in the classroom. Formal preassessments often cause higher levels of anxiety and raise students' *affective filter*. The affective filter has been compared with a defense mechanism that controls the extent to which an individual internalizes input to comprehend or apply it to learning. Krashen (1982, 2000) has argued that raising the student's affective filter can significantly and adversely affect his or her ability to benefit from instruction and other forms of classroom input. Similarly, the stress of testing scenarios can limit students' ability to understand what the test is asking and to produce their highest caliber of work. Standardized assessments frequently do not afford the time needed by many CLD learners to demonstrate the knowledge and skills they possess in the required formal manner.

Standardized tests and subject-area pretests do not measure experiential knowledge, nor are they able to assess the full scope of academic background knowledge a student brings to the classroom. Therefore, although important, formal assessments often are of limited usefulness to teachers as they plan the nuances of their daily instruction. Elsewhere in this book we detail formal preassessment of acculturation (Chapter 4), language (Chapter 5), and content knowledge (Chapter 6). In this chapter, we touch upon formal preassessments that are likely to be most beneficial to obtaining a rough idea of each student's starting point for classroom learning. Our focus, however, is on exploring preassessments that hold the greatest potential for helping teachers to learn more about students and to gather insights that can inform best practices with their specific communities of learners.

Informal preassessment better controls for cultural and linguistic variables by encompassing a continuum of strategies, activities, and techniques. Informal preassessment can take the form of instructional strategies, informal conversations, classroom discussions, and more. In typical classroom practice, preassessment is often limited to a picture walk, a K-W-L chart (see Assessment in Action 3.1), or other activity that is superficial in what it assesses and in the kinds of information it yields. In more dynamic classrooms, however, preassessment is embedded in every lesson and revisited throughout the teaching and learning processes. Preassessment of this nature is intentionally and consistently used to gather information about the knowledge, skills, and capacities of students prior to their participation in a new lesson or course of instruction. Effective teachers assess the language and knowledge of learners and document the background experiences that influence their perspectives. This type of preassessment has the potential to inform both the teacher and the learner.

> **assessment FREEZE FRAME 3.1**
>
> The most effective preassessment practices help us better understand the knowledge, skills, and background experiences students have gained through prior socialization in a particular culture.

For the teacher, preassessment results provide a "point of departure" that guides subsequent decisions about the scaffolding and differentiation required to meet individual student needs. With greater knowledge of learner assets, the teacher is able to create classroom conditions that value all students' contributions to the construction of knowledge, as the community works together to attain the learning goals. For the learner, preassessment provides the opportunity to harness memories, experiences, words, and ideas from across the full spectrum of life that might contribute to the day's learning. An inclusive and professional perspective on preassessment acknowledges that students bring various funds of knowledge to the classroom (Moll et al., 1992). As with many other students, much of what CLD students know and many of the skills they possess were not learned exclusively at school. The most effective preassessment practices help us better understand the knowledge, skills, and background experiences students have gained through prior socialization in a particular culture.

Information gathered from preinstructional assessments is critical for appropriately planning and delivering a lesson. This is especially true for students whose backgrounds contain a particular gap in or wealth of knowledge related to targeted concepts and skills. The classroom teacher's awareness of the needs and assets CLD students bring to each lesson will enable her or him to:

- Create a community that values every members' contribution
- Maximize instructional time by avoiding redundancy
- Connect new learning to prior knowledge and frames of reference
- Directly address misconceptions and gaps in conceptual understanding
- Adapt lessons to enhance authenticity and meaning for students

Teachers' ability to deliver content successfully reflects not only their level professional mastery but also the degree to which they understand and respond to what each individual student brings to the classroom. Unless teachers understand and account for what students already know, student responses to instruction and performance on postinstructional assessments may not clearly reflect their potential or allow the teacher distinguish new learning from old knowledge. Such distinctions are necessary for evaluating both the effectiveness of instruction and the true learning outcomes of students.

The focus of this chapter is on the power that insights gathered through preassessment have for keeping the teacher and student alike advancing in the reciprocal process of teaching and learning. For all educators, implementing productive assessment practices begins with understanding factors that influence CLD student success in the classroom. Student histories are some of the richest and most illuminating sources of preassessment information. Educators who attempt to teach without these insights often miss the mark in their efforts to instruct, accommodate, motivate, and challenge CLD students appropriately.

HISTORY/HERSTORY: WHAT THE CLD STUDENT BRINGS TO THE CLASSROOM

The following phone conversation illustrates how Mrs. Pham, a classroom teacher, obtained information from another school about her student, Aida.

> **Mrs. Pham:** Hello, I'm a science teacher at Champion Middle School. We have a new student here named Aida Galvan, and our records indicate she was in your school and class last year.

Mr. Dansby: Oh, yes, I remember her. How can I help you?

Mrs. Pham: I notice that she received an "L" in all content areas, including science, on her last report card. According to your system, "L" stands for "learning in progress." As we're not familiar with this type of grading, I was wondering what else you could tell me about Aida's knowledge and performance that might be helpful.

Mr. Dansby: To be honest, I didn't determine her grade. Although Aida was assigned to my class, most of the kids like Aida actually got their content-area instruction from the ESL teacher.

Mrs. Pham: Was Aida with grade-level classroom peers for any academic subjects?

Mr. Dansby: Well, the ESL students always returned to class during the last part of the block when we performed experiments but, since I never knew what they were learning on any given day in ESL, I just had them do worksheets, like word searches, while the rest of the class finished their projects and experiments.

On the surface, this conversation may seem rather uninformative, but it was actually enlightening to Mrs. Pham, who could now better understand Aida's current knowledge and skills in terms of her previously restricted opportunities to learn. This interaction shed light on gaps in Aida's grade-level skills that could be addressed by providing highly contextualized, sheltered opportunities to participate in a rich and challenging curriculum.

Information that can prove crucial to instruction often shows up where it's least expected. At other times, as in the previous scenario, it results from a teacher's purposeful efforts to explore the student's background. Teachers can reach out to colleagues, parents, and the student to gather information and insights that might help to explain observations of student behavior and learning during instruction.

Keep in mind that each student arrives with *a story* (be it his-story or her-story). This history or biography is too often ignored amidst the many challenges of teaching a student with atypical needs and circumstances. Yet it is often this history of prior experiences, prior schooling, and prior learning that unlocks classroom adaptations and instructional accommodations necessary for ensuring success. Simply put, the classroom teacher's diligence in exploring student histories is often the key to success with CLD learners. Figure 3.1 depicts a CLD student biography card, a tool that teachers can use to record biographical information on individual students and later access as a quick reference. Teachers can modify and adapt the biography card to include information that is most applicable to their teaching context.

Teaching Tips:

Complete CLD student biography cards at the beginning of the year (or whenever a new CLD student arrives in your classroom). Then use the biography cards as:

- Cues to remember unique characteristics of the learner
- A support system for making decisions about group configurations
- Tools for planning instruction
- Tools for entering into conversations with families
- Tools for engaging with learners in conversations about socioemotional and academic challenges and successes.

Figure 3.1   CLD Student Biography Card

Teachers can use CLD student biography cards such as this to gather valuable data about their students that can help guide their classroom instruction.

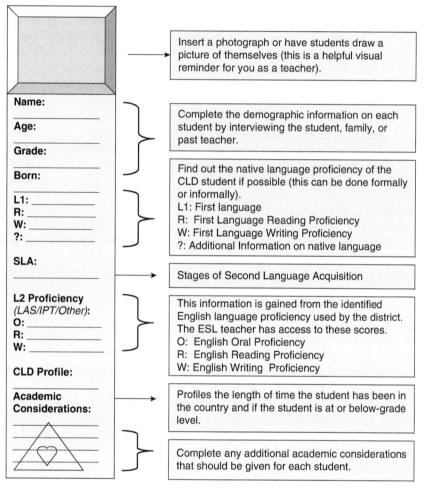

Source: Herrera (2007), p. 101. Used with permission of KCAT/TLC, Kansas State University.

As teachers, it is impossible for us to simply remember all the dimensions of each of our learners. Tracking information with the aid of a computer can help us compartmentalize what we know. However, a tool in our hand can be a constant reminder of what is relevant and important to the learners in our classroom communities. Acting on this information sends the message that we care about our students as individuals. As such, biography cards support teacher efforts to create optimal conditions for learning. With knowledge of students easily within reach, teachers can better differentiate and scaffold instruction.

Biopsychosocial History of the CLD Student

Mr. Kim was an experienced ESL teacher assigned to serve a growing population of newcomers at Southeast Magnet. His early interviews with students revealed that many were finding the transition from rural Mexican settings to urban multiethnic

---

VOICES *from the* FIELD 3.1

One of the most important and most powerful preinstructional assessments that a teacher can collect for each CLD student in the classroom is a student biography card. These biography cards are a starting point and a roadmap that the teacher can use to build a student-specific path to success. Completing a biography card is crucial because it allows the teacher to see and record the assets that each student brings into the classroom. Knowing these assets helps the teacher to plan more meaningful and challenging activities that tap into each student's background.

At the beginning of the year, I make sure to collect a biography card for all of my students; as the year goes on, I believe it is important that I refer back to these cards frequently. As I look back over the biographies, I am not only reminded of where each student comes from, but I also ask myself if any data needs to be changed. Have the students improved in certain areas? Have I learned more about their prior experiences? I feel this reflection on the students' biography cards is important because the students change immensely from the beginning of the year to the end of the year.

Karen Farrell, Third Grade Teacher

---

apartments quite "scary." They reported that the police were called often to their complex and children were rarely allowed outside to play. These insights proved relevant when teachers brought a number of Mr. Kim's newcomers up for discussion with the problem-solving team. In all, nearly one fourth of his class had not done well on initial universal screeners, but unlike English learners at his previous school, several had also done poorly with classroom probes that allowed them greater time and alternative means to demonstrate learning of targeted skills.

As the team discussed the need for interventions, Mr. Kim noted that the words *distracted*, *edgy*, *anxious*, and *forgetful* were used repeatedly to describe the students' performance. Another picture began to emerge. Mr. Kim appreciated the opportunity to share and invite consideration of the children's psychological state as factors in their ability to attend to, make meaning of, and recall academic information. It was clear that several students would benefit from instructional supports that were socioemotional in nature. The team agreed that proactive attention to the students' emotional stress and cognitive fatigue through differentiated instruction, thoughtful grouping configurations, and mindful relaxation techniques would support the learners' psychological state. As they discussed ideas for their English learners, participating teachers began to comment that many of the other students could benefit from these supports as well. They agreed to collaborate with the school counselor in learning how to implement socioemotional and academic strategies that provided all learners with enhanced opportunities to be successful. Mr. Kim left the meeting extremely pleased to be part of a team that was so responsive to indicators of students' multifaceted needs.

Much of a classroom teacher's success with CLD students depends on his or her understanding of the learner's biopsychosocial history. Although the word *biopsychosocial* sounds complex and intimidating, it is simply an adopted descriptor for the core aspects of human experience (Engel, 1977; Gates & Hutchinson, 2005; Saleebey, 2001). For example, if we examine the *bio* portion of a CLD

SNAPSHOT from *CLASSROOM PRACTICE*   3.1

This image illustrates a CLD student biography card reflecting one of the learners in Ms. Meier's second-grade classroom. With this type of information about her students, she is better able to support cross-cultural sharing, tailor language development efforts, and configure pairs and small groups to foster productive student interaction.

Tamara Meier

Name:
Mario Segura
Age: 7

Grade: 2nd

Born:
Mexico

L1: Spanish
R: Fluenty reads English
W: writing is on grade
***:** level in English

SLA: 2

L2 Proficiency   KELPA
(LAS/IPT/Other):
O: Intermediate
R: Advanced
W: Intermediate

CLD Profile:

Academic Considerations:
Excellent Student
Participates in class though
he can be quiet.
Prefers independent work
but will always work with
partner/groups when asked

student's *biopsychosocial history*, we are concerned with his or her health, as well as physical and mental readiness for schooling. More specifically, educators are concerned with questions such as the following:

- In the home country and in the United States, has the student received (and is the student currently receiving):
  - Adequate nutrition?
  - Opportunities for medical, dental, and vision checkups, as well as intervention as needed?
  - Periodic assessments of hearing and speech capacities?
  - Immunizations as recommended?
  - Appropriate opportunities for rest and sleep?
  - Periodic assessments of physical and mental stressors that may compromise the student's well-being (e.g., after-school work, living conditions)?
- What are the natural abilities of the student (e.g., giftedness in drawing, learning languages, using social-affective skills)?
- What personality traits (e.g., introvert vs. extrovert) influence the student's learning?

Factors that may affect the answers to *bio* questions include the socioeconomic status of the family, the English proficiency of family members, the health and responsibilities of parents or guardians, family awareness of and access to appropriate services, the number of persons living at home, family immigration status, and the degree of family isolation from others of the same ethnic or cultural heritage. Without physical readiness for instruction, CLD students are unlikely to achieve their full academic potential. Without opportunity to share unique hidden abilities, the learner is left to be measured by a standard that does not fit his or her history.

Equally important and useful to teachers is the *psych* aspect of the biopsychosocial history of the CLD student. For example, teachers benefit from preassessment information gained from answers to the following sorts of questions:

- Has the CLD student recently emigrated from a country that has experienced any of the following problems?
  - Violence or war?
  - Weather or environmental calamities (e.g., earthquakes, floods, famine, hurricanes)?
  - Oppressive governmental or political regimes?
- What is the current sociopolitical dynamic of the receiving country?
- In what ways has the acceptance or nonacceptance of the language majority group had an impact on the learner?
- What measures have been taken to reduce the student's anxieties and concerns about stressors such as moving to a new country, attending a new school, or acquiring a new language?
- Does the student show any symptoms that might indicate persistent homesickness, excessive stress, withdrawal, depression, or anger?

Answers to such questions may reveal a variety of previously hidden factors that can powerfully influence student performance. Such factors include:

- Psychological disorders (e.g., sleeplessness, nightmares, hysteria) arising from traumatic experiences with violence, war, and weather or environmental calamities

- Psychological trauma arising from the arrest, incarceration, or torture of family members at the hands of oppressive regimes
- Psychological reactions related to transition or school-related adjustments (e.g., homesickness, lashing out, withdrawal, depression).

These are especially important factors for problem-solving teams to consider any time a student is not responding as expected to instruction.

In addition to *bio* and *psyche* considerations, teachers who preassess the readiness of students are concerned with the *social* aspect of the CLD student's history. For instance, teachers who capitalize on the many advantages of home visits and prelesson opportunities to document what the learner brings to the lesson, gain useful information related to the following sorts of social (sociocultural) questions:

- Did the CLD student emigrate from another country and, if so, how recently?
- What role did the student have in the decision to come to the United States?
- How is the student adjusting to a new country, a new language, a new educational system, a new community, and/or a new school?
- How stable and how stressful are employment opportunities and work schedules for family members?
- What access does the family have to other families of the same ethnicity or home culture?
- How dissimilar are the home culture and the school culture?
- What is the social climate of the school?
- What social messages are sent about the student's place/belonging within the new school?
- What experiences outside of school has the learner had that will contribute to the lesson?
- What socioemotional factors can be addressed through the social and academic ecology of the classroom?

Answers to such questions offer classroom teachers valuable insights into the challenges and processes students and family members face at the sociocultural level (Gates & Hutchinson, 2005), as well as ways the school can adapt/change business-as-usual to support CLD students in becoming part of the social fabric of their new environment.

Elsewhere, we have referred to this biopsychosocial aspect of the CLD student's history as the *sociocultural dimension of the CLD student biography* (Herrera & Murry, 2016). This dimension involves some of the most critical precursors to academic success, including self-concept, self-esteem, social identity, cultural identity, and student motivation. Accordingly, successful teachers of CLD students are careful to preassess processes and challenges of this dimension, especially the process of acculturation.

Preassessment of Level of Acculturation   As previously discussed, students enter our schools with a wealth of information and experience they have accrued throughout their lives. This knowledge is acquired in the context of their *culture*, which has been defined as "the totality of socially transmitted behavior patterns, arts, beliefs, institutions, and all other products of human work and thought typical of a population or community at a given time" (Berube et al., 2001, p. 102).

Finding oneself immersed in a new culture can be disorienting because one's normal ways of thinking and interacting are suddenly out of sync with those of others. Such challenges are part of what we refer to as *acculturation*—the process of adjusting to a culture different from one's home culture.

The *U-curve hypothesis* (Cushner et al., 2009; Trifonovitch, 1977) is one of several prominent models used to describe the process of acculturation. According to this model, there is often at first a sense of novelty to the unfamiliar situation and culture. This honeymoon stage is frequently followed by one of hostility, as reality dampens idealized dreams. During this stage, the behavior patterns of students either are misinterpreted by others or are ineffective for interacting within the norms of the new culture. CLD students in the hostility stage often feel overwhelmed and disheartened and, as a result, are more likely to exhibit behavioral outbursts, not engage in learning, or drop out of school. However, with adequate support and understanding, students can progress through the hostility stage to one in which they see the humor of cross-cultural experiences from both sides. In the best of circumstances (especially circumstances of accommodation), the student transitions to a new sense of home. In this home stage of acculturation, he or she feels equally at home with both the old and the new cultures. Figure 3.2 illustrates these stages of the acculturation process.

Another oft-cited model of acculturation is Schumann's (1978) model, which provides a framework for understanding the particular relationship between acculturation phenomena and second language (L2) acquisition. Schumann's model contributes a great deal to our understandings and discussions about the impact of certain external factors on L2 learning. At its core, this model contends that the success of L2 acquisition is highly influenced by the social and psychological distances that exist between the L2 learner and target language community (e.g., native English speakers). Schumann defines this distance in terms of eight inherently social variables and four psychological variables that influence the nature of, and learner's response to, various types of contact with the target language community. Insights to these variables (detailed in Chapter 4) can be gained through preassessment methods designed specifically to aid the teacher's understanding of factors potentially influencing the language acquisition of CLD students in his or her class.

Teaching Tips:

- Ask questions to familiarize yourself with how the learner is interpreting his or her surroundings
- Take time to compare and contrast old ways of doing and the new ways

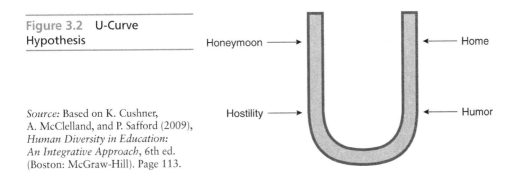

Figure 3.2   U-Curve Hypothesis

Source: Based on K. Cushner, A. McClelland, and P. Safford (2009), *Human Diversity in Education: An Integrative Approach*, 6th ed. (Boston: McGraw-Hill). Page 113.

- Group students with peers that will support the CLD student in adapting to the new routines
- Allow for adjustment time

Common to most acculturation models is the notion that, as an individual becomes involved in the process of acculturation, the clash of cultures that occurs may result in "extreme resistance to adaptation" or "a series of small maladjustments that are overcome one by one" (Lewis & Jungman, 1986, p. 4). How a teacher interprets and responds to the behaviors and reactions of students in various stages of acculturation can profoundly affect both students' ability to benefit from instruction and their positive adaptation to the new cultural environment. Therefore, preassessing the CLD student's level of acculturation is crucial to the classroom teacher's ability to accommodate student needs and assets effectively.

One of the easiest ways to discover more about a student's acculturation experiences is through an informal conversational interview, using a bilingual interpreter when necessary and feasible. Observing students' performance during the lesson and while interacting with others is another way to gain insights. The value of preassessing students in these ways goes well beyond the immediate information acquired. Teachers can develop a foundation for ongoing communication and reflection when they periodically talk with students about what the students already know and would like to know, as well as what they currently feel and think about themselves, school, and the learning process. If there are discrepancies between what the student says (e.g., "Everything is good.") and what the teacher has observed (e.g., frustration, apathy, sadness), these differences provide the basis for deeper conversations. This type of informal, communicative relationship empowers teachers and students to understand and respond to each other's teaching and learning needs.

Teachers who talk with students are better able to recognize and respond to actions that signal student disengagement from or rebellion against the new culture. Such behaviors and reactions include (Herrera & Murry, 2016, p. 20) but are not limited to:

- A sense of alienation
- Actions that are interpreted as hostile
- Patterns of indecision
- Feelings of frustration and sadness
- An intense desire to withdraw from situations
- Symptoms of physical illness
- Exhibitions of anger grounded in resentment

Many students who are dealing with issues of acculturation or even culture shock (see Chapter 4) struggle to function in an environment that limits their effective use of communication. More than just a pedagogical tool, language is the means by which we establish, mediate, and maintain relationships. It allows us to hear and be heard. Teachers can help students deal with acculturation stress by providing sheltered or translator-assisted opportunities to discuss feelings, thoughts, and experiences.

The details of formally assessing a student's acculturation level are more thoroughly explored in Chapter 4. Nevertheless, the Acculturation Quick Screen III (AQS III) (Collier, 2016) is worth mentioning here because it is a well-recognized assessment of acculturation that is widely used as a preassessment tool by classroom teachers and is strongly recommended by an increasing number of school districts throughout the nation.

The AQS III is a commercially available, research-based tool designed to measure a CLD student's level and rate of acculturation to grade-level school culture (Collier, 2016). The AQS III is grounded in research conducted in both rural and urban school districts and is helpful for placing and monitoring CLD students from migrant, refugee, and immigrant families whose first language (L1) is not English. This assessment tool has been used effectively to monitor and plan assistance for students from Alaska Native, American Indian, Asian American, African American, Hawaiian Native American, Latino American, and other CLD populations throughout the United States and Canada (Collier, 2016).

According to Collier (2016), among the many uses of the AQS III are the following:

- To inform instructional decision making and development of appropriate interventions during problem-solving processes and follow-up
- To inform instructional decision making for prevention (of culture shock) or intervention (for difficulties with acculturation, academics, etc.) activities in the classroom or the school
- To aid in the collection of data needed to separate difference from disability concerns when CLD learners exhibit problems with learning or behavior

The findings from preinstructional use of the AQS III are especially valuable for establishing a baseline for monitoring the CLD student's progress in acculturation and adaptation. Such formal monitoring is typically conducted on an annual or semiannual basis (compared with informal monitoring, which is ongoing). When used to gather baseline data, the AQS III should be administered no later than four weeks after the student begins classes at the new school. (For additional information on the AQS III, see Chapter 4.) Beyond using student conversations, classroom observations, and the AQS III, the teacher also can gain an understanding of the learner's acculturation level and other important information by making a home visit or by visiting with family members during school conferences.

> **assessment FREEZE FRAME 3.2**
>
> How a teacher interprets and responds to the behaviors and reactions of students in various stages of acculturation can profoundly impact both students' ability to benefit from instruction and their positive adaptation to the new cultural environment.

Education History of the CLD Student

Jorge's parents were pleased and excited to learn that his new school offered language arts instruction in Spanish as well as English. Learning to read in English had been difficult for Jorge, and he remained about a year behind his English-speaking peers. The teacher last year had told Jorge's parents this was "normal" for students learning to read in their second language. However, Jorge's parents thought he could do much more if given the chance to do schoolwork in his primary language. On learning about the bilingual offerings at the new school, they were thrilled and assumed Jorge would now have the opportunity to catch up.

Nonetheless, within a few weeks, Jorge was complaining that he didn't like Spanish and didn't want to be with the other Spanish-speaking students. His parents found these comments surprising and somewhat hurtful. They wondered if his years with mostly native-English-speaking peers had fostered this negativity. They were confused and distressed. Perhaps it had to do with the teacher. By the first parent–teacher conferences, Jorge was still performing a little below grade level in the

English-speaking teacher's class but was continuing to demonstrate progress. Unfortunately, the Spanish language arts teacher could not offer similarly positive news. Although she acknowledged that Jorge was better able to communicate his ideas verbally in Spanish than in English, he was not completing assignments and had begun to irritate other students during independent work times.

In many ways, the process of reviewing academic records of students such as Jorge puts teachers in the role of an educational anthropologist or investigator. Enrollment staff at Jorge's new school could have made better decisions about Jorge's educational placement if they had given greater consideration to his academic history. Such consideration would have suggested that, despite his Spanish dominance, Jorge had no prior literacy instruction in that language. As a result, many aspects of the Spanish language arts curriculum were beyond his abilities.

As the previous scenario illustrates, effective teachers are concerned with the CLD student's prior education history, in addition to preassessing his or her level of acculturation and other relevant aspects of the sociocultural dimension. The process of gathering information about a student's *education history* often begins with a review of available school records. Generally, these records provide basic details of enrollment, attendance, and achievement for each year of education. Among other data that can be obtained from this cumulative file are evidence of basic health assurances (e.g., inoculations, vision and hearing screenings, etc.), enrollment in special language programs, indications of whether the student has ever been referred to a teacher assistance or student intervention team, and enrollment in special education programs.

Although this is a great place to start, by itself the cumulative folder is a rather skeletal source. Once basic details of student achievement are located, teachers need to gain an understanding of the conditions in which that achievement (or lack thereof) occurred. In essence, educators need to determine the degree to which the curriculum was presented appropriately for the CLD student at each level. If, for example, records indicate a student was classified as a limited English speaker in kindergarten through 3rd grade, the type of instruction the student received during those years will have significantly affected his or her access and success with prerequisite skills and knowledge for subsequent grade levels. When a review of the education history suggests a student's language skills were not at the level needed to benefit from past instruction as provided—or the supports were insufficient to ensure fair access to the curriculum—the student will often lack the skills necessary to function at grade level. Aligning language and academic experiences is useful for native language instruction, too. In Jorge's scenario, neither teachers nor parents initially recognized the variables affecting his academic achievement in his primary language.

Although some schools and districts provide more detailed academic records, it is not uncommon for student files to provide few clues about actual instructional levels, types of accommodations (and the degree to which they have been used), or even the language(s) of instruction. In addition, parents or caregivers may not be aware that the phrase *ESL services* can mean very different programs from state to state and school to school. Parents/caregivers and the students themselves are, however, often the best and most immediate sources for potential data. Even when a particular program cannot be named, a description of the program can often provide enough information for staff members to make an educated guess.

Parent/caregiver and student descriptions of prior development and schooling experiences are aspects of the cognitive and academic dimensions of the CLD student biography (Herrera & Murry, 2016). Among the many challenges for CLD students associated with the *cognitive dimension of the CLD student biography* are:

- Cognitively demanding, decontextualized classroom environments and learning tasks
- Instructional approaches that fail to access the deep prior knowledge these students bring to learning tasks and problem solving
- Reductionist (i.e., basic skills-based and memorization-intensive) curricula and programming that involve few opportunities for higher-order thinking

Challenges associated with the *academic* dimension of the CLD student biography include:

- Academic presentation and textbook formats that involve content-area-specific terminology, unfamiliar grammatical structures, and inordinate assumptions about prior knowledge
- Limited classroom interactions that promote meaningful vocabulary development and familiarity with content-area-specific language
- Classroom curricula focused on preparing for high-stakes assessments
- Lack of reward structures for process learning and incremental gains in academic performance

Elaborating on prior academic knowledge and skills is critical to the ongoing cognitive development of CLD students. Successful classroom instruction focuses on the construction of meaning and helps students develop lasting connections between new learning and existing knowledge. Ultimately, this type of instruction depends on the effective preassessment of students' content-area knowledge, skills, and capacities.

Language History of the CLD Student

In addition to preassessing biopsychosocial and education histories, successful teachers also preassess the *language history* of CLD students. Although language histories have always been important for placing students in language programs (e.g., ESL), they also have powerful implications for classroom instruction.

The process used to identify CLD students who qualify for special language programs usually provides the first level of information about their individual language histories. Student information is often gathered via home language surveys that ask specific questions about current language used by students and their family members in the home. Such surveys may yield an adequate picture of the present situation but often do not gather critical information about the student's prior language acquisition experiences, or changes in language exposure and use over the years. (See Chapter 5 for an in-depth discussion of home language surveys.)

In general, students with stronger L1 skills have greater linguistic resources to draw on as they acquire a second language. These funds of knowledge are an important resource for the teacher as well. An immigrant student with substantial literacy skills in the primary language may initially communicate only in the primary language. However, such a student can often acquire academic English faster than some U.S.-born CLD students who (a) are learning literacy for the

ACCOMMODATIVE ASSESSMENT PRACTICES 3.1

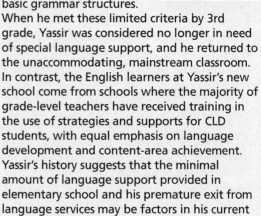

Digging deeper into the realities of students' individual biographies can illuminate best practices for classroom teachers. Often written school records on students' performance and background in school must be taken for what they are—formal records that provide limited context. In many ways, formal records can misinform the teachers, making it critical for the teacher to always dig deeper in informal ways. Consider the following scenario:

Yassir is starting middle school in a new town. His parents report that he began school in the 1st grade speaking no English. Available records indicate that Yassir was enrolled in the ESL program at his previous school, but he was exited during the 3rd grade. Although Yassir appears quite fluent in conversational English, a preassessment of his academic skills indicates that he is performing far below grade level and is having much greater academic difficulty than his CLD peers in the classroom.

Contacts with Yassir's elementary school reveal that the ESL program in which he participated consisted of thirty minutes of pull-out service each day and focused on the students' acquisition of *survival English,* with an emphasis on developing a core vocabulary (e.g., food, clothes, colors) and basic grammar structures. When he met these limited criteria by 3rd grade, Yassir was considered no longer in need of special language support, and he returned to the unaccommodating, mainstream classroom. In contrast, the English learners at Yassir's new school come from schools where the majority of grade-level teachers have received training in the use of strategies and supports for CLD students, with equal emphasis on language development and content-area achievement. Yassir's history suggests that the minimal amount of language support provided in elementary school and his premature exit from language services may be factors in his current lack of academic success.

If Yassir's new teachers had not looked carefully into the differences between the ESL programs in question, they might have arrived at inaccurate conclusions about why Yassir is struggling more than the other CLD students in the same classroom. ∎

first time via their nondominant language, (b) began learning one language at home but shifted to learning English before fully developing the primary language, or (c) are socialized in a family in which English is not the dominant language of parents or siblings but is the language they use most when addressing the student.

Language use patterns can also provide clues to social, emotional, and academic issues that may arise during adolescence. It is not uncommon for parents of CLD students whose L1 is not English to report frustration that they can no longer communicate well with their teenage children. Although this is a sentiment shared by many parents regardless of culture or language, it is particularly distressing for non- or limited-English-speaking parents, who quite literally cannot help with homework or talk about crucial feelings, thoughts, values, problems, and aspirations with their now English-dominant children. Although parents may continue to speak the home language, students can easily become English-dominant through the influences of peers, school, and society. A language barrier between parents/caregivers and children during this critical developmental time can have significant social and educational implications for many CLD students.

Additional considerations during adolescence relate to the student's potential denial of the native language, given the sociopolitical messages the community and school send related to the value of the home language. Often students' identity comes into question. Although the native language could be an excellent scaffold for the teacher and learning strategy for the students, denial of knowing the native language oftentimes seems easier to the learners than making public that they are not like their peers. This challenge can be addressed by what the teacher does during instruction to communicate the message that *being bilingual is an asset.*

Teaching Tips:

- Have materials to preview content in the native languages of the students.
- Remind students how many English words are derived from Latin and are cognates in the native language.
- Highlight the cognitive and communicative benefits of knowing more than one language.
- Remind learners that knowing more than one language is an expectation and reality of most countries outside the United States.
- Encourage students to nurture their native language abilities; bilingual capacities will make them stand out as global citizens.

The native language, when formally preassessed (as possible) and informally preassessed for English learners, has the potential to aid teachers as they attend to the socioemotional, cognitive, and academic needs of each student. Unfortunately, we often are so concerned with preassessment of English and other dimensions of the CLD student biography that preassessment of the native language goes unnoticed. In reality, knowledge and proficiency with English, the native language, and any additional languages the student knows are aspects of the learner's history that elsewhere we have referred to as the *linguistic* dimension of the CLD student biography (Herrera & Murry, 2016). No single biographical dimension is typically any more or less crucial than any other to students' lives and academic success. The four dimensions are interrelated and demand classroom instruction and assessment approaches that target the needs of the whole student. Planning instructional opportunities that support students to use their native language as well as the social language or academic language they have learned in English *as a gateway* to the lesson is the first step to providing and ensuring access for all learners. The words students currently have available for use in classroom engagement become the building blocks for learning and further language development.

Rationale for Assessing Primary Language Proficiency English acquisition and English achievement are the primary focuses of accountability assessments. However, some schools and districts also measure the learning and maintenance of skills in a student's primary language. Districts or schools may choose to assess both L1 and L2 for several compelling reasons. Sometimes such assessment is necessary because the L1 is a purposeful component of academic instruction, as in bilingual or dual language programs. The assessment of L1 proficiency can also be important in understanding issues related to L2 acquisition and student achievement (Rhodes, Ochoa, & Ortiz, 2005). Research and analyses support the idea that skills and knowledge from the primary language are transferable and can be used to support L2 acquisition (Cummins, 1981, 2001; Goldenberg, 2008; Kameenui & Carnine, 1998; Krashen, 1996; Kuo, Uchikoshi, Kim, & Yang, 2016; Thomas & Collier, 2002, 2012; Tong, He, & Deacon, 2017).

Cummins (1984) suggests that once cognitive knowledge is acquired in one language, those concepts become part of a common underlying proficiency (CUP) the individual can access and apply to other languages. This concept is supported by research that demonstrates how students' mastery, continued use, and academic development of their L1 correlates with higher levels of proficiency in English (Hakuta, 1987; Thomas & Collier, 2002, 2012). Information gathered through informal or formal L1 preassessment can aid in monitoring L1 development, as well as provide instructional insights into skills mastered in that language (August & Shanahan, 2006).

By assessing the knowledge and skills students possess in their primary language, teachers can plan optimal levels of academic challenge (and support) during lessons. For example, a teacher may facilitate instruction differently for a student is already familiar with targeted academic concepts in the primary language than for one who lacks related understanding in either language. For the student who has preexisting knowledge, presenting new vocabulary with pictures, graphics, or L1 translations may be sufficient to promote the transfer of a concept to the student's new language (Herrera, 2016; Klingner, Hoover, & Baca, 2008). However, for the student who lacks preexisting conceptual knowledge, the foundational referent does not exist. Therefore, the teacher may be more successful teaching the new concepts through demonstration, hands-on experiences, or other explicit teaching methods that help the student learn the *meaning* associated with the new concept. Even when learners do not possess the knowledge or language of particular lesson concepts, they bring experiences and language that are available to use as catalysts to accelerate their learning of new concepts and words.

---

assessment FREEZE FRAME 3.3

Creating opportunities before, during, and after the lesson for students to document and share their ideas and understandings in both the native language and English informs the teacher of students' existing conceptual and linguistic knowledge bases; it also provides evidence of learning that has taken place during the lesson.

Creating opportunities before, during, and after the lesson for students to document and share their ideas and understandings in both the native language and English informs the teacher of students' existing conceptual and linguistic knowledge bases; it also provides evidence of learning that has taken place during the lesson. Unfortunately, assessing native languages is often absent from the work educators do in school. Rarely do teacher preparation models provide guidance on how to make native language support happen during instruction. It takes creative and innovative teachers to see value in preassessing the native language and then maximizing its benefits for learning. Chapter 5 provides additional information on the formal and informal assessment of students' native language proficiencies.

Discourse Patterns   Language also influences the discourse patterns of the learners we teach. Educators often comment on how English learners seem to have trouble getting to the point when telling stories or writing. This may reflect differences in *discourse patterns*, the patterns through which a person expresses his or her thoughts on a subject (Herrera, 2001). English speakers of the dominant culture in the United States tend to use a linear discourse pattern, one that is highly sequential and focused on succinct resolution. Speakers from other cultures often follow very different discourse patterns in which narratives, by contrast, may seem circular, repetitious, or digressive (Herrera, 2001). However, every language exhibits particular syntactic and lexical structures that are generally comprehensible to speakers from that culture.

Figure 3.3 illustrates one perspective on the directionality of discourse patterns that may be associated with various languages. Considerable debate persists about the patterns illustrated for specific languages (Kaplan, 2005). For example, Kaplan notes that "every speaker perceives his/her language as linear and all others as nonlinear" (p. 388). Nonetheless, Figure 3.3 does convey the less controversial notion that there are perceptible differences in rhetorical preferences across languages to

Figure 3.3 Directionality of Discourse Patterns

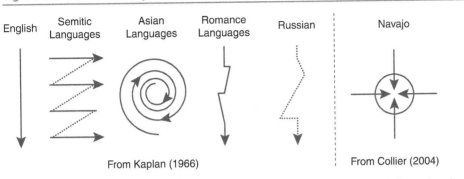

From Kaplan (1966)

From Collier (2004)

Source: Adapted by permission from R. B. Kaplan (1966). Cultural thought patterns in intercultural education. *Language Learning* 16(1), 1–20; and C. Collier (2004). PowerPoint image. Ferndale, WA: CrossCultural Developmental Education Services.

which teachers should attend as they assess their CLD students (e.g., their content-area writing attempts in English). For these and other reasons, many classroom teachers can broaden their own sociocultural competencies by learning about the interaction styles of other cultures and how these styles may influence personal and academic communication in diverse classrooms.

Keepers of Students' Stories: Parents, Caregivers, and Families

Parents, caregivers, and family members are key to our success with students. Teachers of CLD students who conduct home visits not only create opportunities for observing language use in context but also gain valuable information for preassessing the student's level of acculturation, academic background, and more. Although parent conferences at the school offer considerably less contextualized information about the student's home environment, these conferences also provide helpful preassessment information. During these interactions, teachers often find that their initial impressions gave them few or misleading insights into a student's talents and skills.

When talking with parents and caregivers of CLD students, it is helpful to remember that the majority of parents/caregivers may regard teachers as extremely knowledgeable and worthy of their utmost respect. In fact, some parents/caregivers may defer entirely to the teacher on academic issues, placing their complete trust in the teacher's ability to do what is right for the child. This level of trust may compel some to respond in ways that signal agreement with a teacher's comments rather than offering contrary opinions or evidence on the child's abilities and difficulties. Therefore, when visiting with parents/caregivers, it is essential for teachers to look for and ask about evidence of student skills and knowledge in multiple contexts, as the following scenario demonstrates:

> Ms. Adams was somewhat nervous about her home visit to meet Tamara's family. In addition to getting acquainted, they would be discussing the kindergarten placement test that demonstrated Tamara's lack of academic readiness. As Ms. Adams talked about Tamara's inability to do basic tasks such as sorting and matching blocks by color, Tamara's mother nodded. Not having blocks at home, she had never seen her daughter use that skill either. Tamara's mother appreciated the teacher's concern and agreed to purchase blocks if that would help Tamara learn to match.

Although this response initially pleased Ms. Adams, she noticed that while they had been discussing Tamara's skills, the girl had dutifully sorted a large pile of family socks by size and color, laying them in perfectly coordinated sets of two. Laughing aloud, Ms. Adams explained her observation to Tamara's mother and said, "Never mind the blocks . . . unless she wants them for play." From that point on, Ms. Adams eagerly asked parents for alternative evidence of skills at home and, over time, became quite an advocate for the many ways that curricular skills can be taught and assessed through home routines.

Parents such as Tamara's, who do not feel that their own observations and ideas are relevant to academic learning, will often not volunteer potentially critical information. Therefore, cross-culturally sensitive teachers encourage parents/caregivers to share related perceptions and experiences about their children. Figure 3.4

Figure 3.4   Home Skills Survey

Academic Skills Demonstrated with Clothes/Laundry

Can your child:

Yes	No	Unsure	Sort laundry by *color*?
Yes	No	Unsure	Locate items that *match* (e.g., socks)?
Yes	No	Unsure	Tell you which shirt or sock is *bigger/smaller*?

Academic Skills Demonstrated in the Kitchen

Can your child:

Yes	No	Unsure	Sort items by *color* or *shape?*
Yes	No	Unsure	Sort boxes or cans by *size* (e.g., large cans/small cans)?
Yes	No	Unsure	Sort items *in order* from smallest to largest?
Yes	No	Unsure	Show you which cup is *empty* and which is *full?*
Yes	No	Unsure	Identify items from the same *group* (e.g., fruits, vegetables, desserts)?
Yes	No	Unsure	Pick out foods having a particular *characteristic* (e.g., sweet, smooth)?
Yes	No	Unsure	Tell you which bowl has *more* (e.g., ice cream, beans)?
Yes	No	Unsure	Tell you which container has the *most* or *least* (e.g., grapes, chips)?
Yes	No	Unsure	Tell you which foods he or she *does* or *does not* like?
Yes	No	Unsure	Demonstrate that he or she knows *where* to find or put things in the kitchen?
Yes	No	Unsure	Demonstrate that he or she understands that the refrigerator is *cold* and the stove is *hot?*
Yes	No	Unsure	Select the correct *number* of spoons/napkins to help set the table for a family meal?

depicts an example of an informal assessment tool that could be used with parents/caregivers to gather evidence of a student's curricular skills (see also the appendix resources). Educators can tailor such tools to meet the needs of their grade level and content area.

Educators can lay the groundwork for an informative home visit in many ways. Because communication is often an issue, following up with verbal confirmation of written communication (and vice versa) ensures that the family is aware of the time, place, and purpose of the visit. Some teachers also use such contact opportunities to ask a few questions ahead of time so that family members can think about the related issues or confer with a partner who will not be present. For example, a teacher might inform family members that the following questions will be asked during the upcoming visit:

- What would you like me to know about your child?
- What do you think she or he does particularly well?
- What are the family's favorite stories?
- Which songs do you sing with your children?
- Who is your and your child's favorite singer?
- Do you have any concerns?
- What would you like to see your child accomplish this month, semester, or year?

Open-ended questions such as these invite parents and others to share knowledge and insights about the student that the teacher might otherwise miss. In addition, if family members are able to provide responses before the scheduled visit, this input can help the teacher more personally frame the conference objectives in terms of the family's concerns and wishes for their child.

When necessary, the teacher should bring a trained interpreter who, ideally, is also familiar with the community and particular culture of the student. Before the visit, the educator should brief the interpreter on the goals for the meeting and expectations for the interpreter's involvement. Although time constraints and norms of their primary culture may compel some educators to get right to business during the visit, many parents feel more comfortable if a little time is allowed for general social niceties in accordance with the community norm.

After the visit, teachers should document positive observations and insights gathered about the sociocultural, cognitive, academic, and *linguistic dimensions of the student's biography*. Thorough reflection on the home visit often illuminates details that can significantly inform instruction and assessment practices. Home visits also help lower the affective stress CLD students often feel when their home environment does not match that of the school. Thus, what is learned can also support teachers in attending to the socioemotional dimension of the learner. In addition, teachers can easily complete a brief write-up of key information to be added to the student's cumulative folder. Figure 3.5 illustrates one way of summarizing a student's cultural profile. A profile sheet of this kind serves as a quick reference for the current teacher as well as the student's future teachers.

Most of the aforementioned considerations for home visits with CLD families are equally applicable to school-based conferences. Although such meetings are typically less informative and take place outside the context of the home, they do provide opportunities for collecting useful preassessment data. Schools or teachers who report lower participation by CLD parents/caregivers in such conferences may want to examine the cultural and linguistic climate of the setting, as well as the supports available

Figure 3.5   Cultural Profile Sheet

Cultural Profile from Home Visit

Student Name:

_____

Ethnicity:

_____

Country of Birth:

_____

Native Language/Other Languages Spoken at Home:

_____

Second Language Proficiency (LAS score/Information on parent questionnaire or survey):

_____

Family Specifics:

_____

Cultural Characteristics:

_____

_____

_____

_____

Other Information:

_____

_____

_____

to parents and family members. When regular home visits are not undertaken, parent participation in school conferences can be increased by doing any of the following:

- Hold CLD parent conferences at alternate times (e.g., evenings and weekends) or places (e.g., a community center).
- Hold parent conferences (or additional opportunities to conference) preceding or following high attendance events, such as music concerts and sports events.
- Designate a school area as a resource room for CLD parents and families—an area where they can confer with one another and school personnel.
- Provide interpreters so the student is not in the position of interpreting for his or her own conference.

- Provide child care for parents/caregivers during conference times.
- Provide food (pizza, popcorn, ice cream) or drinks during conferences.
- Invite community resource representatives from medical and dental clinics, social services, and police and fire departments to familiarize parents with available services and answer general questions.

Although central to this discussion, parent conferences need not be the only means by which teachers and schools develop relationships with parents and family members. Schools can create welcoming environments that foster increased mutual understandings and family participation by:

- Hiring a parent coordinator to facilitate language-specific calling trees, activity participation, and informed representation of parent/caregiver perspectives
- Translating all or parts of the school newsletter into home languages other than English
- Providing office personnel or other means (phone, computer, symbols) to assist non-English-speaking parents/caregivers in conveying important messages
- Inviting parents to volunteer in the classroom (e.g., make materials, tutor basic skills, provide teacher-directed L1 supports, share cultural knowledge and experiences)
- Hosting regular events such as Muffins for Moms, *Pan Dulce para Papas* (*Pan Dulce* for Parents), Donuts for Dads, Grandparent/Neighbor Appreciation Days, and so forth

Teachers and schools that create a welcoming environment that takes interpersonal and cultural variables into consideration and respects parents and families as valued educational partners are able to form solid bases for collaborative "parent–teacher" relationships.

Teaching Tips:

- Use information gained from home visits, parent conferences, and classroom conversations to build deeper relationships with the students.
- Bring what was learned into instruction whenever possible.
- Ask students to share with classmates the stories or songs they know.

PREASSESSMENT IN LESSON DELIVERY

Mr. Carlson begins his unit on predators and prey by showing a YouTube video on predators and prey. He asks the students to write words (in whatever language they choose) or draw pictures they think of as they watch the video. For the next 10 minutes the students watch the video. Mr. Carlson stops the video a couple of times to have partners share what they have written. Throughout this process, he listens attentively to what students are discussing and observes what they have written and drawn.

When they finish watching the video, Mr. Carlson begins to weave a story about predators and prey, combining students' knowledge and pieces from the video. The class is fascinated by student tales of what they have seen eaten by *what*, *where*, and their guesses as to *why*. Sometimes, as with the praying mantis and grasshopper on Samuel's porch, these descriptions also include a rather detailed *how*.

Mr. Carlson is thrilled by the excitement of his students as he draws on their experiences to introduce new vocabulary and concepts.

> **Mr. Carlson:** What makes a predator successful, Sasha? (After a long pause) Think about the cat you observed. What made him a good hunter?
>
> **Sasha:** I couldn't see him in the tree at first because he's grey like the grey part of the tree . . . the trunk. He moved real slow and was quiet, but when he got close to the bird, he was fast!

Many hands are raised as Sasha finishes, and other students discuss the traits of predators they have seen in real life, on TV, or in the video. Mr. Carlson marvels at the way their prior experiences enhance their understanding of the curricular objectives regarding physical adaptations, prey–predator relationships, and human and environmental influences on that balance.

Students' knowledge of content-area material, as well as related skills and capacities, are among the most vital areas for teachers to preassess. Sometimes this information is gathered through written pretests, but there are many other ways to begin identifying and tapping into what students already know. Opportunities to preassess students' background knowledge from the home, community, and school must be intentional at the beginning of the lesson and continue throughout the lesson (Herrera, 2016). Students' initial schematic connections to the topic, concepts, and key vocabulary influence what they bring into working memory as they construct meaning during the lesson (Sousa, 2017). Planning for and using strategies and techniques that elicit such connections before and during the lesson promotes engagement and fuels students' motivation to learn more.

Teaching Tips:

- Plan for and implement opportunities at the opening of the lesson to collect words, stories (experiences), and language from your community of learners.
- Document what is shared orally to use as you teach.
- Weave the target content vocabulary into the "stories" you tell.
- Use your instructional conversations—now loaded with culturally relevant references—to guide students to reach the learning goals.

Preassessment of this kind can help identify sources of family knowledge from which the student and class can all benefit (Moll et al., 1992). The following scenario describes how Ms. Engelken draws on content-related knowledge from her students' parents:

> Every time the class prepares to begin a new theme or unit of study, Ms. Engelken sends a note home about the upcoming topic. Even though the notes are translated into the native languages of parents, she ensures that there is at least one content-related picture for those with limited literacy skills. The notes are designed not only to inform parents about the lesson topics but also to encourage them to share any of their own related stories, knowledge, and experiences.
>
> Last month the class began a unit on volcanoes by listening to Kita tell the Hawaiian tale of how the Goddess Pele came to be responsible for the eruptions of Kilauea. In addition, Arturo had seen Popocatepetl puff steam while visiting family in Mexico City. Rick's mom had downloaded pictures of Mt. St. Helens from the Internet, and Andre's grandmother actually visited the classroom and told the whole class about how her cousin's house had been buried by ash in Montserrat. Listening to these tales and experiences validated the parents' knowledge and fueled the students' interest in, and ability to relate to, the topic.

Although they gather information in different ways, Mr. Carlson and Ms. Engelken both use what they learn through preassessment to help students make connections between their background knowledge and new content-area concepts. The teachers in these scenarios understand that the pooled knowledge and experiences of students and families offer a library of resources. Some teachers never realize the value of such resources, and others fear to venture beyond their predetermined curriculum. Those who do take advantage of these funds of knowledge access a wealth of ideas and approaches to enhance the instructional experience for everyone involved.

Teachers can use quite a number of different strategies to probe students' current understandings of targeted curricular concepts. Here are some examples:

- Traditional subject-matter pretests (written and oral)
- Class discussions that focus on related experience or knowledge (which may include fictional references)
- Questionnaires
- Student interviews
- Creative student work (e.g., drawings or stories related to the content)
- K-W-L and K-W-L-H charts (see Assessment in Action 3.1)

Although critical preassessment information can usually be gathered easily, sometimes it is revealed only by chance. As illustrated in the following scenario, unexpected details can significantly inform educators about how to enhance academic opportunities for students.

Marisa was referred to the counselor's office early in the second semester at Northfield High. She had begun the school year unremarkably. She always attended class and met the expectations of her teachers. However, she had already accumulated five unexcused instances of tardiness and three absences since the new semester began. On review of Marisa's file, Ms. Lujano, the counselor, discovered that Marisa entered school in August as a newcomer from Guadalajara, Mexico. Because she had no prior English instruction, Marisa was assigned to Mr. Campbell's ESL class every morning. There she received most of her content-area instruction. Given her age and limited English proficiency, this seemed an ideal placement.

At the start of the scheduled counseling visit, Marisa appeared apprehensive about the session. However, she spontaneously returned Ms. Lujano's smile when greeted in Spanish. Ms. Lujano kept the tone informal and allowed social discourse to precede "business." As she listened to Marisa discuss her family and recent changes, Ms. Lujano identified many issues pertaining to acculturation and related adjustments. These seemed to be compounded recently by Marisa's sense that she had been identified as "dumb" (*una burra*). Marisa further explained that school here was boring and that she would rather be helping her mother at home than "wasting time" at school. When asked if she had felt that way in Mexico, Marisa replied, "No, I liked school there." Realizing there were a multitude of issues involved, Ms. Lujano decided to focus temporarily on school, and the following conversation ensued in Spanish:

Ms. Lujano: What is different about school here?
Marisa: They think we're dumb. We color pictures and copy sentences and learn how to say things in English.
Ms. Lujano: Like what?

> **Marisa:** We learned the names of the continents and some of the countries. We learned that Egypt has pyramids, but that's all. I already know that and a lot more . . . in Spanish.
>
> **Ms. Lujano:** You have already learned about the pyramids?
>
> **Marisa:** Yes! I know how the pyramids were built. It took more than 20 years and 20,000 people to make just one! They worshipped these different gods and put things in the sarcophagus with the mummy. I know why they did that too . . . so the dead person had what he needed for the next life. They have pyramids in Mexico, too, but my family left before I got a chance to study them.

Ms. Lujano was amazed at the enthusiasm, detail, and vocabulary of Marisa's response. Without context, even she herself would not have understood the word *sarcophagus* in Spanish. They ended the visit by agreeing to meet later that day with Mr. Campbell, the ESL teacher.

Mr. Campbell was also surprised by Marisa's depth of knowledge in many areas. As he thought about ways they might better address her academic needs, he suddenly realized what had never occurred to him—that Marisa's Spanish skills and knowledge could be an asset to her learning *in* English. Perhaps instruction for Marisa had focused too excessively on English acquisition.

Over the next several weeks, Marisa led a team that searched Spanish Internet resources, downloaded pictures, and conversed with grade-level peers in Mexico (via email) to develop a comprehensive report that compared the pyramids of Giza in Egypt with Mexico's pyramids at Teotihuacán. The team was encouraged to involve more proficient ESL and native-English-speaking peers from Spanish class in the process of developing Spanish and English versions of the report. Not surprisingly, the outcome was tremendous—and Marisa stopped skipping school.

Although identifying the root of an issue is not always this easy, conversations like the one between Marisa and Ms. Lujano can yield key information. When educators focus on practices that connect the prior learning, experiences, and relevant interests of students with current academic goals and opportunities, students continue learning at multiple levels.

The details of formally assessing content-area knowledge and skills are explored thoroughly in Chapter 6. Nevertheless, the Snapshot Assessment System is worth mentioning here because it is a well-recognized assessment that has been widely used as a preassessment tool by classroom teachers throughout the United States. The relative ease of its implementation facilitates its use for both formal and informal preassessment of content-area learning.

The Snapshot Assessment System (Rangel & Bansberg, 1999) is used to identify the knowledge and skill levels of CLD students in core curriculum areas. The degree of formality associated with the system is low; it can be administered quickly and easily. The Snapshot prompts CLD students to perform a series of tasks that are aligned to content standards in mathematics, science, and language arts. The standards and benchmarks targeted by the system are grade-level appropriate and considered fundamental to understanding future content. Teacher-researchers helped develop the system, and content-area experts identified critical, overarching concepts essential to each content area assessed. The Snapshot tasks are designed to be as free from cultural bias as possible and are especially valuable for English learners.

ASSESSMENT IN ACTION 3.1

K-W-L charts are a common way to provide a framework for tying prior knowledge and student motivation to new learning. Students begin a K-W-L chart before a new lesson by listing what they already **k**now about the topic and what they **w**ant to know. This serves to engage both interest and prior learning as students construct new knowledge during the course of instruction. After the lesson, students list what they have **l**earned and compare that with what they already knew or desired to learn. Some teachers add an "h" component to create K-W-L-H charts, which require students to think about **h**ow they learned and what strategies or resources worked best for them. This adds a dimension of metacognition (thinking about one's own thinking) to the students' self-assessment efforts. The following Assessment Artifact illustrates a completed K-W-L-H chart about the monarch butterfly.

■ Assessment Artifact: K-W-L-H Chart

Monarch Butterfly

K	W	L	H
• Has wings • Has antennae • Is black and orange • Comes from a cocoon • Is only here for part of the year	• What does it eat? • Where does it live? • Where is it flying?	• Life cycle: egg, caterpillar, pupa, adult butterfly • Caterpillar eats milkweed leaves • Butterfly eats flower nectar • Found all around the world • Migrates in the winter to warm places like California and Mexico	• Internet • Personal observation

VOICES *from the* FIELD 3.2

There are many preinstructional activities I can have the students do to assess their prior knowledge on the subject and curriculum that will be taught in the lesson. A tool to use with informal assessment is open class discussions. Drawing upon the CLD students' own culture can bring an abundance of information to the lesson. If the student has knowledge or artifacts about the subject from his or her native homeland, I encourage the student to share with the class. Open discussions show me how much prior knowledge the class or individual students have. This is imperative when preassessing the students because I may need to adjust the presentation of the subject and the time frame allotted for the content.

Tammie Heathman, Second Grade Teacher

ACCOMMODATIVE ASSESSMENT PRACTICES 3.2

The preinstructional assessment of a student's education history can reveal significant prior schooling experiences outside the United States. Yet some teachers tend to hold unverified assumptions about the prior schooling of CLD students. Specifically, some tend to assume that most schooling experiences undertaken outside the country are inherently inferior to those undertaken by students in the United States.

In reality, this is often not the case. For example, middle- and high school–age students who emigrate from Mexico have often pursued studies in mathematics that are equivalent to, or frequently above, the grade level to which they are assigned in U.S. schools. This is especially the case for students who have attended private schools in Mexico. The fact that a CLD student is struggling to acculturate to a new country and school and may be wrestling with comprehending a new language does not necessarily indicate that she or he is unable to perform at grade level in any given content area, including mathematics. It is important to keep in mind that the validity of such assumptions is easily tested with even a limited number of informal, content-area preassessments. For example, an informal conversation/interview with the student will often suggest the genuine extent of his or her background knowledge and skills in a particular subject. ■

SUMMARY

When working with CLD students, educators have many types of preassessment at their disposal. Teachers can gain information from the results of formal preassessments. However, such results must be interpreted in light of evidence gleaned from informal assessments that are situated in more authentic contexts of communication and learning. Much can be learned simply by holding informal conversations with the students themselves. Point-in-time assessments allow teachers to gain an inside perspective on students' current skills, knowledge, and interests. With this information, teachers are better able to plan lessons and target instruction to meet students' needs, while using their assets to accelerate learning.

Teachers who are especially successful in promoting the linguistic and academic development CLD students are effective because they have developed a holistic understanding of each learner. Responsive teachers find creative ways to unearth information related to each student's biopsychosocial history, education history, and language history. Educators who recognize the wealth of knowledge that can be gleaned from conversations with parents, caregivers, and family members also find ways to maximize the potential of home visits, parent-teacher conferences, and informal conversations as they gather information about their community of learners.

Unfortunately, the reality in U.S. schools is that preassessment often is overlooked, or only minimally utilized, in the actual planning and delivery of instruction. Teachers wonder: *How can I find the time to gather information that may or may not prove useful to teaching the lesson? Is it really valuable?* Long-standing research and literature in the field, including that of Bransford, Brown, and Cocking (2000), Marzano (2004), Jensen and Nickelsen (2008), and Walqui and Heritage (2012), remind educators of the importance that background knowledge has on new learning. Vygotksy (1978) and Krashen (1984/2005) relate learning to the educator's ability to guide students to move one step beyond where they currently are in language and knowledge. If this holds true, then it is imperative that educators approach students' background knowledge from an asset perspective—valuing and building on even the smallest words or digging deeper to unlock the relevance of what initially seem unrelated experiences, can turn the tide on student learning. When teachers preassess background knowledge rooted in the home, community, and school, they are able to anchor lesson objectives, concepts, and vocabulary in what learners already know. By leveraging the cumulative knowledge of the classroom community throughout the lesson, teachers promote students' sense of belonging, reassure them that they matter, and propel their learning forward.

KEY CONCEPTS

Academic dimension
of the CLD student
biography

Affective filter

Acculturation

Biopsychosocial history

Cognitive dimension of the CLD
student biography

Culture

Discourse pattern

Education history

Language history

Linguistic dimension of the CLD
student biography

Preassessment

Sociocultural dimension of the CLD
student biography

U-curve hypothesis

PROFESSIONAL CONVERSATIONS ON PRACTICE

1. Discuss why teachers benefit from assessing each dimension of the CLD student biography—sociocultural, cognitive, academic, and linguistic—before instruction.

2. Discuss the difficulties associated with relying too heavily on tools designed for formal, as opposed to informal, preinstructional assessment of CLD students.

3. Discuss how preassessment during lesson delivery can be used to gather insights into students' background knowledge from home, community, and school.

QUESTIONS FOR REVIEW AND REFLECTION

1. What are the advantages to classroom teachers who conduct preassessments with CLD students? Specify at least three.

2. How can the affective filter influence students' demonstration of knowledge and skills on preassessments? Explain.

3. As teachers preassess the biopsychosocial history of a CLD student, what three critical aspects of the student's history are assessed? Briefly explain each.

4. Briefly describe the process of acculturation. How does the U-curve hypothesis illustrate this process? Explain.

5. Why is the degree of similarity between the home culture of a CLD student and the school culture important to the classroom teacher?

6. Cross-culturally sensitive teachers often preassess the CLD student's level of acculturation informally through conversational interviews. How do the benefits of this sort of preassessment transcend the value of the immediate information acquired?

7. What are at least two challenges of the cognitive dimension and two challenges of the academic dimension of the CLD student biography? List each.

8. What are at least two reasons for assessing the native language proficiency of CLD students?

9. How can schools and educators collaborate with CLD families to gather information about students and gain insights into the family's funds of knowledge? Briefly describe at least three strategies.

10. What sorts of informal assessments can teachers use to preassess the content-area knowledge, skills, and capacities of their CLD students? Briefly describe at least two ways of informally gathering this information.

CHAPTER 4

ASSESSMENT OF ACCULTURATION

Using student biographies and my parent interviews has opened up my eyes to the very differing needs, experiences, and supports my students have. The student bio cards are completed by me with the help of the students. The parent interview questions are written by me (and with the help of the students in the 4th/5th grades), and the interviews are given by the students as a family history project right at the beginning of the year. This is our investigative writing that we use for writing class, and counts as part of CCSS (Common Core State Standards) as well as a writing unit. However, this project has become my "double-edged sword," serving not only as a way to gauge students' written work, but also as an insightful way to capitalize on the experiences, traditions and heritage each family can bring to our classroom.

Lindsay Smith, K–5 Special Education Teacher

Learning Outcomes ■■■

After reading this chapter, you should be able to accomplish the following:

- Detail the influences of socialization and acculturation on student-teacher classroom dynamics.
- Formally and informally assess acculturation of your CLD students.
- Use acculturation assessments to positively guide your instruction.

■■■

INTRODUCTION

Isamari arrived midyear in a small Midwestern town as a 5th-grade student. A very short biography provided by the school stated she had received schooling in Mexico up to the 2nd grade. Her score on the language test indicated that she was a non-English speaker. Informal assessments indicated she did not know the majority of her letter sounds in English or Spanish and that she struggled to read at a 1st-grade level in her language.

Fortunately, one of the members of the special education (SPED) prereferral team took it upon herself to further explore the sociocultural background of the student. What she learned was that Isamari had been sent to the United States by her mother to learn English (by herself) at the age of 7. She had moved in with her aunt, who enrolled her in school a few months later. After attending school for 6 months, the family began to have financial difficulties and decided they could no longer keep her. She was then sent to live with another family member and was enrolled in a new school. However, it was not long before this family suffered a financial setback as well and, again, Isamari was sent away, this time out of state. On arrival in her current school district, she was again enrolled in school and (as previously mentioned) was found to be lagging behind grade level, as assessed through both formal and informal measures.

Families and students come to the United States for different reasons. Some arrive in search of opportunity, some come to escape the problems of a war-torn country, and many are recruited by industries to work in high-need areas. Very seldom do children, adolescents, or young adults arrive in this country by their own choice. For newly arrived CLD students, stress related to changes in environment, language, and schooling places a strain on their capacity to learn. Educators often overlook these stressors as they scramble to plan for these new arrivals.

In situations similar to Isamari's, we educators often focus on what students know or do not know academically, without exploring the acculturation stressors they may have experienced since arriving in the United States. Questions or assessments for documenting socioemotional and psychological dimensions of the learner have yet to be a significant part of the conversation for placement or planning of instruction for CLD students. This often leads to lack of understanding surrounding low performance that moves beyond language and academic assessment. Lack of knowledge and understanding about the impact of the acculturation process on the CLD student may lead to inappropriate placement, as was almost the case for Isamari's prereferral for special education testing.

Often as teachers we are not prepared to begin with what many would consider the most fundamental information needed to be gathered before deciding education programming. Ask yourself the following questions:

- How might this additional background information cast new light on the ability of assessments to provide critical information about the student?
- How might stressors associated with the acculturation process affect learning for this student?
- In what way does the student's acculturation process and the teacher's own culture interact to accelerate or hinder learning?

ACCULTURATION AND ITS ROLE

Acculturation and Enculturation Processes

From the moment we are born, we immediately are enculturated into "our" way of viewing and interacting with the world. *Enculturation* refers to our *initial* socialization to the norms of our culture or group. This is the process by which we as children acquire the foundational values, behaviors, and language appropriate for the contexts in which we will physically, cognitively, and socially develop. It is evident across different cultures that the way we use language to meet our needs, the way we position ourselves in relation to the world, and the way we come to learn information is intimately tied to our primary caregivers, our community, and our culture. Often culture is not limited to our place of origin. Rather, our culture is multifaceted, comprising many complex and dynamic dimensions of who we are and how we define ourselves within any situation.

On the other hand, *acculturation* is "a natural process of adaptation to a new cultural and social environment" (Collier, 2016, p. 4). In this case, a person who is already socialized to a particular set of norms comes into contact with others of another culture, whose norms or ways may be markedly different. When the learner, as self, comes to school, this person begins the process of transforming, acculturating, and fitting in within a new space and place. This acculturation process can be complex, painful, and humiliating, and it may lead learners to develop a cognitive belief system that reflects the belief that they have no knowledge worth sharing. Therefore, what we as educators do to bridge the learner to new norms during the acculturation process is critical to teaching and learning.

Important questions for educators to consider include:

- Why must classroom teachers and other educators understand the values and beliefs to which they themselves have been enculturated?
- How can these values and beliefs influence educators' responses to, and relationships with, their students?
- What conditions must be present to provide the learner support systems during the acculturation process?
- What may be signs of acculturation stress?
- How can the family be involved to support the process of bridging from the home to the school?

The Teacher's Enculturation and Cultural Lens

The process of enculturation leaves individuals with a sort of filter or lens through which they interpret the behaviors and interactions of others. We become accustomed to our own patterns of response because they generally work effectively with people who have been socialized in the same, or a very similar, culture. However, when we try to read situations and behaviors that result from different cultural norms and experiences, inaccurate assumptions and misunderstandings often follow. This is true for both teachers and students.

Teachers' reflection on their own enculturation can be an eye-opening experience. Teachers who are able to identify their own cultural lens (or way of viewing the world) are generally much better able to recognize how that lens colors or distorts their perceptions of other people and events. The culturally reflective teacher also understands that CLD students have often been thrust into an environment in which their own lens are suddenly an unreliable guide for social interaction. This can lead to confusing (and inadvertently punishing) situations in which previously appropriate behaviors garner unpredictably negative reactions. In the following scenario, Fadi's experience is a prime example of these compounding misperceptions:

> Fadi is a very bright Palestinian student. He seems to be doing well with sheltered instruction in Mr. Tennyson's class, but he is frequently involved in playground conflicts. Although it's not unusual for 4th-graders to prefer same-sex playmates, Fadi's constant touching of the other boys has led to many problems, given the

policies of the school. Fadi disregards the looks and body language warning him to stop but becomes overly upset and cries when his actions result in name-calling, hitting, and alienation from those he considers his friends and reprimands from teachers. For Fadi, school has become an unpleasant place. His increasing visits to the nurse and number of days home sick only add to the Mr. Tennyson's concerns that Fadi will not be successful academically and will never fit in with his peers.

In this scenario, Fadi has failed in becoming part of the community of learners. Lack of understanding surrounds the reality that Fadi's sociocultural norms are clashing with the norms of many of his peers and those of the school. His teacher, Mr. Tennyson, has failed to understand the cultural norms for play that Fadi learned from his immediate enculturation. Fadi is, in fact, just behaving as expected of a boy with his background. He has been socialized in a culture that does not stigmatize males for platonic physical contact. Touching is common during play as a way to communicate friendship. Mr. Tennyson's view of expected behaviors for Fadi to include keeping his hands to himself while students line up during transition time in school and during play are in complete conflict with how Fadi has been socialized to behave in and out of school. He has been used to holding hands or draping his arms around peers as he transitions between activities and classes. Touching during play is just what boys in his culture do.

In this situation, Fadi and the other boys perceived and responded to one another's behaviors according to their own socialization or frameworks of thinking. Mr. Tennyson's interpretation, similar to that of the boys, was enhanced by professional training about the potential negative significance of Fadi's actions. Unfortunately, these ways of thinking led to a web of assumptions and reactions that initially interfered with appropriate resolution of the conflict. Therefore, as students acculturate to new school norms, it is important to check the assumptions we as educators hold in relation to what we perceive regarding behaviors that may not meet the norms of the new classroom and school.

Teaching Tips:

- Learn about the country of origin for new students.
- Investigate how a behavior in question is perceived and addressed within the primary culture of the learner.
- Have conversations with the family and the student to discuss the "why" of the observed behaviors.
- Bridge from the students' cultural norms that you learn to the cultural norms of the new community and school.

Acculturation Dynamics

The relationship between enculturation and acculturation is fascinating but not always easy to understand for those who have not experienced it firsthand. Imagine the frustration you would feel if suddenly the function keys on the familiar television remote were randomly reassigned. Now, pressing any of the automatically understood keys (those to which you are enculturated to use) results in a completely undesired response. How might you feel and react?

Students often get so many mixed messages from media, social media, their parents, and their peers that often the acculturation process becomes a psychological crisis, as they struggle to know when to behave how and for whom. Often immigrants are told, "You are in the United States now. You must speak only English and act like an American." Educators that do not recognize the psychological trauma that students and families experience often have difficulty understanding the student actions and responses that they witness at school. It is important to keep in mind that acculturation does not necessarily occur at the same rate or to the same degree among individuals, even among members of the same immigrant group or family. Most models of acculturation recognize that students often go through a variety of phases characterized by the following:

1. *Euphoria.* There is a curiosity and enthusiasm about the host culture.
2. *Culture shock.* Novelty gives way to reality. Irritability, anger, grief, and sometimes depression ensue.
3. *Anomie.* Individuals begin to understand and sort out their role in each culture. Frequently, however, individuals feel they are in a cultural "no man's land," estranged from the home culture but not yet accepted into the mainstream of the host culture. This period can be short-lived or persist throughout an individual's lifetime. Anomie is often associated with negative overall socialization. By contrast, the ability to adapt to the norms of the new culture while retaining affiliation with the old correlates with much more positive acculturation.
4. *Adoption/Adaptation.* Individuals may fully adopt the new culture as a replacement for the primary culture (assimilation) or adapt to it in a manner that allow them to function authentically within both (integration).

Acculturation can affect people in many different ways. The types and degrees of difference between cultures are also factors in acculturation. As the degree of difference between the cultures increases, so does the likelihood that the norms of one will violate the norms of the other—and that the process of acculturation will also be accompanied by culture shock.

> **assessment FREEZE FRAME 4.1**
>
> Acculturation does not necessarily occur at the same rate or to the same degree among individuals, even among members of the same immigrant group or family.

Culture shock commonly occurs as the novelty of the unfamiliar evolves into a frustrating reality for which there is no quick or easy remedy. In addition to sudden changes in language, recently immigrated students are often dealing with issues of loss associated with the friends, family, and community they left behind. Depending on the reasons for immigration, there may be increased family tensions and insecurities. Language barriers, social isolation, finances, and work schedules can leave some parents less able to provide the emotional support their children need during this critically stressful time. For students who are not recent immigrants, but whose culture is different from that of the school, it may take time to get into the rhythm and routine of the classroom and school setting.

Students who experience culture shock may demonstrate anger, irritability, disorderly behavior, signs of depression, emotionality (e.g., crying), increased somatic complaints (e.g., headache, upset stomach), homesickness, excessive sleeping, overeating or loss of appetite, social withdrawal, or loss of interest in previously enjoyed activities. These symptoms are significant areas of concern for educators because they not only impair a student's ability to learn but also are serious indicators of psychological and physical distress. Because students experiencing acculturation "may behave in a manner that is similar to students with a learning or behavior disability or other inhibiting factor" (Collier, 2016, p. 4), and because erroneous placements only compound the problems, it is essential for teachers to understand and be able to assess as much as possible their students' levels of acculturation. An understanding of the multiple factors contributing to a student's behavior enables teachers and other educators to make informed decisions about appropriate programming, instruction, and assessment.

Like students who struggle with other forms of trauma, learners experiencing dysregulated states (i.e., responding negatively or emotionally out of fear or stress) because of acculturation challenges need caring adults who can provide a calming, safe, and stabilizing influence. Efforts to reason, restate consequences, or enforce control will do little to move learning forward if, in that moment, what the student really needs is acceptance, connection, and relationship (Sporleder & Forbes, 2016). When students are functioning in a fight or flight survival mode, it is "physiologically impossible for them to function appropriately and constructively in the classroom or on the playground" (Sporleder & Forbes, 2016, p. 27). With this in mind, learning will get back on track most quickly if teachers first listen to the child and respond to needs of the heart (emotions) before trying to connect with the intellect.

Regardless of whether a student experiences culture shock, there are psychological, linguistic, and cultural changes related to the acculturation processes. Depending on individuals and their context, acculturation can result in assimilation, integration, rejection, or deculturation. It is extremely helpful for teachers to understand what each means for CLD students in their classroom.

Assimilation   Assimilation occurs when students replace their native cultural patterns and language with those of the new (or host) community. Among overt indicators are style of dress, customs, religious practices, and espoused beliefs. Assimilation represents a sacrifice rather than integration of or adaptation to new cultural and linguistic norms. Not all students want to look and act like everyone else, yet the need to feel accepted often forces CLD students to replace their previous ways with those of their host culture peers. Rapid assimilation to a new culture or language may result in a disconnection between CLD students and parents or family members that undermines family cohesiveness and strength (e.g., the ability to guide, support, solve problems, and communicate values).

Teaching Tips:

- Regularly remind students of the value of their languages and cultures.
- Share with the class the cultures and languages of CLD students. Encourage students to discuss relevant connections during daily lessons.
- Allow students' use of the native language during instruction.
- Create opportunities for students to highlight their unique backgrounds whenever possible.

Integration   Integration or adaptation reflects the degree to which the CLD student is capable of and comfortable participating in the norms and customary routines of different groups. Some indications of integration include situationally appropriate language, style of dress, and food preferences, but other signs are more subtle. It is important to note that behavioral acculturation (e.g., language, social skills, customs) and psychological acculturation (e.g., values, belief systems, attitudes) often do not occur in a parallel manner. Therefore, it may not be appropriate to infer acculturation levels based on single indicators, such as language or style of dress.

Teaching Tips:

- During instruction, group students in configurations that provide the learner the opportunity to interact socially and academically with students from the different cultures.
- Share out, when appropriate, the similarities and differences between the new culture and the culture of the learner.
- Celebrate the foods, languages, and traditions of the learners in your classroom on a daily basis.
- Select strategies and use techniques that provide ongoing opportunities to use the cultural assets the student brings to the community of the classroom.

Rejection   Attending to the culture of the learner during instruction sends the message that the learner is important and bolsters the psychological dimension of the acculturation process. Not attending to culture in the classroom can push students toward rejecting the new culture. Rejection reflects the conscious choice an individual makes to shun either the host or the home culture. Rejection of the new culture is sometimes prevalent among immigrants who choose to isolate themselves from nearly everything about the new culture.

On the other hand, individuals may come to believe that customs and behaviors associated with the old culture are undesirable or a threat to their security. Unfortunately, there is little evidence that directing such negative emotions toward one's own group eases conflicts of the acculturation process. Instead, remaining connected to core cultural values can serve as a source of resilience for students and as a protective factor against substance abuse and other risky behaviors (Sue & Sue, 2015).

The goal of any classroom is to create a space and ecology of trust through the activities the teacher selects and the ways in which instructional conversations support the building of community throughout the lesson. The goal is an ecology where the individual members of the learning community come to understand each other in relation to who they are and how they learn.

Teaching Tips:

- Select academic activities that allow learners to share who they are and how they bring meaning to the text or learning.
- Provide opportunities for talk where there are no right or wrong answers, and where there are opportunities to share experiences and knowledge from home, the country of origin, or previous schooling.
- Enter into conversations with your students that remind them of the contributions their parents make through their work in the community.
- Through whole-class instructional conversations, make public for the community of learners what is similar and different about each member's socialization, highlighting the diverse strengths of individuals and of the group.

Deculturation   Deculturation describes the cultural anomie or "no man's land" that some immigrants experience as a result of the disconnection from the home culture and language that occurred before, or in absence of, positive acculturation to the new community, culture, and language. According to Durkheim (1951), who first described the term in depth, anomie occurs when cultural norms break down as a result of rapid change. When CLD students' ties to their primary culture are weakened or broken due to factors such as language loss or societal negativity, the social norms of that home and culture may no longer influence their behavior. Unless positively integrated into the host culture, deculturated individuals may experience dissatisfaction and conflict for years as they struggle to find their place in society.

Teaching Tips:

- Attending to the diversity in the classroom through activities that highlight the uniqueness of every student and family may encourage the student to keep connected to the home culture and language.
- Through instructional conversations, highlight the assets of every student.
- Connect the content of the curriculum to the student's background whenever possible.
- Affirm student contributions, especially those that are linked to the home culture and language.

ACCOMMODATIVE ASSESSMENT PRACTICES 4.1

As Ms. Wessels prepared notice letters for the year's first conferences, she recalled that Enrique's enrollment listed Spanish as the home language. To verify this, she asked, "Your parents speak Spanish, right?" "No," Enrique said, with noticeable irritation. "We speak only English." Because the enrollment form could certainly be in error, Ms. Wessels asked the school's bilingual aide to be on the extension as she called home to make arrangements for the conference.

"*Bueno?*" on the other end of the line cued the aide to ask Enrique's mom her preferred language. She replied that, although she was trying to learn English, she would not be able to communicate well without an interpreter. When Ms. Wessels shared her confusion about Enrique's comments, there was a long sigh. "Yes," said his mother. "He tells me to only speak English, but I can't. Then he says he wants hot dogs and macaroni and cheese . . . no more *taquitos*. That upsets us and we don't know what to do." Ms. Wessels agreed that these were important issues they would follow up on during their conference.

By the time she hung up the phone, Ms. Wessels decided to add a new word to this week's vocabulary list. As the class reviewed the list of words later that day, nearly all the students knew each word until they got to *facile*. Enrique looked up but remained silent. The others shook their heads or frowned when Ms. Wessels asked if anyone had ever heard that word before. Then she put the word in a sentence: *Basketball is a facile sport for Michael.* "What do you think that means?" Among the shrugs and puzzled faces, Ms. Wessels saw Enrique's hand. He blurted, "That means it's easy for him. Basketball is easy for him."

"Wow!" she exclaimed. "You're right! How did you know what *facile* means?"

Without hesitation, he answered, "Because I know *fácil,* and that means "easy" in Spanish."

"So you have two languages' worth of vocabulary words?"

"Yes," he smiled.

To the class, she asked, "How many of you would like to learn some of the extra vocabulary words Enrique knows?" Of course, hands flew in the air, and Ms. Wessels had the perfect opportunity to begin her "Double Value" word wall, which Enrique assisted with every week thereafter. ∎

Students who go through deculturation are the most difficult to support. Often, they are resistant to offering insights about their culture and language and would rather go unnoticed. A fine line exists for the teacher who wants to support students in being proud of who they are and where they come from and not further alienating them in the classroom. The best course of action in this case is to build a relationship of trust and hold one-on-one conversations with the students about their background.

The process of acculturation is unique to each individual student. Many factors, including those related to the home, school, and larger society, influence a student's ability to adapt positively to the new culture. Although educators cannot control the myriad complexities of a student's acculturation process, they *can* work to ensure that the school environment both values students from diverse cultural and language backgrounds and encourages their successful integration. For example, school gatekeeping staff (e.g., secretaries, administrative assistants, office aides, administrative specialists, school–community liaisons, social workers) can significantly contribute to the acculturation difficulties CLD students and families face at school. Without recurrent professional development in cross-cultural and cross-linguistic sensitivity, these staff members are often unaware of the influences they have on family perspectives about the school, its mission, and its faculty members. Accordingly, successful classroom teachers of CLD students are persistent advocates for appropriate and progressive professional development for school staff, faculty members, and administrators. Table 4.1 details ways a school environment either encourages or discourages each form of cultural adjustment.

Educators often wonder how to address the acculturation needs of their students given the limited time they have for instruction and the curriculum they have to cover. Due to how important it is to attend to the acculturation process to open up pathways for learning, teachers can find ways "in the moment" that are creative and bring the community of learners together. These simple opportunities allow CLD learners to see themselves as valued participants in the classroom. Something as simple as including a word that would be recognized and creating a Double Value word wall was sends the message that languages other than English have value.

Relationship Between Cultural Identity and Acculturation

How well CLD students acculturate—and the attitudes about self and others that are formed during this process—can profoundly affect the students, their families, and their communities. Recent studies on the relationship between cultural identity and student wellness (and achievement) have yielded the following findings:

- Ethnic identity is the strongest predictor of overall wellness for CLD students (Dixon Rayle & Myers, 2004; Molix & Bettencourt, 2010).
- Higher levels of positive socioemotional development are consistent with students' positive identification with both their own and the majority group's culture (Chen, Benet-Martínez, & Bond, 2008; Shrake & Rhee, 2004).
- Disengagement with one's own ethnic identity, characterized by negative attitudes toward one's own group, can result in psychological distress, including feelings of marginality, low self-esteem, and depression (Jensen, Arnett, & McKenzie, 2011; Sabatier, 2008).

Table 4.1 Acculturation Environments

Acculturation Experience	School Factors That Contribute to This Experience	School Factors That Limit This Experience
Assimilation	• Requires that only English be spoken • Mandates strict adherence to a single school uniform • Celebrates only Christian holidays • Forbids prayer • Allows only specific types of responses during classroom instruction and activities • Maintains and promotes only Western views on issues (e.g., medicine, the meaning of life, legitimate sources of knowledge)	• Supports and incorporates use of the native language • Allows for variation within the school dress code • Encourages students to learn about and celebrate the holidays of multiple cultures • Allows private prayer (appropriate to the religion of the student) • Encourages multiple forms of response during classroom instruction and activities • Views open-mindedness as an asset to the construction of knowledge
Integration	• Investigates discrepancies between student behavior and expected behavior to determine the crux of the matter as well as the most appropriate course of action • Recognizes the value of communication in the native language, even if the speakers are able to communicate in English • Encourages students to see themselves as capable of understanding, appreciating, and working from multiple perspectives	• Punishes all deviances from behavior that is expected in academic situations • Expects CLD students to speak only in English, especially if monolingual-English speakers are present • Encourages the perspective that there is only one right way to think, speak, and behave
Rejection	• Allows discrimination based on language, religion, or culture to persist • Encourages students to view differences in customs, behaviors, and so forth, as either good or bad	• Prohibits all forms of discrimination and promotes a climate that embraces difference • Views differences in customs, behaviors, and so forth, as simply differences, with no inherent values attached
Deculturation	• Encourages CLD parents to speak only English with their children • Makes few attempts to involve parents in the learning process • Continues to use a curriculum that offers limited connections to the experiences of CLD students • Puts forth little, if any, effort to ensure that students maintain ties to their primary culture	• Encourages CLD parents to speak the native language with their children • Promotes parent involvement both at home and within the classroom • Incorporates into the curriculum the cultures and languages of the students • Encourages students to research and celebrate their primary culture

Ethnic or cultural identities are particularly significant components of a CLD student's self-identity. Research suggests that CLD students who have a positive association and affiliation with their own cultural group are less likely to experience internal or external conflicts in their own identity development and are more likely to develop positive relations with members of other groups (Sabatier, 2008; Shrake & Rhee, 2004; Umaña-Taylor, 2011). Students with a strong sense of ethnic or cultural identity also rate higher on measures of emotional wellness that correlate with higher student achievement (Caldwell & Siwatu, 2003; Dixon Rayle & Myers, 2004). In essence, students who are able to maintain a positive ethnic identity throughout the acculturation process demonstrate:

- Better overall mental health (Dixon Rayle & Myers, 2004; Umaña-Taylor, 2011)
- Fewer somatic symptoms (Rogers-Sirin, Ryce, & Sirin, 2014; Wright & Littleford, 2002)
- Improved academic achievement (Caldwell & Siwatu, 2003; Umaña-Taylor, Wong, Gonzales, & Dumka, 2012)
- Lower teen pregnancy rates (Goodyear, Newcomb, & Locke, 2002; Jarrett, 2011)
- Less drug and alcohol use (Kulis, Napoli, & Marsiglia, 2002; Hendershot, MacPherson, Myers, Carr, & Wall, 2005; Umaña-Taylor, 2011)

As a result, teachers who encourage CLD students to maintain their cultural or ethnic ties promote their personal and academic success. Educators have the power to create a classroom ecology that encourages students to explore their identity. This is one of the most crucial opportunities that we can provide for CLD students (Reyes & Vallone, 2007).

Tools such as the one depicted in Figure 4.1 help teachers gather useful information for understanding cultural aspects of a student's identity. This identity survey is an informal assessment in that it is teacher-created and serves classroom purposes. It is also authentic in that it uses information about what is relevant to CLD students and their real-world experiences. Information gathered from the identity survey can be used in the following ways:

- Brainstorm connections between the content you teach and the information students document. Integrate details or experiences from students' lives into lessons.
- As you hold sociocultural conversations, get students to elaborate on what they have shared. Make connections to similar experiences you may share with the student.
- Hold instructional conversations during the lesson that bridge the learner with the rest of the community. Look for similarities and highlight them during instruction.
- Use the survey to assess where the student may have difficulty during classroom instruction. Make notes for yourself to include additional supports (e.g., peer collaboration with a classmate who speaks the same language or shares the same culture), as needed.

Cultural identity and the acculturation process are so complex and unique to the individual that educators must account for the variables that affect the family and the student at the individual level. Creating or utilizing surveys and classroom activities that inform us as teachers is critical to creating and managing an environment where the dynamic nature of every student's culture is integrated and bound within the academic content that is taught. What we learn helps us create

Figure 4.1 Assessment Artifact: Identity Survey

IDENTITY Name _____ Block __1__

Make a list of ideas that are important to you personally or culturally.

1. What roles do you play within your family? *Im the baby of the family*
at school? *the student*
at work? *Dont have a job*
among your friends? *Im the joker I make them laugh.*

2. How do you change your appearance for different roles?
I don't change my roles I act the same in front of any body

3. What ancestor from your family tree came to the United States most recently?
How many generations have lived in the United States? *2*
What would one of your ancestors be well-known or famous for?

4. What did your ancestors do for a living? *Work hard, + made us understand things*
Where did they come from? If not another country, then another area of the U.S.
Mexico

5. What celebrations are unique to your culture?
The day of the dead

6. Does your native culture wear any special clothing or folk costumes?
cowboy stuff, and sometimes ponchos.

7. What animals or plants carry special meaning in your culture? What do they
symbolize? *Catuses they carry water for us into the*
desert.

8. Photocopy, Print from the internet or Sketch a piece of artwork from your native
culture. Explain why it was made or how it was used.

9. Briefly describe a tale or folklore story from your native culture.
Bloody mary killed her kids and at night you here calling for her kids

10. List some cultural beliefs that are important to you.
Jesus, virgen mary, working hard, living a good life

11. Describe some music instruments or songs that are unique to your heritage.
Trumpet, acordian, mariacies.

12. What personal qualities do you strive for? What are your outstanding personality
traits or character strengths? How do others see you?

13. What have been some of the most important events in your own life?
My tia died, when I saw my grandma + granapa, when my consin
got married.

14. How do imagine yourself in the future? In your dreams? Goals?
Working hard, having my own house, and passing.

15. What is your proudest moment in life so far?
When I made varsity in long Jump for track.

16. Do you identify with a group of friends at the high school? Would you refer to them
in any general term such as Brains? Jocks? Nerds? Slackers? Movers and Shakers?
Rebellious trouble makers? Good students? Loners?

17. What one event or person influenced you most in life? why and how?
My uncle he more like a father to me telling me to finish school + always be
there for me.

18. What activity or hobby would you like to spend more time doing?
Playing baseball + working more heavier for track.

The responses of one CLD student to this secondary-level survey are illustrated. Questions 1 through 11 assess the student's perspectives on family, home culture, and ethnic heritage. Questions 12 through 18 assess level of acculturation, as well as how the CLD student is responding to a variety of acculturation challenges. Asking students about people or events who influenced their life is an excellent way to build community. Nine times out of ten, the person who has most influenced the student is a teacher, grandparent, or parent. Creating categories from the questions and using the information to build bridges among students often helps with the acculturation process for all students. Using the identity survey and looking for other creative ways to assess the personal common threads that students share go a long way in softening the acculturation process.

VOICES *from the* FIELD 4.1

It was the month of Ramadan and a lot of our students were fasting during the month. It has been a tradition of our school to provide snacks to students every day especially when they come back from recess. One day when we were doing the snacks, some of the students noticed that their friends were not eating. This started a discussion in our usually inquisitive 6th-grade classroom. When the students found that their Muslim peers were fasting and would not be having any water or food during the day, the entire classroom voted to not have snacks during the month of Ramadan. This definitely made me very proud of my students. Our class, and the school as a whole, is really becoming more of a community.

Kendra Metz, 6th-Grade Teacher

---

the micro-world within the classroom that we would like to see students experience outside of the classroom.

Other factors contributing to the differing acculturation experiences of CLD students include the extent of their primary language development; second language acquisition experiences; and access to, interest in, and acceptance by the host community. Schumann's (1978) Model of Acculturation was the first to call strong attention to the correlations between second acquisition and acculturation. Schumann held that second language acquisition was significantly affected by eight key social and four psychological variables. Each of these variables is described in terms of its impact on the degree of distance created between second language learners (L2 group) and the host or target language community. According to this theory, social and psychological distance influences the nature of interactions between groups and thus the ability of second language learners to positively acculturate to and acquire the language of the target group.

The social variables included in Schumann's model are:

1. *Social dominance*—Second language acquisition is negatively affected by the perception that either the target language group or the language learner group has higher economic, political, or cultural status. This component of the model suggests that resistance to learning another language can occur when use of that language is associated with change in social class or with a community considered disparate from one's own group. By contrast, second language acquisition is facilitated by relative equality between groups.
2. *Assimilation, preservation, and adaptation*—These are responses to the acculturation process (described further in this chapter) that Shumann correlated with specific identifiable effects upon second language acquisition. Schumann surmised that a new language is best learned when both the new and host groups desire assimilation/adaptation of the new group.
3. *Enclosure*—This concept can be pictured as one of intersecting circles, with circles representing the social spheres of each group (e.g., church, school, neighborhood, work settings). A greater number of shared settings results in

ASSESSMENT IN ACTION 4.1

◼ Student Interview/Survey

STUDENT NAME:_____   **DATE:**_____

1. Write or draw a picture of your family. How many people live in your home? Do you have any pets? Is there extended family that lives with you?

2. Write or draw about things that are important to your family. Are there any specific things you do on a regular basis?

3. Write or draw about the things you and your family like to do on the weekends. What do you like to do for fun? Are there certain things you do every weekend? Are there things you only do on special occasions?

4. Write or draw about your parents' work. Do your parents work outside the home? Do they work during the day? Do they work at night? Are they gone for extended periods of time?

5. Write or draw about the most important person in your life. Who is the person that helps you the most? What does this person do that makes him/her important?

6. Write or draw about the things you do at home. What responsibilities do you have? Do you do chores? Do you have to watch your siblings?

7. Write or draw a picture of your favorite food. Are there any foods your family avoids? Are there any allergies in the home? Are there special foods for the everyday and special occasions?

8. Write or draw about your favorite song or TV show. Do you watch television at home? Do you watch the same shows or listen to the same songs as before?

9. Write or draw about your favorite holiday. How is it similar or different from the holidays we celebrate in class? What are some special foods, and things that you do for your holiday?

10. Write or draw a picture about your grandparents. Where do they live? Do you visit them? What do you do there?

Teachers can develop their own tools for exploring their students' cultural backgrounds. This Student Interview/Survey is ideal for use with elementary CLD students. The first part of the Student Interview/Survey (Questions 1–4), gives the educator insight about students' home life. Even if students are not able to vocalize it, these four initial questions can provide insight on family values, immediate and possible extended family, socio economic status, and dietary lifestyle. Question 5 informs us about students' support system and why they value the adults in their lives. Question 6 gives us not only a glimpse about students' roles and responsibilities in the home but also cultural insight on possible gender roles. Question 7 informs us about the nutritional customs of students' homes.

Question 8 can provide us with information about students' preferences outside of the classroom. This can be useful in order to include relevant material in daily lessons. (For example: A student in kindergarten that was having trouble learning his colors in English mentioned he loved animal shows, specifically shows about snakes. By including pictures of different colored snakes in the lesson, the teacher piqued his interest and he no longer had a problem remembering the names of colors in English.)

Question 9 can help teachers gain cultural information about holidays that are important to students and their families. The teacher then can put students in the role of "expert" and allow them to share information about a unique celebration with classmates. Question 10 can give us insight on students' heritages. With information from this tool, educators are better equipped to build relationships with, engage, and support students to feel like valued members of the classroom ecology.

a lower degree of "enclosure" and a greater likelihood of contact between the new and host groups. Situations of low enclosure foster greater language acquisition than those of high enclosure, in which there are fewer shared social settings and resources.

4. *Cohesiveness*—Schumann proposed that a group's cohesiveness affects language acquisition because less cohesive L2 groups are more likely to have increased contact(s) with the host or target language group.

5. *Size*—Individuals in large L2 communities may have fewer opportunities for contact with the host or target group.

6. *Congruence*—Contact between groups occurs more often and to a greater extent when the L2 and target language groups are more, versus less, similar. Examples of this are when different language communities share similar values, faith, socioeconomic status, and so forth.

7. *Attitude*—Language acquisition is facilitated when each group holds essentially positive attitudes about the other.

8. *Intended length of residence*—The intent of second language learners to stay longer in the host community appears to positively affect second language acquisition.

Schumann's model contends that the combined influence of external social variables and psychological factors such as language shock, culture shock, individual motivation, and ego development account for level(s) of target language proficiency that a second language learner could attain. Aspects of this model later came under scrutiny, such as the emphasis on group-level factors over individual-level factors, as well as the lack of attention to the role of language instruction (Bluestone, 2009; Mondy, 2007; Zaker, 2016). Yet the core premises remain worthy factors for consideration when exploring factors that can influence CLD students' variable rates of acculturation and language acquisition.

The Role of Acculturation and Emotions in Learning

Learning occurs interdependently with an individual's emotional state (Immordino-Yang & Faeth, 2010; Jensen, 2000; Sousa, 2017). The emotional climate of a learning situation can either hinder or facilitate a student's ability to make enduring meaning from learning experiences. When emotions are involved, it is a powerful whole-body experience. At their most basic level, emotions can boost, imprint, delay, or short-circuit almost any transmission of meaning. Stressed or disconnected students are unlikely to learn as well as those who feel secure and engaged. Because of the difficulties CLD students experience during acculturation, it is critical for teachers to determine the emotional readiness of students and create positive learning experiences for them.

Among their observations, Immordino-Yang and Faeth (2010) note:

> If students feel no connection to the knowledge they learn in school, then the academic content will seem emotionally meaningless to them . . . if the curriculum does not support the development of emotional reactions . . . then the effective integration of emotion and cognition in learning will be compromised. For effective cognition

assessment **FREEZE FRAME 4.2**

The emotional climate of a learning situation can either hinder or facilitate a student's ability to make enduring meaning from learning experiences.

to manifest itself in the classroom and beyond, emotions need to be a part of the learning experience all along. (p. 78)

Source: Immordino-Yang, M. H., & Faeth, M. (2010). *The role of emotion and skilled intuition in learning.* In D. A. Sousa (Ed.), Mind, brain, and education: Neuroscience implications for the classroom (pp. 69–83). Bloomington, IN: Solution Tree Press, p. 78.

This notion underscores the importance of teachers deliberately considering emotions in the planning and delivery of their lessons. They can provide natural opportunities for students to share their emotions within the context of curricular learning by allowing them to document and discuss their personal connections to the content. When teachers encourage students to identify connections to their knowledge and experiences from home, community, and school, emotion-laden connections frequently are shared. Teachers can then use this information to inform the way they interact with students to make the content relevant, provide emotional support, acknowledge challenges, and build on demonstrated assets (e.g., novel ways of thinking about lesson topic). Considerations for planning and delivering instruction that supports learners' acculturation and emotional well-being are provided later in this chapter.

ASSESSING LEVEL OF ACCULTURATION

Ms. Cantu was concerned from the outset about the veiled new girl in her class. Although Nashida was from Michigan and spoke English with virtually no accent, her style of dress suggested that she was far less acculturated than her classmates who struggled with language but had adopted much more "American" ways. Ms. Cantu worried that Nashida would be uncomfortable with the informality and open conversations about religion common among the 11th graders in this history class and wondered if she should revert to more of a traditional lecture approach to reduce the possibility of unintentional offense.

Ms. Cantu was apprehensive about her upcoming visit to the home of Nashida. She knew that inadvertent disrespect could get any relationship off to a poor start. So Ms. Cantu did some reading and contacted the local Islamic center for help. Although these efforts provided valuable insights, her anxiety rose as she approached Nashida's door. She was already slipping off her shoes as planned when a young woman in jeans, T-shirt, and flowing hair answered the door. For a second, Ms. Cantu thought it was the wrong house. Then she recognized Nashida, who excitedly welcomed her in and proceeded with introductions.

Nashida's mom noticed immediately that the teacher had removed her shoes before entering, and she smiled. Ms. Cantu could hardly take her eyes off Nashida. She looked so . . . so *American* in her trendy T-shirt and jeans. Nashida's mom requested a few moments before they started, so Ms. Cantu quietly observed as they all sat together on the couch. Nashida's mom read aloud from a list she was writing. Ms. Cantu guessed it was a grocery list because several of the words, such as *sucar* and *roz,* were similar to food words used in her childhood home. Glances at the muted television revealed an oddly familiar picture. Other than a few unrecognizable printed words, it looked exactly like the sort of variety show her parents still watched every Saturday night. Suddenly, two little boys, powered by sound effects and dishtowel capes, sped through the room. Nashida's mom said something softly, and they answered in English, "Okay, but can we go out back?" She nodded.

During the conversation about her daughter's education, Nashida's mom smiled and nodded frequently as Ms. Cantu discussed Nashida's performance and opportunities at school. Nashida beamed and giggled at her mother's periodic and obviously humorous quips in their native language. As the visit ended, the group headed toward the door. Nashida's mom handed Nashida the list, and when they neared the door, Nashida reached behind it, quickly cloaking herself to leave. Car keys jingling, she bid Ms. Cantu a cheerful goodbye. Ms. Cantu was struck by her own surprise. Why had she just assumed Nashida didn't, couldn't, or wouldn't be allowed to drive? Why did Nashida seem so different to her now? Why had she assumed so many things based on Nashida's style of dress? Ms. Cantu realized that for all her cultural sensitivity, the limitations of her own experiences had led to a very limited perception of this student.

Acculturation is generally understood to impact the learner at two levels: the behavioral and the psychological (Berry, 1992; Searle & Ward, 1990). Behavioral aspects include areas such as language, social skills, and customs, whereas the psychological aspects have more to do with values, belief systems, attitudes, and preferences. This is important to bear in mind because assessment perspectives that emphasize primarily the behavioral or observable aspects of acculturation (e.g., customs) can lead to inappropriate assumptions about what the learner may be going through as well as inappropriate educational decisions for English learners and other CLD students.

As Ms. Cantu's scenario illustrates, it is important to avoid making assumptions and drawing conclusions about a student's level of acculturation based only on a single source of information. Rather, educators need to use multiple types of assessments to gather information for making informed educational decisions. Acculturation is often part of conversations in both preservice and in-service preparation/professional development programs for teachers and administrators. Yet determining which tools to use and how to use the results for instructional purposes often is not clearly delineated. Given that the dynamic, complex process of integration and adaption to a new community or school may progress differently for each student, both formal and informal assessments of acculturation can provide valuable insights.

Formal Assessment of Acculturation

It is unfortunate that the assessment of acculturation does not play a significant role in decision making for placement, programming, and assessment. Few tools are systematically and consistently used in schools, making it hard to be explicit on how and when to use such tools. When tools are not readily accessible or used in schools, educators run the risk of making assumptions about the psychological state of the learner. Therefore, it is important to avoid misperceptions and to assess acculturation in a standardized way. In this section, we highlight tools that are available for this purpose. Each assesses somewhat different parameters or characteristics. Therefore, an informed review of such tools is recommended to determine which assessment tool best fits the community and targets the desired acculturation information. One of the most popular formal assessments of acculturation is the Acculturation Quick Screen III (AQS III).

The AQS III is capable of measuring the level and rate of acculturation to grade-level school culture. In addition to the uses described in Chapter 3, the AQS III (Collier, 2016) often is used (a) to make decisions about the modification of testing, evaluation, and other assessment procedures and (b) to provide an early warning system to alert that placements, services, assessments, and other aspects of schooling may be compounding the student's acculturation challenges. When the AQS III is used soon after the English learner's arrival, the findings are especially valuable for establishing a baseline from which to monitor the CLD student's acculturation and adaptation progress. In fact, the AQS III is recommended for routine use among CLD students in newcomer programs (Collier, 2016).

For purposes of monitoring, students should be reassessed using the AQS III at the same time each year. The findings of the AQS III provide a map of acculturation patterns from less acculturated to more acculturated, according to a 48-point scale. Five levels of acculturation are measured by the AQS III, ranging from "significantly less acculturated" to "in transition" to "significantly more acculturated." Long-term results have indicated that the average rate of acculturation falls between 10 percent and 12 percent each school year, and varies according to the type of assistance offered to the student (Collier, 2016).

The cultural and environmental factors identified as significant by the AQS III can serve as an index of important areas to assess, regardless of the particular tool or method used. Most acculturation assessments require the school to gather information related to the following:

1. *Number of years in the school district.* In most cases, students who have been in a new country a relatively short time are less acculturated than those who have lived there many years. The number of years in a given school district may suggest greater or lesser acculturation, given the time in the country, due to the transitions and acculturation adjustments associated with mobility.

2. *Number of years in ESL/bilingual education.* Knowledge of a student's educational history is essential to making decisions about appropriate placement and programming.

3. *Native language proficiency.* The strength of a CLD student's proficiency in the first language (Cummins, 1984; Szapocznik & Kurtines, 1980) is positively correlated with acculturation because students are able to draw on first language knowledge to facilitate second language understandings and skills.

4. *English language proficiency.* An understanding of a student's second language proficiency is needed for teachers to be able to accommodate the student's instructional and assessment needs appropriately.

5. *Bilingual proficiency.* Proficiency in both the first and second languages correlates with indicators of mental health (e.g., lower incidence of social and emotional problems) as evidence of bilingualism and biculturalism increases (Szapocznik & Kurtines, 1980).

6. *Ethnicity/nation of origin.* A CLD student's ethnicity and nation of origin play an important role in acculturation because of the degree of similarity or difference between the new culture and the native culture (for example, those coming to the United States from western European countries versus eastern European countries or Pacific Islands).

7. *Percentage of students in the school who speak the CLD student's language or dialect.* The percentage of others in a particular school who speak the CLD student's language or dialect can also affect acculturation (Juffer, 1983). The more interaction students have with the host population, the more likely they are to acculturate to that population.

In addition to the AQS III, a number of other instruments are available to assess student acculturation formally. A representative sample can be found in Table 4.2. Because no two students will experience acculturation the same way,

---

assessment FREEZE FRAME 4.3

The strength of a CLD student's proficiency in the first language is positively correlated with acculturation because students are able to draw on first language knowledge to facilitate second language understandings and skills.

Table 4.2   Formal Acculturation Assessments

Acculturation Assessment	Development/Key Characteristics
Acculturation, Habits, and Interests Multicultural Scale for Adolescents (Unger et al., 2002)	The Acculturation, Habits, and Interests Multicultural Scale for Adolescents (AHIMSA) generates four subscores: United States Orientation (Assimilation), Other Country Orientation (Separation), Both Countries Orientation (Integration), and Neither Country Orientation (Marginalization). Three of the subscales were correlated with the subscales of a modified Acculturation Rating Scale for Mexican-Americans-II, with English language usage, and with generation in the United States providing evidence for the validity of the scale.
Acculturation Rating Scale for Mexican Americans-II (Cuéllar, Arnold, & Maldonado, 1995)	A revision of the Acculturation Rating Scale for Mexican Americans (ARSMA) that found a strong link between communication and acculturation. This tool assesses a student's cultural orientation toward Mexican and European American cultures. Results can be generated that describe multidimensional acculturation types.
Acculturation Scale for Southeast Asians (Anderson et al., 1993)	The responses of 381 Cambodian, 359 Laotian, and 395 Vietnamese research participants (age 18–89) living in the United States were analyzed in the areas of language proficiencies and language, social, and food preferences. Inter-item reliability and construct validity were demonstrated. Among the sample population, males tended to show higher scores for the proficiency in language subscale, with Laotian and Vietnamese females scoring higher than males on language, social, and food preferences.
African American Acculturation Scale (Landrine & Klonoff, 1994)	The African American Acculturation Scale is a 74-item scale that has been demonstrated to have good internal construct and validity (Landrine & Klonoff, 1994). This scale examines acculturation in terms of eight dimensions of African American culture: (a) traditional African American religious beliefs and practices; (b) traditional African American family structure and practices; (c) traditional African American socialization; (d) preparation and consumption of traditional foods; (e) preference for African American things; (f) interracial attitudes; (g) superstitions; and (h) traditional African American health beliefs and practices.
Asian American Multidimensional Acculturation Scale (Gim Chung et al., 2004)	The Asian American Multidimensional Acculturation Scale (AAMAS) was developed to be easy to use with a variety of Asian American ethnic groups. It includes questions relating to cultural identity, language use, cultural knowledge, and food preferences.
Bidimensional Acculturation Scale for Hispanics (Marin & Gamba (1996))	The Bidimensional Acculturation Scale for Hispanics (BAS) uses 12 items (per cultural domain) that measure three language-related areas in order to provide an acculturation score for two primary cultural dimensions (Hispanic and non-Hispanic domains). To develop and validate the scale, researchers surveyed a random sample of 254 Hispanic adults. Resulting scores indicated high internal consistency and validity coefficients. The scale can be used effectively with Mexican Americans and Central Americans.
Suinn-Lew Asian Self-Identity Acculturation Scale (Suinn, Richard-Figueroa, Lew, & Vigil, 1987)	The Suinn-Lew Asian Self-Identity Acculturation Scale (SL-ASIA), modeled after the Hispanic acculturation scale (ARMSA), was designed to assess the acculturation of Asian-heritage students. The SL-ASIA measures similar factors to the Hispanic ARSMA and is sensitive to determining Western acculturation among Asian individuals.
Vancouver Index of Acculturation (Ryder et al., 2000)	This instrument includes 20 questions that assess interest/participation in one's "heritage culture" and "typical American culture." It is a self-report instrument that assesses several domains relevant to acculturation, including values, social relationships, and adherence to traditions. Evidence is provided for its validity. This tool is a multicultural assessment that can be used with students from all cultural backgrounds.

it is important to assess the acculturation of each individual student rather than draw broad comparisons between potentially dissimilar peers.

Formal assessment tools serve to inform teachers' instructional efforts and shed light on decisions about placement and special programming, such as special education. Often acculturation challenges are at the root of observed difficulties in the classroom. When decisions are high stakes, it is critical that the student's level of acculturation and psychological and emotional stress be considered. Decisions about programming often have long-term implications for the student.

As discussed in Chapter 1, CLD students are a highly diverse group with a wide variety of educational, linguistic, economic, and even traumatic backgrounds. Traditional lenses or screeners of academics and emotional health frequently fail to inform practices that lead to mutual adaptation of CLD students and staff. Assessments of acculturation, especially when used in a proactive rather than reactive manner, have the ability to shed timely light on individual or system needs. The insights gained regarding each student's level of acculturation serve educators in the following ways.

- Encourage consideration of factors beyond language proficiency that may impact student response to school settings, materials, and interactions.
- Lead to instructional accommodations that increase student access to learning.
- Inform the selection and interpretation of other forms of assessment (e.g., achievement, cognition).
- May reveal systemic barriers to acculturation growth, such as reliance on ESL or "tracked" courses.
- Serve as a springboard for discussions to promote CLD student participation across inclusive settings.
- Can be monitored over time as an additional or alternate indicator of educational "progress." This is especially important for accountability at both the school and individual level when supporting CLD students with limited previous schooling.

Informal Assessment of Acculturation

Whereas formal acculturation assessment tools may not be at the discretion of the classroom teacher with regard to when and how they will be utilized to inform practice, informal assessments of acculturation can take many forms, and teachers have a great deal of liberty with regard to their development and use. Home visits are an excellent way of gathering authentic insights into the culture of students and their families. Strategic use of school records and observational checklists and rubrics also yields insights into students' levels of acculturation. Activities often can be integrated into lessons without much preparation. Sometimes it is what one gathers through classroom observation and student products that best informs planning, lesson delivery, and assessment. Much can be learned about CLD students in these various ways. We will briefly discuss each.

Home Visits   Beyond the classroom walls, one of the most powerful methods of informal assessment is the home visit. When teachers visit the homes of students, they create opportunities to observe students, caregivers, and other family members in the home environment. As a result, these educators are better able to sense the stressors and challenges students and their families face on a daily basis. Although teachers may initially be apprehensive about conducting home visits due to potential language and cultural differences, such obstacles can be easily overcome with the help of a linguistically and culturally competent translator. For a more detailed discussion of home visits, see Chapter 3.

School Records   Another way to gather information on acculturation is to review a student's school records. Useful information might include the following:

- Number of years the family has been in the country
- Whether students arrived at the same time as their parents
- Country of origin
- Number of siblings and their grade levels
- Language spoken in country of origin. How does it approximate the English language?
- Family literacy practices
- Reason for move
- Parent level of education

Observational Checklists and Rubrics   Teachers can collect data through observational checklists or rubrics (see Figure 4.2), which can be used to assess many kinds of behaviors. Examples of such behaviors include the following:

- Communicative effectiveness with native-English-speaking peers
- Choice of language when addressing bilingual peers or those who speak English as a second language
- Large-group participation (e.g., calling out or hesitation to volunteer in large groups)
- Small-group participation (e.g., willingness to serve as group leader or offer suggestions)
- Miscommunications with culturally dissimilar peers
- Learner preferences (e.g., individual versus collective, demonstration versus recitation)

Teachers' situational monitoring of student behavior enables them to recognize signs that a CLD student may be experiencing acculturative stress or shock. Teachers can note objective physical indicators such as absenteeism, increased misbehavior during instruction, and lack of participation during class time, Indicators of social or psychological stress may be observed in school, during home visits, or as reports from a parent or guardian. Such indicators include personality changes; withdrawal; over- or undereating; behavioral incidents or referrals; conflicts with siblings or parents; and rejection of home language, customs, and foods. Teachers familiar with these issues are much better able to reduce the impact of acculturative stress on CLD students.

Activities   Throughout the acculturation process, students are aware of and question their position in the classroom. Culturally and linguistically diverse students recognize their differences, and due to this it can be hard for them to be part of the cohesiveness that teachers essentially want in their classrooms and from students. All students have moments where it is difficult to see beyond themselves and understand

Figure 4.2   Level of Acculturation Observation Rubric

LOA* Observation Rubric			
Student:			
Date of Observation:		Time of Observation:	
Criterion	**Range and Rating**	**Anecdotal Notes**	**Monitor Status****
Level of affect	5 Upbeat 0 Sullen and/or Angry		
Data:	5 - 4 - 3 - 2 - 1 - 0		
Level of interaction with peers of a similar culture and/or language	5 Highly Interactive 0 Withdrawn		
Data:	5 - 4 - 3 - 2 - 1 - 0		
Level of interaction with peers of a different culture and/or language	5 Highly Interactive 0 Withdrawn		
Data:	5 - 4 - 3 - 2 - 1 - 0		
Communication effectiveness with peers of a different culture and/or language	5 Highly Effective 0 Ineffective		
Data:	5 - 4 - 3 - 2 - 1 - 0		
Level of participation in group learning	5 Highly Participative 0 Nonparticipative		
Data:	5 - 4 - 3 - 2 - 1 - 0		
Level of student engagement with classroom learning activities	5 Highly Engaged 0 Not Engaged		
Data:	5 - 4 - 3 - 2 - 1 - 0		
Legend:	* LOA = Level of Acculturation ** Status Range = Enhance, Maintain, or Reduce Monitoring of LOA		

the diversity that exists within the classroom. To help alleviate this, activities that create an ecology where learners see themselves as part of the learning community, can help set conditions to support a culture of acceptance and learning.

Following are four sample activities: (1) My World, Your World, Our World, (2) Heritage Poem/Oral History, (3) Cultural Quilt, and (4) Sociocultural Mind Map. These activities can stand alone or be integrated into English Language Arts or Social Studies/World History lessons.

My World, Your World, Our World

Grade Level: PreK–6

Materials:

- Large poster board, cut into puzzle pieces as shown in Figure 4.3
- Crayons, markers, or colored pencils for each student
- For very young children or students with interrupted formal schooling, use of magazines with pictures representing possible aspects of their backgrounds or computers with Internet access are recommended.

Directions:

1. Distribute a puzzle piece to each student. Explain that they are going to use it to draw or write their thoughts and feelings about who they are/their identities. They are to be guided by the following questions:

   a. My family (defined as the person who takes care of me), has lived in the following places.
   b. My family speaks _____ at home. (Examples: Spanish, English, Arabic, German)
   c. My family and I love to _____ when we are together.
   d. My favorite food is _____.
   e. My favorite song is _____.

2. After the students have finished (and depending on language level) have them turn their puzzle piece over and write something they would like the teacher to know about them or their family.

3. Have students do a connected talk where they share out things they wrote on their puzzle pieces. After one student shares, other students—one by one—add their own realities (from the puzzle pieces). This highlights for students the different ways they are connected to one another. Facilitate the conversations/sharing as needed.

4. As students share, begin to put the puzzle pieces together. Remind the students that this classroom community is not complete unless we put the pieces together. Each holds a piece of the puzzle that tells the story of this community.

5. Explain once the puzzle is together, emphasize that the final puzzle illustrates that each student brings a unique cultural and linguistic perspective, as well as other attributes, talents, and international (in some cases multinational) experiences that—when combined—make them ROCK STARS!

Observing Students:

As students work on their puzzle pieces, ask questions and hold conversations that provide you a glimpse into the social lives of students and also help them and you make needed academic associations. These instructional conversations will help students see themselves more as a part of the learning community. They will also support you to identify how students are feeling about the learning community and how they see themselves as learners.

Differentiating Instruction:

- Think about your content standards and document for yourself links to what you are learning about the students.

Figure 4.3   Assessment Artifact: My World, Your World, Our World

For this activity, Ms. Armijo, a third-grade teacher, asked her students to think about their families and the languages they speak at home, as well as their own personal likes (e.g., favorite hobbies, sports, food). She invited them to include on their puzzle piece anything that was important to them. Students were excited to create this reflection of their lives, especially since the teachers in their building had posted their own similar puzzle pieces on one of the school bulletin boards. Reflecting on the success of this activity, Ms. Armijo shared:

> As a teacher, I saw that my students were very eager to share about their lives. I felt like this activity communicated to my students that they matter and that they are a part of our classroom community. This activity helped me to remember that all my students' voices matter, and that students really want to share a part of themselves.

This activity provides ready links to the sociocultural and linguistic dimensions that teachers can use to build relationships of trust with their community of learners. The connections likewise can serve as entry points to subsequent curricular conversations.

Source: Natalie Armijo. Reprinted by permission.

- Jot down notes that will support you in making decisions about grouping configurations when you plan your lessons. You will learn your students' stories as they share, and these stories will help you make many decisions about their instructional needs.
- Make a note of those students that may need your smile and attention a little more often throughout each day.

Additional Notes:

This activity can be repeated three times during the academic school year. Often teachers use this as an activity immediately following standardized testing at the beginning, middle, and end of the year to informally assess changes that may have occurred in students' lives.

Heritage Poem/Oral History

Grade Level: 8–12

Materials:

- Resources (websites, articles, books) based on the countries, states, and communities represented in your classroom
- Guiding questions
- Sample of a heritage poem/oral history (See Figure 4.4)

Directions:

1. Discuss with your students what can be gained by understanding our cultural heritage (we all started somewhere).
2. Share your own heritage and how it has influenced your own life.
3. Have students write a version of an "I Am" poem. To do this, provide students with the following prompts/guiding questions.

Possible guiding prompts:

- Ancestral ties (Where did I/we begin our journey? What roads have been traveled?)
- Family members and relatives (Let me tell you about my roots, where I come from, the people who inspire me to keep learning and moving forward. They come from . . . , I have learned . . . , I am inspired by . . . .)
- When I think about where I come from and what I what I would tell others about who I am, what I want, and what I think, I would tell them the following: _____ (e.g., place of birth, about me, my highs and lows, personal goals).
- Places of residence: _____ (A written history of stops along the path that has led me here today.)
- Family customs (I am . . . languages, holidays, celebrations, traditional clothing)
- Favorite food(s) (I live for eating _____ at my _____ house.)
- Challenges of adjustment (I face challenges . . . I am driven forward by. . . .)
- For my continued journey, I wish the following: _____.

Figure 4.4   Assessment Artifact: I Am Poem

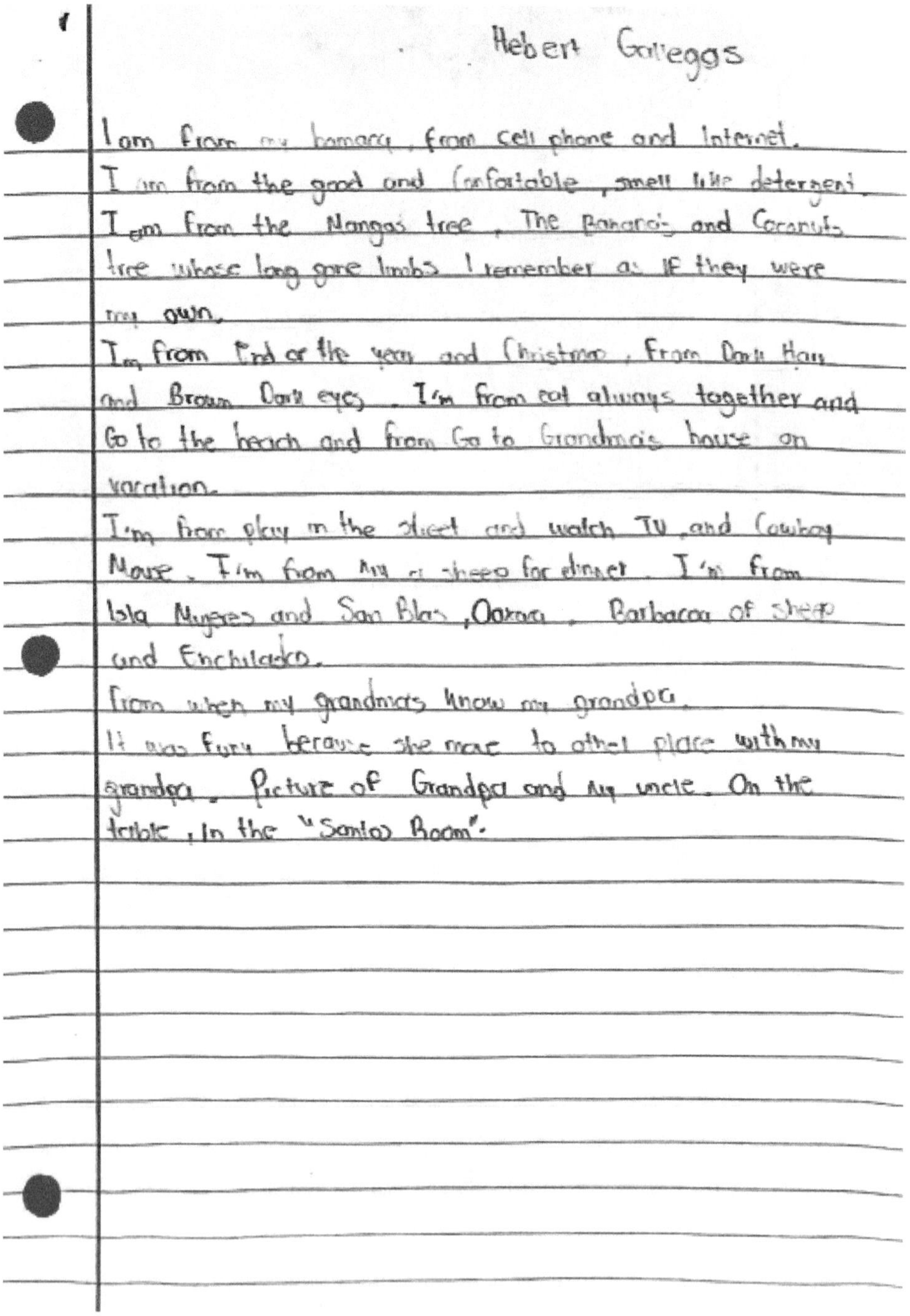

Hebert Garreggs

I am from my hamaca, from cell phone and Internet.
I am from the good and confortable, smell like detergent.
I am from the Mangas tree. The Banana's and Coconuts
tree whose long gore limbs I remember as if they were
my own.
I'm from End of the year and Christmas, from Dark Hair
and Brown Dark eyes. I'm from eat always together and
Go to the beach and from Go to Grandma's house on
vacation.
I'm from play in the street and watch TV and Cowboy
Movie. I'm from My a sheep for dinner. I'm from
Isla Mujeres and San Blas, Oaxaca, Barbacoa of sheep
and Enchilados.
From when my grandma's know my grandpa.
It was Funy because she move to other place with my
grandpa. Picture of Grandpa and my uncle. On the
table, In the "Santos Room".

This poem reflects the writing of a Hebert, a high school student at the early intermediate level of English proficiency. From this poem, the teacher is provided with many points of entry into conversations about his background and potential connections to the curriculum. For instance, the prominence of mangos, bananas, and coconuts in his home country help provide a setting for past experiences. Important celebrations in his life include Christmas, end-of-year festivities, and beach-time vacations with his grandmother. Hebert shares information about leisure activities and foods connected to personal memories, and he references extended family members who have played a role in his life. The "Santos (Saints) Room" is another connection that the teacher could easily inquire about in order to better understand Hebert's home culture.

Observing Students:

As the poems are being written, enter into conversations with students that support each to think deeper about who they are and where they fit in your classroom.

Differentiating Instruction:

As you read the poems, document important information that will support your planning and delivery of lessons. For example, you may find out that some students work all night to help support the family financially. From your observations, create a "Find Some Who" activity to have students learn about each other (see Figure 4.5). Your making students' lives a part of the daily curriculum will speak volumes about the level of your inves tment in them, as unique human beings and as learners in your classroom.

Additional Notes:

This activity is used to build relationships with students and is recommended to be used at the beginning of the year or as new students arrive. It is not intended to be completed for assignment of a grade. The information provided sets the stage for entering into both academic and sociocultural conversations. The prompts, when possible, should be developed by the teacher based on the culture of the school, the content area being taught, and what teacher knows and would like to know about the community of learners.

Cultural Quilt

Grade Level: PreK–6

Materials:

- 3 × 5 cards (six per student)
- Crayons, markers, or colored pencils for each student
- Yarn (Enough to sew all the cards together at the end to make a quilt for each student)
- For very young children or students with interrupted formal schooling, magazines with pictures representing their background can also be used.
- Sample of a cultural quilt (see Figure 4.6)

Directions:

1. Give each student a set of six 3 × 5 cards.
2. Explain that each student will use these cards to share about their life using drawings (and words for older students). Highlight that students each have their own story. Some might have been born in the local community. Others have traveled long distances to be here.
3. Share with students that they have two options regarding their quilt.
   - They can use the cards to create a timeline of their journey.
   - They can use the cards to write about themselves.

Figure 4.5   "Find Someone Who" Activity

Find Someone Who . . . !!!		
Find someone who is from Mexico. Name:	Find someone who grew up with mango trees. Name:	Find someone who comes from a big family. Name:
Find someone who makes empanadas. Name:	Find someone who celebrates Ramadan. Name:	Find someone who is from Guatemala. Name:
Find someone who celebrates Christmas. Name:	Find someone who is from Afghanistan. Name:	Find someone who has gone to the beach. Name:
Find someone who is from Honduras. Name:	Find someone who makes tamales. Name	Find someone goes to church on Sundays. Name:

Possible prompts to generate thinking about a journey:
- In what country were you born?
- How old were you when you came to the United States (e.g., baby, young child, a specific age)?
- Who came with you when you traveled?
- What type(s) of transportation did you use to get here?
- Did you stop at other places on the way to this community?
- What does your home look like here?

This activity was created using the "I Am" poems written by high school students at the early intermediate level of English proficiency. In the photograph, students race to ask and answer questions about themselves in order to complete each box on the sheet. The teacher enjoyed this activity because it prompted all students to produce language. Students were engaged with everyone else in the class, communicating with peers who speak different native languages as well as those who share the same home language. When teachers use students' reflective writing to build up the classroom community, they send the message that they care about each individual learner and their lives beyond the classroom.

Figure 4.6   Assessment Artifact: Cultural Quilt

Ms. Clark implemented the Cultural Quilt activity with her fourth-grade students to support them, and herself, in learning more about their class as a community and as individuals. In addition, she decided to take the activity to the next level by involving parents and families in the process. Ms. Clark explained:

> I made this a home/family activity. Students were able to tell me what they knew about their family, culture, language, and themselves here at school and then they took their project home for their family to help them add any other things to their cards. . . . I was able to tell which students love to be creative and draw and which ones do not. I also used it this week in our language arts lesson. This week's topic is culture and about passing down stories. I had one student who on his culture card wrote "telling stories." I had him share with the class what kind of stories his family shared and why that was important to him.

Overall, the activity provided the opportunity for students to discuss their lives with one another. It also provided the teacher with a source of connections to students and their families, cultures, and languages that she could then draw upon to enrich her instruction.

Source: Victoria Clark, Reprinted by permission.

Possible prompts to generate thinking about themselves:
- The most important thing about my name is _____.
- The most important thing about me is _____.
- The most important thing about my family is _____.
- The most important thing about my language is _____.
- The most important thing about my culture is _____.
- The most important thing about my school is _____.

4. Ask students to draw a picture for each of the prompts. Younger children may use pictures from magazines if desired. Older students can add words for each picture.
5. Use yarn to sew together the quilt pieces.
6. Have students share their finished quilts with their peers.

Observing Students:

Observe students as they create their cultural quilts. Hold a conversation with students who struggle, so that you can listen to their ideas and give suggestions regarding what they might draw on their card.

Differentiating Instruction:

- Help students see the similarities and differences in their cultural quilts: family, favorite things, etc. Also have students explore similarities and differences in journey timelines. Highlight the uniqueness of each student's life. Make notes about these aspects of your students' lives for your own future reference. These insights will inform your decisions about grouping and can energize your efforts as you find ways to relate the curriculum to students' lives.
- Have students find commonalities that they all share. Record these on chart paper and post for the class's future reference. Even in very culturally diverse classrooms there are commonalities that we can all relate to that help bring us together. When misunderstandings or tensions among students arise during the year, as they inevitably do, remind learners of the aspects that unite them as equal members of the learning community.

Additional Notes:

Select literature that can take the class back to their quilts during the year. This will help students to see themselves in text and in the curriculum. You might also find it useful to use literature prior to having students create their quilts. For example, the teacher might begin a 2- or 3-day project by reading *The Josefina Story Quilt* (Coerr, 1986). In the story, the protagonist creates a quilt of her journey to California. To help students apply the concept to their own lives, the teacher then would ask students to create their own cultural quilts.

Sociocultural Mind Map

Grade Level: 4–12

Materials:

- One blank piece of paper for each student
- Crayons, markers, or colored pencils for each student
- Sample of a mind map (see Figure 4.7)

Directions:

1. Provide each student with a piece of paper and writing/drawing utensils.
2. Explain to students that they will create a mind map using pictures and words to represent themselves. Possible ideas include perceptions of self, personal goals, academic interests, career goals, friendships, family, and cultural or language transition experiences.
3. For students who need additional support, have them begin by creating a Cultural Mosaic (see Figure 4.8).
   - To do this, have students capture the same ideas using only drawings.
   - Then discuss the mosaic with the student. Jot down words, phrases, and ideas that the student connects with the illustrations.

Figure 4.7   Assessment Artifact: Sociocultural Mind Map

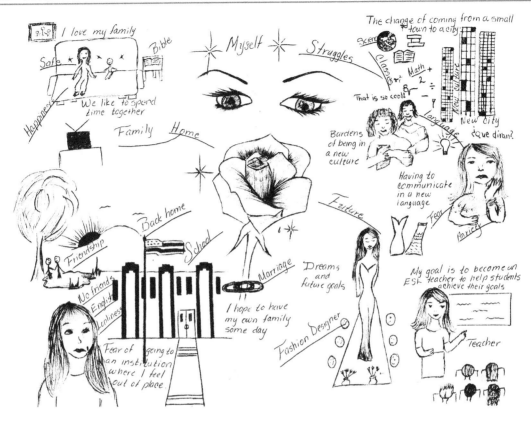

- Have students use the words you recorded to support their addition of words to their mosaic. The end result is a mind map.
4. Have students share their mind maps with a partner or small group.
5. Display completed mind maps to celebrate the richness of the community of learners.
6. As an extension of the activity, have students write an explanation of the various elements of their mind maps.

Observing Students:

As students work on their mind maps, ask questions and hold conversations that provide you with insights into their cultural and linguistic backgrounds, struggles, hopes, and dreams. Attend to acculturation challenges that surface. Make note of support systems available to students (e.g., family members, friends). Listen for career goals and other interests that serve as sources of motivation for learners.

Differentiating Instruction:

- Document notes for yourself that can later support decisions about grouping.
- Record ideas for making lessons relevant to learners, based on what you learned.
- Make note of students whose work product or conversation with you provide an indication of significant emotional challenges or other struggles. This will enhance your ability to provide them with supports that can increase their engagement and success.

Figure 4.8   Assessment Artifact: Cultural Mosaic

Additional Notes:

This activity can be repeated three times during the academic school year. Often teachers use this as an activity to find out about their students' backgrounds at the beginning of the year. Then they have students create a new mind map midyear, after teachers and students have had a chance to develop higher levels of trust. Using the tool at the end of the year provides students with opportunities to envision and incorporate new goals and aspirations that can carry them through the summer and into the next academic year.

Mind maps (Buzan, 1983) are increasingly being used for both instruction and assessment in both elementary and secondary classrooms. The potential contributions of mind maps to assessing CLD students are multifaceted. A mind map often brings to the surface information relating not only to acculturation and the sociocultural dimension of the CLD student biography, but also to the cognitive, academic, and linguistic dimensions. The following scenario illustrates these potentials:

Julianna, an 11th-grade student who arrived 6 months ago from Mexico, developed a mind map (see Figure 4.7) from the cultural mosaic (see Figure 4.8) she was asked to create in Mrs. Villareal's language arts class. In an informal interview, Julianna discussed her mind map with Mrs. Villarreal. Their discussion revealed details of Julianna's prior socialization patterns, as well as her new acculturation experiences in the United States.

From this conversation, Mrs. Villarreal learned that the rose in the center of the mind map portrays Julianna's love for nature. Julianna was born in a rural community of Mexico and has found the transition to urban living difficult. She misses the time, access, and friends with whom she used to enjoy nature and the outdoors. The rings, on the other hand, depict Julianna's desire to someday have a family.

The illustrations in the upper left-hand corner of Julianna's mind map portray the relative safety, comfort, and pride she recalls about living in Mexico. Her drawings indicate that family and religion were of particular comfort to her, despite the poverty in which she and her family lived.

To the right of this point in the mind map, the illustration of the eyes represents Julianna's soul. She told Mrs. Villarreal, "If you pay attention [to these eyes], you can see what's inside me [e.g., the tears that have fallen upon the rose]." Like many other CLD students, Julianna often feels ignored and sometimes lost in many of her classes.

In the upper right-hand corner, the buildings characterize the new city in which Julianna lives. For Julianna, the many sociocultural transitions from rural small-town life to urban living have been challenging. Note the illustrations and passages below and to the left of the buildings. The phrase "*Que diran?*" expresses her concerns about what other adults and fellow students will think and say about her appearance, her culture, and her language.

The light bulb and associated passages represent the knowledge Julianna feels she brings to the classroom—knowledge she believes is little recognized by her new teachers, especially her prior knowledge of science and mathematics. Julianna considers herself a good student in science and very much enjoys studying this subject. According to Julianna, the illustration below the buildings further depicts her sadness about the fact that no one knows about her knowledge, her aspirations, and her desire to make new friends like those she had in Mexico. For Julianna, friends have always been the source of her strength and her motivators in school. Now that she lives in a new city and has few friends to turn to, she increasingly struggles to cope with the many challenges of immigration and academics in a new school system.

The illustrations and passages in the lower left-hand corner of Julianna's mind map show the difficulties she faces trying to succeed in a new school system. Her lack of friends, difficulties with the English language, and increasing loneliness each further complicates the fears she already has of "feeling out of place." In fact, the illustrations that surround the tree indicate that Julianna, amidst her many struggles, is often drawn to memories from her prior socialization, especially memories of nature and fun with her friends.

Finally, the illustrations and passages in the lower right-hand corner portray her dreams, goals, and aspirations for the future, including her future beyond school. Along with her desire to have a family, Julianna's mind map suggests that she envisions herself as a career woman. She considers both a career in fashion design and a career as an ESL teacher to be within reach.

In summary, Julianna's mind map reflects the powerful potential of this tool to accomplish the following:

- Prompt CLD students to explore and discuss difficult issues they might not otherwise talk about.
- Reveal student interests and academic potentials.
- Assess student struggles with acculturation issues.
- Serve as a focal point of discussions for assessing sociocultural, academic, cognitive, and linguistic experiences and challenges.

The aforementioned activities constitute but a sample of the many informal classroom assessments teachers can use to gather information about CLD students and their acculturation experiences. Activities and projects that involve parents and other family members are especially helpful for promotihg family ties that support students through the acculturation process. Informal assessments that incorporate multiple forms of communication (e.g., drawing, discussion, writing in either the native language or English) enable maximum participation of CLD students who are in the beginning stages of acquiring English and transitioning to a new culture. Such opportunities allow students to share their unique perspectives in multiple and often surprising ways.

SNAPSHOT from *CLASSROOM PRACTICE*   4.1

This picture depicts an informal way through which Ms. Foiles, a 4th-grade teacher, decided to gather information about her students. Often students feel shame about living with grandparents, aunts, or host families, especially in the case of refugee children and adolescents. Informal activities such as this, which provide a canvas for students to share who they are, create a space for them to disclose personal information in a nonthreatening way. Using students' responses to the activity as a starting point, the teacher can gather more information about the family, and the country of origin. The teacher also can gather books that may interest the student. Building relationships begins with cultivating connections that have been shared by the student. A teacher's creativity and imagination is the only limit for what is possible.

Carol Foiles

I am in __4__ grade.
I am (ethnicity): __Chinese__
I speak: __Chinese__ (L1)
__English__ (L2)
My family is from (country of origin): __United States__

Here is a picture of my family:

Here is a picture of one of our cultural traditions/celebrations called: __Chinese New year__

Here is a picture of the country I am from. The name of the country is: __China__

Here is a picture of me doing my favorite thing, which is: __swimming__

Here is a picture showing what I like most about my culture. It is a picture of: __Chinese Noodles__

Here is a picture of one thing that has been hard about "fitting in." It is a picture of: __Making new friends__

One thing I wish my teacher(s) knew about my culture was: __the chinese language__
我喜欢我的学校

USING ACCULTURATION INFORMATION TO INFORM INSTRUCTION

The assessment tools discussed in the previous sections support educators in making decisions about the best course of action to take when planning, delivering, and assessing instruction. Formal assessment tools provide point-in-time information, whereas informal assessments provide in-the-moment guidance to keep the student moving forward as the lesson unfolds.

Planning Tips:

- Look for ways to connect concepts and other content to what is learned from formal and informal acculturation assessments, such as family traditions, literacy practices, countries of origin, and community experiences.
- Learn about the grammatical structures of the student's language and hold individual instructional conversations to point out similarities and differences. Help alleviate student stress by supporting learners to understand that they often are merely transferring what they already know to a new language.
- Provide personalized feedback to students on written work that clearly communicates your awareness of their background by calling attention to things you remember learning from them during formal or informal assessments.
- Make notes on your lesson plans to remind you of the little things that will make the student feel part of the learning community.

Instructional Tips:

- Start the lesson by sharing your content and language objectives. Remind students that they are learning new words that they may already know in their language. That is, they are acquiring new labels for existing concepts.
- Explicitly make sociocultural connections to content throughout the lesson. For example, keep in mind what the student may already know about the content you are teaching (e.g., What does the student know about war, multiplication, rainforests?).
- Throughout the lesson, build in opportunities for students to discuss connections to their native languages and home cultures with peers. As a teacher, it is important to understand the language and culture of each student. These opportunities for discussion allow teachers to glean insights through purposeful listening. They also support the building of trust that leads students to feel safe and accepted in a new learning environment.
- Scaffold learning for students, as needed, to bridge from the schooling context of their primary socialization (e.g., in the home country) to the new one. For example, explaining differences in the way math problems are worked in the home country versus the new country can go a long way in reducing confusion for students.
- When configuring pairs or small groups, think about where the student is in the acculturation process, and group students based on their sociocultural and linguistic needs. Think of students in your classroom that are accepting of others and who will help the CLD student become part of the learning community. Small groups allow for students to interact with additional peers, each of which can provide a different kind of support (sociocultural, linguistic, cognitive, academic). All students have something they can learn from others.

In classrooms where teachers are faced with students from different socioeconomic backgrounds, languages, and countries of origin, the art of assessing who students are and what assets they bring to the classroom is critical. A growing number of schools, districts, and states recognize the relationship between acculturative adaptation (which does not negate the student's primary cultural and language identity) and student academic success. "Knowing that many ELLs [English language learners] define their 'cultural identity' by the *language* and *ethnicity* of the sociocultural group to which they feel connected supports the necessity to include students' native language during instructional and non-instructional time" (Indiana Department of Education, 2005, p. 2). Policies that value native language use stand in stark contrast to past policies, which often promoted academic environments in which students were humiliated, punished, or forbidden from using their home language at school. For many students, hearing and seeing their native language as part of the environment and during instructional time serves to validate their language and culture—and themselves as individuals. Chapter 5 discusses the role of the native language and how teachers can incorporate native language support into their instruction.

Cultural Differences as Learning Assets

A group of Midwestern teachers reviewed the following dilemma:

Mrs. Bingham is concerned because Joel rarely completes his math homework. The homework usually consists of 20 to 25 practice problems involving computation skills he has learned and has been able to perform in class. Joel's mother is single, and her evening attention is split among cooking, cleaning, laundry, and bathing the little ones. However, she tries her best to help Joel in whatever ways she can. Joel has several older and younger siblings, so Mrs. Bingham is concerned that the home environment is interfering with his ability to do homework. She suggests to his mother that Joel be provided a quiet place to work without distraction for a certain period every night. Joel's mother agrees to keep his siblings out of their shared bedroom, but they continue to play at the door. The teacher then advises her to "shut the door for half an hour . . . or until Joel gets the work done." After several weeks, there is little improvement in Joel's homework. When the group of experienced teachers was presented with this scenario, their comments and observations included the following:

- "I feel sorry for the mom."
- "That's the problem with so many of our students."
- "Clearly, there is no way he can study in *that* home."
- "Perhaps there is an after-school program where Joel could do his homework."

Although their comments reflect empathy for Joel and his mother, this empathy is inadequately rooted in preconceived ideas about what constitutes study and the notion that large families are distractions rather than resources. The teachers' comments were in response to the following question, which had been crafted to inspire insights about cultural assets: "Given Joel's collectivist culture, what other kinds of solutions may have been generated if Joel and his mother were involved in identifying their own resources and solutions?" Despite this prompt and the teachers' previous exposure to professional development (which included the cultural concepts of individualism and collectivism; see Table 4.3), only one teacher made a comment that reflected the desired consideration: "Maybe Joel isn't comfortable being

Table 4.3   Key Features of Individualism and Collectivism

Individualism	Collectivism
Home Cultures That Value and Promote Individualism	Home Cultures That Value and Promote Collectivism
Encourage the understanding of the physical world as knowable or manipulable, irrespective of its meaning for the members of the culture	Encourage the understanding of the physical world in the context of its meaning to the members of the culture
Promote independence across members of the culture and individual achievement	Promote interdependence among members of the culture and group success
Value egalitarianism, role flexibility, and upward mobility	Value stable, hierarchical roles associated with gender, family background, age, etc.
Foster self-expression, self-directedness, and personal choice	Foster adherence to cultural norms, respect for authority, deference to elders, and group consensus
Favor individual ownership and private property	Favor group ownership and shared property

alone . . . isolated. Is there a way the kids could do their homework together?" This particular teacher was from a CLD family herself, and she more readily saw that the family might be more comfortable working together.

Once the educators discussing Joel were allowed to benefit from another perspective, they were able to see how the dynamics of his home situation could facilitate his learning in a variety of ways. Additional ideas generated included have Joel use interactive games and activities to practice skills with his siblings. One teacher, who had characterized the original situation as "a mess," suddenly realized the inconsistency of her own views. After all, she was a strong proponent of cooperative education as a way to provide authentic, differentiated, and natural models for learning. Why had she not seen before the benefits of bringing these practices home where they could be made even more powerful by involving parents or siblings? As a result of this professional conversation, several teachers added optional forms of home practice (e.g., games) that resulted in more actual opportunities to practice the concepts and skills than the old worksheets.

Many teachers of CLD students have discovered that acculturation can prove a mutual (and mutually beneficial) process. Increased contacts with diverse students often result in the type of reflection that fosters significant personal and professional growth among education personnel. The ability to identify cultural assets to which one is not accustomed and view them from an alternate perspective is similar to experiences with optical illusions. Many of us have looked at a picture, certain of the *one thing* it depicts . . . only to have someone else point out a completely different image or way of perceiving the work. Suddenly, those things our minds did not allow us to see before become glaringly obvious.

It is important, therefore, for educators to realize that cultural assets enhance the student's acculturation process—not detract from it. The scenario provided at the beginning of this section illustrates, for example, the characteristic of *familism,* the tendency to value family and family goals above those of the individual. When this trait is studied in CLD families, high degrees of familism correlate with positive interpersonal relationships, strong family unity, the ability to work with others toward shared goals, and close ties to extended family (e.g., Esparza & Sánchez, 2008; Garriott, Raque-Bogdan, Zoma, Mackie-Hernandez, & Lavin, 2016). Indeed, many in the fields of education and psychology have extolled the importance of cultural values, such as familism, to the health, engagement, and persistence of CLD students (e.g., Germán, Gonzales, & Dumka, 2009; Romero, Robinson, Haydel, Mendoza, & Killen, 2004). One need not sever ties nor abandon values to build new relationships within, and learn the alternate norms of, a new society. We as teachers simply need to explore alternative ways of interpreting the world, through the eyes of students and families, and seek input from cultural insiders when outcomes do not match what we hoped to achieve.

Knowledgeable educators recognize that there are many ways to incorporate and affirm the strengths and cultural assets of CLD students. Supportive teachers (and schools):

- Convey a climate of affirmation and celebration of the languages and cultures represented.
- Make use of professional development opportunities in the areas of acculturation and second language acquisition, to inform their instructional practices.
- Regard CLD student cultures and languages as enriching assets.
- Advocate for curricula and use resources that reflect the cultures and values of the student populations represented.
- Build in opportunities in every lesson for students to share with peers how the content connects to their worldviews.
- Create home–school connections through the following:
  - Opportunities for parents, caregivers, and other family members to share experiences and knowledge related to topics the child is learning
  - Home visits and informal conversations that emphasize relationship-building and respect for the family's knowledge and expertise

> **assessment FREEZE FRAME 4.4**
>
> It is important for educators to realize that cultural assets enhance the student's acculturation process—not detract from it.

Keep in mind that effective student instruction and accommodation require the combined efforts of students, parents, and the community. Families have unique abilities to support and guide students toward success. Community members represent an additional source of knowledge, insight, and experience. Table 4.4 supports educators to examine their own perspectives regarding the assets that students, parents, and communities bring to the education process.

Impact of Acculturation on Appropriate Methods of Assessment

Although a primary emphasis of this chapter is on the assessment of acculturation, it is also important to understand the impact of acculturation on assessment in general. CLD students often arrive with cultural values and behaviors that differ from the Western cultural perspective on which so much of our educational system

Table 4.4 Sociocultural Environment: Educator Views of Student, Family, and Community Assets

| Component | Level of Performance | | | |
	Meets Criteria	Basic Needs	Improvement	Unsatisfactory
Culture	The student's culture is respected and valued as a source of knowledge and experiences that advance learning and enhance the cultural climate of the school. Issues and behaviors related to acculturation processes are identified and mediated with sensitivity and knowledge of research-based approaches that are appropriate for the CLD student/family/community involved.	The student's culture is respected and valued on principle. General implications and stages of acculturation are understood as influencing student learning and behavior. Recognizes but is unable to comfortably mediate cultural misperceptions and conflicts between families and self or other staff.	Behaviors that arise from cultural differences or acculturation are viewed as interfering with student achievement and long-range success. Instructional strategies and interventions emphasize acculturation to the dominant culture.	The CLD student's culture is viewed as a negative influence on the student and school. Cultural considerations are rejected as irrelevant to the development of appropriate instructional practices and intervention
Language	Supports L1 use at home and school. Understands, models, and is able to explain the rationale for L1 and sheltered instructional strategies. Is knowledgeable about language acquisition phenomena, including language loss and implications of language support, or lack thereof, on student achievement.	Supports L1 use at home. Understands basic language acquisition stages and time lines. Can explain the benefits of sheltered instruction. Considers CLD student's language as potentially affecting behavior and/or achievement.	Regards continued use of home language as an obstacle to English acquisition and school success. Is supportive of, but cannot describe or model, instructional strategies that benefit CLD students.	Regards the student's home language as a deficit to be overcome. Is unsupportive of ongoing adaptations and instructional modifications for CLD students.
Academics	Is able to articulate the relationship between L1 and L2 learning and analyze classroom tasks in terms of prerequisite language, academic, or social experiences. Makes specific recommendations regarding instructional modifications and assessment of CLD student progress.	Understands the impact of language and acculturation on CLD student academic progress. Identifies general instructional strategies that benefit CLD students.	Provides strategies to meet the academic needs of general students performing below grade level but does not understand or provide strategies particular to the needs of CLD students.	Considers the academic difficulties of CLD students to be either environmental or innate and therefore is resistant to long-range change regardless of interventions.

(Continued)

Table 4.4 Sociocultural Environment: Educator Views of Student, Family, and Community Assets *(continued)*

| Component | Level of Performance | | | |
	Meets Criteria	Basic Needs	Improvement	Unsatisfactory
Families	Exemplifies a respect for CLD families that is evident through greetings, verbal and nonverbal communication, and overall accessibility. Advocates for programs, events, and activities that engage families. Demonstrates an understanding of, and respect for, culturally different family dynamics. Respectfully mediates cultural issues and behaviors that conflict with a student's positive school participation.	Expresses respect and value for CLD families. Encourages CLD family involvement but has little direct contact with parents beyond those required by policy or events. Recognizes when cultural issues affect school–family communications but does not initiate or engage in actions to address potential conflicts or concerns.	Feels that truly interested families are already involved. Communication with CLD families is limited to required procedural or behavioral matters.	Regards CLD families as unsupportive of education. Is opposed to initiatives or incentives to increase CLD family involvement. Avoids communicating with CLD families.
Community	Is knowledgeable about, and communicates with, community resources that can provide or assist CLD students and families. Regards community resources as potential assets and partners in the educational, linguistic, and social–emotional learning of CLD students. Involves members of the local neighborhood and CLD community in schoolwide events and celebrations.	Is knowledgeable about and appreciates, but does not personally communicate with, community resources that can provide or assist CLD students and families. Recognizes selected organizations (e.g., religious, fraternal) as valuable to the positive overall development of CLD students.	Provides CLD students/families with referrals only to school-based professionals such as social workers, nurses, and counselors. Does not communicate with community or seek additional resources for meeting the essential and/or enrichment needs of CLD students and families.	Speaks in generalities about community support but feels resources and influences in the student's community conflict with school ideals of what "is best" for the student. Is unable or unwilling to provide resources or contacts appropriate to the needs of CLD students and families.

is based. Traditional assessment practices typically value individual achievement, competition (ranking), and recitation of knowledge. Therefore, many traditional approaches to assessment favor students who bring strong, existing competencies in the expectations of the dominant culture. By contrast, the CLD student may not able to do the following:

- Understand the cultural assumptions of assessment prompts that are grounded in the dominant culture (e.g., that pizza slices are cut into even proportions).
- Be comfortable demonstrating knowledge in ways that he or she perceives are condescending or might cause others to lose face (e.g., provide the answer to a question another student missed).
- Be motivated by competition, speed (faster is better), or nonsocial reinforcers (e.g., grades).

Because the goal of assessment is to determine *what* and *how* the student learns in order to inform instruction, assessment methods that do not account for acculturation only serve to cloud the teacher's ability to gain anything valuable from their results.

Understanding how acculturation affects student performance is key to recognizing how inadequate traditional assessments are for measuring what we really need to know: *Is this student learning?* Each CLD student, by the very nature of age and cultural difference, develops along multiple physical, emotional, linguistic, cognitive, and acculturative continua. Testing students according to static, predetermined points of learning, especially when they already feel overwhelmed or unready to demonstrate their capabilities, can lead to frustration and the belief that there is little hope for their success in the classroom. As many of us have experienced on a personal level, being subjected to assessment practices that emphasize what we *don't* know rather than what we *do* know—along with those that result in negative consequences (e.g., failure, overt/covert comparison to others)—can significantly undermine our attitudes about education . . . and ourselves.

Teaching Tips:

- Communicate to students and their families that your focus will be on growth.
- Encourage students by building on the positive (e.g., existing language skills, conceptual knowledge, and academic abilities).
- Assure students that formal tests are just a moment-in-time; they tell us nothing about the student's potential.
- Review assessment materials for cultural bias.
- Hold conversations with students about their thinking processes if they have incorrect responses on an assessment that seem odd, given your formative observations of their learning.
- Explore students' thought processes if you see patterns of incorrect items; rule out the possibility that the student misunderstood the directions or expectations of the item format.
- Explain your perspective on expectations for student interaction, and allow students to share their perspectives/norms with you.
- Through your actions and communications with students and families, demonstrate that you value open, honest, two-way communication about the child's education, including assessments.

PROGRAMMING-RELATED ISSUES: ASSESSMENT OF ACCULTURATION

Issues of placement and programming for CLD students who are acquiring English as a second language are topics beyond the scope of this text. Nonetheless, the results of assessing acculturation, content-area skills and knowledge, and language proficiency can aid decision making associated with these issues. Therefore, the following discussion highlights grade-level issues of acculturation assessment that are relevant to the identification, placement, monitoring, and exit of CLD students. This discussion is by no means exhaustive, but provides a synopsis of issues that should be considered.

Identification

Acculturation status is an essential component of the larger body of information collected when identifying CLD students for alternative language programs. Students with lower levels of English language proficiency may experience concurrent issues of acculturative stress or, in some cases, culture shock. Such stress can affect the ability of students to demonstrate their actual abilities through language and content-area assessments. Therefore, it is important to allay student fears during the formal assessment process and emphasize informal assessment information, which is generally obtained in less anxiety-provoking contexts.

Placement

Levels of acculturation and the degrees of difference between the home and host culture can help determine the most appropriate instructional placement and approaches for CLD students. An unaccommodating classroom can greatly hinder the academic success of students, especially those in early stages of acculturation. Such students may benefit from extensive opportunities to draw on their native language and culture as learning assets.

Monitoring

CLD student acculturation, along with language acquisition, should be monitored across settings. Negative acculturative phenomena, such as deculturation or rejection, will require attention to both individual student needs and the educational environment. Home visits and conversations with parents can provide critical insights into how students can best be assisted through their acculturation journeys.

Exit

It is important to realize that CLD students who have met the language and achievement criteria to exit alternative language programs may continue to require supports and affirmation. Even after students exit a program, such support is often necessary for positive cultural identity development and acculturation processes that lead to integration or adaptation. Students who integrate aspects of the host culture to form a bicultural identity are able to draw on the strengths of both cultures to overcome personal and academic challenges. Such individuals are also better able to help fellow students facing similar acculturation challenges.

SUMMARY

This chapter explored key dynamics of the accultura-tion process as they pertain to the instruction, assess-ment, and building relationships to create a classroom community. The acculturation process is by no means a linear process. It is influenced by external and inter-nal factors that make each student's journey unique. The most effective educators move beyond content delivery and testing in order to explore the student's level of acculturation in creative and innovative ways. The chapter addressed both formal and informal ways of assessing aspects of students' identity, and it has provided considerations for teachers regarding the impact of identity on students' classroom participation and learning. Although many districts and schools choose not to formally assess level of acculturation, it is imperative that teachers explore acculturation in informal ways.

This chapter has provided strategies and activities for educators to learn about the student. These are but the tip of the iceberg of what can be possible when all educators see the importance of acculturation assess-ment for instruction. It is difficult to teach students who may feel marginalized, and who do not see themselves as part of the learning community.

The teacher's journey often requires reflection on self, as teacher, and ways in which instruction is deliv-ered that may contribute to the acculturation stress or success that CLD students and families experience in their school-situated interactions. In like manner, the capacity of teachers to recognize and reflect upon their cultural lenses and the influences they may have on per-ceptions, pedagogy, and expected outcomes among CLD students is pivotal to furthering students' accultura-tion and academic success.

Acculturation is a complex and formidable process for CLD students; learners seldom are nurtured as sensi-tively as they were during the processes of enculturation. Accordingly, teachers benefit from knowledge about the typical acculturation stressors that CLD students may encounter and ways that they can help students maintain low affective filters and experience effective learning in the midst of such stressors. Historically, the goal of school-ing for immigrant, refugee, and other CLD students has been assimilation. Today, theory and research support the preferred goal of adaptation. Teachers, school lead-ers, and other educators can do much to reduce students' stressors and highlight their assets as they target this actualizing goal for CLD learners and families.

KEY CONCEPTS

Acculturation	Cultural assets	Individualism
Adaptation	Cultural lens	Integration
Anomie	Culture shock	Psychological acculturation
Assimilation	Deculturation	Rejection
Behavioral acculturation	Enculturation	
Collectivism	Familism	

PROFESSIONAL CONVERSATIONS ON PRACTICE

1. Discuss the role that prior socialization in a particu-lar culture plays in developing the lens through which a teacher views the abilities, behaviors, and performance of a CLD student. Why is it critical for teachers of CLD students to recognize, understand, and monitor this lens? Why should teachers want to know about the origins of that lens?

2. Review the case of Nashida discussed in this chapter. Discuss the pitfalls of informally assessing level of acculturation according to a single continuum of acculturation development or progress (i.e., behav-ioral or psychological). How can relying on a single source of assessment information foster inappropri-ate assumptions about CLD students?

3. Discuss how assessing acculturation of CLD students can encourage the teacher to use appropriate instructional and other classroom accommodations with these students. How can classroom teachers better identify and reduce acculturative stress with CLD students?

4. Discuss what the goal of assessment should be. How might traditional assessments detract from that goal, especially in the case of the CLD student?

QUESTIONS FOR REVIEW AND REFLECTION

1. What is acculturation, and how does it differ from enculturation?

2. What does the phrase *cultural lens* mean, and why must teachers learn to recognize its influence on their perceptions of, expectations for, and pedagogical actions with CLD students?

3. Name at least five behaviors a student may exhibit as a result of culture shock.

4. What are key differences between assimilation and adaptation or integration as potential outcomes of the acculturation process?

5. How can emotions, especially emotions associated with the challenges of acculturation, affect CLD student performance and achievement?

6. Along what two continua is acculturation generally understood to develop?

7. What are specific advantages of a home visit for informally assessing the level of acculturation of CLD students?

8. Describe at least two informal assessments of acculturation a classroom teacher might use with CLD students.

9. What are at least three effective actions schools can take to reduce acculturative stress with CLD students?

10. Define *familism*. What is the relationship between familism and the acculturation challenges confronted by CLD students?

CHAPTER 5

ASSESSMENT OF LANGUAGE PROFICIENCY

Before reflecting upon my assessment practices, I was not considering any language difficulties when giving students assessments. After having the chance to reflect on my biased assumptions and actions, I changed my assessments to fit the needs of my CLD students. Instead of written responses, multiple-choice quizzes, and cumulative tests on paper, I began to assess some students orally if needed. I also allowed students to show me what they knew by doing hands-on assessments that were more appropriate for students who struggled with language skills. Having visuals and experiments allowed my kinesthetic and visual learners the chance to express their knowledge and level of understanding without the stress of knowing all of the words and spellings that would be on a written test.

Morgan Walton, Second Grade Teacher. Reprinted with permission.

Learning Outcomes ▬▬▬

After reading this chapter, you should be able to:

• Detail three dimensions of language that provide a foundation for language acquisition and learning.

• Hold informed conversations with administrators, colleagues, parents, and students about formal language assessments.

• Informally assess the language skills of your CLD students.

• Use language assessment results to inform your instructional planning and delivery.

• Provide an overview of the process used to identify, place, monitor, and exit students from language support services.

▬▬▬

THREE DIMENSIONS OF LANGUAGE

As educators, language acquisition is the first concept that we grapple with as we begin helping students transition to their linguistic journey in a new language. However, the first question that we often ask of ourselves is, "How proficient is the student in his or her language abilities?" We want to have a baseline measure of students' language abilities. Language acquisition and language proficiency are two related but distinct concepts that need to be unpacked as we think of assessments, interventions, and instructional decisions for students.

Language acquisition is the process of becoming successful at understanding and using a language. Although different theories exist to explain the phenomenon, typically developing children are able to associate abstract features of a language they hear (or see) with inherent rules about the content, form, and use of that language (Bloom & Lahey, 1978; Wright & Kersner, 2015). For this natural process of first language acquisition to happen, children must be exposed to authentic communication and have opportunities to use the language for real purposes. Culturally and linguistically diverse (CLD) students likewise must have opportunities for authentic and purposeful use of English if they are to acquire the language.

Language proficiency, on the other hand, refers to students' ability to perform in a language. Four domains of language typically are assessed: listening, speaking, reading, and writing. Ideally, the assessments we use to evaluate language proficiency yield results that inform our understanding of individual students' progress in English language acquisition.

A brief exploration of isolated features of language will support our ongoing discussion of the relationship between language proficiency—assessed through both formal and informal means—and language acquisition, which should be one of the targeted goals of our daily instruction. We will frame this exploration around the three dimensions of language: form, content, and use.

Form

Form is the structural aspect of language that involves attaching some symbol to the meaning being expressed. The symbol can include the spoken word, a picture, or a gestured sign. Form also refers to the structures we create by combining symbols such as words to make sentences (*syntax*). It includes additive forms, such as suffixes, that we add to words to refine the meaning of our message (*morphology*). It also includes the sounds and patterns of sounds in a language that we use to form words (*phonology*).

Syntax   Syntax refers to language-appropriate word order. Chomsky (1968) has argued that all languages and dialects share a universal grammar. Humans are predisposed to attend to and develop detailed patterns of language. The features each group chooses to highlight, or mark, may differ but each is complex in its own way (Fenk-Oczlon & Fenk, 2014). Yet the conventions of "standard" English are among the benchmarks by which a person is deemed proficient in the United States. As with all skills, the ability to use English syntax in ways that reflect those of native speakers is acquired developmentally over time.

For example, young native English speakers, as well as new-to-English speakers who have yet to distinguish between subject and object pronouns, commonly produce sentences such as "Her went to the store." CLD students who are acquiring a second language (L2) may initially combine L2 words and first language (L1) syntax patterns. For example, the Spanish sentence "Yo tengo un perro *chiquito*" ("I have a *little* dog") is structured with the modifier following, rather than preceding, the noun. For this reason, many native Spanish speakers initially produce sentences such as "I have a dog *little*." With time and experience, most CLD students can automatically differentiate these patterns as specific to only one or the other language.

Teachers often conduct assessments of syntax in their classrooms when they give students a set of words and ask to put them in order. Careful attention to students' responses enables educators to understand gaps in syntactical understanding. They then plan interventions and instructional practices accordingly.

Morphology   Morphology refers to the rules and patterns for changing words to alter meaning by way of tense, person, number, and so forth. For instance, the addition of *ed* to most verbs tells us we are referring to a past event ("I walked"), but the addition of *s* to many verbs usually indicates a present-tense action by a third person ("She walks"). It violates the commonly accepted rules of English—and therefore sounds awkward—to say "I walks" or "She walk." As with syntax, CLD students must not only master English morphological conventions but also differentiate those from the conventions of their first language.

Consider how additions of prefixes such as *dis* or *un* can completely change the meaning of a word (*dis*agree, *un*tie). Although students might be fully aware of the added prefix or suffix, they may not be able to grasp the changes in meaning as a result of the additions. As we support learners to attend to such additions to words, it is important to highlight contextual use of the words. This allows students to understand the meanings of the words themselves, as well as their constituent parts.

Phonology

Ms. Murillo presented Ezequiel with a quick set of prompts to check his knowledge of opposites.

> **Ms. Murillo:** What is the opposite of *up*?
> **Ezequiel:** Down.
> **Ms. Murillo:** Empty?
> **Ezequiel:** Full.
> **Ms. Murillo:** Dead?
> **Ezequiel:** Mom.
> **Ms. Murillo:** (pause) . . . Um, not Daaaaaad . . . *dead*.
> **Ezequiel:** Oh, alive!
> **Ms. Murillo:** Heavy?
> **Ezequiel:** Not heavy.
> **Ms. Murillo:** False?
> **Ezequiel:** Stands.

Ms. Murillo noted four out of five correct on Ezequiel's chart. Which response did she consider incorrect? Ezequiel realized that *heavy* is an adjective with which it is appropriate to use the modifier *not*. Ms. Murillo knows this realization demonstrates an important element of linguistic comprehension but does not demonstrate Ezequiel's ability to provide an appropriate opposite. By contrast, his most blatant "error" came when he heard Ms. Murillo say *falls* instead of the word *false*. Seemingly incorrect, Ezequiel's response of *stands* is actually an appropriate opposite for the word he believed Ms. Murillo to have said: *falls*.

In this scenario, phonology lies at the root of the misunderstanding. Phonology refers to the sound system of a language, the manner in which phonemes (distinct sounds) can be combined to create meaning. Phonemes in one language may not be phonemes in another. If a sound is phonemic, it may change the meaning of a word.

For example, the sound /z/ (as in *zip*) is not a phoneme in Spanish. The Spanish language does spell words with the letter *z*, but the sound produced is like the English language *s*. For instance, *taza* (cup) sounds like *tasa*. There are no sounds in Spanish like the one English speakers associate with the letter *z*. Consequently, native Spanish speakers such as Ezequiel are not as attuned to distinctions between

ASSESSMENT IN ACTION 5.1

Assessments can provide invaluable insights into students' developing language skills. One area of assessment that is growing in importance and relevance is preassessment of phonological skills. Phonological skills refer to the student's ability to recognize, discriminate, and manipulate the sounds or sound units of language. Research on English speakers has shown that phonemic awareness skills are strongly predictive of literacy development (Yesil-Dagli, 2011).

For CLD students, phonological skills in the primary language have been found highly predictive of literacy success in both L1 and L2 (Branum-Martin, Tao, Garnaat, Bunta, & Francis, 2012; Durgunoglu, Nagy, & Hancin-Bhatt, 1993; Yeung & Chan, 2012). Because a child's brain has had more exposure to the sounds and patterns of his or her primary language, the child will often initially be more adept at demonstrating and learning these skills in that language (Coleman & Goldenberg, 2010). Transfer of skills from one language to another suggests there is value in measuring and teaching these skills in whatever languages possible in a given setting (Cárdenas-Hagan, Carlson, & Pollard-Durodola, 2007; Kuo, Uchikoshi, Kim, & Yang, 2016; Luo, 2014; Sun-Alperin & Wang 2009).

Following are a few assessments that would be considered as point-in-time assessments. Even if conducted over time and incrementally, assessments such as these only give us a snapshot of students' skills. These assessments are beneficial, however, because they can point us in the direction of interventions and instructional practices that are likely to help students' advance in second language acquisition.

ASSESSMENT OF PHONEMIC AWARENESS FOR PRE- AND NONREADERS

1. **Imitation of Auditory Patterns***

    Instructions: Tap or knock *X* number of times. Encourage the child to imitate by saying, "Do this," and by using the equivalent saying in the child's native language (e.g., "Haz esto" for Spanish speakers), or by using gestures to convey the instruction. Note the child's response by recording the number of times he or she tapped.

	Student Taps
1. X	_____
2. XXX	_____
3. XXXX	_____
4. XX	_____
5. X	_____
6. XXX	_____
7. XX	_____
8. XXXXX	_____

2. **Syllable Segmentation with Physical Cues**

    This may be done using native language words, English words, nonsense words, or a combination of these. (Please circle stimuli types used for this task.)

    Instructions: Say a word with the targeted number of syllables. Say it again slowly, tapping, clapping, or jumping once to each syllable count (e.g., Tap two times as you say "*ca-sa*" [Spanish for *house*] and three times as you say "bas-ket-ball"). Ask the child to join you. Once he or she can perform this task well in unison, have him or her imitate your performance with new words, tapping for each of the syllables. If this is easy, give the child words to segment independently. Use two to three words comprising the different numbers of syllables and note the child's responses. (Use "+" to indicate a correct response, and "−" to indicate an incorrect response.) Teachers can then use these data to inform their instruction of readiness skills.

(imitation)	L1	L2	Nonsense
1 syllable			
2 syllables			
3 syllables			
4 syllables			

(independent)	L1	L2	Nonsense
1 syllable			
2 syllables			
3 syllables			
4 syllables			

3. **Auditory Discrimination**

    Instructions: The student will need to understand the concept of sameness. If the student is young, point to his or her shoes, nod, and say, "Same" ("*Iguales*" [Spanish translation], etc.). Then put your shoe next to one of the child's, shake your head, and say, "No, not same." Do this several times with environmental objects (e.g., pencils, blocks).

    Using two identical objects such as blocks or pennies, touch each as you repeat the same word "car–car." Do this several times and model a "thumbs up" or nod as you affirm their sameness. Then take two dissimilar objects (e.g., a block and an eraser) and touch each for dissimilar words "car–milk." Shake your head and model "No, not same." It is not necessary for the student to use words such as *same, different,* or *not same* to perform this task. Any reliable gesture

ASSESSMENT IN ACTION 5.1 (*continued*)

(head shake/nod or thumbs up/down) will do. Encourage the student to watch your mouth as you say the words and note if he or she can determine whether the following pairs of words are the same (head nod) or not (head shake).

L1 words:

car–car	spoon–spoon	_____
milk–milk	spoon–soon	_____
candy–candy	chair–chair	_____
apple–dog	made–mad	_____
apple–apple	eat–eat	_____
banana–spoon	cup–come	_____

4. **Structured Rhyming**
    An example of how to elicit structured and independent rhyming is included in a subsequent section of this chapter (see the Oral and Written Cloze Assessments section). Although it is not necessary to probe the student's skills using all stimuli types mentioned below, the distinction of language used will inform instructional planning for this student.

	L1	L2	Nonsense
Recognizes rhyme	yes/no	yes/no	yes/no
Selects rhyming word	yes/no	yes/no	yes/no
Offers rhyming word	yes/no	yes/no	yes/no

5. **Sound–Syllable Blending**
    Instructions: To determine the level(s) at which the student is able to blend sound segments into words, you say variously sized segments of the word aloud, and the student then combines the segments to produce the whole word. You may need to begin by using something visual or tangible to demonstrate the desired behavior. For example, lay a token down for each syllable as you say "back-pack" or "wa-ter-fall." Then push the tokens together and say the entire word. The student's familiarity with the vocabulary will be a factor in his or her ability to understand the purpose of this task. Familiar words from the child's L1 and L2 as well as nonsense words can be used for this assessment. Children who are shy or not yet comfortable speaking the target language can demonstrate skills by pointing to the appropriate picture among a set provided by the teacher. Present several words for each of the

following three levels to discover the student's instructional readiness. Note the student's responses.

	L1	L2	Nonsense
1. By syllable ("bu-tter-fly")			
2. Initial sound + remainder of word ("r-ock")			
3. By sound ("d-e-s-k")			

6. **Phoneme/Syllable Deletion**[†]
    Instructions: This skill is often not evident in the preschool years but becomes very relevant for previously unschooled students or struggling early readers. This skill can also be demonstrated with colored blocks or other items to represent the sound or syllable segments being manipulated. To assess elision (the deletion of a sound or syllable), tell the student:

    1. Say "hot dog." Student: "hot dog"
        Now say it again, but don't say "hot." Student: "dog"

    2. Say "hamburger." Student: "hamburger"
        Say it again, but don't say "ham." Student: "burger"

    3. Say "baloney." Student: "baloney"
        Say it again, but don't say "low." Student: "bunny"

    4. Say "bake." Student: "bake"
        Now say it again, but don't say "b." Student: "ache" (Be sure to pronounce sounds rather than say letter names.)

    5. Say "meat." Student: "meat"
        Now say it again, but don't say "t." Student: "me"

    6. Say "cloud." Student: "cloud"
        Now say it again, but don't say "k." Student: "loud"

    Feel free to substitute words with similar patterns and expand on this list. Note below words and responses generated while assessing elision in the student's primary language:

    _____
    _____
    _____

Source: Selected items adapted from the *Spanish/ English Preschool Screening Test* (Kayser, 1998) and the [†]Test of Auditory Analysis Skills (TAAS)(Rosner, 1993)

/s/ and /z/ as are native English speakers, for whom *zip* and *sip* are very different words with very different meanings.

Language production "errors" are often recognizable as features of a person's accent. However, teachers' interpretation of student performance becomes more accurate when they are aware of ways phonological perception may influence what students hear and how they answer. This awareness also helps the teacher highlight pronunciation differences in strategic ways during daily lessons, especially when students are learning new content vocabulary.

Content

Teachers had come from different schools to staff a newly opened elementary school. The students were largely CLD learners who had been transferred from overcrowded schools in adjacent areas. Their principal, Ms. Houston, had been fortunate to attract many talented teachers to the new school. Within a month, however, the excitement began to wane.

It appeared that the students had widely varying skill levels. Many didn't return homework and "lacked the oral language" needed to talk about content, much less learn new vocabulary at the recommended pace. Prescribed lessons entailed heavy use of repetitive response drills to help students remember the word definitions and examples provided by curricular scripts. Fidelity to scripts was promoted to ensure that all students received the same instruction, with nightly homework sheets to cement the skills. Teachers noticed that those students who *already* were successful participated the most, and with greater success.

Other students could repeat back the prompts used to teach, but they not discuss the material or apply concepts with any depth. It reminded Ms. Sami of how she only memorized terms long enough to pass the high school anatomy tests—until the chapter on skin. She had been to a dermatologist and she also liked having her nails done. Word parts like "derma" and "cutaneous" (cuticle!) hit home. This prompted Ms. Sami to wonder aloud, "Is it possible that all the structure designed to *equalize* access may actually be *impeding* some students' more personal and powerful connections to the vocabulary words?"

Another teacher jumped in, "How do we know our families *don't* have experiences with the concepts represented by academic vocabulary? I can't tell you how many times a cognate or discussion of home experience has given instant *life* to "new" words. It's so much more powerful than memorization. Besides, the only students completing the homework pages regularly are those who already find it easy, or have parents who do." Others agreed.

Ms. Houston summarized, "So, I'm hearing a few themes. One is that the district-provided lessons don't necessarily facilitate connection. The other is that homework may not be helping. In fact, many of you feel the practice sheets:

- Reinforce students' self-perceptions as either a learner or a struggler
- Further disadvantage parents who have less time to sit with each child or who are less proficient in the school language
- Don't significantly impact oral language development

These are keen observations. Homework is definitely an area we can adapt." Together they decided to try something radically different. Students in all grades would have no homework assignments other than vocabulary, and the format of the vocabulary homework also would change.

Figure 5.1   Questions for Parent and Caregiver Conversations

---

Conference Dialogue Questions

- What would you like me to know about your child?
- What are your child's interests?
- What activities does your child like to do?
- Does your child like to read?
- What excites you about your child?
- What does your child like to do with friends?
- How does your child feel about school?
- Where does your child feel the most success?
- What do you like to help your child with the most?
- If you could choose a goal for your child, what would it be?
- We need your help with homework. *(Describe the vocabulary activities and how those at home can help.)*

Source: Michele Ingenthron, Wichita, KS. Reprinted by permission.

Teachers used the subsequent fall conferences to learn more about students (see Figure 5.1) and gain insight to home language development. They explained the new homework approach to parents. A letter also was provided, translated into the languages spoken by area families (see Appendix B). Each week, all students would be assigned targeted vocabulary, just as before. Several teachers, however, wanted to add power by opening with a strategy to activate background knowledge. They were willing to share these ideas and experiences during professional development time. Insights gained during conferences and through activation could then be referenced while teachers presented the standard district materials and visuals.

There were minor differences in the formats used for home practice. In all cases, students had opportunities to learn and talk about the words before taking them home. Most homework involved taking home a graphic organizer, with individual or group notes developed during activation and connection in class. Students were not required to rewrite or memorize definitions. Instead, the only requirement was to go home and talk to a parent, grandparent, aunt, uncle, neighbor, or sibling. Students were to share their understanding of what these words meant and *listen* to the thoughts, examples, or questions parents had for each word. The parents' job was simply to talk, adding personal connections and home language words (or dramatizations) wherever possible for each idea. Above all, these conversations were to occur in the language of the home and heart.

The next morning, students had a chance to share with tablemates what they had learned or heard in those home discussions. Ideas were written on sticky notes, which were added to the vocabulary organizer or poster used by each class (see Figure 5.2). There was an immediate positive response from all stakeholders. Teachers noticed not just improved scores on weekly quizzes but increased oral and written use of the new words across settings. These were truly evidence-based results!

Figure 5.2   Assessment Artifact: Vocabulary Insights from Home

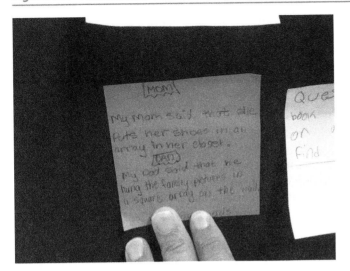

Students have the opportunity to talk to parents, caregivers, and others about their connections to words being studied at school. In this example, the student provided the perspectives of both parents on the word "array."

Images Source: Natasha Reyes, Wichita, KS. Used with permission.

Teachers can display, celebrate, and build upon home vocabulary connections during instruction. Doing so communicates the shared community of the class and the unity among parents, students, and teachers as they work toward common goals. Facilitating connections between background knowledge and the curriculum also promotes student comprehension and retention of learning.

The voices of the following teachers illustrate the benefits of the new homework policy for the learning community:

I have never had parents and kids so excited to do homework before. The parents can go home and have conversations with their kids and there's no right or wrong answer. It's just using the vocabulary. And we found that kids are vertically aligning their vocabulary K–5. That's the way the district is set up, so it's nice to have brothers and sisters able to have conversations about the same words and they can build relationships that way, too. So it's all about building relationships and making parents confident to talk to their kids at home.

Chelsea Johnson, Second Grade Teacher. Reprinted with permission.

I got a very positive response from parents and students about it. The students that even had behavior issues at home and school said, "I love it because I can sit with my mom or my dad and just talk, and I'm not in trouble." And it's very positive. Parents said that they loved it because it was stress free and even my student that had a lot of behavior issues said, "I love that my Dad will just talk to me and it's one of the only times that we really do talk." So it was a very positive experience in my classroom.

Bridget Lujano, Fifth Grade Teacher. Reprinted with permission.

This scenario illustrates the power of building vocabulary instruction upon the existing languages and experiences of students, families, and community members. It also highlights how teachers' willingness to think outside the box can set into motion more effective teaching and learning practices. With relatively little effort, teachers were able to increase the relevance of their grade-level curriculum for students while also supporting stronger bonds within families and the community.

Most of us master the form (syntax, morphology, and phonology) of our primary languages as children. However, our skill with the content, or meaning, of language continues to develop and grow throughout our lives. *Semantics* relates to the meanings of words, phrases, and sentences. Meaning can be expressed by our choices of words, their endings or prefixes, and the order in which we arrange them. Therefore, most of us choose our words rather carefully based on the meanings we believe they hold and the message we want to convey in a given context. For teachers, it is important to remember that vocabulary, to a large extent, is gained and retained through interactions with people and print outside of educational settings. With this in mind, homework of the nature described in this section's vignette is beneficial to advancing students' (and families') continually developing semantic knowledge.

Semantic knowledge is the most readily transferred aspect of language. It is much easier to connect the new form (word) with an already understood concept than it is to learn a concept one has never been exposed to (in a language not yet fully understood). Even if there is not an exact translation, every word has semantic features or meaning associations that function like Velcro hooks. These understandings provide added "stickiness" for new related words. The more words known in the native language, the easier it is to learn new words in *any* language.

As we teachers work to support students to develop semantic skills, we also must consider the difference between a child's ability to make meaning when words are present in isolation versus when words are utilized within a context. If you have ever closely listened to English learners reading or performing on a proficiency test or a state assessment, you likely noticed the frustration they feel at times in their ability to understand the words and phrases within the context of a paragraph. With enough knowledge of phonological awareness and isolated discrepancies in morphology, our language learners often are able to connect the isolated sounds to form words and the words to form sentences. However, these abilities do not guarantee that they have been able to master the art of the language, which lies in meaning making. We do not want to leave students stuck at the level of being "word callers." We must continuously look for ways to support learners on their path toward greater understanding and comprehension.

assessment FREEZE FRAME 5.1

The more words known in the native language, the easier it is to learn new words in *any* language.

Use

CLD students are learning not only new sounds and words but also detailed, yet often unspoken "rules" about how such words can be marked and combined (or not) to communicate effectively with the new language "code." Actual use of a language requires an understanding of how to use the language in varying contexts and for a multitude of purposes. *Pragmatics* refers to ways in which social context and experience influence the interpretation of language. Such influences depend on the speaker, listener, setting, and intent rather than on just the static meaning of the spoken words.

For example, depending on the people and their relationship, interaction style, situation, and nonverbal cues, the word *great* can be used as a sincerely positive or a sarcastically negative comment. Let's consider a simple exchange:

> **Jack:** It's starting to rain.
> **Saul:** Oh great.

This dialogue is difficult to interpret unless the author provides us with some context, along with descriptive or stylistic cues such as punctuation or italics to inform us about the pragmatic aspects of the message. The study of pragmatics encompasses a variety of both blatant and subtle, as well as verbal and nonverbal, features of language. These features can dramatically influence how a message is delivered and perceived. Most people generally understand language pragmatics as the appropriateness of the communication action or intent in context.

The pragmatics of a situation always should be considered an influence on a student's response. For example, in many languages—including English—it can be considered redundant to repeat the subject of a question in the response. For most of us, "What is the boy doing?" will elicit a response that directly answers the question, such as "Riding a bike," without the additional phrase "The boy is . . . " Unfortunately, it is common to find prompts requiring an artificial construction (e.g., repetition of the subject when the subject is already understood) on tests intended to measure a child's content knowledge or language skills. Such prompts may penalize students who provide the more natural fragmented response.

Language is complex, and mere knowledge of its structure is insufficient. Language also is acquired at the level of *communicative competence*. Effective communication demands that we know what to say, when to say it, to whom to say it, and under what circumstances (Kayser, 2008). The answers to such questions typically lie in the dynamic norms of varying linguistic and social groups.

In addition, most speakers, regardless of background, shift their manner of speaking or style depending on the situation. To illustrate, depending on the formality of a workplace, it may seem unusual to hear someone speak to a boss in the same manner he or she would use with close friends or family. In addition to tone of voice, speakers who are *style shifting* also unconsciously adjust vocabulary, syntax, intonation, and grammar to fit the discourse style necessary for that particular setting or purpose. Style shifting is a sophisticated skill, and weaknesses in this area can be socially awkward. CLD students who demonstrate communicative competence are able to communicate effectively in a variety of social groups.

ASSESSING LEVELS OF LANGUAGE PROFICIENCY

Federal legislation often stipulates that schools must meet certain requirements in assessing the English language proficiency of CLD students. These criteria seek to enhance the alignment of instruction, learning, and assessment while increasing school and district accountability for student success. Standardized tests are usually a key component of recommended guidelines. This can move the focus of language assessment from communicative authenticity (informal assessments) to the type of validity attributed to well-developed standardized assessments (formal assessments). Both types of assessment provide important information for identification, placement, monitoring, and exit from language programs.

Formal Assessment of Language Proficiency

The formal assessment of CLD students whose primary language is not English has become a recurrent focus of policymaking, research, reform, and debate in education. Educational reform initiatives, especially those at the federal level, are often the impetus behind these trends in education. The most recent of these reform initiatives have advocated standardized formal assessments, the results of which are thought to be comparable across school districts and across states. Consequently, the emphasis of language programming for CLD students is increasingly grounded in standardized assessments of language proficiency.

A variety of formal assessments are available and have been used to assess different aspects of language proficiency. These generally include specific tasks designed to measure students' listening, speaking, reading, and writing capabilities. Most formal assessments are not conducted by classroom teachers and therefore are beyond the scope of this text. However, intuitive teachers of CLD students use the results of such assessments in planning and delivering accommodative classroom instruction. These teachers learn about the nature of formal assessments used by their school district, as well as general guidelines for interpreting the student outcome reports (results) generated by each type of assessment.

Table 5.1 provides examples of formal assessments of language proficiency. Classroom teachers are encouraged to visit the testing agency's website or contact the agency's commercial or institutional representative for more specific information about particular versions of formal standardized assessments. Teachers can also benefit from reading the work of researchers who strive to contextualize the assessment process for schools and educators who serve CLD students (e.g., Rhodes, Ochoa, & Ortiz, 2005).

Formal standardized attempts to measure the *overall* language proficiency of emergent bilinguals often involve administering essentially monolingual tests in two or more languages (e.g., the native language and English). Although this approach to testing CLD students does provide information about separate language skills, these assessments may not tell us much about the larger body of language competencies a student may draw upon for learning. Emergent bilinguals develop language competencies that often reflect the intertwining of linguistic features from the native language and English (García, Ibarra Johnson, & Seltzer, 2017).

Some formal language assessments have been developed to permit CLD students to demonstrate more holistic language knowledge and competency. Generally, this means that students are assessed in one language and are either simultaneously or sequentially prompted to provide missing or incorrect information in the alternate

Table 5.1   Formal Assessments of Language Proficiency

Assessment	Key Characteristics
The Dos Amigos Verbal Language Scale (Critchlow, 1996)	This assessment uses 85 pairs of opposites in Spanish and English to measure conceptual linguistic knowledge. Qualitative results provide information about relative proficiency in each language. The provision for qualitative interpretation also facilitates a more holistic picture of proficiency levels in the two languages as they are demonstrated separately and in unison.
Preschool Language Assessment Scale (Pre-LAS 2000) (Duncan & DeAvila, 1998)	This assessment is designed to measure the developing language and preliteracy skills of preschool-age children to inform the placement of these young language learners into the most appropriate classroom settings. It is available in English and Spanish.
Language Assessment Scale—Oral (LAS—O) (Duncan & DeAvila, 1990)	This assessment measures the listening and speaking skills of students in grades 1 through 6 and 7 through 12. Like the Pre-LAS, it is available in English or Spanish and is useful in assessing primary language development or to identify students for placement in, and exit from, bilingual/ESL programs. The LAS—O contains an optional observation form that can be completed by another examiner to further support or triangulate findings used to determine whether a student is ready for redesignation.
The Bilingual Verbal Ability Tests Normative Update (BVAT-NU) (Muñoz-Sandoval, Cummins, Alvaredo, Ruef, & Schrank, 2005)	This assessment takes into consideration both the native and second language and comprises three subtests from the Woodcock-Johnson III Tests of Achievement (Woodcock, McGrew, & Mather, 2001) that have been translated into 18 languages (now including Hmong and Navajo). The BVAT scoring software generates a report that differentiates among the student's bilingual verbal ability, student's cognitive academic language proficiency (CALP) skills, and relative language proficiency in languages assessed.
Language Assessment Scale— Reading/Writing (LAS—R/W) (Duncan & DeAvila, 1990)	This assessment measures reading and writing skills in English or Spanish L1 ability levels. It may be used to identify students for placement in, and exit from, bilingual or ESL programs. The test combines selected response and writing sample evaluations to assess vocabulary, fluency, reading comprehension, mechanics, and usage.
IDEA Proficiency Test (IPT) (Ballard & Tighe, 2004)	This assessment offers oral, reading, and writing versions available in Spanish and English. It is also designed to assess both social and academic language. Like other assessments of this type, the IPT may be used to measure primary language skills but is most often employed for the identification, placement, and (re)classification of CLD students who are acquiring English in appropriate classroom contexts.
Woodcock-Muñoz Language Survey Revised (WMLS-R) (Woodcock, Muñoz-Sandoval, Ruef, & Alvaredo, 2005)	This assessment is another popular measure of Spanish and English that comes with a computerized scoring program. This scoring program generates a narrative that describes the CALP in English or Spanish, or the relative proficiency between languages if both versions of the test are administered.
Receptive One-Word Picture Vocabulary Test (ROWPVT) (Brownell, 2000b) and its companion, the Expressive One-Word Picture Vocabulary Test (EOWPVT) (Brownell, 2000)	These assessments, originally developed for English speakers, have been translated into Spanish and are normed on bilingual students in the United States. These assessments credit correct responses in either language (conceptual scoring) in addition to rating relative proficiency in Spanish and English.

(continued)

Table 5.1 *(continued)*

Assessment	Key Characteristics
Stanford English Language Proficiency 2 (SELP2) assessment (Harcourt Assessment, 2003)	This assessment measures the English listening, reading, writing, and speaking skills of K–12 students. Now with four forms, SELP 2 can be used at the beginning of the school year to establish a baseline and then administered periodically to obtain multiple data points to evaluate progress. SELP 2 assesses student language proficiency and mastery of skills included in the CCSS and WIDA standards and is a predictor of how well students will perform on high-stakes state assessments. If employed during the school year, results can be used to help prepare students in advance of the standardized testing required by states.

language. These approaches are based largely on Cummins's (1984, 1996) conceptualization of a bilingual person's *common underlying proficiency* (CUP). They operate on the theory that a CLD student's structural and communicative language knowledge is best demonstrated through assessment in contexts in which both languages are accessed, even though one language may be dominant.

These assessments are standardized and have been normed using performances of similar bilingual students under similar conditions. Such norming better accounts for relevant linguistic and cultural factors. Two assessments of this kind are the Dos Amigos Verbal Language Scale and the Bilingual Verbal Ability Tests Normative Update.

The Dos Amigos Verbal Language Scale (Critchlow, 1996) is easily administered and uses 85 pairs of opposites in Spanish and English to measure conceptual linguistic knowledge. Qualitative results provide information about relative proficiency in each language. The provision for qualitative interpretation also facilitates a more holistic picture of proficiency levels in the two languages as they are demonstrated separately and in unison. This is significant because bilingual students often exhibit a home and community vocabulary in the primary language that is broader than the academic vocabulary they can demonstrate in English. Therefore, assessing language proficiency in one language alone can provide misleading information about the student's overall vocabulary knowledge.

Analyzing response differences and performance can also demonstrate whether the student is accessing L1 knowledge to help him or her process concepts in L2. For instance, a student may correctly respond that *"blanco"* is the opposite of *"negro."* However, the same student may respond to the English prompt that the opposite of *"black"* is *"brown."* Such responses indicate that the student can use words to make the targeted conceptual connection in the L1 but does not yet grasp L2 words in ways that demonstrate a similar level of processing.

The Bilingual Verbal Ability Tests Normative Update (BVAT-NU) (Muñoz-Sandoval, Cummins, Alvaredo, Ruef, & Schrank, 2005) also takes into consideration both the native and second language and comprises three subtests from the Woodcock-Johnson III Tests of Achievement (Woodcock, McGrew, & Mather, 2001) that have been translated into eighteen languages (now including Hmong and Navajo). The BVAT scoring software generates a report that differentiates among the student's bilingual verbal ability, *cognitive academic language proficiency* (CALP) skills, and relative language proficiency in languages assessed.

For some CLD students who are acquiring a second language or are using their first language less, there may be a significant difference between their expressive and receptive skills. This disparity may not show up on assessments that measure all language competencies with tasks requiring a verbal response. Being aware of this disparity can help the classroom teacher plan lessons that are comprehensible at higher levels and still provide necessary supports and modifications for verbal participation.

Examples of assessments developed to separate the receptive and expressive domains are the Receptive One-Word Picture Vocabulary Test (ROWPVT) (Brownell, 2000b) and its companion, the Expressive One-Word Picture Vocabulary Test (EOWPVT) (Brownell, 2000a). These assessments, originally developed for English speakers, have been translated into Spanish and are normed on bilingual students in the United States. Like the BVAT, these assessments credit correct responses in either language (conceptual scoring) in addition to rating relative proficiency in Spanish and English. More recent research suggests that total vocabulary (count of all correct words) may be an even more reliable measure of vocabulary growth in bilinguals than conceptual scores (Core, Hoff, Rumiche, & Señor, 2013). Situational priming and inhibition also impact bilingual students' ability to access words in L1 or L2 during naming tasks (Anaya, Peña, & Bedore, 2018). Because of the great variance in home language lexicons and experiences, caution is recommended in the interpretation of any formal measures of vocabulary.

Educators often are at a loss when determining the level of language proficiency of their English learners. Having knowledge of tests available and the potential of each to provide the necessary information for decision making related to program placement, services, and instruction is critical.

Teaching Tips:

- Use the findings of standardized tests to make decisions about necessary adaptations to the curriculum.
- Configure groups based on students' L1 and L2 proficiency to maximize oral language development.
- Use standardized test scores to set the baseline and create checklists to monitor student progress (more on this in the upcoming discussion of informal assessments).
- Create materials aligned with content standards that will be accessible to the student based on language proficiency.

State-Developed or State-Adopted Variations   In response to state and federal accountability requirements, as well as historic inconsistency in state testing practices, there is a growing trend among states to develop (or subcontract the development of) their own assessments for English learners. For instance, Kansas uses one such tool called the Kansas English Language Proficiency Assessment 2 (KELPA2). KELPA2 assessments are divided into four parts corresponding with the four domains of the English Language Proficiency Standards: listening, speaking, reading, and writing. KELPA2 assessments are fully computer-based for students in 2nd grade and beyond. K–1 learners take a mostly computer-based exam, while also completing a small number of writing items using paper and pencil. KELPA2 assessments are implemented every spring, along with regular Kansas Assessment Program (KAP) summative assessments in English language arts and math.

Similarly, Texas uses the Texas English Language Proficiency Assessment System (TELPAS). TELPAS fulfills federal requirements for assessing the English language proficiency of K–12 English learners in the four language domains: listening, speaking, reading, and writing. TELPAS assesses students in alignment with the Texas English Language Proficiency Standards, which are part of the Texas Essential Knowledge and Skills (TEKS) curriculum.

Many states around the nation alternatively have joined a consortium. As a consortium member, the state has access to tools its schools can use to assess CLD students' language proficiency. The assessment results then are used to determine the extent of language services needed by each student.

For example, members of the World-class Instructional Design and Assessment (WIDA) consortium use ACCESS for ELLs 2.0. This is a secure, large-scale English language proficiency assessment administered to K–12 students who have been identified as English learners. Developed by WIDA, ACCESS for ELLs 2.0 is aligned with the WIDA English Language Development Standards and assesses each of the four language domains of listening, speaking, reading, and writing. It is given annually to monitor students' progress in acquiring academic English. ACCESS for ELLs 2.0 is only available to school districts within the states that are part of the WIDA consortium. This assessment serves multiple purposes for the states administering the test. First, it helps students and families understand learners' current levels of English language proficiency along the developmental continuum. Second, it serves as a measure for determining whether students are prepared to exit English language support programs. Third, it provides districts with information that helps them evaluate the effectiveness of their ESL/bilingual programs.

The ELPA 21 assessment is another large scale utilized by a group of consortia member states that designed and developed an assessment system for English learners. The system is based on English language proficiency standards and addresses the language demands needed for students to reach college and career readiness. This exam assesses students' English abilities in speaking, listening, reading, and writing and scores them according to different levels. It is administered at the beginning of the school year or at the time of a student's arrival at a new school system. The summative assessment is taken annually at the end of the school year by students who were designated as English learners. The results of the summative assessment are used to monitor students' progress in English language acquisition.

In short, different states use different English language proficiency assessments to identify, monitor, and exit their students from language services. States decide which assessment they will use, based on their own state-specific educational policies. All of these assessments are intended to provide insights into students' language levels and abilities across the four domains of listening, speaking, reading, and writing.

Interpreting Results   Formal standardized assessments of second language proficiency generally measure a CLD student's competency with targeted skills such as reading, writing, speaking, or listening. The results are reasonably assumed to represent new learning and are used to compare individual or group growth toward the standard on which it is based. In best practice, second language proficiency assessments should rarely be interpreted to infer anything about a student's innate linguistic or cognitive abilities.

Unfortunately, the results of language proficiency assessments are not always interpreted cautiously, especially when the assessment is administered in the student's primary language. Although there are certainly reasons to gather information about an English learner's primary language, relying on formal assessments or inappropriate testing procedures can lead to erroneous findings, inaccurate assumptions, and the potentially harmful placement of the student.

For example, it is not uncommon for students who were raised in bilingual U.S. communities to perform poorly on language proficiency assessments (for languages other than English) that were developed and normed in countries outside the United States. This is especially true if these students received classroom instruction only in English. When combined with apparent evidence of a student's limited English proficiency, these results are sometimes misinterpreted to indicate innate language or learning problems.

In reality, the results more often reflect cross-cultural discontinuities or differing expectations and norms across educational systems. Educators should carefully examine the normative basis of such assessments to ensure that they are valid for the population (and specific backgrounds) of students served. By giving serious consideration to the appropriateness of assessments and by being knowledgeable about language acquisition variables, we help ensure that results actually lead to unbiased instructional decisions and practices.

It is also important to remember that not all standardized assessments of language proficiency are created equal. Some may be designed with vocabulary or constructs seemingly unrelated to classroom goals and objectives. Other problematic content or stimuli include culturally or experientially narrow items (e.g., picture prompts of men panning for gold), which inevitably measure content-area knowledge as well as language.

Effective teachers of CLD students are concerned as well with the currency of language proficiency assessments. They check to ensure that the pictures and references in an assessment are relevant to modern-day life. For example, classroom teachers often report that many students misidentify pictures of televisions and typewriters as computers. Others do not recognize pictures of corded phones or bar soap. Similarly, CLD students often arrive with varied experiences and provide alternate answers that make sense to them (and indeed demonstrate the targeted skills), only to have these answers marked incorrect on the assessment.

Examiners should scrutinize both the assessment and the student's performance. One can ask the student to explain answers different than those cited as "correct." Atypical responses may reflect either a culturally different interpretation of the prompt or a correct (albeit nontraditional) application of the targeted skills and understandings. For this reason, it is critical to be aware not only of what each assessment actually measures, but also the student skills the assessment might potentially fail to take into account.

When students take assessments, teachers can ask proctors to add anecdotal notes on students' performance behavior during implementation of the test. These notes on the academic and linguistic behaviors exhibited by a student during the assessment can provide valuable insights for the teacher. The teacher can consider both noted challenges and indications of the student's successful strategy use when planning instructional interventions and daily lessons.

As this chapter discusses, language can be defined in so many ways and along so many continua that there is no one, agreed-upon set of skills that truly reflects this amazing human gift. Therefore, it is not uncommon to find that different language assessment developers have chosen radically different tasks to measure the same skill (for example, language comprehension). This, along with the fact that many language assessment developers customize their assessments to align with individual state standards, reminds us that we must always

---

assessment FREEZE FRAME 5.2

Although there are certainly reasons to gather information about an English learner's primary language, relying on formal assessments or inappropriate testing procedures can lead to erroneous findings, inaccurate assumptions, and the potentially harmful placement of the student.

critically analyze and reflect on assessment results. The best way to know what our language proficiency assessments are—*and are not*—telling us, as well as how reliably they inform us about CLD student learning, is to consistently align their findings with those of other assessments of language performance and achievement.

Informal Assessment of Language Proficiency

Language is a rich and complex system of sounds, words, sentences, nuances, and gestures that is, by its very nature, reciprocal and spontaneous. Other than for distinct purposes, such as formal speeches, language is incredibly interactive and socially dynamic. For example, it is quite natural for teachers to adapt their style and pace or stop for clarification when reading to students who appear confused or inattentive. These subtleties, which make replicating language with technology so difficult, also hamper our use of formal assessments to measure a student's grasp of a language. Any time we seek to assess language, we must understand not only what our tests can tell us but also what they *cannot*. In this section, we discuss a variety of informal assessment techniques for developing a clearer picture of a CLD student's language profile and proficiency level.

The value of informal assessment data frequently depends on the types and numbers of settings in which we observe the student's use of language—as well as the perspectives through which we interpret that language usage. For example, because language can be so situation-specific, it is unwise to assume that a single sample of CLD students' language is fully representative of their broader linguistic abilities. What CLD students may not be able to properly express in one language, manner of speaking, or situation, they may be perfectly capable of expressing in another.

Reflect back to the three dimensions of language we discussed earlier: form, content, and use. It is through the informal assessment of language proficiency that we can gauge more clearly how our students are progressing in their acquisition of English and in their understanding of these dimensions of language. We also can look for language performances that do not match our contextual expectations but might be quite appropriate from the perspective of a different cultural norm.

For instance, some children may feel that to answer questions with obvious answers is disrespectful, or they may avoid eye contact as a sign of respect, despite the teacher's insistence to "look at me when I'm talking to you." Other children may call out agreement or commentary as the teacher speaks. We all attend to different cultural norms that affect our communication style in various settings. How might we be judged if, while in church, we respond to the sermon in a manner appropriate for a football game? How many of us find "table talk" quite different at our own house than it is at the homes of our in-laws or neighbors?

Just as it takes any child time to learn the subtleties of when and what to say where, CLD students will, if not demeaned for their culture's rules, learn additional cultural norms for effectively communicating with multiple groups in multiple settings. Teacher actions that demonstrate concern for the affective side of learning, and especially language learning, are key to this process. Arnold (2009) defines affect as the area of feelings, emotions, attitudes, moods, and beliefs that influence students' behavior. Students who feel supported and encouraged to take risks in their new language and communicative interactions will progress more quickly and easily along the path toward more proficient language use. As we explore informal ways of assessing language proficiency, consider how teachers can use such approaches to

---

assessment FREEZE FRAME 5.3

Any time we seek to assess language, we must understand not only what our tests can tell us but also what they *cannot*.

gather information—while simultaneously providing students with affirmation and assurances of their capacities, progress, and potential.

Home Language Surveys   Linh's kindergarten teacher referred her to the student intervention team because she was "still not speaking English in class." The teacher felt something was very wrong because other teachers noted that Linh's brother began speaking with peers "nearly right away" and their father was reportedly able to convey basic information in English to staff members. The teacher was concerned that Linh might be developmentally delayed.

In reviewing the home language survey, the intervention team quickly noted that, although the father had some English proficiency, Vietnamese was reported as the only language spoken in the home. This was logical because Linh's mother did not speak English at all. Despite the initial impressions of the teacher, the team concluded that Linh probably was not developmentally delayed, but rather had had very limited exposure to English prior to her first preschool year.

The survey used in this school also asked about the dominant language of the child at home (in this case, Vietnamese) but did not ask for any information about the child's perceived proficiency with that language. To meet Linh's needs effectively and help her achieve in school, it was decided that the team needed more information about her first language proficiency and use.

In this scenario, a misunderstanding about language acquisition processes almost resulted in an inappropriate assessment of the student's actual communicative competence. *Home language surveys*, such as the one depicted in Figure 5.3, are one of the most common ways that schools and districts gather initial

---

Figure 5.3   Home Language Survey

The home language survey is given as soon as a student from a diverse language or dialect background enrolls in the school district. Besides the date and the student's name, additional information is gathered: country of origin, whether the student has been in a school in a language other than English, how long and in what language was the schooling, the student's first language, etc. The home language survey is to be kept in the student's cumulative file to inform all education personnel.

Date _____ School _____ Grade _____ Student's Name _____

Parent or Guardian's Name _____

1. What is the student's country of origin? _____
2. What language did your child learn when first beginning to talk? _____
3. What language does your child most frequently use at home? _____
4. What language do you most frequently speak to your child? _____
5. What language does the primary caregiver speak to your child? _____
6. What is the language most frequently spoken at home? _____
7. Has the student had academic instruction in a language other _____
   than English? Yes ❑ No ❑ How long? _____ Language? _____
8. Please describe the language understood by your child. (Check only one.) _____
   a. ❑ Understands only the home language and no English.
   b. ❑ Understand mostly the home language and some English. (and Spanish)
   c. ❑ Understands the home language and English equally.
   d. ❑ Understands mostly English and some of the home language.
   e. ❑ Understands only English.
9. If available, in what language would you prefer to receive communication from the school? _____

Source: Collier, C. (2015). *Separating difference from disability workbook.* Ferndale, WA: CrossCultural Developmental Education Services. Page 36. Reprinted with permission.

information about the language(s) used in a student's home. These assessments of language proficiency help teachers understand more about students' level of exposure to English and their linguistic foundations in the primary language.

Home language surveys are included as informal assessments in this text because districts have considerable flexibility in the way they create and administer the survey. Federal mandates only ask that some sort of screener be used to determine which students need to be formally assessed for language proficiency. Home language surveys fulfill this purpose. Districts also administer home language surveys in informal ways. Parents frequently complete them at a welcome center or other location as part of the registration process.

Although home language surveys can serve a variety of additional purposes, they are generally the first and broadest step toward identifying students who may qualify for additional language services. When the home language survey indicates a primary language other than English is spoken in the home, the student is often referred. Postreferral assessments help determine whether a student is proficient enough in English to participate fully in classrooms where instruction is delivered only in English.

Whether home language surveys are simple or complex, school personnel who review them should bear in mind that some parents will lack the literacy skills (in either English or the first language, or both) to complete these forms without additional support. Other parents might misinterpret the meaning or intention of survey questions due to language dialects or translation quality. Some parents, unsure of the degree of trust they should place in school officials and systems, will require additional information about the process and its possible outcomes for their child before they will feel comfortable completing the survey.

Examiner Tips:

- Explain the survey's purpose.
- Ensure privacy of information.
- Explain how the results of the survey will be used.
- Provide assistance to parents in completing the survey.
- Verify the parents' interpretation of provided information during translator-assisted conferences. This effort provides valuable opportunities as you establish lines of communication with parents or guardians and seek additional information about the funds of knowledge students bring to class.

With conscientious use and interpretation, assessments such as the following similarly can be used in informal ways to elicit key information about primary language development.

- Bilingual Language Proficiency Questionnaire (Mattes & Santiago, 1985; Mattes & Nguyen, 1996)
- Communication and Play Screening Instruments (Kayser, 2008)
- Adapted, parent-friendly version of the Student Oral Language Observational Matrix (SOLOM) (California Department of Education, n.d.[a]) (see Figure 5.4 for adapted version in English and Appendix B for a Spanish translation)

Information gathered with these tools can allay the teacher's concerns about students who exhibit longer-than-expected silent periods. A *silent period* is part of the preproduction stage of the second language acquisition process (Krashen & Terrell, 1983). During this period, CLD students may communicate

Figure 5.4   Parent-Friendly Student Oral Language Observation Matrix (SOLOM)

Parent/Teacher Language Observation
(Adapted from the Student Oral Language Observation Matrix)

Student's Name:				Grade:	Date:
Home Language(s):			Completed By (signature):		
	1	2	3	4	5
A. Comprehension	Doesn't appear to understand any conversation.	Has difficulty following everyday social conversation, even when words are spoken slowly and repeated.	Understands most of what is said at slower-than-normal speed with repetitions.	Understands nearly everything at normal speed, although occasional repetition may be necessary.	Understands everyday language and normal family conversation without difficulty.
B. Fluency	Speech is so limited that conversation is virtually impossible.	Student attempts to speak but has periods of silence due to limitations.	Speech in everyday conversation is frequently disrupted by the student's search for words.	Speech in everyday conversation is generally fluent, with occasional lapses while the student searches for the correct manner of expression.	Speech in everyday conversation is fluent and effortless.
C. Vocabulary	Vocabulary is so limited that conversation is virtually impossible.	Difficult to understand because of limited vocabulary and misuse words.	Student frequently uses wrong words: conversation somewhat limited because of inadequate vocabulary.	Occasional use of inappropriate terms and/or rephrasing of the ideas because of limited vocabulary.	Vocabulary and idioms approximately those of a native speaker.

(Continued)

141

Figure 5.4 (*continued*)

Parent/Teacher Language Observation
(Adapted from the Student Oral Language Observation Matrix)

Student's Name:

Home Language(s):

Grade:

Date:

Completed By (signature):

	1	2	3	4	5
D. Pronunciation	Pronunciation problems so severe that speech is virtually unintelligible.	Difficult to understand because of pronunciation problems; must frequently repeat in order to be understood.	Concentration required of listener; occasional misunderstandings caused by pronunciation problems.	Always intelligible (understandable), although some sounds may be in error.	Pronunciation and intonation approximately those of a native speaker.
E. Grammar	Errors in grammar and word order are so severe that speech is virtually unintelligible.	Difficult to understand because of errors in grammar and word order. Rephrases or limits speech to basic patterns.	Frequent errors in grammar and word order. Sometimes hard to understand meaning.	Occasional errors in grammar or word order. Does not interfere with meaning.	Grammar and word order are approximately those of a native speaker.

Source: Adapted SOLOM, Natasha Reyes, Wichita, KS. Reprinted by permission.

in only nonverbal ways as they primarily listen to the new language and try to understand its patterns and rules before attempting to produce in that language.

When classroom teachers are aware of criteria incorporated on such assessment measures, they can better attend to language development throughout the instructional day. For example, a teacher who is familiar with the school district's language acquisition rubric is often much more aware of the need to develop descriptive vocabulary among CLD students. This teacher might then purposefully elicit words such as *crunchy, gooey, delicious, crisp,* or *sweet* during nonacademic periods of the day, such as snack time.

Home Visit Interviews

During a *home visit interview*, teachers asked a few more detailed questions about Linh's use of language in the home. The team was able to observe Linh's interactions with her family, who shared the same cultural and linguistic knowledge base. Because these assessments were conducted in Linh's language of comfort, they were more likely to yield genuine information about her true linguistic abilities.

The responses the teachers received and the language performance they observed indicated that Linh actually began speaking at an early age. She was able to speak in complete sentences, and she used language effectively to tell her parents about her day at school. These findings reassured the team that Linh possessed a strong language base rather than a possible developmental delay.

The home visit also provided additional information that her teacher could use to enhance the home–school connection. Aided by a translator, the teacher encouraged the parents to talk about and build on school topics they could glean from translated newsletters, notes, and Linh herself. The parents were reassured that doing so in the home language would facilitate Linh's classroom learning and confidence and enhance her ability to transfer her primary language skills to the new language.

The next month, during a class discussion on weather, Linh raised her hand excitedly to share, "My dad say Vietnam so much rain."

"Yes," the teacher replied, "Some places like Vietnam get much more rain than we do."

Along with other class members, Linh walked over to the globe to find Vietnam. Together, they talked about the weather in Vietnam, Mexico, Israel, and even Chicago, where Jason said his grandmother calls wind "the hawk." It was amazing how a few simple strategies for helping Linh's parents enrich her learning had such an impact on the learning experiences of others.

Observational data gathered through home visits can greatly enrich and validate findings from other types of language proficiency measures or surveys. Observing language use in context allows educators to see how students actually use the relatively decontextualized skills measured by formal tests. Seeking this kind of additional data was essential in Linh's case, as teachers felt they simply did not have enough information to make appropriate decisions about her instruction based solely on the home language survey. The team followed up the standard survey with a home visit interview, knowing that a genuine developmental delay or learning concern would be evident in Linh's home environment as well.

A parent or caregiver's observations of a child's language use in the home and with family can greatly inform the assessment process. Ideally, teachers will have the opportunity to meet with parents or caregivers at home. Parents and students often are more comfortable in their home environment, and such opportunities allow educators to observe student behavior in a setting that is familiar and nonthreatening. Translators involved in this process should know the teacher's agenda for the meeting and should be trained (in both linguistic and cultural competencies) to provide parents/caregivers and the teacher a reliable interpretation of the messages exchanged.

A guide or prepared list of questions may be helpful, but the astute interviewer also invites parents to "tell me more" or to "think of a time when" the student demonstrated the skill being discussed. Checklists of communication functions (i.e., how the student uses language in context) are also useful for obtaining information about a student's overall communication proficiencies. Such checklists allow teachers to note the child's use of L2 at school and then probe parental perceptions about how the child uses language in the home or community. When a teacher has more clues about a student's particular language strengths and preferences, he or she can more appropriately accommodate that student's learning and L2 acquisition needs.

ACCOMMODATIVE ASSESSMENT PRACTICES 5.1

Ms. Kole used a simple checklist of communication functions (see Figure 5.5 and the related appendix resource) to quickly note language skills she had observed with CLD students in various classroom contexts. Although Jean, a CLD student, was demonstrating several important skills, such as describing experiences and expressing imagination, he struggled to follow sequential directions in class. Ms. Kole doubted that language was a factor because Jean understood each step perfectly when instructions were broken down into smaller units. Therefore, she decided to explore other issues that might be involved.

During conference week, Ms. Kole met first with the French interpreter to discuss Jean's progress and her concerns before they met with Jean and his mother in the home. Ms. Kole also discussed the communication inventory with the interpreter so they were both aware of particular language skills to ask about in the home language setting.

Jean's mother was expecting them and left her supper to simmer while visiting with the guests from school—she was so pleased to meet them! After exchanging greetings with the teacher, Jean's mother turned to her son with several comments, and he headed over to the open kitchen. Ms. Kole noticed the interpreter watching him as she and Jean's mother resumed the conference. After a minute or two, Ms. Kole cleared her throat ever so slightly to regain the translator's attention. The translator smiled and told the teacher that Jean had just carried out every one of the four things his mother told him to do in the kitchen, precisely as directed.

Momentarily putting the agenda aside, Ms. Kole commented on the interpreter's observation.

Ms. Kole: Some children have trouble following directions even when they try. Does Jean usually follow directions this well?
Mom: Oh, yes. Back in Port-au-Prince, I could send him to my sister's apartment or to the market, and he always remembered all the things I said to do and get. He's a good boy.
Ms. Kole: That's great! I always forget things on my grocery list. How do you remember everything, Jean?
Jean: Sometimes my mother sings while she's doing her chores. So when she tells me lots of things to do, I make a song in my head, too. Hey, that rhymes!

Ms. Kole gained many valuable insights about how to work more effectively with Jean, such as using music and rhyme in the classroom as mnemonic devices.

Classroom teachers should always keep in mind that CLD student performance may be affected by variables other than language. Students of all cultures and linguistic backgrounds can benefit from the careful differentiation of instruction to meet their particular needs. ∎

Figure 5.5   Communication Functions Checklist

Please indicate whether the following communicative behaviors are:

        Observed (+)   Reported (R)   Not Observed (–)

Student Name: _____

	L1	L2
1. Student comments on actions of self or others.		
2. Student initiates conversations.		
3. Student maintains a topic in conversation.		
4. Student follows multipart directions.		
5. Student uses language to request (action/object, assistance, information, clarification, etc.).		
6. Student uses language to tell (needs, feelings, thoughts, answers to questions).		
7. Student describes experiences (retells events).		
8. Student predicts outcomes or describes solutions.		
9. Student expresses and supports opinions.		
10. Student uses language to express imaginative and creative thinking.		

Classroom-Based Measures   Classroom-based measures of language proficiency provide the flexibility that teachers need to observe, document, and monitor students' use of language skills in low-risk, low-stress situations.

Checklists   In addition to developing social language—or *basic interpersonal communication skills (BICS)*—CLD students must acquire the CALP necessary for classroom success. These language skills include but are not limited to inquiring, classifying, describing, comparing, contrasting, explaining, analyzing, inferring, supporting one's opinions, persuading, synthesizing, and evaluating. It is often easier and more authentic for a teacher to evaluate how students demonstrate language skills with activities and materials he or she already uses than it is to create unrelated or isolated assessments to measure the skills. The checklist depicted in Figure 5.6 provides examples of skills related to BICS and CALP development (see also the related appendix resource). Using a checklist such as this, teachers can observe a student in the course of daily instruction and update the checklist accordingly.

Anecdotal Logs   Much can also be learned about the academic language proficiencies of students through *anecdotal logs*. These are important components of observational assessment. Although it is certainly easier to set aside distinct times and

Figure 5.6 BICS and CALP Checklist

Basic Interpersonal Communication Skill (BICS)

L1	L2	Listening
O	O	Understands school/classroom routines
O	O	Responds, with little hesitation, when asked to perform a nonverbal task
O	O	Follows oral directions at the end of lesson (with familiarity and modeling)
O	O	Listens to peers when process is provided
O	O	Becomes distracted when lesson is not differentiated
O	O	Distinguishes sameness or difference between English sounds

L1	L2	Speaking
O	O	Is comfortable with groups speaking English
O	O	Communicates with peers in social settings
O	O	Responds to questions in class when the question is context embedded or the teacher provides scaffolding
O	O	Is able to retell a pictured, cued, or scaffolded story
O	O	Can describe the topic of the lesson using limited vocabulary
O	O	Struggles with concept retelling when topic is not contextualized
O	O	Withdraws when group discussions go beyond known vocabulary
O	O	Is eager to participate when language demands are supported

L1	L2	Reading
O	O	Recognizes common language of school
O	O	Recognizes environmental print (e.g., signs, logos, McDonald's)
O	O	Can match or read basic sight words
O	O	Reads best when material is contextualized
O	O	Demonstrates limited use of reading strategies
O	O	Volunteers to read when material is known

L1	L2	Writing
O	O	Writes personal information (e.g., name, address, phone number)
O	O	Writes with contextual and/or instructional scaffolding
O	O	Writes with some spelling errors
O	O	Writes with many spelling errors
O	O	Writes with moderate to high levels of syntax errors

(continued)

Figure 5.6 (*continued*)

Cognitive Academic Language Proficiency (CALP)

L1	L2	Listening
○	○	Is able to carry out academic tasks without language support
○	○	Understands vocabulary in different content areas (e.g., *sum* in math vs. *some* in science)
○	○	Understands process/sequence across content areas
○	○	Uses selective attention when taking notes
○	○	Understands teacher idioms and humor
○	○	Understands English language functions
○	○	Comprehends teacher lecture, movies, and audiovisual presentations

L1	L2	Speaking
○	○	Asks/answers specific questions about topic of discussion
○	○	Uses temporal concepts (e.g., first, next, after) appropriately
○	○	Recognizes the need for, and seeks, clarification of academic tasks or discussion
○	○	Expresses rationale for opinion
○	○	Poses thoughtful questions
○	○	Actively participates in class activities and discussions
○	○	Volunteers to answer subject-matter questions of varying difficulty

L1	L2	Reading
○	○	Demonstrates knowledge and application of sound–symbol association
○	○	Demonstrates phonemic awareness skills such as sound blending, elision, and rhyming
○	○	Regards print with appropriate spatial skills and orientation (e.g., left to right, top to bottom)
○	○	Interprets written words and text as the print representation of speech
○	○	Understands differential use of text components (e.g., table of contents, glossary)
○	○	Reads for information and understanding
○	○	Reads independently to gather information of interest

L1	L2	Writing
○	○	Performs written tasks at levels required by the curriculum
○	○	Uses complex sentences appropriate for grade level
○	○	Writes from dictation
○	○	Writes for audience and purpose
○	○	Understands purposes and application of writing conventions
○	○	Uses writing as a tool for personal means (e.g., correspondence, notation, journaling)
○	○	Writes compellingly or creatively (e.g., editorials, poetry, lyrics, stories)

Source: Based on B. Bernhard & B. Loera (1992). Checklist of language skills for use with limited English proficient students. *Word of Mouth Newsletter,* 4(1). San Antonio, TX: Lauren Newton.

situations to observe specific students, those moments are unlikely to yield the quantity and richness of results one can achieve by also noting incidents that arise naturally during the school day. The possibilities for this sort of observation are unlimited, and the various systems creative teachers develop to record and manage such data never cease to amaze.

One example of an anecdotal log is a flip file, created by taping the top edge of overlapping index cards onto a clipboard (see Figure 5.7). Virtual or actual sticky notes can work as well. Each card lists a student's name and specific goals, if desired. As language-related or other significant actions are observed, the teacher writes a date and a short comment on that student's card. The cumulative

Figure 5.7   Assessment Artifact: Flip File

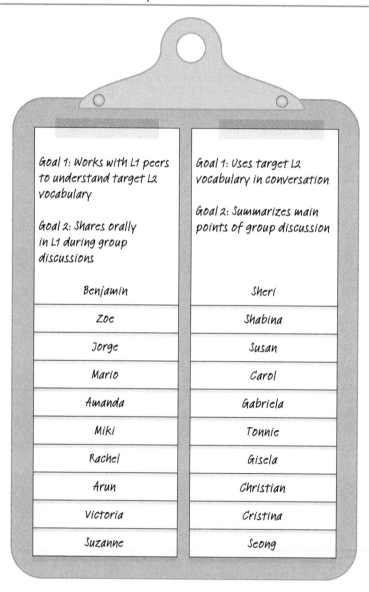

VOICES *from the* FIELD 5.1

As a teacher I know that I cannot always rely on the assessments that are done two to three times per year. I have come to realize that I need a system in place where I can find out different abilities that my students possess. To do this, I have started doing lots of informal assessment, including taking anecdotal notes during the lesson. I usually keep a clipboard next to me with a chart with names of students on it and take quick notes regarding my students during the activity. I always go back to the notes at the end of the day as I am reviewing my students' work.

Cali Nossaman, Second Grade Teacher. Reprinted with permission.

assessment information from these cards/notes can then be used to inform decisions about group configurations, support rubric assessment, and share authentic evidence with parents or other evaluators.

Another type of anecdotal log calls for the teacher to write (either on computer or by hand) the class roster or targeted students' names on sheets of removable labels. These can also be positioned or transported on a clipboard. As interesting language behaviors occur—or do *not* occur (lack of expected behavior is also noteworthy)—the teacher jots the date and comment on that student's label. For example, "10/2, short sentences—small group" may allow the teacher to counter another individual's impression that "Lise doesn't talk." At the end of the day or week, these labels are moved to a page in the student's folder. This strategy (easily adapted for tablet technologies) builds a chronological and reproducible record of language acquisition in progress.

Matrices and Rubrics   Tools such as matrices and rubrics may be used with either naturally occurring language samples or those elicited through story retelling or other more standardized contexts. Preexisting video or audio can also be rated to demonstrate growth, or lack thereof, to the present day. Because pragmatics and context influence the student's response, the teacher should note how the sample was obtained. This information assists reviewers as they interpret the results and compare them with other samples of the student's language.

Because the teacher can make more accurate and revealing observations once the student is more familiar with the teacher and setting, language observation rubrics may not be as informative for initial placement decisions as they are for monitoring ongoing growth and readiness for reclassification. Teachers who gather observational data frequently find it is a powerful tool for measuring learning over time. This ability to aid ongoing instructional planning is a distinct advantage over most formal measures of language, and there are many ways in which teachers can adapt rubrics to gather the specific type of information they need.

Although some classroom teachers prefer to use multiple sheets to note behaviors on different dates, others like to plot skills observed over time (by date) on the same page. Figure 5.8 illustrates one way of recording ongoing observations. Teachers who plot skills over time may then color-code data by setting (playground, large group, individual) or register (academic, social, with peer, or with adult) for a more holistic view of the student's language acquisition progress.

Figure 5.8   Plotted Skills

The teacher used the same rubric to plot Karina's expressive language skills observed in the fall and in the spring. From these results, the teacher can visually see the improvement in the student's message effectiveness, language structure, and pronunciation. Karina demonstrated the same level of skill with vocabulary at both points in time. The teacher then could use this information to focus efforts on promoting Karina's incorporation of vocabulary in her language production.

Expressive Communication Rubric

Student Name   _Karina T._

Date(s) Completed: X above _9/22/05_   X below _2/28/06_

	Level 1	**Level 2**	**Level 3**	**Level 4**
Message effectiveness	Unable to understand intent/ meaning.	X Difficult to understand.	Able to understand most but not all of message. X	Message is easily understood.
Language structure	X Multiple errors with word order and grammar.	Noticeable errors but student able to convey aspects of the message. X	Uses mostly correct structures with some errors.	Use of language structures is similar to that of a native speaker.
Vocabulary	Incorrect word choices and/or limited vocabulary hinder social and academic communication.	X Relies on a limited range of vocabulary to communicate. X	Vocabulary is not usually conspicuous but is rarely specific or elaborate.	Varied types of words, including idioms, are used with facility.
Pronunciation	Speech is often unintelligible.	Speech is understandable with careful listening and known context.	X Speech is generally understandable to familiar and unfamiliar listeners.	Speech pronunciation is similar to that of a native speaker. X

Observational matrices and rubrics such as the Student Written Language Observation Matrix (SWLOM) (California Department of Education, n.d.[b]) are also helpful tools for assessing writing to inform placement decisions and track student progress. Teachers using such approaches may wish to identify representative yet varied samples of writing, such as narratives, journals, blogs, and social network pages, for different audiences before rating skills according to the matrix. Inconsistencies in performance, such as improved voice or sentence variety in journal or letter writing—compared with essay attempts—can give teachers ideas for bridging strengths from one format to another (e.g., "Why don't you start by writing a letter to Joe about your book, and then we'll turn it into a book report"). These tools can also be adapted to rate a student's writing ability in his or her primary language. Personnel who are trained with the matrix and are both fluent and literate in the student's home language are able to most accurately interpret the data.

To monitor the overall growth in a student's language abilities, teachers can use tools such as an adapted or adopted continuum of skills. In the example presented in Figure 5.9 (and the related appendix resource), benchmarks of language

ACCOMMODATIVE ASSESSMENT PRACTICES 5.2

Below is the story Miguel made up to narrate an eight-part wordless cartoon after viewing several times on a classroom tablet. Mr. Mahon let each student determine his or her own readiness to retell their version of the story to him. He used a rubric to note key elements and transcribed the stories of those he most wanted to monitor. If words were too unclear or indecipherable in the audio recording, he simply left blank lines (blanks) as placeholders in the transcription. Miguel had made significant progress and was now quite a talker.

Transcription of Miguel's response:

"Yesterday Johnny was walking with the dog and he opened the door and the dog bark and Johnny put the dog inside his backpack.

Johnny came inside and his mom gave him cookie and he started, he hurt his stomach and he went to his room.

Johnny was in his room and he open his backpack and the dog came and he bite his sock, and he started to pull and his mom.

Johnny went to his room and he went to his bed and his mom came and the dog growled and his mom, is thinks it is Johnny's stomach.

Johnny, he growled his stomach and his mom got idea and his mom went, get out of his room.

Johnny get up, waked up and he put the dog right next to that window.

His friends came and the friends got the dog and get the mitten and his mom is get upsets.

His mom said, "Let's go to his bed," and he went to his bed and his friends, Johnny

friends get away and the dog is so sad. And the mom give it medicine and he don't like it. The End."

How would you rate Miguel's skills using the rubric provided in Figure 5.8? What are his strengths? His needs? How might this information aid planning for Miguel's ongoing language development?

In Miguel's case, Mr. Mahon provided the following ratings for performance on this task:

- Message effectiveness: 2–3
- Language structure: 2–3
- Vocabulary: 3
- Pronunciation 4

Considering Miguel's performance on the narrative assessment, Mr. Mahon decided that his focus for the next month would be *language structure*, as this is the key area impacting *message effectiveness*. Mr. Mahon planned to address these skills first by ascertaining whether Miguel recognizes incomplete or vague sentences. This could easily be incorporated into a quick classwide game of "Which sentence sounds better, one or two?" If Miguel's listening skills reveal underlying grammar recognition, Mr. Mahon will further support him this month by offering "better" or "worse" sounding alternatives to phrases Miguel uses in classroom work. This will serve to affirm both Miguel's well-worded original sentences *and* his ability to select those that sound "better" to his competent ear. Mr. Mahon is confident that this is all Miguel would need to be then ready to self-rate and edit his own recorded stories. ■

Figure 5.9 Continua for the Assessment of English Language Development

Student Name: _____

	Preproduction	Early Production	Speech Emergence	Intermediate Fluency	Advanced Fluency
Date					
Listening	• Cannot yet understand simple expressions or statements in English.	• Understands previously learned expressions. • Understands new vocabulary in context.	• Understands sentence-length speech. • Participates in conversation about simple information. • Understands a simple message. • Understands basic directions and instructions.	• Understands academic content. • Understands more complex directions and instructions. • Comprehends main idea. • Effectively participates in classroom discussions.	• Understands most of what is heard. • Understands and retells main idea and most details from oral presentations and conversations.
Date					
Speaking	• Is not yet able to make any statements in English.	• Uses isolated words and learned phrases. • Uses vocabulary for classroom situations. • Expresses basic courtesies. • Asks very simple questions. • Makes statements using learned materials. • Asks and answers questions about basic needs.	• Asks and answers simple questions about academic content. • Talks about familiar topics. • Responds to simple statements. • Expresses self in simple situations (e.g., ordering a meal, introducing oneself, asking directions).	• Initiates, sustains, and closes a conversation. • Effectively participates in classroom discussions. • Gives reasons for agreeing or disagreeing. • Retells a story or event. • Compares and contrasts a variety of topics.	• Communicates facts and talks casually about topics of general interest using specific vocabulary. • Participates in age-appropriate academic, technical, and social conversations using English correctly.

Date					
Reading	• Is not yet able to read any words in English. • Is not yet able to identify the letters of the Roman alphabet. • Is not yet able to decode sounds of written English.	• Reads common messages, phrases, and/or expressions. • Identifies the letters of the Roman alphabet. • Decodes most sounds of written English. • Identifies learned words and phrases.	• Reads and comprehends main ideas and/or facts from simple materials.	• Understands main ideas and details from a variety of sources.	• Reads authentic text materials for comprehension. • Understands most of what is read in authentic texts.
Date					
Writing	• Is not yet able to write any words in English. • Is not yet able to write the letters of the Roman alphabet.	• Copies or transcribes familiar words or phrases. • Writes the letters from memory and/or dictation. • Writes simple expressions from memory. • Writes simple autobiographical information as well as some short phrases and simple lists. • Composes short sentences with guidance.	• Creates basic statements and questions. • Writes simple letters and messages. • Writes simple narratives.	• Writes more complex narratives. • Composes age-appropriate original materials using present, past, and future tenses. • Writes about a variety of topics for a variety of purposes.	• Write summaries. • Takes notes. • Compares and contrasts familiar topics. • Uses vivid, specific language in writing.

Source: Wichita Public Schools, Wichita, Kansas. Reprinted by permission.

acquisition in the areas of listening, speaking, reading, and writing are arranged in the order of the stages commonly associated with second language acquisition (i.e., preproduction, early production, speech emergence, intermediate fluency, and advanced fluency). Teachers who understand the skills involved in, and potentially elicited by, particular curricular activities find it much easier to assess after instruction whether students have demonstrated these skills, given appropriate opportunities and facilitation. Even in the absence of deliberate preplanning, it is often not difficult to note whether and when the hallmark skills of language development have been attained.

> **assessment FREEZE FRAME 5.4** 𝕏𝕏𝕏
>
> Teachers who gather observational data frequently find it is a powerful tool for measuring learning over time.

Narrative Assessment   The conditions in which a student produces a sample of oral language can significantly affect how well this sample represents his or her actual language competence. Many linguists contrast a person's *language competence*—what she or he knows or can do—with *language performance*, how this knowledge is used in a particular circumstance (Byram, Holmes, & Savvides, 2013; Freeman & Freeman, 2014). The best measures of language proficiency elicit student performance that genuinely reflects language competence. In nearly all cases, this involves going beyond standardized assessments to demonstrate how students use language in authentic, real-life situations. Such opportunities easily found in the home with family and in unstructured social situations, can also exist at school when teachers create the right conditions. *Narrative assessments* often provide teachers with similar opportunities.

The ability to develop cohesive narratives (storytelling structures) is a critical component of second language acquisition for several reasons. Of primary interest to educators, this skill is essential for literacy development that goes beyond associating sounds with symbols/letters and decoding words out of context. An underlying knowledge of narrative forms and structures helps students better understand both written passages and orally presented material. This knowledge enables the reader to skim text for essential content, as well as comprehend narrative formats used to inform or persuade.

There are many ways to look at and sample narrative language. Assessing a CLD student's ability to produce narratives in the primary language can provide valuable insights into foundational knowledge and skills. As mentioned earlier, this information can greatly aid instructional planning, especially when paired with measures of narrative development in the second language.

Activities and techniques for eliciting student narratives can yield especially rich samples of language. However, the type and quality of sample a student produces depends on a variety of variables. Sometimes a teacher who is not fluent in the language or comfortable with the interaction patterns of the CLD student attempts to elicit conversation or narrative using prompts in the L1 that exhibit simplified grammar and vocabulary. Students perceive the teacher's limitations and naturally respond by simplifying their own vocabulary and sentence structures to better communicate with the teacher. Unfortunately, these efforts to facilitate communication may then be perceived as limitations of the student rather than the teacher. Such misperceptions can negatively affect a student's education because the teacher who believes a student's L1 skills are limited may fail to draw on the student's prior linguistic knowledge as a learning asset.

Contradictory perceptions that students are simultaneously low in overall language yet possess "enough English" to achieve can result in decisions and practices that lead teachers away from the interventions most likely to resolve perceived learning concerns (i.e., L1 instruction, L2 accommodations). For this reason, it is important to note variables inherent to the situations in which we observe student language. Because we so often use language to assess language, it is always important to consider how the teacher's own language skills, speaking style, choice of wording, and subject of conversation may influence a student's response. The material a teacher uses to stimulate a response should also be familiar and meaningful to the student (Kayser, 2008).

Some narrative ratings also assess cohesion or *flow*. Student samples containing frequent word and grammar revisions (changes, false starts, self-corrections) are often perceived as evidence of poor vocabulary or language weakness. Because many English learners function bilingually, narrative reviewers should bear in mind insights from research on bilingual versus monolingual revision rates. Results of a study by Gámez and González (2017) compared the story structure complexity of bilingual students with those who were monolingual in English or Spanish. While using English or Spanish, the bilingual students used more revisions than others *as they increased narrative complexity*. Contrary to the perception of linguistic weakness or breakdown, these revisions were more positively correlated with word diversity and therefore considered evidence of deeper linguistic application.

Narrative tasks can yield terrific samples of language, or merely highlight the disconnect between prompts and purpose. Regardless of materials, educators will want to define the skill, behavior, or knowledge they hope to see evidence of in a sample. Which would you rate higher, the elaborate, well-developed story that is rife with grammar errors, or the incomplete retelling comprised of short, error-free statements? It depends on what you are assessing.

Awareness of the *what*, allows us to better recognize those capacities in real life. Teachers can be attuned to and inquire about evidence of narrative skills (e.g., telling jokes or stories, sharing anecdotes, describing movie plots) and proficiencies in other contexts. These insights prove especially valuable when assessing a relatively unschooled student.

Teaching Tips:

- Remember that asking students to "tell me a story" is often too vague, unless you provide the CLD student enough examples of the expected type of response.
- Provide samples or do a walk through (joint production) of an example story before expecting the student to generate his or her own original narrative from a prompt.
- Sources of inspiration for narratives can include wordless picture books, muted videos or computer stories, photos of class activities, and family photos.
- Topics might include popular movies, video game adventures, television shows (Spanish language novelas, for example, have clearer story lines than English language soap operas), current events (especially dramatic ones), or field trips.
- Wherever possible, document spontaneous narrative activities because they are often the best evidence of student skills. Significant events, such as playground fights, can elicit excellent (though unpleasant) examples of settings and characters with unique attention to sequence, antecedent, consequence, problem, solution, and alternate ending.

ACCOMMODATIVE ASSESSMENT PRACTICES 5.3

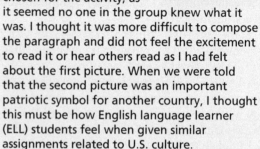

The importance of student familiarity with material used to prompt their narrative responses was underscored during a professional development exercise. Teachers from the dominant culture were asked to write narratives about photographs of familiar (e.g., Statue of Liberty) and unfamiliar (e.g., India's Red Fort) cultural icons. The following was excerpted from a participating teacher's reflection journal about the exercise.

When we began this assignment, I thought it was an interesting way to involve students in a group writing activity and something I might like to use in class. It seemed easy to think of words to describe the Statue of Liberty because I was so familiar with it and visited it last summer. Our group had fun brainstorming words and then writing the paragraph. I thought everyone was very proud of the symbolism the Statue of Liberty provides to the United States—a place of freedom, equality, beauty, diversity, opportunity and patriotism. I thought the paragraphs that each group wrote were extremely creative and enjoyable to hear.

As we looked at the second picture of the large stone building (India's Red Fort), I had a hard time thinking of descriptive words because I was unfamiliar with the building. Looking at it brought up no past experiences or memories, no feelings or ideas. I wondered why this picture had been chosen for the activity, as it seemed no one in the group knew what it was. I thought it was more difficult to compose the paragraph and did not feel the excitement to read it or hear others read as I had felt about the first picture. When we were told that the second picture was an important patriotic symbol for another country, I thought this must be how English language learner (ELL) students feel when given similar assignments related to U.S. culture.

During another group's discussion of this activity, one teacher mentioned that, although she and other African Americans understood and appreciated the symbolism, not all would associate the Statue of Liberty with the idea of unequivocal freedom that was expressed by others. This comment enabled other teachers to see that perceptions and cultural experiences influence a student's ability to respond authentically (or as predicted by a teacher) to a given prompt. This scenario reminds us as teachers to reflect on the student's familiarity with images, settings, plot lines, and other elements that can affect his or her performance and lead to invalid interpretations of assessment results. ■

Story Retelling Assessment   *Story retelling assessment* is another method of eliciting oral or written narratives from CLD students. Such tasks are a common component of language proficiency assessments. For some students, story retelling facilitates language production. The opportunity to hear a story first provides a model that students can use for retelling the story. These productions can reveal much about individual proficiency levels. Nonetheless, issues such as auditory memory, cultural norms, and task familiarity can confound the ability of other students to perform this essentially expressive task. Because factors other than targeted skills can have such a strong influence, some researchers argue against story retelling as a means of assessing linguistic ability (Gutierrez-Clellan & Quinn, 1993). This view is supported by the research of MacSwan, Rolstad, and Glass (2002), who found that 20% of the 38,887 Spanish-speaking students sampled for their study (students who took the Spanish version of the IDEA Proficiency Test—Preschool [IPT-P]) did not respond at all when prompted to retell a story. The inordinately high percentage of students who did not respond on this subtest suggests that teachers or examiners should consider alternative methods of eliciting narratives for students who don't perform under structured conditions.

In practice, there may be a number of reasons why students do not respond at all or with the desired detail when asked to retell a story they have just heard. For instance, it can seem artificial and pragmatically inappropriate for the student to restate details of a story that the evaluator has just told. Clearly, the evaluator already knows it! This obstacle can often be overcome by asking the student to retell the story to another person or a puppet, or to record it for someone else.

A student may also have an unclear understanding of the expected response. Students often wonder, "Is it the topic (what it's about), the gist of what happened, or the whole thing that you want?" Being explicit about expectations and modeling an appropriate response help students better understand the task.

There may also be times when the conditions, story situation, or narrative format are culturally unfamiliar or uncomfortable for the student. Attending carefully to nonverbal signals from students and providing alternative conditions, stories with different plots, or stories with different narrative formats oftentimes can yield more desirable results. Teachers of CLD students who are reflective and creative are more likely to discover their students' true proficiencies and needs.

Native Language Writing Samples   When teachers assess academic language proficiency, they should keep in mind that, at times, it may be beneficial to allow students to use their native language to demonstrate content-area knowledge and skills. For example, Figure 5.10 illustrates one first-grade student's writing that was produced when the teacher allowed her to write in Spanish. Students in the class worked in small groups to produce books about whales (*ballenas*), and this student participated fully by writing her page in Spanish. The writing sample enabled the teacher to determine that the learner, a newcomer to the school in the earliest stages of English language acquisition, could construct a nonfiction text. Although the student was still developing the English skills needed to complete the task in her second language, she possessed the cognitive, academic, and linguistic skills to respond adeptly to the task in her native language.

Oral and Written Cloze Assessments

First-grade teacher Mrs. Wesley asked Ms. Buremen, the ESL teacher, for help teaching students to rhyme. She had tried everything to encourage them, but most just "didn't get it." Ms. Buremen was happy to plan her next whole-class lesson around this challenge and started by reading the rhyme-laden book *If You Give a Mouse a Cookie* (Numeroff, 1985). She read the first line of each rhyme and showed the corresponding picture. Then, paying very close attention to cadence, she read the second line and paused ever so slightly before saying the final rhyming word.

By the fourth rhyme, some of the students were calling out the rhyming words. Mrs. Moran nodded and continued without breaking the gentle flow of the poem's meter. To close the lesson, students used props to retell the story together as Ms. Buremen probed other language skills, such as sequence and vocabulary.

Mrs. Wesley took notes as Ms. Buremen started a new activity by laying four of the props from the story in a row. The broom, comb, bed, and chair provided a limited range of familiar responses from which the students could choose their rhymes.

Ms. Buremen: I like the way rhymes sound. Let's see if we can make some of our own. *Wake up, wake up you sleepy head, it's time now to get out of _____.*
Class: Bed!

Figure 5.10 Assessment Artifact: Primary Language CALP

English Translation:
Whales
All whales eat meat, fish, mussels, crabs, and seals. The humpback whales eat plankton, it is so thick that it covers the water like a green carpet. There are fish that have plankton and humpback whales eat them and submerge underwater.

In this writing sample, the student's rich vocabulary and understanding of the content concepts is apparent. She is able to use figurative language, as is evident from her inclusion of the simile comparing plankton with a green carpet. With this evidence of knowledge and learning, the teacher is able to confirm that the child's performance demonstrates attainment of the grade-level standard.

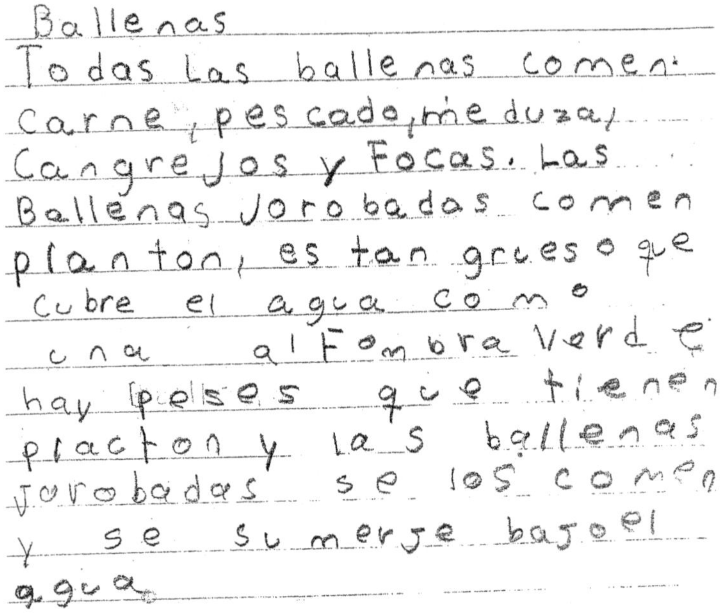

> Ballenas
> Todas Las ballenas comen:
> Carne, pescado, meduza,
> Cangrejos y Focas. Las
> Ballenas Jorobadas comen
> planton, es tan grueso que
> cubre el agua como
> una alfombra verde
> hay peses que tienen
> placton y las ballenas
> Jorobadas se los comen
> y se sumerje bajoel
> agua

Source: Angela Sesti. Reprinted by permission.

> **Ms. Buremen:** *If you're hungry, grab a pear, and then come sit down on a*
> _____.
> **Class:** Chair!
> **Ms. Buremen:** *But looking at this dirty room makes me want to use a* _____.
> **Class:** Broom!

The students responded well to this oral cloze format. It provided semantic cues as well as auditory patterns and limited choices. By the end of the session, students were also having fun completing oral cloze rhymes *without* visible choices (e.g., *My little brother likes to eat. His favorite food to eat is* _____). Mrs. Wesley was pleased to learn that 90 percent of the spontaneous and sometimes silly responses produced actually rhymed. After listening to one another's choices, the students developed a word bank of possible answers (*meat, wheat, feet, seat, beet,* and so forth), some of which they were now generating without the scaffold of an oral cloze prompt. By using this approach, Mrs. Wesley determined which students did not demonstrate language proficiency levels sufficient to support this skill and which students were ready to recognize auditory patterns, given appropriate methods and supports.

Oral and written *cloze assessments*, in which words are deleted intentionally from the larger passage or text, can be used in a variety of ways to gather information about the student's progress in language acquisition and content-area learning. According to A. A. Ortiz (2004), the elements of most languages are remarkably redundant. As a result, we can comprehend messages that are distorted or missing a number of elements (e.g., articles, prepositions) by accessing our prior knowledge and applying our understanding of the system for that language. Knowledge of language patterns appears to correlate highly with one's overall proficiency in that language. Eventually, the language learner senses the absence of mandated elements.

There are multiple ways to construct oral and written cloze assessments. When a fixed ratio format is used, every *nth* (e.g., seventh) word is deleted throughout the passage. This is generally used to sample a student's more holistic knowledge of the language. However, teachers can choose to omit certain types of words, such as pronouns or past-tense verbs, to measure particular aspects of morphologic and syntactic development. Figure 5.11 is an example of a teacher-created, fixed-ratio cloze assessment in which every eighth word is deleted. Oral cloze assessments are especially powerful and highly adaptable ways to gather information about a student's emerging language acquisition and mastery of skills. They can help a student bridge simple recognition of language patterns with the emergence of new expressive skills. They also work well with story retelling to assess comprehension of auditory or text input.

Teachers can follow up reading a story by asking students to "help me with the story." The teacher retells the story using an oral cloze format with regularly spaced pauses. At each pause, he or she gestures to students, asking them to fill in the missing word. Pacing is important for maintaining a natural flow and supporting student comprehension. Many CLD students initially unresponsive to story retelling tasks do well with this approach. When students provide appropriate answers, they demonstrate both comprehension and retention of the original material.

Figure 5.11   Assessment Artifact: Written Cloze

Word Bank				
was	Zoo	Zebras	And	to
and	And	Little	Feet	elephants
they	with	Monkeys	To	

On a hot and sunny day, Letica _____ her mother decided to go to the _____. They brought sunglasses, bottles of drinking water, _____ a camera. The first exhibit they saw _____ the home of two gray elephants. The _____ were enormous! They had huge ears, big _____, and very long trunks. Next they went _____ the building where the monkeys lived. Some _____ were busy eating and others were playing _____ old tires. Letica's favorite monkey was the _____ baby monkey. Letica and her mother continued _____ visit the many animals in the zoo. _____ took pictures of the lions, tigers, and _____. At the end of the trip, Letica _____ her mother were both very tired.

Listening Skills Assessments

Josue and Abram are working as a team to help their sophomore ESL class win a pizza party—but the students will win pizza only when everyone in the class successfully completes the task. The students are highly motivated as each person in each pair takes turns being the *giver* or *receiver* of directions. The partners are separated by a piece of cardboard so that neither can see what the other is doing.

Josue and Abram's first attempt to arrange five geometric shapes identically ended in surprise disaster. As they worked together, they felt sure they would win. However, they didn't realize until the final moment that failure to clarify had led to fundamental misunderstandings neither had recognized.

Their teacher, Mr. Sing, loved it when students discovered these moments for themselves. He had often wondered how frequently miscommunications occur in teaching and learning. Over the years, Mr. Sing had noted with concern how many CLD students did not actively listen or seek clarification regarding unfamiliar, ambiguous, or confusing material. He had begun to speculate on whether the students had become accustomed to simply "getting the gist," even though their language skills had developed sufficiently for deeper comprehension.

As a rule, Mr. Sing praised those students who asked for definitions of unfamiliar words as he taught, and he at times intentionally used nonsensical terms just to see who was listening. He encouraged all his students to ask clarifying questions because he believed it was the students' job to listen with their *mind* as well as *ears*—to listen to understand, recognize when they did not comprehend, and do something about it.

Josue and Abram had been watching other teams win and lose just as they had, but they were ready to try again. Josue considered the twenty shapes of varied form, size, and color. He needed to use only five. It seemed so easy.

Josue: Take the big yellow rectangle and put it in the middle.
Abram: The one that looks like a box or a French fry?
Josue: The rectangle. It's long from top to bottom and skinny side to side. Yeah, it looks kinda like a French fry.
Abram: Okay, I got it. Put it in the middle?
Josue: Yeah. (*Remembering another team's problem*) Make it vertical.
Abram: Vertical?
Josue: Vertical is up and down like a basketball pole.
Abram: Okay, I put the big, yellow rectangle up and down, vertical . . . in the middle.
Josue: Take the medium-size purple circle and put it on top.
Abram: On top of what? The paper?
Josue: Put the purple circle on top of the yellow rectangle.
Abram: On top . . . in the middle?
Josue: No, not laying on it . . . on top . . . *above* it, like a lollipop.

By the time all five pieces were in place, Abram and Josue had practiced academic listening and natural clarification skills, with repetition that was natural to the context of the activity. Mr. Sing assessed Abram as having grown so much in clarification ability that he planned to pair Abram next with Saul, who still did not recognize communication breakdowns. The students were becoming more aware of their own learning because they were motivated to earn the pizza party. Mr. Sing planned to later add a sphere, rhombus, cylinder, cube, and cone to their list of choices for this exercise.

Like Mr. Sing, many teachers find it easier to plan language assessment when they are able to identify the linguistic demands of their curriculum. Listening skills can be assessed in a variety of contexts, but observers should be acutely aware of environmental cues that can facilitate comprehension. When CLD students are unable to adequately comprehend the language of instruction, direction, or assessment, they more keenly attend to available physical, interpersonal, and nonverbal cues. Although this serves as a testament to their resourcefulness, it can also prompt the teacher to overestimate a student's L2 competencies and subsequently misinterpret his or her academic struggles. Conversely, when provided accommodative teaching, some students may, in fact, understand the material far better than their oral or written responses suggest.

Wherever possible, teachers should require CLD students to demonstrate listening skills in ways that do not involve spoken language (e.g., perform a task or make a physical signal of understanding). If, for example, a student's understanding of a story is evaluated solely on his or her ability to retell it or to answer questions (especially in L2), the teacher will likely find it nearly impossible to distinguish between the student's oral language skills and his or her comprehension. This is especially important when students are verbally limited in L2, but it also applies to the performance of seemingly fluent CLD students and native English speakers. Although students may be talkative, it can be difficult to determine whether these students really understood the targeted material. Therefore, careful evaluation of CLD students' listening skills includes tasks that do not combine performance and skills in other domains, as well as those that do.

The specifics of these tasks will, of course, vary greatly by grade level but may include:

1. Following oral instructions:
   * Give students simple one-step directions such as, "Get out a crayon."
   * Add modifiers such as, "Get out a *blue* crayon."
   * Increase the number of steps such as, "Open your health book and turn to page 14."
   * Gradually incorporate linguistic concepts (*of, unless, however, whether,* and so on) such as, "*Unless* you brought your lunch today, please line up at the door."
   * Direct students to perform an experiment or create a product while checking to see how students respond to step-by-step instructions. This process better assesses listening skills than does providing detailed instructions all at once (the latter is often a memory issue rather than a language issue).
   * Ask students to relay instructions to a peer in the L2. Alternatively, separate L2 *listening* skills from L2 *verbal* skills by having the student relay his or her understanding of L2 instructions to a peer in the L1.
2. Responding to questions:
   * Students answer yes or no questions orally, with a head shake or nod, or thumbs up/thumbs down.
   * Provide the CLD student with a closed set of responses from which to orally or physically select an answer (e.g., pictures, words, or sentences from which to choose; questions phrased with modeled choices such as, "Who invented the light bulb, Edison or Einstein?").
3. Demonstrating curricular learning:
   * Have students identify main characters, story sequence, problem/resolution, or content-area answers by pointing to or otherwise nonverbally selecting depictions of the appropriate response.

- Direct students to create a picture or product representing a core concept.
- Have students use graphic organizers to display their understanding of concepts or relationships using pictures or writing.

Among the more authentic ways to assess the listening skills of a CLD student are situations in which the student's ability to perform a task requires him or her to integrate listening skills and clarification strategies effectively. The scenario with Josue and Abram illustrated this type of activity. *Barrier games* are among the more broadly referred to *information gap activities* that compel students to draw on and value active listening skills that are not commonly addressed in traditional classrooms. Barrier games require one student to give another student directions to perform a task or to replicate a design, despite a physical barrier (e.g., open file folder, piece of cardboard) that prevents each student from seeing the other's referent. One of the most powerful features of barrier activities is that, after initial training and modeling, students can engage in skill building with very little input or interference from the teacher.

Oral Skills Assessments   Oral language acquisition is part of the human development process that occurs naturally through authentic communication. What we often tend to overlook is the fact that oral language is not so much a biological inheritance, but a cultural product. Children acquire increasing levels of language skills as they develop throughout their lives. With each linguistic interaction, they gather information and feedback regarding pronunciation, word order, word meanings, idiomatic expressions, and effective as well as ineffective ways of expressing needs, desires, and so forth *within a particular culture*. Learners process this information in largely subconscious ways. We later apply in our own speech language patterns and frames we've heard used by others. Oral language development is an ongoing process that requires repeated, meaningful practice.

Language is a vehicle or tool for communicating ideas, and this is true for both oral and written language production. Students' cultural backgrounds play an integral role as they become increasingly active members of classroom activities and conversations. Culture influences how we interpret the language we hear and read, and it shapes how we express our own ideas (as well as the ideas themselves). English learners benefit from plentiful opportunities to interact with peers and share their unique perspectives about the curriculum and about themselves.

Formal oral skills assessment can provide a starting point for teachers as they gauge where their students' language skills are. However, from there such assessments should be considered as benchmarks to determine how students are progressing in response to daily instruction. Informal assessments of orals skills, on the other hand, can do much to inform teachers about how they might structure individual learning opportunities in the classroom.

Oral language samples often are most reflective of students' actual skills when they are gleaned in connection to daily lessons. Because oral production of language can be context reduced, where students have to form their oral language by relying heavily on their cognitive abilities, it is critical that we provide students with a context or structure to support their expansion of language. Personal connections to a recently discussed topic or an engaging book read with the class can provide a conceptual foundation for students as they harness their cognitive energy to produce oral language.

Free recall or a picture prompt can be used to elicit an oral language sample. The teacher simply asks the student to recall events from a story or events from their day (i.e., provide a context). Because the goal is for the student's response to reflect oral language abilities, it is critical that the recall or the retelling task occur as soon as possible after the event takes places or after the story is read, so the assessment does not end up becoming a test of memory.

The following illustrates a sample procedure:

1. After you have finished reading a picture book to students, choose a picture and select the device you will use to record the student's language.
2. Have the student share with you what is happening in the picture. You may prompt the student by saying, "Tell me a story about this picture" or "Using complete sentences, tell me three things you can share with me about this picture."
3. You may further prompt the child by saying, "Tell me more," or "What else can you say?" Remember to keep the prompts open ended, so the prompts do not lead students to the answers or anticipated language.
4. Transcribe the student's entire response.
5. You may create a checklist or use an oral language rubric (see Figure 5.12) to gauge students' oral language skills.

Figure 5.12   Sample Oral Language Rubric

Oral Language Rubric

Name: _____

Grade: _____

Syntax:

4—Uses appropriate syntax of the English language with complex sentences. Grammar is used correctly. Appropriate use of tenses in the sentences.
3—Uses appropriate syntax of the English language with simple sentences. Grammar is used correctly. Switches the tenses as inserting them in sentences.
2—Uses correct English syntax for very simple sentences. Inappropriate use of grammar and tenses in sentences.
1—Uses very little correct syntax of the English language. No complete sentences used.

Vocabulary:

4—Uses many descriptive words and adjectives. Uses a variety of words to explain thought process.
3—Uses basic language consisting mostly of nouns and verbs with some use of descriptive words and adjectives.
2—Uses very simple, basic language and short phrases consisting mostly of nouns and verbs with little use of adjectives.
1—Uses only isolated words to describe the picture and/or unable to do any retelling.

Fluency:

4—Uses lots of connected, descriptive details when talking about the visual and/or the story. Oral sharing is well organized and well thought out.
3—Uses some descriptive details while talking about the visual and/or the story. Oral retelling is somewhat organized.
2—Uses only a simple sentence or two when talking about the visual and/or the story. Oral retelling is very limited.
1—Uses simple labels with one or two words (e.g., rock, boy) for elements in the visual and/or the story.

Consistent and meaningful practice with oral language builds students' listening skills and increases their desire to use language for other purposes as well, such as reading and writing. Through the different opportunities that teachers provide, students can learn to use English to articulate their words and express their thoughts clearly. The following activities can be used to support learners as they enhance their oral language skills, along with their listening, reading, and writing skills.

Phrase It and Stick It

Grade Level: 2–6

Materials:

- Pictures representing the topics being covered in the class
- Set of sentence starters or stems to guide students' phrase development (optional)
  - Sentence starters/stems can be created and provided to students if they struggle to come up with an original phrase. These starters/stems might require that students only have to add an original word to complete the phrase.
- Sticky notes

Directions:

1. Explain to the students that we will work on an activity that helps us practice our oral language skills. Our task is to create an original phrase in response to the pictures we see. The phrase might explain what the picture is about or what is in the picture.
   - For instance, in response to a picture of a house, the original phrase might be "*A mighty house.*"
2. Place students in small groups, and give each group a set of two or three pictures that reflect the topic being covered or the book being read.
3. Have each small group select one of the visuals.
4. Ask each student to think of an original phrase in response to their group's picture.
5. Have students take turns sharing their original phrases with group members.
6. After each student has shared their own original phrase, give each group sticky notes (enough for each student to have one).
7. At this point, the task for each student is to choose any *one* of the original phrases shared by anyone in the small group and write it on the sticky note.
8. Then have students add their sticky notes to the picture.
9. Have groups repeat this process for all the pictures.
10. Next have each group select one picture that they will use to share out to the class their sticky note phrases.
11. Recap for students by explaining that in this activity, they started with sharing and building oral language and then transitioned toward advancing their own writing.

Observing Students:

As students are working, document their oral language production as they create original phrases. Consider the way students use grammar, tenses, adjectives, and so forth in their language production. You can also do an authentic error analysis of students' language production in real time. As they are creating phrases, gauge the kinds of errors they are making and record your findings.

Differentiating Instruction:

- Jot down notes about the patterns of errors students are making in their language production. These notes will support your instructional conversations and language modeling in subsequent lessons.
- Focus on students' written language development as they transfer original phrases to the sticky notes. Your knowledge of students' strengths and challenges can inform decisions about supportive group configurations.
- For students who are able to complete the activity with relative ease, encourage them to try to link together all the sticky note ideas to create a connected description of the picture. Phrases should be arranged so that they make sense syntactically as well as semantically. This extension can be taken a step farther by your asking students to write this connected description.

Additional Notes:

This activity can be repeated as often as desired throughout the academic school year.

I Learn, I Extend, I Remember

Grade Level: 5–8

Materials:

- Curricular materials
- Blank pieces of paper (one per student)
- Writing utensils

Directions:

- Have students begin by using a blank piece of paper to create a three-column chart for taking notes. They can simply fold a piece of paper to create three columns or you can give them a template with three columns drawn on it.
- Next have students write at the top of the first column, "What did I/we learn?"; at the top of second column, "How did we learn it?"; and at the top of third column, "How can I connect it to the outside world?"
- As you read the book or cover the lesson material, have students stop at strategic points and add their ideas to the three-column notes.
  - At each stopping point, have students first share what they learned in their small groups.
  - After students have orally synthesized what they have learned and how they learned it, ask them to transfer their thoughts onto the three-column chart. Providing the opportunity to complete this process orally first will result in students generating and recording a much more elaborated response.
  - Another way to support students to orally express and expand upon their thoughts is to have students first record a visual depiction of their learnings

in the first column and then describe their visuals orally to their small group. Subsequently, students can expand their documentation by adding writing to accompany the visuals on their three-column notes.

- Next have students discuss real-world applications of their learning. Have students add their ideas to the chart as they discuss. Be sure to emphasize these connections during your instructional conversations with students (small groups, whole class, and individuals).

Observing Students:

As students work on their activity, observe them and listen to their discussions so you can see how their oral language is evolving. You can integrate a simple oral language development checklist to gauge how your students are developing over time.

Make sure to ask probing questions. As you ask questions, again allow students to first discuss the answers as partners or small groups. Through these conversations, you can hear the kind of language students are using to form their arguments.

The activity itself can become a form of formative assessment for language development as students attend to the task. Collect the chart from students at the end of the lesson to see how their writing is progressing. Give them feedback on their writing skills to support continued development.

Differentiating Instruction:

- Through concurrent discussions while the activity is unfolding, you will be able to provide instructional support based on the formative data you are gathering.
- As the activity progresses, consider the degree to which your students are making appropriate gains toward the associated outcomes. Make adjustments during the course of the activity to redirect learning, as needed.
- Your observation of challenges and successes during group and partner work will inform how you redirect the interaction component of future activities.

Additional Notes:

This activity can be utilized within any content area to support students' comprehension and retention of the curricular material. It is ideal for prompting students to extend their ideas to real-world applications. This activity also supports the teacher's informal assessment of students' language skills in real time.

Marketed Instructional Materials   Although spontaneous human language is dynamic and best assessed in authentic, interactive contexts, students must also learn to mediate the more structured language of academic instruction and curricular texts. Talented teachers find multiple ways to use marketed materials. The key is always to begin with a firm grasp of the desired outcome or benefit. The prevalence of fun, colorful, ready-made activities can steer us toward products that don't meet our needs or can't be modified or adapted for individual gain. On face value they are convenient—"everything you need" in one book, box, or link. Minutes gained in lesson planning are lost tenfold by lack of instructional benefit.

Avoid activities for the sake of activities. Instead, consider whether the task complexity and/or scaffolding can be easily targeted, tracked, and incrementally ratcheted to measure and advance language growth. The student's performance on similar tasks over time may also be cited as indicators of progress monitoring for the purposes of response to intervention (to be discussed in Chapter 7).

Teaching Tips:

When purposefully selecting marketed materials, consider:

- What skills are important for my students to gain, strengthen, or practice?
- Do these materials foster deeper connections to particular concepts, or application of skills?
- Can the materials be used to create or support a strategy my students use to aid their own learning?
- Are the stimuli used (pictures, reading level, experience assumptions) appropriate for my students?
- Will use of this material be inclusive (adaptable), or stratifying?
- What will I learn by observing my students use of this material?
- How will insights gained inform my instruction?

USING LANGUAGE INFORMATION TO INFORM INSTRUCTION

Throughout this chapter, we have presented an in-depth review of both formal and informal assessment tests, tools, and strategies that can be used in practice. These assessments can provide educators with information on the language acquisition and proficiency of the learner. Our individual context and role as an educator often determine how and when we use particular assessments, and for what purposes.

In this chapter, we have tried to provide a blueprint for making decisions on diagnostic assessments, placement, instruction, and ongoing monitoring. Standardized assessment must always be approached with caution, given the multitude of variables that can influence scores as well as the high-stakes nature of many educational decisions. Informal, ongoing assessments can provide us with a closer look at the potential of the learner within different situational contexts.

Language acquisition is a dynamic process influenced by a student's unique biography as well as the teaching and learning context. We always must remember that assessment and instruction are interrelated. Assessment provides a baseline, or the point of departure, for making decisions about what is best for the learner. With regular use, assessments can allow us to chart growth as students continue to progress on their language acquisition journeys. What happens between each data point—daily instruction—is at the heart of the language acquisition process. Classroom instruction can either help accelerate language development or inhibit progress.

Teachers can increase the effectiveness of their daily instruction by using language assessment results in the following ways:

- Plan specific activities and strategies for students, to build on identified strengths and target areas for growth.
- Plan appropriate interventions for students.
- Place students in pairs and small groups that ensure a balance of challenge and support.
- Implement scaffolds during instruction to bolster language comprehension and production.
- Gauge what is working during instruction and what needs to be adapted or modified.
- Make adjustments to grouping configurations.
- Monitor effectiveness of interventions.

Regardless of professional role or context, understanding language assessment is essential when serving CLD students. As educators, our knowledge, action, and advocacy often determine the quality of our students' educational journeys.

PROGRAMMING-RELATED ISSUES: ASSESSMENT OF LANGUAGE PROFICIENCY

Issues of placement and programming for CLD students who are acquiring English as a second language are topics beyond the scope of this text. Nonetheless, the results of assessing language proficiency can aid decision making associated with these issues. Therefore, the following discussion highlights how language proficiency assessment is relevant to the identification, placement, monitoring, and exit of CLD students. This discussion is by no means exhaustive, but it provides a synopsis of issues that should be considered.

Identification

Assessing English language proficiency is critical in determining whether a CLD student can participate in the curriculum without additional supports. This determination should be, but is not always, based on a combination of factors. Standardized assessment results, informal assessment outcomes, observation, and parent and teacher input all serve to inform our understanding of a student's language abilities. Students whose English language proficiency does not meet stated criteria are often identified as limited English proficient and, as a result, are entitled to instructional modifications and access to language programs designed to alleviate language issues in content-area learning.

Placement

Careful consideration of language proficiency data and academic skills, combined with knowledge of available programs (e.g., transitional bilingual, dual language, content-based ESL), is necessary for identifying the setting that will provide the CLD student maximum access to the curriculum. The appropriateness of student placement is determined through ongoing assessment of language acquisition, social adjustment, and curricular learning.

Monitoring

Alternate versions of formal assessments that can be readministered at midyear provide a useful update on student progress and can be used to help determine whether to reassign a student to grade-level classes. Informal assessment approaches and other forms of data gathering discussed earlier are also vital in helping teachers monitor student status and progress relative to changing curricular demands.

Exit

The redesignation of CLD students has the potential to affect perceived student or program success. Students must typically meet language proficiency and academic criteria to be exited from the English learner (EL) designation. Because higher-performing students who exit a language program are continually replaced by lower-proficiency students entering the program, it is nearly impossible for this group as a whole to demonstrate the type of progress required by state or federal mandates.

ASSESSMENT IN ACTION 5.2

Teachers can use a portfolio to document a CLD student's development in all four language domains (i.e., listening, speaking, reading, and writing). A portfolio is the most comprehensive method of understanding the students' linguistic assets and needs. The following checklist provides possible items to be included in the ongoing assessment and monitoring of language skills.

Portfolio/Cumulative Folder Checklist

Items to Be Included			Date
Home Visit Interview or Parent Survey on Language Use			
Home Language Survey			
Initial Language Test (e.g., LAS)			
Subsequent Language Tests	Grade	Score	
	Kindergarten	/	
	First	/	
	Second	/	
	Third	/	
	Fourth	/	
	Fifth	/	
CLD Student Biography Card or Background Survey			
Informal BICS Evaluation (L1 and L2)			
Informal CALP Evaluation (L1 and L2)			
Native Language:			
• Literacy Screening (Grades K–5)			
• Reading Benchmark (Grades 3–5)			
• Writing Sample (Grades 3–5)			
English Language:			
• Literacy Screening (Grades K–5)			
• Reading Levels (Grades 3–5)			
• Early Writing Assessment			
Cognitive Learning Strategy Use (classroom observation notes)			

Historically, such a scenario has tempted states to enact policies to keep redesignated students in this EL category for up to 2 years (Abedi, 2004), or simply delay the redesignation of qualified students. This practice effectively denies otherwise capable students access to a more appropriate and challenging curriculum (Abedi & Dietel, 2004).

Today, federal law requires local education agencies (LEAs) to submit to their states data on the number and percentage of EL students who:

- Are making progress toward English language proficiency
- Attain proficiency needed to exit EL services, and
- Have been classified as EL for more than 5 years

Additionally, LEAs must also provide information regarding the number and percentage of former English learners who meet academic content standards for 4 years after exiting English development programs. The rationale for this is to ensure that the overriding emphasis of programming for English learners relates to academic access.

Educators are well advised to consider multilevel educational and linguistic criteria, rather than political agendas, to determine when students are ready to participate in the full curriculum of an English-only classroom environment. Central to these considerations is the acknowledgement that data regarding reclassification and achievement reflect not only on the English learners described, but also on the degree to which instructional methods used are effective in the promotion of language proficiency and academic success.

SUMMARY

This chapter explored the language dimensions of form, content, and use. These dimensions serve as the foundation for discussions related to students' language acquisition processes. They also inform our ability to interpret and make use of results from language proficiency measures, including both formal and informal assessments.

The purpose of increased accountability related to the language development of English learners is to ensure that all children have a legitimate opportunity to succeed in school. We want to make certain that the educational needs of CLD students are not brushed aside. Educational reform efforts attempt to target inequities in student learning through measures that hold schools and districts accountable for student academic success. Nevertheless, this drive for accountability fosters an increased emphasis on standardized testing—an effort that often fails to measure relevant progress or achieve intended results.

Informal language assessments help to fill in the gaps of our understanding related to what students know and are able to do with language. They allow the teacher to connect language use to the daily realities of the classroom, authentic text, and students' lives. Informal assessments allow us to capture language samples during the course of student communication in settings that are low-risk and in ways that account for students' affect.

Classroom teachers ultimately have the privilege and responsibility of helping students open new doors to communicating with the world. Remembering that language develops best when students have opportunities to use their linguistic skills for authentic, purposeful communication is key to creating contextualized and meaningful language development experiences. Through interaction and dialogue with peers, CLD students gain and share valuable insights into the curriculum, themselves, and the world beyond the classroom.

In order for students to reach their linguistic potentials, educators at all levels must coordinate their efforts. From initial intake of students to the school or district, to the identification of English learners, to the subsequent formal assessment of their language proficiency, to placement in language assistance services and programs, to teachers' development and use of informal assessments, to their creative use of assessment results to inform their responsive instruction of individual students—CLD students look to us as educational professionals to support them on this language acquisition journey.

KEY CONCEPTS

Anecdotal logs

Barrier games

Basic interpersonal communication skills (BICS)

Cloze assessments

Cognitive academic language proficiency (CALP)

Common underlying proficiency (CUP)

Communicative competence

Home language surveys

Home visit interviews

Information gap activities

Language competence

Language performance

Morphology

Narrative assessment

Phonemic awareness

Phonology

Pragmatics

Semantics

Silent period

Story retelling assessment

Style shifting

Syntax

PROFESSIONAL CONVERSATIONS ON PRACTICE

1. Discuss why classroom teachers of CLD students should understand the form, content, and use of language. What implications does this knowledge have for their professional practice with CLD students?

2. Discuss why classroom teachers of CLD students should use home visits. What are some advantages of home visits for CLD parents and guardians?

3. Discuss types of formal assessments of language proficiency. What is the importance of ensuring that these assessments have been normed on similar English learners, assessed under similar conditions?

4. Discuss types of informal assessments of language proficiency. With which are you most comfortable? Which do you intend to emphasize with students as a result of reading this chapter?

QUESTIONS FOR REVIEW AND REFLECTION

1. What are syntax, morphology, phonology, semantics, and pragmatics? Briefly describe each.

2. What are at least three formal standardized assessments of language proficiency? List and briefly describe each.

3. Why have some states developed their own formal standardized assessments of English language proficiency?

4. What are the purposes of home language surveys for data collection? List and describe each.

5. What are at least three advantages of a home visit interview for collecting data about the background experiences and language proficiency of a CLD student? List and describe each.

6. How can the pragmatics of languages make it difficult to assess CLD students in English?

7. Why might it be difficult to rely on a single sample of a CLD student's performance on a narrative assessment task? What can teachers do to gain the most accurate data from narrative assessments?

8. What are the advantages of matrices or rubrics for informally collecting data about language proficiency?

9. What are potential problems with story retelling as a means for informally assessing language proficiencies of CLD students? What can classroom teachers do to avoid these pitfalls?

10. How can assessing the English language (L2) proficiency of a CLD student benefit the teacher in planning and delivering classroom instruction? List at least three benefits and briefly describe each.

CHAPTER 6

---■■■■■---

ASSESSMENT OF CONTENT-AREA LEARNING

When students' language, culture and experience are ignored or excluded in classroom interactions, students are immediately starting from a disadvantage. Everything they have learned about life and the world up to this point is being dismissed as irrelevant to school learning; there are few points of connection to curriculum materials or instruction and so students are expected to learn in an experiential vacuum. Students' silence and non-participation under these conditions have frequently been interpreted as lack of academic ability or effort; and teachers' interactions with students have reflected their low expectations for these students, a pattern that becomes self-fulfilling.

Jim Cummins, *Negotiating Identities: Education for Empowerment in a Diverse Society*

---■■■■■---

Learning Outcomes ████

After reading this chapter, you should be able to:

- Defend the use of content-area assessment with students still developing English proficiency.
- Implement and interpret the results of formative content-area assessments.
- Design and prepare students to succeed on summative content-area assessments.
- Implement and advocate for assessment practices that appropriately maximize students' native languages.
- Audit classroom-based assessments for potential bias.
- Use content-area assessment results to inform your grading practices.
- Hold informed conversations with administrators, colleagues, and parents about implications of content-area assessment for CLD students' programming.

████

INTRODUCTION

When it comes to content-area learning, teachers and school administrators look at multiple factors to determine the kinds of assessments they need to utilize to create a cumulative picture of students' skills and performances. Content-area learning is often categorized in terms of outcomes and learning objectives. The assessments that U.S. school districts plan for students are designed to document student achievement, measure gains, and indicate which aspects of the curriculum need to be revisited.

In many instances, state and local education agencies have responded to legislative initiatives by utilizing overarching standards of achievement, which support assessment of student progress and alignment of instruction. Many districts follow state-directed criteria related to standards that are intended to provide guidance, consistency, and accountability for what is taught in U.S. classrooms, regardless of the setting, teaching style, and student demographics. These standards and criteria serve as the contextual framework for teachers to plan and deliver their instruction. They also provide a blueprint of sorts for school districts to maintain accountability regarding the achievement of *all* students, including historically excluded groups such as English learners and those with special needs (Herrera & Murry, 2006; Lara & August, 1996; Rhodes, Ochoa, & Ortiz, 2005).

Long-standing gaps in student achievement are evident in comparisons between mainstream students and English learners. For instance, average scores for English learners in grades 4, 8, and 12 on the 2013 National Assessment of Educational Progress (NAEP) in reading and math were significantly lower than those of native speakers of English—a gap that continued to widen with increasing grade levels (Office of English Language Acquisition, 2015). Research has demonstrated that issues with reliability and validity can exist when assessments developed mainly for native English speakers are used with English learners (Abedi, 2006). In addition, one of the main reasons we have seen this gap in achievement is because we often categorize the needs of English learners under a broad umbrella of language proficiency. We hold the notion that English learners will not be able to perform well on content-area assessments while they are still developing their language proficiency. Although this notion does remind us of the necessity to minimize bias in content-area assessment—because lack of language proficiency can lead to a lack of understanding of questions on a given assessment—we need to be able to utilize student performance data to inform our instruction.

Most teachers readily recognize the difficulties that language can present to student achievement. In their efforts to address these challenges, however, teachers may create an imbalance in their instruction. They may tend to follow either an inadvertent or an intentional focus on language development while at the same time overlooking the importance of students' acquiring core grade-level concepts. Although teachers may have the best of intentions, such actions may actually widen the learning gap for CLD students (Collier & Thomas, 2004, 2009; Ramírez, Yuen, Ramey, & Pasta, 1991; Thomas & Collier, 2002, 2012).

Although the level of second language (L2) acquisition positively correlates with academic success, we also know that it generally takes a minimum of 5 to 7 years for students to learn a second language to the level necessary for full participation—without accommodation—in classroom instruction. Keeping this thought in mind, it becomes necessary to think in terms of classroom accommodations and interventions that can help ensure students make gains both academically and linguistically. Language and content development need to happen simultaneously, or CLD students will find it nearly impossible to catch up to their native-English-speaking peers.

Content-area assessment plays a very definite role in teaching and learning. It is essential for informing us about how well CLD students are learning academic material during the period in which they are also acquiring English. Given the myriad languages, cultures, and backgrounds of our students, a great deal of reflection and planning is needed as teachers find ways to access, uncover, and maximize the content-area skills and knowledge that CLD students bring to the classroom.

The following questions can guide teachers as they plan their own approach to content-area learning and assessments:

- What am I trying to find out about my students' learning?
- What learning goals or outcomes do I want to measure?
- What kind of evidence do I need to show that my students have achieved the goals/outcomes?
- What kind of assessment will give me that evidence?

When working with CLD students, it especially important for teachers to consider instructional elements that will support their ability to gather valid and reliable assessment information. The following questions reflect attention to student learning dynamics that are key to attainment of our assessment-related goals:

- Which strategies will guide students to reach intended language and content objectives of the lesson?
- Under what conditions (levels of support) does each particular student learn best?
- What can students do with what they have learned?
- In what ways will students' linguistic and academic growth be documented during the lesson?

Given the learner's ability to drive his or her own instruction, teachers are challenged to go a step further to consider how assessment can be used to increase students *desire* to learn and their feelings of competence that they are *able* to learn (Herrera, 2016; Ruiz-Primo, 2011; Stiggins, 2002). Assessments that are aligned with standards and curricula; chosen, developed, or accommodated to be reliable indicators of learning; and valued by students and teachers for their authenticity will support us to reach these goals.

In this chapter, we highlight specifics of assessing CLD students' content-area learning. Our discussion focuses on both formative and summative assessment measures. We explore the value of using different types of assessments in different ways, and at different times, to better understand the dynamic relationship between teaching and learning, while also preparing students to demonstrate their knowledge and skills on high-stakes tests. We also delve into what we can learn from such assessments and how we can use resulting information in our instruction to promote the achievement of all students.

VOICES *from the* FIELD 6.1

I have learned to think critically about assessments in class. Does this assessment truly measure mastery of the content? Should this assessment be viewed in a formative or summative way? Does this assessment need to be for a grade or not? What feedback will this assessment give my students? Will students be able to use this feedback to improve their own learning and understanding of their progress? How will this assessment impact student motivation?

Travis Hampl, Middle School, Social Studies Teacher. Reprinted with permission.

FORMATIVE CONTENT-AREA ASSESSMENT

Formative assessments are tools and strategies employed by grade-level and other teachers to determine what and how their students are learning so that instruction can be modified accordingly while it is still in progress. This process is somewhat like referring to a compass every few miles to check your direction rather than waiting until you have reached the end of the line (or not) to realize you were on the wrong track. Formative assessments enable educators to make teaching more responsive. They largely depend on teachers' knowledge, their ability to create classroom environments that invite student engagement and expression, and their observational skills (Herrera, 2016; Johnston & Afflerbach, 2015). For instance, as Johnston and Afflerbach illustrate, "we can learn a lot about children's word knowledge from their invented spelling, provided the classroom environment encourages it and teachers know how to interpret it." Formative assessments can be either informal or formal. Both types are discussed in this chapter.

Informal Formative Assessment

Perhaps no single form of assessment is as effective for the teacher or as beneficial for the CLD student as informal formative assessment. The tools typically associated with this type of assessment hold the capacity to reveal the nature and strength of *incremental* academic progress. For the teacher, the assessment of incremental progress provides a more realistic, authentic portrait of the student's capacities as well as her or his strides in both language acquisition and content-area learning. The knowledge gained from these assessments reduces the potential frustration of many teachers and keeps their instructional accommodations focused on incremental, but ongoing, progress.

VOICES *from the* FIELD 6.2

In my kindergarten classroom, small centers are a way students are assessed informally. Each center has an objective, which most students will meet at about the two-week mark. Students must complete activities at their center by either playing a game, completing a puzzle, sorting objects, answering questions, matching letters or numbers, or reading sight words. The activities completed in small centers are designed to help students advance by providing various ways of completing the same objective. Since small centers are focused on individual skill areas, it is easy to see where students are struggling. The consistency of working on specific content areas and then retesting helps give me a good perspective on where my students are and how much they have progressed over a couple of weeks. This helps me modify activities and ways of teaching for the students who are struggling. I constantly speak with the paras [paraeducators] and ESL [English as a second language] teachers who are also involved with students in my classroom. We talk about what we see and discuss different strategies to help students learn difficult content.

Donita Estes, Kindergarten Teacher. Reprinted by permission.

For CLD students, the assessment and documentation of these incremental gains tend to both lower the affective filter and enhance motivation for new learning. Too often, formal assessment measures fail to provide these students with any sense of progress and accomplishment. In contrast, informal formative assessments provide opportunities to encourage, motivate, and challenge these students to higher levels of academic achievement and language acquisition.

Inquiry Assessment/Inquiry-Based Learning

Before reading *Bob the Snowman* (Loretan & Lenica, 1993) to her kindergarten class, Ms. Lam asks if anyone has ever seen a snowman. Most have not, but several volunteer that they have indeed seen a *real* one on TV or in a movie. Ms. Lam begins reading the story of a snowman living up North who is told by a migrating bird how beautiful everything is, and how much more fun it is, in the South. Bob decides he'd like to go there, too. Ms. Lam draws the students' attention to the picture of Bob in the snowy North and the bird in the sunny South and asks the class if Bob should go. They respond with a resounding "Yes!"

Ms. Lam: Look at where Bob lives now. Is it hot or cold?

Several voices: Cold!

Ms. Lam: How can you tell it's cold?

Juan: (He raises his hand and then points to the picture of a boy in a coat.)

Ms. Lam: Good thinking! I wear a coat when it's cold, too. Who wore a coat to school today? (Several heads shake "No.")

Ms. Lam: Why didn't you wear a coat, Marisa?

Marisa: It's too hot!

Ms. Lam: What's it like in the South? Is it hot or cold? (The picture shows the bird in a palm tree on a sunny beach.)

Class: Hot! (Ms. Lam turns the page as Bob begins his journey.)

Ms. Lam: As Bob heads for the train station . . .

Marco (in an apparent non sequitur): Bob's got a snow cone head!

Ms. Lam: Yes, his head and body are made of snow like a snow cone. How many of you have ever had a snow cone? (Eight hands fly into the air.) What happens to snow cones on a really hot day?

Julia: My snow cone melted in the park.

Juan: It gets water.

Marisa: Bob's going to melt!

With this revelation, the class revises their advice to Bob, although he travels anyway. Eventually, he does melt, turns into a puddle, evaporates, becomes a fluffy cloud, blows north, gets heavier, and returns home in the form of new-fallen snow. This wonderful story has different levels of concepts that range from basic vocabulary and emotions to prediction, sequencing, weather, states of matter, life cycles, cause-and-effect patterns, and story format.

Ms. Lam had used this book easily in her previous school but had never encountered a group like this, in which no one had experience with snow. She was ill prepared for the initial inability of her students to see a problem with Bob's plan. By relating Bob's head to a snow cone, Marco provided a context that bridged others' prior learning with unfamiliar concepts and allowed the students to work at higher levels of understanding throughout the remainder of the story. Ms. Lam decided, and noted in her reflection journal, that when she introduces *Bob the Snowman* next year, she'll remember not to limit prior learning connections to the snows of her New England past but also include the snow cones of her students' Laredo, Texas, present.

One of the most common types of informal formative assessment occurs in the dialogue of teaching, as exemplified by this vignette. The information teachers receive from the process of *inquiry-based assessment* can inform them about students' developing language skills and content knowledge. Dialogue that evolves during the inquiry-based learning process is a product of real-time formative assessment that occurs as the learning unfolds. When students engage in social learning of this kind, they have opportunities to receive various types of embedded feedback (Learning and Teaching Coordinating Network, 2016).

Research demonstrates that teachers who recognize and differentially respond to student learning behaviors (e.g., individual responses to questions) during spontaneous interaction positively influence student learning (Ruiz-Primo, 2011). For some teachers, this begins rather intuitively, is reinforced through experience, and is best validated by the success of their students. It becomes a natural part of how they teach. These teachers catch those on-the-fly moments in which clarification, connection with prior learning, and probes of higher-order thinking keep all learners engaged with the curriculum and continuing to move forward.

To get a reliable window into the content-area learning of English learners, teachers particularly need to take care when structuring the types of questions posed. For example, newcomers like Juan in the scenario can often demonstrate comprehension of targeted information by pointing to an object, word, or picture or by responding yes, no, thumbs up, or thumbs down to simple questions. Teachers can accommodate students' language levels by using basic "wh" questions, and then "how" and "why" questions, before they attempt more abstract prompts or complex questions. Sample prompts and questions in a discussion about *Bob the Snowman* might include the following:

- "Show me the snowman."
- "Where is it cold?"
- "Who spoke to Bob?"
- "Should Bob go south?"
- "Why not?" (Students with limited proficiency in English can demonstrate advanced thinking by pointing to the sun, just as Juan pointed to a jacketed child to answer the inferential question, "How can you tell it's cold?")

Inquiry assessment can also take the form of a whole-class inclusion activity. For example, prompts like the following could be used for an activity in which each student has a sheet with pictured objects and animals:

- "Point to the cheese."
- "Who ate the cheese?"
- "Point to all the animals."
- "Which animal is bigger, the dog or the horse?" (answer embedded)
- "Which animal [vehicle, dinosaur, etc.] do you like best?"
- "Raise your hand to tell me *why* you like it best."

In a science conversation about plants, questions might include:

- "Does our plant need water?" (thumbs up, thumbs down)
- "Does our plant need soil, or dirt?"

- "Does our plant need ice cream?"
- "Does our plant need sun?"
- "Does our plant need snow?"
- "Raise your hand to tell me why you think it does or does not need snow."
- "Raise your hand to tell me how you think the plant gets food."

Open-ended questions are more difficult but have value as a modeled and anticipated form of query that can be answered by others or with the support of native language partners until CLD students are ready to respond independently. Figure 6.1 summarizes types of questions and prompts that are appropriate for students in different stages of second language acquisition.

In all cases, visual referents and use of the native language as a resource provide much-needed support until a student's performance suggests that she or he no longer needs the assistance. Thinking of instructional questions as keys rather than probes is helpful. Each is uniquely shaped to open a specific door, inviting a student to bring his or her knowledge into the learning zone. In constructive

Figure 6.1   Questions and Prompts According to Stage of SLA

The sentence/questioning stems included here are categorized by a specific stage of language acquisition for illustration purposes only. Students may move rather quickly through the stages, or they may be ready for more advanced questioning despite the majority of their language skills reflecting a lower level of proficiency.

Preproduction	Early Production
Questions or directives that students can respond to or follow before they are ready to speak • Where is _____? • Show me the _____. • Bring me the _____. • Point to the _____. • Touch your _____. • Who is wearing _____? • Put the _____ on the _____. • Give _____ the _____. • Who wants _____?	Yes/no questions • Is this a _____? • Is a spider an insect? Either/or questions • Did Billy go to a store or park? • Is this food or clothing? One- to two-word response questions • Who is the line leader today? • What is Kenya riding? Questions that elicit naming items from groups or categories • What animals did we see at the zoo? • Which of these were marsupials?
Speech Emergence	**Intermediate Fluency**
Questions that require elaboration • *Why* did Will miss the bus? • *How* did he get to school? • *What happened* when he got to school? Questions that ask for more information • *Tell me about* your vacation. • *Describe* your favorite place.	Questions that inspire/probe higher-order thinking skills • What will happen if? . . . • How are _____ and _____ alike? • How are they different? • What would you do if . . . • What do you think about . . . • How did you vote and why?

Source: Based on Alaska Department of Education and Early Development (n.d.). Sample assessment instruments. Curriculum Frameworks Project. Author.

classroom environments, this door remains open for access to prior knowledge and experiences that are the bricks and mortar of each student's ability to construct new knowledge.

When classroom teachers use predictable patterns of conversation assessment, students begin to anticipate questions and think about the material in terms of inquiry. This can occur, however, only when adequate time is provided for responses. It is not uncommon for teachers to wait less than one second for a response after they pose a question. If no student response is provided in that time, they are likely to either ask another question or answer the question themselves (Bond, 2008; Echevarria, Vogt, & Short, 2004; Kaur & Hashim, 2014). This practice excludes the CLD student, who requires more time to process language, and all students need time to be able to formulate their thinking. As Bond (2008) explains, before students can reply, they must hear the question, determine whether they understand the question, and recall information from memory. All this takes time.

If we teachers want serious thinking from our students, we must be willing to provide them the time necessary to make it happen (Sun, 2012). The only kinds of questions a student can answer within a very short time are generally those requiring very little thought or formulation. Rather than facilitating or assessing higher-level thinking, these types of questions merely probe the efficiency with which students memorize facts.

To develop questioning as a formative assessment tool, we must go beyond the standard questioning procedure. We cannot merely ask the question, have students respond to it, and move on. Questioning in itself is a strategy that becomes formative in nature when we pose questions to seek information that we then interpret and use to enhance and develop our students' language and content knowledge (Jiang, 2014). As Jiang explains, to facilitate this process we should:

1. Pose questions that are pivotal to students' construction of understanding.
2. Seek responses that make known students' thought processes, which provide teachers with the most useful information for instruction.
3. Respond by providing meaningful interventions that guide students along the way to achieving their learning objectives.

---

assessment FREEZE FRAME 6.1

Thinking of instructional questions as keys rather than probes is helpful. Each is uniquely shaped to open a specific door, inviting a student to bring his or her knowledge into the learning zone.

Teaching Tips:

- Adapt the language of the question for maximum comprehension.
- Formulate questions that elicit deeper levels of thought but can be answered without complex language.
- Allow adequate time for responding.
- Affirm "I don't know" answers as opportunities to engage the class in brainstorming ways to make sense of the material.
- Use questions as a means for reciprocal language use; as the student provides an answer, use that answer to further probe with how or why questions.
- Leverage questions to elicit interaction among learners; when posing a question, ask students to dialogue with each other in pairs or small groups before formulating a response.

As students' language proficiencies increase, their attention to the higher-level language in cognitive prompts and responses of others encourages their own processing of the concepts at more advanced levels. The objective of this type of assessment approach is to determine what the student has learned from the lesson and what that implies for instruction.

U-C-ME (_Uncover, Concentrate, Monitor, Evaluate_) Strategy

Grade Level: 2–12

Materials:

- Copies of the U-C-ME template (one per student)

Directions:

- *Uncover*
    - Place students in small groups and give each student a blank U-C-ME template.
    - Have students write the name of the topic/concept that is the focus of the lesson around the outside of the center oval.
    - Ask students to write down everything they "bring to the table" or know about the topic/concept in the center oval. Encourage students to write down information in their native language if they prefer.
    - Have students discuss ideas with peers.
- *Concentrate*
    - Ask students to think of specific questions they may have about the topic. Model this first by posing sample questions for two or three of the spokes. Generate questions that require students' higher-order thinking skills.
    - Have students work as a class to pose their own questions for the remaining spokes. Together, the questions will become the guide for student learning.
    - During instruction, make sure to concentrate on information that can be used to answer the questions.
    - To guide students, you may want to create a whole class U-C-ME template on which you model how to document key learning.
- *Monitor*
    - Have students monitor their learning by placing responses to each of the questions posed in the corresponding ovals (see Figure 6.2).
    - Provide opportunities for students to discuss their responses with peers in their small group.
- *Evaluate*
    - The final evaluation of student understanding can be done by having students use what was written in the ovals to summarize what they learned about the topic or concept.
        - Persuasive or narrative paragraph
        - Oral conversation with a peer (discussing what was learned and where or how it was learned)

Figure 6.2   Assessment Artifact: U-C-ME

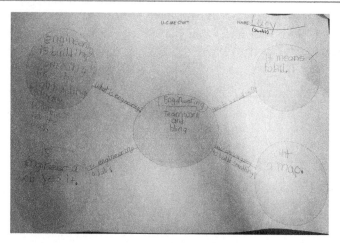

This artifact depicts the completed U-C-ME graphic organizer of a second grader who is a native Swahili speaker in the Speech Emergence stage of second language acquisition. The teacher, Mr. Gruber, adapted the standard strategy template to meet the developmental needs of his learners. Reflecting on his use of the strategy, he shared:

> As a second grade teacher, I was impressed at how fast students picked up the understanding of engineering ideas and how quickly vocabulary words were being used independently. . . . The chart [U-C-ME template] can be adapted to fit the abilities of all students. Teachers may have to lead the students in younger levels whereas older students can be more independent with using this chart. Overall, the goals of developing students' vocabulary, proper English comprehension/usage, and content knowledge can be met by using this strategy.

Observing Students:

Circulate among students to note their connections to background knowledge as they uncover what they know. Pay attention to what students subsequently share with one another in their small group conversations. Resulting insights can be used to highlight predictions about the topic and unique skill sets or knowledge among the community of learners. Similarly observe students as they monitor their understanding. Information gathered will support your ability to emphasize key aspects of the curriculum and the learning process and redirect if necessary. Continued observation of students during the evaluation phase of the strategy will enable you to provide additional targeted feedback to individuals and to the whole group.

Differentiating Instruction:

- Jot down notes about student thinking and performance as you proceed with the lesson. Anecdotal notes on students' connections to background knowledge will inform the links you make to boost relevance of the content.
- Make sure to document students who struggle with the process of generating questions. This skill is critical for active reading, and it can be revisited as students proceed with reading the text during the lesson.
- Student thinking that stands out as an example of innovation, collaboration, personal progress, struggle, or self-doubt will inform your in-the-moment response as well as your evaluation and feedback on the final product/performance.

Additional Notes:

This strategy can be used with any content area and repeated as often as desired. After initial modeling and with consistent use, this strategy can quickly become a student learning strategy that CLD students are able to apply to learning in other areas of their life.

Source: Adapted from Herrera (2016), p. 171.

Observation Assessment

> José struggles self-consciously and quits prematurely when called on to read in class. It seems he is still a nonreader. One day Mrs. Kay notes that he follows along well with his fingers as other students read aloud, pausing precisely where they do. In that moment, she makes a preliminary assessment that he may in fact be reading silently but is not yet able or ready to read aloud unsupported. She alters her instruction by having the whole class read the next paragraph together. Ms. Kay watches as José reads the entire paragraph aloud with the class and makes a note in her anecdotal log. She excitedly decides to have students do this again tomorrow, alternating choral reading with student-read sentences to see if José will be more comfortable or capable of reading smaller segments by himself.

Through cycles of observation and modification, teachers such as Ms. Kay are informally assessing their students throughout the day. *Observation assessment* is another type of informal formative assessment that is particularly useful in the accommodation of CLD students. Teacher observations made during instruction can provide information that may be crucial to determining the root of a student's difficulties, or a particular strength, with content-area material. Such observations also enable teachers to provide students with opportunities to build their confidence and readiness to attempt higher levels of classroom involvement.

The advantage Ms. Kay has is that she also documents these instances of informal assessment and uses the new information to alter her instruction according to the learning responses of her students. This ongoing refinement (similar to the kind of responsiveness previously discussed in relation to questioning) allows her to zero in on the zones in which her students are capable of maximal growth as she adjusts her teaching to those levels.

A potential drawback to a reliance on unplanned informal assessment is that even highly significant observations that occur in the course of instruction are likely to remain unrecorded. The primary reason is that too much is happening in a dynamic classroom. That's one reason that ready-made or teacher-created observation checklists are popular. These can take many forms, limited only by the teacher's creativity, preferences, and time. One method, adaptable to any setting, involves listing all or selected students along the left side of a single page and targeted curricular behaviors along the top. As illustrated in Figure 6.3 (and the related appendix resource), a teacher can easily note with narrative detail or a simple checkmark the occurrence of observed behaviors during specified or unspecified activities. Checklists are especially helpful when educators observe students in action, working collaboratively, or exhibiting unpredicted or spontaneous evidence of skills (e.g., correctly counting change for the vending machine). Documentation of the conditions in which a behavior occurs, as well as those in which it does not, can be instructive in the design of future learning environments, activities, and interventions.

Informal observation assessment can also look at how well students learn through their own observations. Many of us can cite examples of students learning

Figure 6.3 Observation Checklist

Student Name	Follows directions without a model	Uses nonverbals to communicate understanding or express needs	Uses single words to answer questions or express needs	Uses simple sentence structures for social purposes	Uses simple sentence structures for curricular purposes	Other comments or observations
Ahmed A.	X	X	X	X		Said, "I play too?" on playground
Feliciana G.		X				Hasn't cried all week
Mindy H.		X	X	X		Needs to watch before doing
Luciano L.	X	X	X			Words just now emerging
Ghassem M.	X	X				Joins play during recess
Van N.	X	X	X	X	X	Volunteers during whole group
Sara N.	X	X	X	X		Talkative in Housekeeping Center
John (Kang) V.	X	X	X			Asks for help/chooses snack

ACCOMMODATIVE ASSESSMENT PRACTICES 6.1

Effective use of scaffolded observation is demonstrated in the following scenario:

> Ms. Reyes looks out on eight kindergarten students circled in front of her on the carpet. They excitedly eye her plain brown bag. They've seen it before. It always holds something different . . . but it's always something fun! Ms. Reyes carefully removes each item, labeling, describing, and discussing its use. There are two cans of frosting (vanilla and chocolate), several toppings (shredded coconut, yellow candy stars, and red sprinkles), plastic knives, spoons, paper napkins, plates, and two kinds of cookies. Ms. Reyes intentionally calls on those with the strongest language and academic skills first. All eyes are riveted on the cookies.

> **Ms. Reyes:** Josh, would you like a cookie?
> **Josh:** Yes, please.
> **Ms. Reyes:** Which kind would you like, a white sugar cookie or a brown chocolate cookie?
> **Josh:** A brown chocolate cookie.
> **Ms. Reyes:** Let's put your cookie on a plate. How would you like me to decorate it? I have . . . (she points while naming all the options).
> **Josh:** Chocolate frosting.
> **Ms. Reyes:** Here's the chocolate frosting. What should I do with it?
> **Josh:** Put it on the cookie. (Ms. Reyes puts the can of frosting on the cookie. There is silence and then the students laugh.)
> **Josh:** No, you have to open it. (She opens the can.)
> **Josh:** Put it on the cookie . . . please. (She begins to set the can on the cookie a second time.)
> **Josh:** Not the can; put the *frosting* on the cookie! (Ms. Reyes looks into the can, puzzled.)
> **Josh:** Put the knife in. (She puts the knife in and leaves it.)
> **Josh (laughing):** Scoop it out and put it, no, *spread* it on the cookie!

> This pattern of scaffolding, modeling, and self-expansion continues through all

phases of decoration. The finished cookies are set aside until all are completed, and the process becomes more efficient with successive student turns, even though several students face communicative challenges. The language use of CLD students is noticeably more specific and complex under these conditions than during regular classroom discourse. The students enjoy the humor of the lesson but also realize Ms. Reyes will follow their instructions explicitly, attending to words such as *in, on, more, as much, enough, spread, shake, sprinkle,* and so forth. Academic vocabulary pertaining to color, size, position, and quantity concepts also becomes meaningful in this context.

Ms. Reyes observes when students are unable to produce the targeted structures and modifies her prompts accordingly. For example, Nahla has been in school 2 months and has little prior exposure to English. Observation checklists reveal she uses mostly single words and gestures to communicate in the classroom. By the time her turn arrives, Nahla has been watching intently. She knows what she wants and has grasped the most significant words that will make that happen. With every classmate's previous turn, she has very likely rehearsed her own requests.

> **Nahla:** Cookie . . . chocolate!
> **Ms. Reyes:** You want a chocolate cookie? Here's a chocolate cookie. Do you want frosting?
> **Nahla:** Chocolate frosting . . . please. (Nahla does not wait for a prompt.) Put knife . . . frosting on cookie.

Later, in response to Ms. Reyes's sprinkling of only a tiny amount of red candy on top, Nahla shakes her head and before a model can be provided says, "Not enough . . . more candy, please."

Although the lesson seems simple, in a very short time Ms. Reyes has added another important dimension to her own

(Continued)

ACCOMMODATIVE ASSESSMENT PRACTICES 6.1 *(Continued)*

knowledge about how Nahla and the other students learn. This informal yet deliberate assessment has indicated that several students not previously thought to have acquired many kindergarten concepts did indeed have the cognitive ability to learn curricular material in a highly communicative lesson that maximized the learning potential of anticipatory observation. Given other indicators, Nahla was only expected to use single words and perhaps demonstrate recognition of one or two colors. Instead, after observing others' work, she responded at multiple levels by using expanded utterances and grasping unanticipated curricular concepts.

As illustrated in this scenario, one of the most exciting aspects of differentiated instruction is that it also allows for differentiated assessment. Such purposeful differentiation can occur in a variety of contexts at all academic levels. ■

---

negative behaviors by watching others, but this natural tendency to learn by example can also be drawn on positively during classroom instruction. Children have been found to learn just as effectively through intently observed activities as those experienced hands-on. This is particularly potent for CLD students who are going through periods of relative silence or acculturation (as discussed in Chapter 4) but who may be able to learn well through scaffolded observation and instructional accommodations. Central to the concept is that the observed activity is understandable and that there is an anticipation of imminent or eventual participation (Rogoff, 2014).

Structured Authentic Assessments

Ms. McKinley knows that CLD students in the early stages of second language acquisition might have difficulty comprehending a science unit on plant parts. Therefore, she and some of her fellow teachers designed a science activity with language modifications that would enable the participation of all students in the class. The activity involves having students work in heterogeneous (Spanish and English) pairs to identify the parts of an illustrated plant. As one modification (see Figure 6.4), the students are given an unlabeled diagram of the plant along with word cards in Spanish and English for the different plant parts. The partners take turns placing the Spanish and English words in the appropriate blanks. Students check their work using a plant diagram that is labeled with terms in both languages. When the activity is used as an individual assessment, each student is given an unlabeled diagram and a set of the Spanish and English word cards. The student then glues the word cards in (or near) the blanks.

Although educators occasionally are fortunate to observe behaviors related to desired skills in unplanned situations, most of the time the skills demonstrated by students will depend on the opportunities inherent in the educational activities that teachers plan. As explored in depth in Chapter 2, the design of structured authentic assessments reflects teacher efforts to develop activities that maximize student demonstration of curricular knowledge and skills. The preceding vignette illustrates that teachers of CLD students also plan modifications that will help ensure students' assessment performance accurately conveys their abilities related to target knowledge and skills. Authentic assessments such as this provide learners the opportunity to demonstrate conceptual knowledge without being hindered by language challenges.

Label these parts of this plant:

Figure 6.4 Plant Part Identification

flower	flor
flowers	flores
stem	tallo
leaf	hoja
root	raíz

Another of the many ways to assess students in authentic contexts is to develop situations or scenarios in which students exhibit targeted skills while working toward the creation of a project or product. In such contexts, students are engaged and motivated to draw on all their skills and resources to achieve an identified goal. The following scenario illustrates the effective use of an authentic, cooperative group assessment with CLD students.

Ms. William's 2nd-grade class is studying living creatures and their environments. They recently had the opportunity to visit the local zoo and see many animals. The zoo guide was interesting but talked much too fast for some of the English learners. Fortunately, Ms. William had made sure that native-English-speaking peers were included in each group of students to facilitate understanding. She knew that using the native language helps students learn, but some of the English-speaking students also do a very nice job of retelling information in creatively comprehensible ways.

During the zoo visit, the students were encouraged to take notes or draw pictures to remind themselves of the most interesting details about the animals or places they saw. Later, each group used this information to develop questions for the other students. The questions often required that students give detailed descriptions of the animals or their environment. A checklist guided the students to develop at least one question each about an animal classification (e.g., Turtles and snakes belong to which group?), a geographical region (e.g., Name three animals that live in the jungle.), animal eating habits (e.g., What do ducks eat?), and a predatory relationship (e.g., What animal likes to eat ducks?). As students quizzed one another, they noticed how many different correct answers were elicited from each group.

The next day, students continued to work in groups to design their own zoos. Ms. William informed them that the zoo would be located just outside town, so they needed to consider the region's weather conditions and determine each animal's appropriateness for the zoo or need for shelter. Students were asked to include at least one type of animal that did not live in the zoo they had visited the previous day. The plan of the new zoo was to have more animals living together in realistic habitats than in the current zoo. The primary task for students was to create three habitats where at least 15 animals (five in each habitat) could live safely.

As they worked together, the students pooled their previously learned (but still fresh) knowledge. Jesse wanted the zoo to have chickens but knew from experience that chickens shouldn't live anywhere near foxes or snakes. Linda wanted prairie dogs in the farm habitat because cows, goats, and horses don't eat them. However, Sam knew that prairie dog burrows could break the horses' legs. When they finally finished, each group prepared to present its zoo to the class.

The class checked the ideas of each group by using a rubric to determine whether the group could (a) describe each habitat; (b) explain the reason for its plants, shelter, and boundary type; (c) explain why each animal was chosen; and (d) describe each animal's main traits. When Ms. William heard the groups share their final presentations, she was confident that all the students in her class had gained a far greater and more durable understanding of the curricular concepts (as well as greater ability to generalize them) than if she had just spent an entire week on verbal lessons followed by a paper-and-pencil test.

Teachers can also follow this type of collaborative activity with individual tests, a group test in which all members work together to discuss and record the answers, or a combination of both.

---

assessment FREEZE FRAME 6.2

The design of structured authentic assessments reflects the efforts of teachers to strategically select strategies that maximize assessment of curricular skills and knowledge.

Teacher-Made Tests

Mr. Jin places on the floor three pictures (covered, or pasted inside down-turned paper plates), which will serve as the possible answers to a question. He then explains to the class that one of these is the correct answer to the question he is going to ask, but rather than focusing on the choices, they should first try to see if the answer pops into their heads. He reads the story-based question from the board.

Mr. Jin: What was the main setting for *Charlotte's Web*? (As he nods to their raised hands, the students volunteer "a farm" and "a fair.")

Mr. Jin: Are those names for the same place, or were there different settings in this story?

Class: Different settings.

Mr. Jin: Yes, let's reread the question together.

All: What was the main setting for *Charlotte's Web*?

Mr. Jin: The question asks for the *main* setting. What does that mean?

Sara: Where they were most of the time.

SNAPSHOT from *CLASSROOM PRACTICE*   `6.1`

Ms. Lewis tries to incorporate authentic activities and assessments into her classroom assessment practices. To help her students learn the parts of a cell, she had students build models that include various cell parts and descriptions of their corresponding functions. This photograph depicts the work of a CLD student who labeled her animal cell model in both her native language and English.

In a reflection about this activity, Ms. Lewis wrote:

> I have taught this science lesson for 3 years, and this is the first year that I had students make a model of the cell. Usually, we cover the lesson and do some worksheets. I think the model representation helped [CLD and other students] to remember the parts of the cell. We also viewed a video on cells this year, so students could visually see movement of live cells as well as different cell types and structures. I feel that I am growing professionally because I am now incorporating language support into my lessons, and I am focusing more on the needs and learning styles [preferences] of all of my students. The cell model offers an alternative form for assessing students.

Teachers such as Ms. Lewis who adapt and modify lessons to increase student engagement often have to "step out on a limb." After trying activities they have never previously used, effective teachers reflect on ways in which the lessons and related assessments succeeded and/or require further refinement.

Sheila Lewis

Mr. Jin: Do you all agree?

Class: Yes!

Mr. Jin: What do you think was the main setting for most of the book?

Class: The farm.

Mr. Jin: Let's see if the farm is among our answers. (He reveals a picture of a school.)

Class: No, that's a school.

Mr. Jin: (Reveals the next picture of a market.)

Class: No!

Kenji: (laughing) That's where Wilbur was gonna end up!

Mr. Jin (impressed with Kenji's inferential thinking but keeping the class on track): If we know for sure that the school and the market were not the main setting, what can we guess about the last choice?

Class: It's a farm.

Mr. Jin: Yes, because we knew the answer without looking, it should be a farm. Let's look. (Reveals the third picture.)

Class: It's a farm!

Mr. Jin: What if our last choice was a picture or word we didn't recognize (he replaces the farm with a word written in Chinese), but we knew the other two answers were wrong? Would this be a good guess?

Sara: Yes, I bet that says *farm*!

Mr. Jin: If you guessed this was the right answer because you knew the other two answers were wrong, that would be a good guess. And you are right . . . it does say *farm*!

Students are not born savvy test takers. They develop testing competence through ongoing attention to characteristics of question formats they encounter. It is important for students to understand that test taking, just like playing videogames or basketball, requires a set of skills and involves more than subject knowledge—it also requires heightened awareness and practice. A teacher might introduce approaches to multiple-choice testing, for example, at very early levels by using strategies such as those demonstrated by Mr. Jin in the previous scenario. Students who have been exposed early in their education to mediated examples of test-taking strategies in formats that continually adapt to their skills and curricula will, by later years, be able to employ these strategies independently across test-taking contexts.

Teacher-made tests can complement all other forms of assessment, but the development of classroom tests that are appropriate for CLD students requires the careful consideration of several factors. The content tested should, of course, reflect what has been taught and should be probed in the manner best suited for students' demonstration of knowledge. Task analysis skills should be separated into their component parts so that mastery of subskills can be determined. Factual or memorized material can be assessed via formats that have pictures or mastered vocabulary presented in a familiar test design (e.g., matching, multiple choice). The correct answer should be easy to distinguish from incorrect answers, given an understanding of the concepts being measured. Vague or ambiguous prompts are essentially meaningless and sometimes punitive because they tell us only about a student's language and testing finesse rather than the student's content-area comprehension. Assessment in Action 6.1 provides additional guidelines for creating effective prompts/tests.

Although "objective" tests might seem less complicated for CLD students, these learners may actually find it easier to tackle questions that require synthesis, explanation, or analysis through short-answer essays if they are supported with access to graphic organizers and bilingual dictionaries (as applicable). When teachers grade the essays of CLD students, they may choose to focus solely on content rather than incorporating literacy criteria. Alternatively, teachers can provide separate scores for each skill area.

Teaching Tips:

Additional tips for developing teacher-made tests (Educational Testing Service, 2003; Missouri National Education Association, 2011; Salend, 2005) include the following:

- Identify the purpose of the test.
- Determine what type of test would be most appropriate based on the material, student variables, and what you want to measure.
- Control the language level of the test unless that is the curricular area being assessed. Avoid ambiguous or vague prompts. Linguistically complex forms (e.g., unless, although), clausal constructions, and negatives often lead to misinterpretation of the question.
- Keep questions short and specific to lessen the impact that differences in reading speed and fluency have on indices of content learning.
- Allow students some choice in selecting the questions they will answer or demonstrating their knowledge/skills (e.g., options for essay questions, choices of the structure/organization of the response).
- Include questions that reflect varying degrees of complex thought.
- Consider the element of time when developing a test. Inadequate time or time pressure injects several biasing elements into the testing situation that detract from a teacher's ability to distinguish results based on knowledge from those resulting from testing conditions.

Educators who develop effective teacher-made tests remember that it is essential to give students mediated opportunities to work with these formats so they are better equipped to interpret them in higher-stakes testing situations. Many test-taking skills can be learned while applying similar skills during instruction. For instance, the skills of isolating information, synthesizing, and summarizing that frequently are needed to succeed on tests are best developed during daily instruction. The more students practice these skills in academic contexts, the better prepared they will be for actual tests.

The tips provided in Figure 6.5 offer educators guidance for teaching students how to strategically approach test formats such as multiple-choice, matching, true/false, sentence completion, and essay questions. When sharing these tips with CLD students, however, teachers need to incorporate appropriate examples and scaffolding, depending on the academic and language proficiency levels of their students.

Point-in-Time Assessments   *Point-in-time assessments* are those quizzes or tests that a teacher employs to gather immediate quantitative feedback about student learning. Often, but not always, such assessments involve the measurement of skills that are acquired hierarchically. Some skills in mathematics, for instance, are acquired in this way. For example, it is important to check the ability of a given student to add single digits before moving on to double digits and regrouping. Spelling tests and vocabulary quizzes are also among the more common point-in-time classroom assessments.

Many teachers who use ongoing assessments such as portfolios or projects also find value in regular quizzes to check for understanding. Assessments that are capable of measuring incremental progress are especially valuable for CLD students. The teacher can subsequently revise instruction or implement

---

assessment FREEZE FRAME 6.3

Point-in-time assessments are those quizzes or tests that a teacher employs to gather immediate quantitative feedback about student learning.

Figure 6.5 Test-Taking Tips for Students

Testing Tips
Multiple Choice • Read the question and think of the answer before reading the response options. • Eliminate choices that are obviously incorrect or unrelated to the content. • Carefully analyze and choose from among the remaining options. • Look for grammatical clues. • If within the first few attempts you are unable to determine the answer, skip the question and return to it later.
Matching • Make sure you know the rules and understand the directions well (e.g., whether items can be used more than once). • Read the first item in column one and then all possible matches before answering. • First answer items that appear less difficult; skip (and note) difficult items to reconsider when there are fewer possible answers remaining (if one answer per item). • As you proceed, mark out or highlight choices that have been used to focus your attention on responses remaining for review.
True or False • Words that qualify statements (such as *rarely, sometimes, most,* and *usually*) are more likely associated with correct answers than words that make the statement 100% true or false (such as *always, never,* and *every*). • Read each item carefully; mark it false if any part of it is not correct or true. • Highlight prefixes and negative words, and consider their power to change meaning.
Sentence Completion • To help determine the answers, convert these items into questions. • Pay attention to grammatical clues as well as length or number of blanks to identify targeted responses.
Essay • Highlight key words related to directions (e.g., *explain, compare, describe*). • Read the question, note important points to address, and outline your response before beginning to write. • Rephrase the question as the first sentence of the answer, detail your response accordingly with transitions between ideas, and summarize main points in your closing statement(s). • If you are unable to complete an item fully, note its key points and create an outline. • Proofread your response for legibility, spelling, grammar, and style.

Source: Based on Salend, S. J. (2005). Creating inclusive class- rooms: Effective and reflective practices for all students (5th ed.). Upper Saddle River, NJ: Prentice Hall.

interventions at the most opportune time rather than waiting until the student is significantly behind.

More frequent, short tests over specific content can benefit students who struggle to remember vast quantities of information (Salend, 2009a). In addition, providing frequent quizzes requires students to consistently recall information (Paul, 2015). Paul accentuates the importance of this process, explaining that retrieval practice alters our memories, as our brains elaborate and enforce connections that likely will be needed in the future. Such retrieval practice boosts students' retention of the material and supports subsequent recall. The importance of later explaining and discussing the correct answers with students cannot be overemphasized (Paul, 2015).

Students also need supported to develop metacognitive skills related to their study practices. In fact, some teachers regularly build in opportunities after tests/

ASSESSMENT IN ACTION 6.1

CREATING PROMPTS FOR TEACHER-MADE TESTS

The following guidelines ensure that teacher-made tests are accommodative:

1. When creating questions with multiple choice answers, be mindful of students with varying linguistic skills. Carefully design prompts and foils to avoid creating undue advantages or disadvantages for students. For example, although some students may legitimately know the answers to the following fill-in-the-blank questions, others who are not sufficiently familiar with the content material might be cued by grammar structures that indicate the correct answers.

    i. _____ eat a variety of vegetation, including tree bark.
        a. Moose
        b. Walrus
        c. Penguin
        d. Arctic wolf
    ii. A person who explores caves is called a _____.
        a. entomologist
        b. ethnographer
        c. agronomist
        d. spelunker

2. Consider the range of responses that may be elicited from items. For example, "Tyrannosaurus rex was a _____." (Possible responses include dinosaur, meat-eater, GoBot, etc.). Determine whether to accept all logical responses or revise the prompt to probe the targeted content more specifically. For instance, this item can be rewritten, "Tyrannosaurus rex ate only _____."

3. Avoid using words such as *always, never, all,* and *none* when designing multiple-choice assessments to gather information about content knowledge. These words tend to favor students with greater linguistic experience.

4. Be mindful of the potential for cultural/regional bias in assessments. Depending on the prompt, descriptors such as "Arctic" in the term "Arctic Wolf" might give undue advantage to students familiar with the region's climate, vegetation, and native animals.

5. In many instances, it is best to have students describe the topic/concept in their own words or create a visual (with labels, as needed) to share their understanding of the concept.

ACCOMMODATIVE ASSESSMENT PRACTICES 6.2

On a sentence completion test with picture cues of a cookie, spoon, apple, and cup, Adan circled the cookie as the best response to: "I eat beans with a(n) _____." It seems clear to Mr. Rossi that Adan is either unable to read or did not adequately comprehend the prompt, but he's not sure which. Mr. Rossi hoped this format would give him insights into this student's skills but realizes he won't know much more about Adan's learning if he simply marks the test item wrong. He reads the item again. Perhaps the problem is the preposition *with.* Mr. Rossi had not thought of it when he created the test, but the question could be interpreted as meaning what you eat *along with* your beans, rather than what you use to eat beans. Nevertheless, he thought, it is possible that Adan just couldn't read or understand the words. Mr. Rossi calls Adan to his desk and asks him to read the response to the item aloud. Adan smiles, "I eat beans with a tortilla."

In this case, cultural factors had contributed to Adan's "incorrect" answer. In his family, a tortilla (rather than a spoon or fork) is used to scoop beans from the plate. Given the images provided, Adan's selection of the cookie/tortilla now made perfect sense. Mr. Rossi knows that this student did, in fact, correctly demonstrate the skill being assessed. Based on this experience, Mr. Rossi plans to modify the prompt before using it again. He also is validated about his pedagogical decision to ask students to explain their answers if something seems amiss. ■

SNAPSHOT from *CLASSROOM PRACTICE*   6.2

In her 3rd-grade classroom, Ms. Farrell uses point-in-time vocabulary quizzes to measure the level of student understanding. To support students' ability to fully demonstrate their knowledge, she provides the translated vocabulary term and asks that the students draw a picture and use the word in a sentence.

Karen Farrell

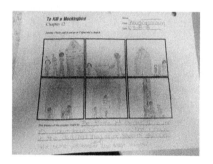

Ms. Sayles, an 8th-grade teacher, uses an activity called "My Learning in a Box" to ascertain what students have gained from the latest chapter in the book, *To Kill a Mockingbird*. During the activity, students draw visuals in each of the six boxes to summarize their learning and then write the theme of the specific chapter. With this information, she is able to determine the degree to which her students understood the essential message of the text and their levels of readiness for proceeding to the next chapter.

Tyherah Sayles

---

quizzes for students to evaluate what studying practices were most or least effective for them. They also ask students to consider modifications to their studying and commit to trying one or more new strategies the next time they study for an assessment (Lovett, 2013; Millis, 2016).

Curriculum-Based Measurement   Another approach to measuring the incremental progress of learners is *curriculum-based measurement* (CBM). Like criterion-referenced tests (which are discussed in a subsequent section of this chapter), teacher-made tests, and point-in-time assessments, CBMs are designed to measure the acquisition of curricular skills directly. Although each of these types of assessment is a form of broader curriculum-based assessment, there are some significant distinctions among them.

To design criterion-referenced and teacher-made tests, long-range objectives are broken down into skills and subskills that are taught and measured sequentially throughout the year. Although it stands to reason that mastery of these distinct hierarchical components will inevitably result in broader core-area knowledge, this cannot always be assumed. For example, a student might be able to demonstrate mastery of addition with and without regrouping during those respective lessons but perform poorly when required to apply those same processes in more global assessments (or when problems requiring these separate processes are presented together) (Fuchs, 2004). Vanderheyden (2005) contrasts this model of *mastery measurement* with *general outcome measurement*.

CBMs are best characterized as general outcome measurements. Instead of measuring the mastery of incremental steps to an academic goal, CBMs repeatedly sample global skills from which a growing mastery of subskills can be inferred. This is similar in principle to what is sometimes referred to as informal differentiated assessment but differs in that CBMs can be standardized in their administration for an entire class or group.

In a process described by Hosp and Hosp (2003), a teacher using curriculum-based measurement first identifies academic goals and objectives the student is expected to master over the course of the school year or semester. The teacher then uses these outcomes to develop minitests called CBM probes, which can be administered at regular intervals throughout the year. CBM probes gauge student progress toward the terminal goal. An advantage to such probes is that teachers can create graphic representations of the data that are easy to maintain and are comprehensible to parents. Using our math example, CBM probes might comprise 25 items that draw on a range of skills expected to be mastered during the year (e.g., one, two, and three place-value addition and subtraction, with and without regrouping). Student progress with subskills and holistic applications will be demonstrated by an increase in the number of correct items or correct steps per item.

A number of studies indicate that CBMs demonstrate good reliability and validity as measures of ongoing student learning (Hosp, Hosp, & Howell 2016; Christ, White, Ardoin, & Eckert, 2013). CBMs also tend to be quality indicators of student performance on certain high-stakes reading assessments (McGlinchey & Hixson, 2004). Additional research is needed, however, in areas related to CLD learners and the contexts of their instruction. It seems reasonable, for example, that CLD students learning to read in their primary language will demonstrate a different slope of skill mastery than those who receive either highly accommodated or essentially unaccommodated instruction that is delivered only in English. CBMs can also be used to determine when students schooled in their first language (L1) have developed sufficient native language skills to support the transition to English academic instruction, and to monitor the progress of CLD students on reintegration or designation into grade-level education classrooms (Harper-Young, 2018).

Because CBMs provide consistent curriculum-based feedback on student progress, these assessments are useful to classroom teachers as they determine the effectiveness of their curriculum-based instructional accommodations for CLD students. Teachers who reflect on and self-monitor their use of CBMs tend to demonstrate a noticeably broader range of instructional modifications than those who do not self-monitor or those who do not use CBMs. Self-monitoring of CBM use has also been correlated with significantly greater student progress (Neuenschwander, Röthlisberger, Cimeli, & Roebers, 2012).

---

assessment FREEZE FRAME 6.4

Instead of measuring the mastery of incremental steps to an academic goal, CBMs repeatedly sample global skills from which a growing mastery of subskills can be inferred.

Self-Assessment In most classrooms, teachers continue to be primarily responsible for rating and evaluating student work. Traditional grading systems are supported for a variety of reasons, which include simple formats for informing parents and the presumed capacity to motivate students. Grade-oriented learning environments, however, can be detrimental to student learning if the grades are considered as the ultimate goal. When grades are not viewed as another means of finding what students are capable of doing, then we risk students seeing themselves in a particular category of grades (e.g., "I'm a C student."), at which point it tends to be difficult for them to envision a different reality. In grade-oriented classrooms, less attention is typically paid to the process, or construction, of learning than to the result (the quality of which is generally determined by someone other than the learner). For many CLD students, such practices reinforce an external locus of control and further reduce their sense of self-efficacy in learning.

The promise of *self-assessment* extends well beyond the ability to provide information about achievement. Through self-assessment, students are guided to reach deeper levels of personal thinking and learning. The goal for students is to develop metacognitive skills, which enable them to be reflective about their own thinking, and to approach learning with a growth mindset (Zubrzycki, 2015).

Self-evaluation systems engage students in their learning and foster relationships with teachers as mentors and guides rather than as omnipotent evaluators. In our efforts to promote self-assessment in the classroom, it is important to help students gain a clear and precise understanding of the learning objectives and outcomes. Expectations might be explained in the form of rubrics with examples, delineation of specific skills, discussion of criteria, or the ideal of a real-world application. Although it is always important for students to understand how they will be assessed, there is significant data suggesting that practicing self-assessment according to such criteria leads to improved academic learning and performance (Dearnley & Meddings, 2007).

Self-assessment charts or graphs can function in a variety of ways depending on grade level and content. Simple formats, such as the one depicted in Figure 6.6, might involve listing tasks, skill competencies, or knowledge areas along one axis and descriptors of comfort or success along the other. These descriptors might correlate directly with objective indices of mastery, such as percentage correct in multiplication tables (ones, twos, threes, etc.), qualitative terminology (e.g., lost, uncomfortable, getting it, comfortable, super), or pictorial representations (e.g., sad, confused, curious, or happy faces; red, yellow, or green stoplights) (Wiliam, 2004). Students are taught to plot and recognize their own progress as they assess themselves along targeted parameters of learning. As with other forms of assessment, it is important to emphasize what has been accomplished and to promote the mutual discussion of ways to address what has not. Innovative educators might also elect to model self-assessment of their own learning of curricular material or a recently undertaken hobby.

Technology can be a great aid for students as they focus on their growth. Technology initiatives and access to computers and tablets have provided teachers with additional means to tailor electronic learning programs according to students' levels and needs. Programs that incorporate data tracking and visual graphs allow students to see how their performance has changed over the course of time. When students complete additional types of assessment, the results can be uploaded on the same devices to provide learners with a cumulative picture of their own performance. Having continuous access to data and associated performance tasks

Figure 6.6   Assessment Artifact: Self-Assessment Rubric

Literature Circle Presentation Preparation
Self-Assessment Rubric

Student Name:
Title of Book:

Presentation Preparation Activities	Please circle the most appropriate response to each statement. 1 = Never 4 = Frequently 2 = Rarely 5 = Always 3 = Sometimes				
1. I came to group meetings prepared (on time and ready to make an honest effort to understand the material).	1	2	3	4	5
2. I willingly read from the book when it was my turn.	1	2	3	4	5
3. I actively participated in discussions.	1	2	3	4	5
4. I listened attentively while members shared thoughts.	1	2	3	4	5
5. I respected the ideas and opinions of other members.	1	2	3	4	5
6. I helped my group discuss the general questions.	1	2	3	4	5
7. I helped discuss the questions specific to our book.	1	2	3	4	5
8. I identified at least one question that needed to be addressed.	1	2	3	4	5
9. I helped define presentation responsibilities.	1	2	3	4	5
10. I prepared for my presentation responsibilities (gathered materials, rehearsed part, asked for advice when necessary, etc.).	1	2	3	4	5

With which group members did you work most effectively?

Additional Comments:

ACCOMMODATIVE ASSESSMENT PRACTICES 6.3

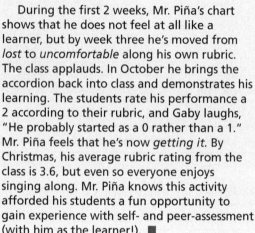

Mr. Piña decided to model self-assessment by using his experiences with playing an accordion. He shares with the class that he has always wanted to learn how to play the accordion and that he recently found one at a garage sale. His 5th-grade class is intrigued by the accordion's buttons and bellows but oddly surprised at Mr. Piña's inability to produce anything that sounds like music. Carla volunteers that her uncle plays the accordion, and he agrees to give Mr. Piña lessons.

The students are doubtful that Mr. Piña will learn to play a song by Christmas. He posts a small chart on the wall on which he will plot how he feels each week about his progress (i.e., lost, uncomfortable, getting it, comfortable, or super). The students want to be involved too, so together they develop their own additional rubric to rate his eventual success:

1. No one can recognize the song.
2. A few recognize the song; there are too many errors; it is way too slow or fast.
3. Many recognize the song; there are some errors; it is a little too slow or fast.
4. Nearly everyone recognizes the song and can sing along.

During the first 2 weeks, Mr. Piña's chart shows that he does not feel at all like a learner, but by week three he's moved from *lost* to *uncomfortable* along his own rubric. The class applauds. In October he brings the accordion back into class and demonstrates his learning. The students rate his performance a 2 according to their rubric, and Gaby laughs, "He probably started as a 0 rather than a 1." Mr. Piña feels that he's now *getting it*. By Christmas, his average rubric rating from the class is 3.6, but even so everyone enjoys singing along. Mr. Piña knows this activity afforded his students a fun opportunity to gain experience with self- and peer-assessment (with him as the learner!). ■

promotes ongoing self-reflection among students related to their learning processes and performances.

As one might expect, both teachers and students need targeted support in becoming adept at using self-assessment to advance classroom learning effectively (Brown & Harris, 2014). The format of self-assessment tasks must be developmentally appropriate and geared toward eliciting the kinds of thinking that promote learning and future application of insights gained. Providing opportunities for students to justify their self-evaluation, for example, challenges them to engage in sophisticated thinking about criteria and their own performance (Brown & Harris, 2014). Brown and Harris also make clear that teacher feedback about the results of self-assessments are instrumental to students' growth in their ability to realistically assess their learning efforts.

Technology-Supported Assessment   Today technology drives our society. In addition to technological applications for everything from household management to entertainment and citizenship (news, consumerism, voting), technology is also uniquely suited to meet some of the critical needs of CLD learners. Carefully chosen technologies can facilitate the CLD student's comprehension and demonstration of content-area learning by providing:

1. Access to native language supports or resources that enhance student comprehension
2. Contextual supports such as pictures, videos, and audio clips, as well as more authentic learning opportunities through simulations and so forth

3. One-on-one instruction that provides immediate feedback at the student's learning level
4. Programmed adjustment of content and complexity that adapts to student responses, scaffolds new knowledge, and engenders a sense of success
5. Added dimensions to cooperative and project-based learning activities, including access to and communication with outside resources
6. Opportunities to access and enhance higher-order thinking skills as the student connects new and prior learning through self-directed inquiry

Technological applications can augment our repertoire of performance and project-based assessments, but they also offer a range of modifications to more traditional tests that were not previously possible or practical for the typical teacher. Some programs allow teachers or students to choose the assessment design, modifications, and response format that is most likely to yield valid information about students' abilities in content areas. Options may include audio presentation, verbal or written response, L1 translation, use of bilingual online dictionaries, extended time, and so forth. For many teachers, these modifications are actually easier to provide via technology than through adaptations, materials, or personnel currently available to them on site.

A strength of *technology-supported assessments* is that they can be designed (or purchased with the design) to respond dynamically to the performance patterns of a single student. For example, computer-assisted tests (CATs) are now available to differentially assess students who are performing above or below assigned grade level on their mastery of targeted knowledge and skills. These assessments are structured so that items answered correctly are followed by more complex or difficult prompts, whereas those answered in error lead to more simplified branches of the material or content. This reduces the number of unnecessary items and provides generally equivalent data in far less time. If the overall pool of test items is large, students are unlikely to take the same test twice. Therefore, CATs usually can be readministered more frequently than traditional forms of standardized assessment (Van Horn, 2003).

When considering the use of technology-supported assessments, recommendations (Chien, Wu, & Hsu, 2014; Salend, 2005, 2009b) include:

1. Scrutinize items or the structure of assessments for cultural or linguistic bias.
2. Carefully evaluate tools for language demands that may unfairly affect the CLD student's demonstration of knowledge and skills.
3. Consider student familiarity and comfort with technology in general when determining the appropriateness of use.
4. Think about the extent to which the format precludes accommodations (e.g., highlighting) that may be particularly relevant and useful for the CLD student.

The Internet can also provide innovative opportunities for our work with CLD students and families (Kingsley & Tancock, 2014; Salend, 2005) that include, but certainly are not limited to:

- Ongoing assessment formats such as electronic portfolios and interactive journals
- Teacher-made assessments to be used as self-assessments and point-in-time measures (www.funbrain.com; www.quia.com)

SNAPSHOT from *CLASSROOM PRACTICE* 6.3

In this middle school science classroom, students use textbooks and the Internet as resources to create a PowerPoint on the Precambrian era. The students were provided a rubric listing the requirements that were expected within their presentations.

- Test-taking resources, practice tests, or computer-assisted tests (www.edutest .com; www.homeroom.com)
- Resources for creating, designing, and interpreting surveys
- Online web pages to inform parents and students about assignments, deadlines, and instructional goals
- Electronic mail to inform parents of grades, absences, concerns, celebrations, and accomplishments. (*Note:* These should be scrutinized for cross-cultural sensitivity and cross-linguistic comprehensibility.)

When use of the Internet is involved in any aspect of instruction or assessment, responsible teachers address the need for students to understand issues of digital citizenship, which include plagiarism, acceptable access, and general matters of e-conduct.

Formal Formative Assessment

Formal assessments encompass more than the periodic high-stakes assessments that tend to dominate conversations in staff meetings and lounges. Like informal assessments, formal assessments are tools that teachers can use effectively to gather data about instruction and learning in their classrooms. This data can be used to diagnose learning needs, monitor progress, and provide students and families with timely feedback (Research for Better Teaching, 2016).

Teachers may consider their high-stakes "look-alike" tests as formal formative assessments, but many districts identify formal formative assessments as the centrally developed or adopted tools used as a barometer of student learning across settings such as classes, schools, or districts. Such assessments include (a) norm-referenced or criterion-referenced tests designed for (or permitting) periodic update, (b) formal assessments that accompany a standardized program of instruction (e.g., Scholastic Reading Inventory [SRI]), (c) assessments that are part of district curricular units, and (d) some assessments that are facilitated by computer (e.g., Advantage Learning, FastBridge Learning: Curriculum Based Measurements, Measures of Academic Progress [MAP], Standardized Testing and Reporting [STAR]).

Formal Formative Assessments as Norm-Referenced and Criterion-Referenced Tests   This section of the chapter discusses those formal formative assessments that are specifically applicable to classroom teachers of CLD students. *Norm-referenced tests* and *criterion-referenced tests* are each useful as formal formative assessments. The differences between these two kinds of tests largely reflect their purposes and the way resulting scores are interpreted (Boehm, 1973; Bond, 1996; Brown, 2014). Norm-referenced assessments are designed and used to measure differences among students. Items mastered or failed by a majority are discarded in favor of those deemed most likely to distinguish among test takers. Often this results in a test with fewer, more heavily weighted items per skill. On the other hand, criterion-referenced tests provide information on the acquisition or demonstration of selected components and target instructional skills among students *without* regard to the relationship between one student's performance and the achievement of others.

In general, reliance on tests that sample skills through a limited number of items is less informative to our teaching than is the use of assessments that include multiple opportunities to probe or elicit demonstration of content-area knowledge. If the primary purpose of formative assessment is to enlighten our understanding of how well a student is learning (and how well the teacher is teaching) the targeted material, there may be particular merit in using criterion-referenced rather than norm-referenced assessments of content-area learning. Regardless of the type used, the assessment should measure what we intend to measure and provide reliable information that is useful. Well-designed criterion-referenced tests not only provide formal formative information about student mastery of specified skills but also give us insight into the levels of prerequisite knowledge necessary to perform the tasks.

assessment **FREEZE FRAME 6.5**
In general, reliance on tests that sample skills through a limited number of items is less informative to our teaching than is the use of assessments that include multiple opportunities to probe or elicit demonstration of content-area knowledge.

Commercially Produced Assessments   The growing population of CLD students in public schools has resulted in an expanding market for assessment tools that aid our understanding of these students and enhance our ability to assess their learning. Marketed tests or *commercially produced assessments* can be very attractive because the majority offer formative numerical indices of student skills, and some are developed for use in other languages. A sole reliance on such tests in the belief that they allow us to easily identify and address discrete areas of student need can result, however, in inappropriate placement and instructional practices for CLD students. Readers are cautioned to review discussions in Chapter 5 regarding the validity of any "normed" tests for diverse populations. Used wisely, however, some of these tools can indeed provide auxiliary pieces of information that may augment a school's more authentic and dynamic picture of student progress in content-area learning.

The Snapshot Assessment System (Rangel & Bansberg, 1999) is an example of a marketed tool that can be used to ascertain information about the content-area learning of CLD students. It is designed to assess the student's related knowledge in Spanish or English but can be administered as a formal formative assessment by teachers who speak only English. In roughly 20 minutes, reading, writing, science, and math can be sampled sufficiently to obtain an overview of a student's L1 or L2 knowledge and skills in core academic areas. One reason the Snapshot is popular among classroom teachers is that it does not simply compare CLD students with an artificial norm to derive a statistic that does little to inform instruction. Instead, this assessment provides tangible evidence of standards-based skills to aid the teacher in developing appropriate instructional plans (see Chapter 3 for additional details).

Dynamic Indicators of Basic Early Literacy Skills (DIBELS) (Good & Kaminski, 2002) is a reading assessment developed to assess K–6 students on the acquisition of literacy skills. The test is designed to measure the National Reading Panel's Five Big Ideas of early literacy: phonological awareness, alphabetic principle, fluency, vocabulary, and comprehension. The tests are short (1-minute) assessments that assist teachers in monitoring the development of students' reading skills. As with any assessment, using DIBELS with CLD learners has advantages and disadvantages. Benefits of DIBELS include the following:

- The test is given to individual learners, thereby making it a convenient screener for students' literacy skills.
- The test can be administered quickly.
- The assessment can serve as one tool for data-driven decisions about the needs of students.

Potential drawbacks to DIBELS with CLD students include the following:

- The timed part of the test (5–7 minutes per student) is sometimes not enough to create a true picture of a student's needs.
- The resulting scores on the test often simply do not provide enough information for teachers to determine students' skills fully.
- The pictures used within the test can create cultural bias for students from different cultures.
- English learners may inadvertently be counted off for using their understanding of the sounds in their native language, especially during administration of the Initial Sound Fluency (ISF) subtest.
- The Nonsense Words Fluency (NSF) subtest can be very confusing for English learners who are still in the initial stages of language development.
- Inordinate emphasis might be placed on results, given limitations of the assessment (e.g., limited predictive ability of Grade 1 Letter Naming Fluency (LNF), Phoneme Segmentation Fluency (PSF), and Nonsense Words Fluency (NSF) subtests for students' achievement beyond Oral Reading Fluency (ORF) performance [Goffreda & DiPerna, 2010]).

AIMSweb (2000) is an assessment, reporting, and data management system commonly used in response to intervention (RTI) or tiered instruction (see Chapter 7 for additional details about these types of data-informed programming). AIMSweb provides very brief (most are 1 to 4 minutes) assessments of reading, math, spelling, and writing that can be generalized to overall academic performance and used for screening/benchmarking and progress monitoring. English and Spanish versions are available. AIMSweb includes an ELL Profile that supports educators to:

- Identify English learners whose academic issues are broader than simply their level of language proficiency
- Establish expectations and goals for individual learners, based on their profiles
- Consider recommendations for instruction and connections to other academic outcomes

The most current version, aimswebPlus (2017), includes tools to screen for dyslexia and behavior/emotional challenges.

Interpreting Assessment Results   In all cases, the usefulness of assessment data hinges on our ability to interpret the results knowledgeably. When teachers are familiar with the formats, implications, and limitations of assessments, they can begin to identify factors in results that lead them to further examine the source of the data or individual student variables before determining success or failure of student learning. Questions to consider include the following:

- Where and how is the content of the assessment represented in the school's curriculum?
- Have the skills and concepts assessed been taught in a comprehensible manner?
- Is there classroom evidence of content learning that contradicts the results of the assessment? If so, why do the discrepancies exist?
- Were sufficient assessment accommodations provided to mediate the linguistic complexity of the assessment?
- How might a student's level of acculturation or task familiarity have affected her or his performance on the assessment?

The answers to these questions should prove extremely informative, especially when combined with knowledge of language acquisition processes and an awareness of the sociocultural contexts of the instruction and assessment being examined. Although necessary for accountability and statistical applications, formal assessments can and should coexist effectively with ongoing informal assessment processes.

SUMMATIVE CONTENT-AREA ASSESSMENT

Summative content-area assessments are designed to measure student understanding following a sustained period of instruction or participation in a series of instructional sequences. Since *summative assessments* are higher-stakes than formative assessments, it is critical to ensure that the assessment aligns with the goals and objectives of instruction. As previously noted, the results we gain from formative assessments inform us of our students' strengths, needs, and gaps so that we can accommodate them strategically and consistently. With such support, we increase the likelihood that students will be able to perform on summative assessments in ways that more accurately reflect their individual potentials.

Summative assessments emphasize the level of student mastery attained and the efficacy of instruction or schooling patterns. From a student perspective, summative assessments are about quantifying performance and determining either grades or sufficient performance to pass to the next level of education or career. From an educator perspective, summative assessments can be used to refine instruction but are more often associated with issues of accountability. From a policy perspective, summative assessments of content-area learning are increasingly about politics, accountability, and rationales for funding decisions.

Informal Summative Assessment: Portfolios as Authentic Assessments

Student assessment portfolios can be used for either formative or summative purposes. As Masters (2013) explains, "When assembled over a period of time, portfolios can provide a valid basis for establishing current levels of achievement and for monitoring progress over time" (p. 38). Summative portfolios focus on learning outcomes and provide evidence of the range and extent of a student's skills and knowledge in the content areas. According to Davis and Ponnamperuma (2005), portfolio assessment can be organized to include the following stages:

1. Students collect evidence to demonstrate attainment of learning outcomes.
2. Students reflect on learning.
3. Teachers evaluate evidence.
4. Students defend evidence (especially in the cases of struggling or borderline students).
5. Teachers arrive at the assessment decision.

In order for portfolios to best showcase student learning, students and teachers may decide to build a portfolio around a combination of teacher assessments and student self-assessments and products that reflect both the process of learning and final outcomes. This type of portfolio development encourages students to take ownership over their learning, as discussed in Chapter 2. The best competency-based portfolios are developed in this manner and emphasize both the student's self-directedness in skill development and self-assessment and the effectiveness of the teacher's instruction. Because a single item of evidence may be applicable to more than one performance indicator or learning outcome, it is often necessary for the teacher to develop an appropriate cross-referencing system for the student portfolio. In some cases, commentary or a caption may also be needed to explain the relevance of an item of evidence.

Formal Summative Assessment: High-Stakes Tests

Formal summative assessments of content-area learning are increasingly at the heart of school reform and educational funding debates as well as educator account-ability arguments. Because the outcomes or results of these assessments have rami-fications for the future education, careers, and life paths of students, such assessments are now synonymous with terms such as *high-stakes tests*. Now more than ever, teachers live and breathe the air of high-stakes tests. It permeates their planning, instruction, and relationships with students and their feelings about their careers. In many places, the results of these tests hold stakes that are just as high for teachers as they are for students and schools. This emphasis on scores has actu-ally prompted some teachers to intentionally disregard administration protocol or to directly teach to the test (Goodnough, 1999; "Under pressure," 2010). The more common response, however, is to focus more intensely on skills and drills in prepa-ration for these tests.

Although such a narrow focus of instruction on the content and constructs of the test has some degree of merit, triangulated studies (e.g., Amrein & Berliner, 2002; Volante, 2004) suggest that the possibility of detrimental trade-offs is high, and that such trade-offs often result in reductionist, skills-bound learning; inability of students to demonstrate higher-order thinking; and low student motivation. These effects have been noted by other researchers as well who contest the predic-tive ability of standardized tests and their power to provide informative data about actual student learning (e.g., Burger & Krueger, 2003).

What, then, can teachers do to promote the success of CLD students on high-stakes tests? First, effective educators recognize the power of both formative and summative assessments to guide them as they facilitate students' construction of knowledge. Second, these teachers strive to:

1. Align their learning goals with state and local standards
2. Define and describe the desired academic outcomes, so that they are transparent for students
3. Ensure the equitable access of *all* students to educational content and learning opportunities
4. Interpret and respond knowledgeably to student learning behaviors in context (which oftentimes means reevaluating instructional practices)
5. Ensure that students enter testing situations with the tools necessary to reduce their affective filters and maximize their performances (e.g., test-taking strategies and skills, experience with modifications, confidence)

Teachers who make these actions part of their daily practices actively promote the classroom engagement and academic success of CLD students. Students who are thus engaged and successful in their learning are, in turn, increasingly self-motivated and prepared to demonstrate their skills and knowledge on high-stakes tests.

THE ROLE OF LANGUAGE IN CONTENT-AREA ASSESSMENT

Mr. Loucks, a 5th-grade teacher, understands the potential benefits of allowing CLD students to use their native language to demonstrate academic capacities. He reflects on his instructional practices to enhance the writing skills of one particular Spanish-speaking student. (For purposes of anonymity, the student's name has been changed to Enrique.)

The practice of having one of my ELL students occasionally complete his Weekend Write-up in Spanish was a highlight for both him and the class. At the beginning Enrique was not a willing writer. When I asked him to write about his weekend, I'd get maybe two or three sentences at best. As time progressed, I realized that Enrique indeed was a fairly fluent writer in Spanish, his L1. Although at first he was hesitant to write in much detail in Spanish, his writing really blossomed when I allowed him to share his writing with the class. Probably the highlight for Enrique and the class was the time I made an overhead transparency of what he was reading and they could follow along. Not only was this an opportunity for my class to realize that it was indeed a gift to be bilingual, but it also helped them realize that there were things they didn't know—like Spanish. Enrique's credibility in the class skyrocketed when he started sharing and claiming his Spanish language, instead of trying to hide it.

As time went on, Enrique's writing continued to flourish. That isn't to say it was perfect. As you can see [referring to a student writing sample] . . . Enrique didn't believe in punctuation. ☺ This was a continual struggle for him. Once he got writing, he wanted to just write, not punctuate. I know he still struggles with this in 6th grade, but at least he was writing. I'd rather allow him to be fluent in writing his L1 than be so preoccupied with the mechanics that he loses his interest in writing.

Enrique was also allowed to write his State Writing Assessment in Spanish. . . . We had already started our first day of prewriting during the State Assessment when Enrique approached me and wanted to know if he could write in Spanish.

When I asked him why he wanted to do this, he said it was because he could do a better job in Spanish. Our curriculum director called the . . . [State] Department of Education and was told that as long as there was a qualified scorer available, Enrique could write in Spanish. As you might suspect, Enrique got hammered in Conventions and Fluency, but scored well in Ideas and Content, Organization, and fair in Voice and Word Choice.

Mr. Loucks recognized that his accommodative classroom practices were pivotal in the appropriate assessment of this student. Because he had previously allowed Enrique to write in his native language, Mr. Loucks saw the validity of Enrique's request to complete the state writing assessment in Spanish.

Cross-culturally competent teachers such as Mr. Loucks advocate on behalf of CLD students for assessment accommodations that enable these students to best demonstrate their abilities. Teachers and administrators who share an inclusive vision of student learning understand that the purpose of assessment, at all levels, is to inform and guide the instruction of students. This can occur only when the manner and the content of student instruction and assessment are aligned. Many schools and districts unfortunately opt to "prepare" their CLD students for high-stakes tests in English by denying them appropriately accommodated classroom opportunities to learn. Students are not allowed to demonstrate their learning through the native language or through modified instructional techniques and assessments. These *un*accommodative practices significantly compromise not only the education of CLD students but also the ability of teachers to understand and differentially respond to their learning processes.

Validity issues arise when linguistic and presentation modifications that were not used during instruction are then used to assess CLD learning on high-stakes tests. For example, most schools and districts that attempt to accommodate students' first language needs either use personnel of varying qualifications to provide written or verbal translation or purchase marketed translations of English-based tests. However, simply translating tests from English to the student's native language does not significantly improve performance unless the student actually received instruction in his or her native language. This concern holds true even for tests (e.g., Supera, Logramos, Aprenda, SABE, Woodcock-Muñoz) that are designed for use with specific CLD populations. If students have not been exposed to the content-area curriculum in their native language or do not possess sufficient literacy skills in the native language, the tests will not yield valid results (Abedi, 2001; Abedi, Lord, & Hoffstetter, 1998; August & Hakuta, 1997; Turkan & Oliveri, 2014).

Because a large number of languages spoken by CLD students cannot be supported by existing materials or testing personnel, and because the majority of CLD students in this country receive their academic instruction in English, it becomes more appropriate for many students to be assessed in English, their nondominant language. For others, the decision is systemic rather than individualized. In either case, however, one must thoroughly consider the impact that language may have on a CLD student's capacity to comprehend what is being asked and to demonstrate acquired knowledge by means of language-loaded assessment formats.

To reduce test anxiety and provide CLD students with appropriate language support, Mr. Wille synthesized the input

---

assessment FREEZE FRAME 6.6

Cross-culturally competent teachers advocate on behalf of CLD students for assessment accommodations that enable these students to best demonstrate their abilities.

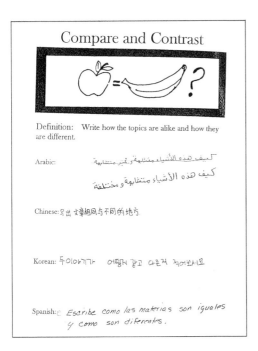

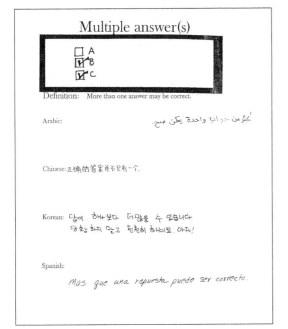

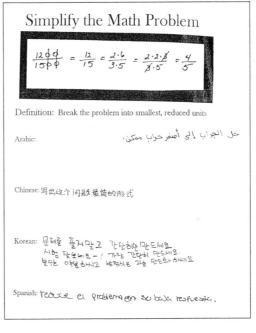

Figure 6.7   Assessment Artifact: Test Vocabulary Handbook

Source: Gale Wille. Reprinted by permission.

of fellow teachers to create a test vocabulary handbook, an excerpt of which is pictured in Figure 6.7. The teachers identified vocabulary terms and phrases frequently found in the instructions of standardized tests. Then they provided an explanation for the testing vocabulary as well as a visual to enhance comprehensibility. The definitions were translated into Arabic, Chinese, Korean, and Spanish. This tool enabled teachers within the school system to use consistent testing language as they prepared students to take standardized assessments. The handbook was beneficial for *all* students because the instructions were simple and precise. The testing language the students used during classroom instruction was the same language they encountered in formal assessment.

BIAS IN CLASSROOM-BASED CONTENT-AREA ASSESSMENTS

As she reviewed her students' scores on a district math assessment, a Kansas teacher was mystified about why so many of her CLD students did poorly on a particular item. The question involved having the students calculate how many checkerboards would be needed for a given number of students to play checkers. Students were required to show their work in mathematical and pictorial form. To her surprise, the teacher noted that most of the CLD students depicted three to four students at a game. Although their related calculations were correct, the students' answers were graded as incorrect. According to the teacher:

> Even though this test question was about something as insignificant as checkers, it served to separate the "haves" from the "have-nots" and the "knows" from the "know-nots," but not in the area of math. To me this is just a tiny example of how entire groups of people can be held back, be it inadvertently or intentionally.

> *Source:* LuAnna Peck. Reprinted by permission.

As this example demonstrates, test items that require cultural knowledge as well as content-area knowledge may hinder appropriate interpretation of assessment results. This scenario also illustrates that bias is not always easy to recognize. The absolute certainty with which we contend that our views and experiences are universal becomes especially problematic when we consider issues of assessment.

Although it is a recognized concern that tests designed for large groups of students must be scrutinized in terms of their appropriateness for all students, similar biases may also exist in teacher-made tests. In the following excerpt, Principal Richard Wirtz poses questions as he reflects on his role as an assessment leader:

> When assessments are designed to test content or prior knowledge, are they free from cultural bias? Do I plan staff development that considers assessment training? Are examples of test items shared that display test bias and some that don't? Do I outline the requirements that make up quality test items . . . guidelines . . . if you will? Are teachers expected to reflect on questions they should ask themselves before attempting to write test items that display cognitive skills without compromising the background of the student?

> *Source:* Principal Richard Wirtz. Reprinted by permission.

These are excellent questions. Effective leaders involve staff in ongoing professional development, discussion, and reflection related to assessment. They directly address and share examples of unwitting bias in tests. They recommend guiding questions for teachers to consider as they work to reduce bias in their assessments. It is difficult to produce test items and tasks that are equally free of bias for all students in today's diverse classrooms. However, our objective in all cases is to identify and rectify, to the greatest extent possible, controllable elements of bias in our assessment tools and procedures.

In reality, a potential for bias exists in all forms of assessment. In some classes, particular students may be perceived as more capable or diligent based on factors such as race, language proficiency, dialect, affiliations, or the teacher's previous experience with similar or related students. Teachers may inadvertently provide differing amounts of support and feedback during ongoing assessments such as portfolios, or allow unrelated opinions or political concerns to influence their subjective ratings of student work. Differences in language, past experiences (personal and educational), sociocultural precepts, and approaches to novel tasks may continue to obstruct the access of CLD students to the learning goals of traditionally designed projects or multimodal activities (Cramer & Bennett, 2015). Although these types of issues can cloud or corrupt the validity of nonstandardized assessments, the capacity of such assessments to influence student learning positively and contribute significantly to what we know about how students learn compels us to improve our control of bias rather than diminish the role of these valuable tools.

The following questions may help educators identify bias within a variety of assessment tools and approaches (Hamayan & Damico, 1991; Ovando & Combs, 2018):

1. Is the content of the assessment linked to known student experiences?
2. Does the assessment take into account the impact of prior school experiences?
3. Have cultural values and practices (e.g., cooperation versus competition, role of time) been considered for their impact on student responses?
4. Is the task appropriate to the developmental level(s) of the students?
5. Have the language demands of the task been adjusted for the language proficiency level(s) of the students?
6. What are the prerequisite skills or knowledge assumed by the task?
   * Are they related to the target being measured?
   * If not, are they known (not assumed) to be familiar to the students?
7. Are the criteria for responses or goal attainment clearly defined?
8. Are assessment accommodations employed during assessment consistent with those used during content-area instruction?
9. Has the assessment process and product been reviewed by others for sources of potential bias?
10. How has rater and inter-rater reliability been addressed (e.g., "blind" grading and exchanges)?

Some teachers who have begun to embrace the promise of better assessment practices now ask, "Will an increase in authenticity and reduction of bias in assessments result in higher demonstrated achievement of CLD students?" The answer is, "Not necessarily . . . but they certainly can." Because the goal of content-area assessment is to measure academic learning, effective assessment practices simply provide a clearer picture of instructional efficacy with a given student or group. Students who are not receiving accommodative instruction that fosters engaged participation in the curriculum will continue to perform poorly. If bias and inequity are not recognized at the instructional level, even the least biased assessments will yield inherently biased results.

---

assessment FREEZE FRAME 6.7

If bias and inequity are not recognized at the instructional level, even the least biased assessments will yield inherently biased results.

USING CONTENT-BASED ASSESSMENT INFORMATION TO INFORM INSTRUCTION

At this point, teachers may be thinking, "Strategies for authentic assessment are all well and good, but what about the grade? How do I determine a grade for CLD students' content-area learning?" This question is one of the most common asked by educators who must document a letter or percentage grade for all students in the classroom. Ultimately, teachers are responsible for reporting whether a student has met the goals set by the curriculum and guiding standards.

Our education system has a history of limiting teachers' views of grading and hindering the potential of the reported results to enhance the student's motivation to engage, aspire, and take risks during learning endeavors. So much is determined by policies that reflect the unquestioned values, norms, and traditions that have been part of school systems for decades. Grading systems were decided long before changing demographics and diversity in classrooms became the norm rather than the exception. It is beyond the scope of this chapter to address the many complexities of fairness issues and the grading policies of school districts across the United States. Instead, the focus of this section is on the need to (1) assess the extent to which students achieved the intended objectives of the lesson/unit/class, and (2) document progress in student motivation, engagement, thinking processes, and social collaboration toward academic achievement and linguistic development.

Effective teachers use assessment results to support future learning and to inform them about appropriate accommodations for the student population served. They move beyond fixating on a grade and the grading system—a system that conveys limited (superficial versus deep) information about the knowledge and skills that were learned and the degree to which they were learned. Rather, reflective teachers are concerned with *understanding* in assessment. Such teachers strive to determine how well students were able to:

- Construct meaning from the unknown
- Incorporate new content and concepts into their preexisting foundations of knowledge
- Build new skills that transcend the content areas
- Collaborate with diverse peers to share, learn, and articulate new information

At first glance, this alternative perspective on appropriate postinstructional assessment may appear to rely on a comparatively subjective foundation. However, this perspective does not eliminate the need to plan for the assignment of a less subjective grade that can be shared with parents and policymakers. Rather, it asks that educators consider ways to provide multiple and varied opportunities for CLD students to enhance their linguistic, academic, cognitive, and sociocultural skills and knowledge *before* using the norms of the grade level to assign a permanent grade. Only through authentic learning experiences and activities, opportunities for student practice, and ongoing process-focused assessments can a teacher appropriately scaffold instruction and provide timely feedback to enhance the product focus of grade-level-appropriate achievement and learning.

As educators embark on the journey toward equitable decisions about grading and the CLD student, they consider the multitude of variables concerning the learner's growth and achievement that might be shared with students, parents, future teachers, and administrators. They also determine the subset of variables they will use to make decisions about the student's grade. The following questions can guide a teacher's decisions about what to include in the final grade for a lesson or unit:

- What are the objectives of this lesson or unit regarding both knowledge (content/concepts) and language (listening, speaking, reading, and writing) skills?
- Will percentage or symbol grades be given to indicate achievement of the selected objectives?
- What are the purposes of the grades or observations that will be recorded?
- In what ways will opportunities for practice and feedback (to assess progress and growth incrementally) be provided?
- Which activities will be assigned a grade for product assessment, and which activities will be used as process assessments to ensure ongoing progress?
- Will there be a homework grade?
- Will there be a cooperative learning grade?
- What checklists, rubrics, or anecdotal notes will be used to document progress and achievement?
- What weight will be given to each piece of the final reported achievement score?

The following additional questions can guide decisions about a student's final grade for the instructional term or year:

- What information will be used to calculate the final grade?
- Will the grade be an absolute measure of achievement?
- Will the grade be reflective of linguistic, academic, cognitive, and sociocultural aspects of learning and academic performance?
- Will some aspects of the practice and application be weighted more than others?
- What roles will attitude, motivation, and cooperation play in the final grade?

Among classroom teachers of CLD students, the assignment of final grades should reflect thorough consideration of these and related questions. Above all, teachers should reflect on whether the assessments used, and grades assigned, provide a multifaceted picture of the potential that CLD students are capable of demonstrating.

PROGRAMMING-RELATED ISSUES: CONTENT-AREA ASSESSMENT

Issues of placement and programming for English learners are topics beyond the scope of this text. Nonetheless, the results of assessing content-area skills and knowledge can aid decision making associated with these issues. The following discussion highlights grade-level issues of content-area assessment that are relevant to the identification, placement, monitoring, and exit of CLD students. This discussion is by no means exhaustive but provides a synopsis of issues that should be considered.

Identification

Ideally, the identification of CLD students for differential instruction is not based solely on a single measure or limited sampling of literacy domains (listening, speaking, reading, and writing). Within each of these domains are innumerable factors that render otherwise identical scores fundamentally nonequivalent. Many protocols for identifying CLD students who are not yet proficient in English gather little, if any, information about content-area knowledge and skills. However, the determination of whether students have a history of prior L1 education or have been exposed to cognitively rich experiences and conversations in L2 is essential to appropriate placement.

Placement

Creative and individualized placement may be needed for CLD students who would benefit in many ways from a newcomer program but who have skills that would not be capitalized on in this environment. Unfortunately, it is common to discover CLD students placed, for example, in remedial math despite mastery of calculus in a prior country or setting. Teachers are encouraged to discover the facets of each student's learning background that expose strengths or resources that can be drawn on in accommodative classrooms.

Monitoring

Ongoing and varied formative assessments provide teachers with (a) information needed to monitor and document student progress, (b) input for appropriate instructional modifications, (c) indicators that a student may need enhanced levels of differential support, and (d) evidence of a student's readiness for redesignation. Unless teachers monitor to maintain a comprehensible level of rigor in their instruction, students may become so accustomed to added support that they doubt their abilities to be successful on their own. Therefore, attention to student empowerment and confidence are encouraged at all times but become especially important as readiness for exit approaches.

Exit

Student performance on content-area assignments and assessments are part of the body of evidence necessary to consider a student's redesignation from differential programming designed to support English language acquisition. Teachers are encouraged to review multiple sources of data when making recommendations about the best instructional situation for a CLD student. When educators monitor student learning closely in various contexts, it is generally apparent when a CLD student is ready to be exited from a program. Although subjective input from teachers can be extremely valuable to the process, sometimes teachers are either inclined to underestimate student readiness or desire to shield students from the accommodated experience. Such resistance to redesignation without sufficient (especially data-driven) rationales can inhibit educational opportunities and growth potentials among CLD students.

SUMMARY

This chapter explored the purposes and formats of multiple types of assessments teachers use to gauge CLD students' content-area learning. At the core of the discussion was the need for us to gain a holistic understanding of the knowledge and skills students possess after their engagement in accommodative, standards-based instruction. Teachers have the most control over the strategies they use to support all students to attain the content and language objectives of each lesson. Our caring, responsive interactions with students during the course of instruction and assessment lie at the heart of gathering data that most authentically reflects their current capacities.

Formative content-area assessment makes it possible for teachers to gather data about students' sense-making processes and levels of understanding while learning is still in progress. Informal assessments of this type are tied to teachers' daily instructional practices. Sources of information include inquiry-based learning, observation, structured authentic assessments, teacher-made tests, point-in-time assessments, curriculum-based measurement, student self-assessment, and technology-supported assessments. Formal formative assessment, on the other hand, often involves norm-referenced and criterion-referenced tests. Many districts rely on commercially produced assessments to gather data for use in monitoring students' growth. Results on such measures then can be compared with evidence of learning demonstrated in the classroom.

Summative content-area assessment enables teachers, students, and families to gain a sense of students' achievement at the end of a longer period of time. Portfolios provide educators with a highly adaptable means of authentically assessing students' performance and progress. At the other end of the spectrum, formal high-stakes tests provide students opportunities to demonstrate their knowledge on comprehensive standardized assessments. The efforts of classroom teachers to engage CLD students in critical thinking and cognitively complex tasks (while providing necessary scaffolds), develop learners' test-taking skills and strategies, and continually build students' self-confidence as capable learners, can go a long way to promote their achievement on high-stakes assessments.

The role of language in the content-area assessment of CLD students must always be taken into account. Providing accommodations on high-stakes tests is valid, if students received the same types of accommodations during the original instruction over the concepts, skills, and processes. Students rely on us to provide the supports that make their access to, and engagement with, the curriculum possible. Likewise, they depend on us to advocate on their behalf for the types of accommodations that allow them to demonstrate most accurately what they know and are able to do on high-stakes assessments.

Because we all view content-area curricula and instruction through the lens of our own backgrounds and socialization, it is important to recognize the potential of bias in our classroom-based assessments. Weighing assessments and test items against the knowledge that we have of our students and their unique backgrounds and needs is a necessary step if we are to identify as many potential sources of bias as possible. Asking colleagues to provide an outside opinion also can be beneficial.

Inevitably, teachers working with CLD students are faced with questions about "the grade" for their content-area learning. Holding a perspective that values process as much as product can go a long way in helping us to devise grading criteria that are equitable for students and that result in grades that provide useful information to all stakeholders. Reflecting on the overall purpose of the lesson/unit/class and its various components and target skills can support us to identify possibilities, weigh options, and make well-reasoned decisions.

Content-area assessment also has implications for programming-related issues. The content knowledge and skills that student may have acquired through instruction in the native language must not be ignored. These assets often are overlooked, when the primary emphasis is on identifying students' skills (and gaps) in English. Our goal, as educators, is to provide students with programs and supports that allow students to best maximize their potential. This might require us to think outside the box with respect to placement, continually challenge students with rigorous curriculum and instruction, and seek data that might indicate a students' readiness for redesignation (while acknowledging the need for ongoing monitoring and support).

KEY CONCEPTS

Commercially produced assessment

Criterion-referenced test

Curriculum-based
   measurement (CBM)

Formative assessment

General outcome measurement

High-stakes tests

Inquiry assessment/Inquiry-based
   learning

Mastery measurement

Norm-referenced test

Observation assessment

Point-in-time assessment

Self-assessment

Summative assessment

Teacher-made test

Technology-supported assessment

PROFESSIONAL CONVERSATIONS ON PRACTICE

1. Discuss why formative content-area assessments might be better than summative assessments for accommodating instruction and promoting learning for CLD students.

2. Discuss the purpose of assessment and ways that high-stakes tests are consistent and inconsistent with this purpose.

3. Discuss how bias may be exhibited in classroom-based content-area assessments. What can teachers do to minimize bias?

QUESTIONS FOR REVIEW AND REFLECTION

1. What are key features of effective inquiry assessment? Describe at least two.

2. What tips can support teachers to develop their own informal content-area assessments for CLD students? List at least three.

3. What are the advantages of point-in-time assessments? Discuss at least two.

4. How do mastery and general outcome measurement differ?

5. What general steps should teachers follow as they develop curriculum-based measures (CBMs) of content-area learning?

6. When considering use of technology-supported assessments with CLD students, what benefits and concerns should teachers keep in mind? List at least three benefits and two concerns.

7. What is the difference between criterion-referenced and norm-referenced assessments?

8. When interpreting the results of formal formative assessments, what considerations should teachers bear in mind? List at least three.

9. What assessment-related problems might occur when translating tests from English to a CLD student's native language? Specify at least two.

10. What questions should teachers ask themselves as they reflect on how to assign a grade for CLD students' content-area learning? List at least three.

CHAPTER 7

DATA-DRIVEN PROBLEM-SOLVING PROCESSES

When gauging the successes of our CLD students, we have to look well beyond a score on a standardized test. It is important to take into consideration their experience with their L1 and L2, their confidence with English, and their support system at home as well. It has been beyond valuable to have a data dialogue where all stakeholders can be involved who are invested in the student—classroom teacher, ESOL teacher, intervention teacher, etc. Sometimes that dialogue paints a better picture of a student than a graph full of data. When we know all the factors that influence students on a day-to-day basis, it makes it easier to problem solve and figure out how to meet their needs.

Chelsea Johnson, Elementary Reading Specialist. Reprinted with permission.

Chapter Outline

Response to Intervention
>   What Does RTI Look Like?
>   Tiers (Not Tracks) of Instruction
>   Bringing Focus to the "Data Daze"

Individualizing for CLD Students

Intensified Needs (Few of the Few)

Problem Solving Versus Referral for SPED

Summary

Learning Outcomes

After reading this chapter, you should be able to:

- Detail the purposes and models of Response to Intervention (RTI).
- Gather data needed to inform interpretation of assessment results.
- Hold informed conversations with administrators, colleagues, and parents about tiers of support available to CLD students.
- Engage in problem-solving processes to address student learning needs.

INTRODUCTION

Assessment is a teaching tool, calibrated chiefly by its appropriateness for the intended group and purpose. Effective use of assessments to measure learning requires teachers to understand, and have taught to, the specific skills and knowledge students need to perform each task. But teaching techniques alone cannot ensure that every student will learn what is taught.

Consider the quarterback on a football team. Mere mastery of the physics and execution of the perfect pass cannot guarantee the ball will be caught. Top quarterbacks understand that the health, psychology, prior training, and motivation of their *receivers* factor into each player's ability to perform under particular circumstances. These quarterbacks respond quickly to missed connections by making changes to their delivery, redirecting team supports, and structuring subsequent plays to the receiver's strengths.

Effective teachers are like winning quarterbacks. Their ability to deliver content successfully reflects not only professional mastery but also the degree to which they understand and respond to what each individual student brings to the game. The focus of this chapter is on the power that insights gathered via preinstructional assessment (Chapter 3) have during response to intervention and other data-driven, problem-solving processes. These types of processes are key to the advancement of both the teacher and the student on the field of educational achievement.

RESPONSE TO INTERVENTION

> Response to intervention integrates assessment and intervention within a multilevel prevention system to maximize student achievement and to reduce behavioral problems. With RTI, schools use data to identify students at risk for poor learning outcomes, monitor student progress, provide evidence-based interventions and adjust the intensity and nature of those interventions depending on a student's responsiveness, and identify students with learning disabilities or other disabilities. (National Center on Response to Intervention, 2010, p. 2)
>
> *Source:* National Center on Response to Intervention (March 2010). Essential Components of RTI – A Closer Look at Response to Intervention, p. 2.

Response to intervention (RTI) is a relevant topic of any text that examines the relationship between assessment and instruction. RTI reflects newer perspectives and practices in the way schools identify and respond to students who are not learning as expected within the *core curriculum*, or general instruction provided all students.

Despite these efforts, nationwide data continue to show that far too many capable students are not acquiring the skills necessary for academic success (Aud et al., 2011; IES, 2015). Although some students enter school with a degree of academic disadvantage (Burkam & Lee, 2002; Hart & Risley, 1995, 2005, Weisleder & Fernald, 2013), it benefits educators to examine instances in which exposure to formal instruction *increases* rather than closes the educational gap.

These phenomena are not limited to isolated cases. Indeed, entire groups of students may "fail" when they are provided with poor curriculum or instructional methods. Situations such as these are beyond unfortunate; they violate the educational rights of all students, exceptional and nonexceptional alike. More insidiously, patterns of student (school) failure can reinforce notions that entire groups of students are inherently less capable of learning than others.

RTI is a conglomerate of practices based on the alternate premise that most students *do* learn well when provided high-quality instruction and close monitoring of educational progress (Echevarria & Hasbrouck, 2009; Fuchs & Deshler, 2007). *In its ideal*, RTI combines systematic, proactive, and responsive elements to improve patterns of student achievement across entire schools and districts.

RTI approaches encourage examination of both the instructional inputs and achievement outputs associated with individual and group learning within the "core." RTI models require that instruction be (a) evidence-based, (b) delivered with fidelity, and (c) consistently informed by dynamic measures of student progress (Bender & Shores, 2007). Frequent assessments of targeted skills provide teachers the information required for timely instructional adjustments to ensure that all students receive the supports necessary to maximize individual success (Hale et al., 2010). RTI speaks so explicitly to the power of *evidence-based* instruction that RTI was included among the criteria schools may utilize to determine a student's eligibility for special education (reauthorized Individuals with Disabilities Education Act [IDEA], 2004). Preventative support structures, such as RTI, along with assurance for supports to meet culturally and linguistically diverse (CLD) student needs, also are promoted in the updated Every Student Succeeds Act (2016).

RTI represents an important shift in the requirements necessary to identify and assist students with a possible learning disability. Previous criteria for determining disability focused on finding a significant discrepancy between the student's overall ability (measured IQ) and performance on standardized tests of academic achievement. As discussed throughout this text, however, factors other than an innate disability can contribute to student achievement, and overreliance on discrepancy models is one of the factors frequently associated with disproportionate referral and placement of CLD students in special education (De Valenzuela, Copeland, Qi, & Park, 2006; Rueda & Windmueller, 2006).

In addition to overidentification at the point of evaluation, adherence to discrepancy models can actually prevent struggling students from receiving the support needed to close emergent achievement gaps before they widen. RTI represents a move away from wait-to-fail models that disregard student struggles until gaps become large enough to merit diagnoses as a disability (Fletcher & Vaughn, 2009; Fuchs, Mock, Morgan, & Young, 2003). It has been anticipated that through more rapid response to concerns and eligibility based on student response to research-based methods, fewer students overall will require special education support (Fuchs & Deshler, 2007).

RTI has greater potential to promote systemic improvement than previous models where focus on assessment and placement (in special education) did little to expand teachers' abilities to assess, interpret, and respond to students' learning needs with targeted and timely supports. Whereas test results provide a score, well-implemented interventions facilitate the cycles of learning, assessment, and modification necessary to determine when, how, and *under what conditions* the student *does learn*. RTI models invite us to think as much about the responsiveness of our instruction to the student's learning, as the student's response to our instruction (Hamayan, Marler, Sánchez-López, & Damico, 2014; Hiebert, Stewart, & Uzicanin, 2010). Teachers who begin to problem solve in this manner not only become more adept at distinguishing disabilities from differences in individual students, they often become more capable and responsive teachers of students overall. This is particularly important with CLD students for whom lack of appropriate teaching methods can seriously affect opportunity to learn.

Some districts frame self-assessment, improvement plans, and instructional practices around *multitiered systems of support (MTSS)*. MTSS structures frequently include RTI, but the terms are not synonymous. Both are considered preventative, but MTSS models tend to be more comprehensive, with attention to varied or multiple *tiers of instructional support*. These support structures may involve nonacademic areas such as social-emotional development and behavior, or system goals (e.g., professional development, learning culture, and parent involvement). Although distinctions exist, the bulk of information and examples in this chapter applies to the data we employ to assess—and assess within—either of these proactive/responsive systems of supports.

---

assessment FREEZE FRAME 7.1

Whereas test results provide a score, well-implemented interventions facilitate the cycles of learning, assessment, and modification necessary to determine when, how, and *under what conditions* the student *does learn*.

What Does RTI Look Like?

Well-designed RTI models include a number of components that enable and support student learning. Central to each is the assurance of high-quality classroom instruction, delivered with fidelity by collaborative and knowledgeable staff who involve parents in supporting the child's educational experience. Students' progress is monitored closely via universal screenings and data derived from student responses to targeted intervention.

RTI models commonly reference a triangular pyramid of tiered supports. Most models delineate three or four tiers, with the largest or core level representing the effective educational practices provided to *all* students. The premise and promise of RTI is that a well-implemented instructional core successfully meets the needs of 70% to 80% of students across settings and populations. When fewer students demonstrate expected growth within the core, schools should examine the following:

- Scope and coherence of curricular content
- Appropriateness of the instructional methods
- Fidelity of implementation
- Validity of data for CLD students
- Correspondence with more authentic or alternate demonstration of skills

Because the proportion of students with innate learning disabilities is generally similar regardless of demographic, it is reasonable to expect that the majority of students, regardless of background, will experience success within a *relevant* and *responsive* core.

RTI structures differ among states, cities, and districts. There are two major types of RTI models, employed either separately or in tandem within a framework of supports. The first is referred to as a *standard treatment protocol*. Within this model, the same research-based treatment is provided to all students at each level, with progress measured against set indicators or benchmarks of achievement. Students who do not meet these criteria receive an additional research-supported treatment of more intensive supports. Literacy models that track student achievement using benchmark and progress monitoring systems, such as AIMSWeb (Pearson) and DIBELS or IDEL (University of Oregon), are examples of standard treatment protocols commonly used in schools today.

Although the models are not mutually exclusive, the *problem-solving model* differs from the standard treatment protocol in several respects. Chief among these is that problem-solving models focus on more individualized interventions and contextually based assessment. Methods outlined for problem solving foster detailed consideration of the experiential or external factors that may be influencing a specific student's achievement (Hamayan et al., 2014). Individualized interventions that prove effective for numerous students may then become incorporated into the core as levels of necessary differentiation for all, rather than as indicators of individual need.

In discussing problem-solving and standard treatment models of RTI, Catherine Collier (2010) notes that the graphics used to describe them (see Figure 7.1 for examples) lend insight to potential weakness or cautions of each. In the multitiered models, student movement between tiers may be based upon universal or larger scale criteria that are not appropriate for CLD students. Although placement within the tiers is ideally fluid (students return to core settings once skill-specific needs are met), the potential exists for the ascending tiers to be misinterpreted as unidirectional steps toward special education.

Conversely, problem-solving models are frequently depicted as circular to represent continuous cycles of instruction, assessment, analysis, and instructional refinement. Although this representation effectively reduces consideration of the process as a path to special education, ongoing treatment outside the standard can fail to illuminate how, when, and *if* the student can be successful within the core. These models are not mutually exclusive, and many schools strive to employ elements of both.

Figure 7.1   Models of RTI

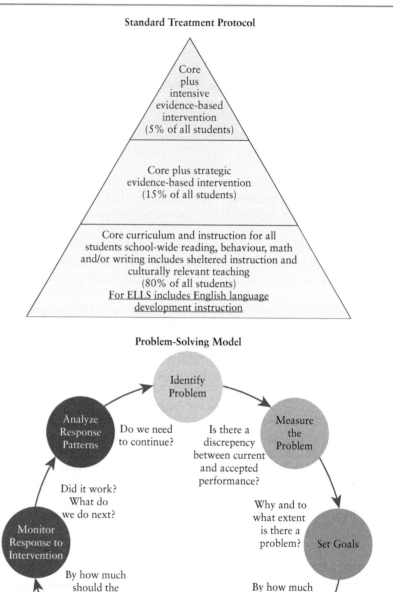

Sources: J. E. Brown, A. Sanford, and E. Lolich (2010, April 29), *RTI for English Language Learners: Appropriate Screening, Progress Monitoring and Instructional Planning.* Webinar presentation by the National Center on Response to Intervention. C. Collier (2010), *RTI for Diverse Learners: More Than 200 Instructional Interventions.* (Thousand Oaks, CA: Corwin Press). Page 5. Reprinted by permission.

Tiers (Not Tracks) of Instruction

Consideration of the appropriateness of a measure for students became the topic for prekindergarten teachers attending a workshop about the new *universal screener* for use in their school.

> **Mr. Mantri:** Well, I think I understand the intention and, yes, it makes a lot of sense to find out early which students need more help than others, but . . .
>
> **Ms. Ordaz:** Will paraprofessional allocations and class size be adjusted for classes with more low students?
>
> **Ms. Lowell:** I don't consider my students "low," but I do worry that a lot of their scores will be. Many of them have never even been exposed to the pictured items they'll be asked to quickly name. Others could easily do that task in their home language—but not in English.
>
> **Mr. Mantri:** That's what bothers me, too. I understand that rapid automatic naming predicts reading success and it's important to have an early indicator of who may need more attention. But for many of our students, this screener won't be measuring how quickly students can name pictures. It will be measuring their exposure to English.
>
> **Ms. Ordaz:** Isn't English vocabulary necessary for reading in English? It seems to me that regardless of why they have trouble, it will show us which ones need more help for whatever reason.
>
> **Mr. Mantri:** What happens if 75% of our students don't make benchmark? Will this screener tell us who needs *which kind* of help?

The teachers in the vignette are asking excellent questions. As mentioned in Chapter 2, it's just as important to understand the reliability and validity of screening tools as diagnostic measures.

Take a few minutes to think about (or discuss) the following:

- Is the picture-naming task a *reliable* measure of students' ability to name pictures in English? (In other words, does it accurately portray the student's ability to name specific *English* words?)
- Is it a *valid* measure of rapid automatic naming? (Does the task distinguish between students who score poorly due to word retrieval and those who simply do not yet know the words?)
- What might it indicate if 75% of Mr. Mantri's class does fail to meet the fall benchmark? Will we be able to answer this question on the basis of screening data alone?

Typically, Tier I of a standard treatment protocol refers to the general or core instruction available to all students. At this level, evidence-based practices and quality resources combine to meet the academic and behavioral needs of *most* students. Of key importance for educators of CLD students is whether the instructional and assessment methods used for RTI are research-based as effective and appropriate for students of all demographics in that setting (Sanford, Brown & Turner, 2012). Attention to appropriateness for CLD students is critical given the (a) predominance of instructional practices touted as research-based for all students that have not specifically been determined as effective for English learners, (b) biased methods used to assess skills, and (c) dissimilarity of peers to which they are compared (Brown, 2013; Brown & Doolittle, 2008; Klingner, Hoover, & Baca, 2008; Reynolds & Shaywitz, 2009). Where such assurances have not been examined and/or cannot be made, RTI runs the risk of misidentifying students by the same faulty criteria as the discrepancy formula it seeks to replace (Reynolds & Shaywitz, 2009).

RTI models reflect the realization that *some* students may require more intensive support to make expected gains in particular areas. It is important, however, for schools to understand the variables that can influence student performance on screenings, and consider alternate probes and core-level accommodations before referral to more intensive tiers of support.

Teaching Tips:

- Review screening data from the teacher's lens.
  - Do the results reflect the student's performance on formal and informal classroom tasks?
  - Do observations by any other staff indicate the student demonstrates targeted skills under differing conditions?
- Review screening results with the child in mind.
  - Does this student *typically* perform well under the conditions in which the skill was screened?
  - Do anecdotal notes indicate the student was unwell or under stress at the time of screening?
- Identify other sources of data that exist or can be gathered to corroborate the student's need for additional support with specified skills.
- Determine scaffolds that will support this student's ongoing participation in a differentiated core.
- Monitor look-alike or alternate indicators of data that demonstrate student growth with the targeted skill.
- Advocate for multidimensional sources of data when identifying the most beneficial settings to advance student skills.

The goal is to ensure that each student is allowed to engage in the core setting for the maximum time possible, while still meeting his or her individual needs. Indeed, recent research has found that among students with similar academic profiles, those who remained in the core setting made greater progress than those receiving the designated intervention (Balu et al., 2015). Further research is needed to understand what's happening when additional "help" serves to hinder rather than strengthen achievement.

Typically, students identified as making insufficient progress within a well-designed and well-implemented core are referred for more targeted levels of instruction in specific areas of need. At any given time, 15% to 20% of students may require Tier II supports for some aspect of the curriculum while continuing to participate in the universal core. An often-cited benefit of Tier II interventions is that they typically are provided in smaller group settings. Each student's progress is monitored more frequently, with probes administered every 1 to 2 weeks. Data points plotted to determine students' rate of growth reveal their response to the intervention. Poor student responses require reassessment of the intervention and a refinement of the methods used with an individual or group of students. Just as with the core, instructional techniques utilized in Tier II need to be effective for the intended group(s) of students, delivered with fidelity, and *responsive* to the learner(s) for whom it is designed.

For many students, early attention to specific needs results in a resolution of difficulties such that they can continue successful participation in an enriching core with minimal additional supports. Student participation in either tier of support is understood to be need-specific and fluid—never a form of (re)designation or tracking. This labeling/tracking may occur overtly, through assignment to leveled classes, or through the more insidious use of scoring terminology to describe a student or group (e.g., "She's below basic," "Most of my class is red").

SNAPSHOT from *CLASSROOM PRACTICE*   7.1

In this picture, Mrs. Thomas is working with a small group of 2nd-grade students to provide them with added support during their reading time. This kind of a guided intervention enables teachers to provide targeted instruction that is responsive to students' individual academic needs.

Jessica Thomas

VOICES *from the* FIELD 7.1

Two years ago, our building switched to a push-in intervention model. We saw huge success with this change and I believe a large part of that success was due to the fact that reading intervention became a part of the homeroom class. Classrooms were no longer a revolving door of students leaving for 30 minutes here, 20 minutes there, and the transition times it took to get to a new location. Our push-in model cut down on the time it took for students to get to reading intervention and allowed them to start working sooner. The push-in model also allowed the planning and intervention process to become more of a collaborative effort between the classroom teacher and innovation specialists. Reading aides and specialists could hear what was going on during classroom instruction and intervene, almost immediately, around that instruction for Tier II interventions. It really took on a "class within a class" feel, which took away the shame that sometimes came with "going to reading." Since all students were working with small groups, and rotating through teachers, aides, and specialists, they felt successful in their own classroom. We were also able to intervene around more students as the transition time from room to room was cut down. There was a bit of push back in the beginning. Teachers were worried that it would be too distracting to students. What we found was that the students transitioned more seamlessly because they weren't leaving the classroom. This kept the focus on reading, the strategies fluid, and the messages the same.

JoAnna Euston, Elementary Instructional Coach

As noted in the conversation between Ms. Ordaz and Mr. Mantri, such thinking can begin to impact school culture and decisions unless data discussions are structured to invite deeper consideration of the results (Datnow, Choi, Park, St. John, 2018).

When discussions are a regular part of data review, trends may be noted that foster ideas for strategic improvement to ongoing practice. This process serves not only to empower teachers, but also to reduce the noise created by responding to each perceived "deficit" by adding a new program or pullout to the curricular routine.

Bringing Focus to the "Data Daze"

The new principal at Roosevelt Elementary, Ms. Drake, was surprised by how many teachers described their students, and the school in general, as "low." This was done in a manner that suggested inherent ability, rather than specifically defined need or skill. To be honest, fall screening data was alarming. Per protocol, Ms. Drake was now required to help staff "drill down" on those multicolored graphs.

Slides presented during this Data Day's meeting confirmed that Roosevelt's reading triangles were indeed "upside down" (see Figure 7.2). This meant that the majority of students scored in red or yellow, with fewer scoring in the green. There was no perceptible cohort scoring "well above."

Figure 7.2   Reading Data

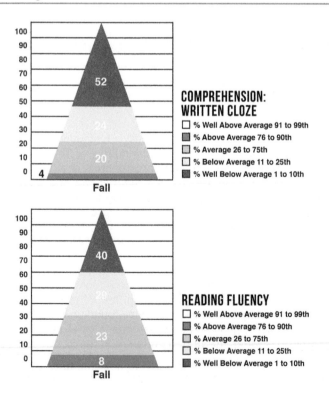

Despite having had time to reflect, Mrs. Ryan blurted, "That's just Roosevelt. We do the best we can with what we get. Have you seen the neighborhood?" Heads nodded. Another person added, "What if the red kids got extra vocabulary homework or we use their recess time for fluency drills?" Mrs. Ryan countered, "I've been here 20 years and it just feels like we're working harder and cramming more into each day, but little changes." Ms. Drake realized this may be a systemic challenge, and likely the reason she was assigned to Roosevelt. What an opportunity to make a difference! She truly believed most people do strive to feel successful, but numbers alone couldn't tell any of them why they weren't achieving desired outcomes at their school.

In addition to screening, there also were demographic data. When Ms. Drake asked about the percentage of students in special education, teachers shared that this had become a district concern, and "now nobody can be referred." Ms. Drake reassured staff that problem solving around student needs actually was *not* a special education process. There may be students whose needs lead to that consideration, but their first step would be "looking beyond these darn triangles!"

Out of the corner of her eye, she caught another teacher's eyes roll and declared, "Let's stop talking and do some walking." Ms. Drake asked teachers to submit the names of students who may benefit from further attention. She clarified, "These should be students whose needs aren't being met in the accommodated tiers. These are students who stand out, even when provided extra support."

By week's end, 4th-grade teachers had submitted more names than 1st-grade through 3rd-grade teachers combined, so they would be the 1st grade-level group to meet. There were far too many referrals to represent exceptionality or to explore each in-depth. However, every child's success mattered, so they would be trying a new approach. Ms. Drake also invited the ESL teacher, counselor, learning coach, and speech pathologist to this grade-level, problem-solving meeting. They would have 1 hour.

Ms. Drake had prepared a few slides to keep the conversation moving. The first was a photo of nurse Jen's office on a typical busy day. More than 80% of her visitors return to class after a short assessment (e.g., temperature reading, sugar level reading, observation) and the indicated "treatment" (e.g., medication, water, listening ear). "Why is the student returning to the classroom important?" Ms. Drake asked. "Students need to be in class to learn," Ms. El-Amin chimed. "Exactly," the principal replied. "It's like our model of MTSS. There are really only a few students who need something very different, but we don't ignore the rest."

To start the problem-solving process, classroom teachers were given a few minutes to jot down up to three primary concerns they had for each student they had come to discuss. Examples were provided regarding the level of detail for this step (e.g., "Sara has trouble answering questions about stories" is more informative than "Sara doesn't understand").

As teachers read aloud concerns, teammates probed details such as, "Were these student-read stories, or does that also happen after hearing *you* read?" This helped the group reach consensus on how to list the emerging themes. For example, Sara's name was added to those of Ian, Josue, Carmen, Jamari, Stephanie, Ixchel, and Kendra on the chart labeled, "Answering Questions after Listening." There was an even longer list for "Answering Questions after Reading," with many of the same names appearing on it. Two teachers commented that they were not sure if those who couldn't respond to reading prompts might have done better orally, so they made a note to follow-up with informal probes to find out. Mr. Vu had a great resource with scaffolded tasks that he was willing to share. All agreed that seeing how each student performed with different response options would add a lot to their understanding of who needed what, and even more importantly, who already *knows* and *can do* when provided an alternate probe.

Another theme emerged that reflected concerns such as, "I never hear him speak," "She doesn't use complete sentences," and "They just don't respond. Crickets!" By the 30-minute mark, chart paper lists revealed common themes around "Speaking in Sentences," "Answering Questions," and "Retelling Stories or Events." Everyone noted the connection to *oral language*, which could also, of course, impact *fluency, vocabulary*, and *comprehension*. Two charts had only one name. The speech language pathologist and counselor would be following up in advance of more individualized problem solving related to those concerns.

Returning to the emergent themes, Ms. Drake drew a frame around each titled skill. She asked the group to reflect on current practices, resources, or routines. Acknowledging full plates and wariness to add-ons, she asked, "Are there any tweaks that could be done to get more power, more language use, and growth from what we *already do*?" They took a few minutes to note individual thoughts before sharing. The ESL teacher opened by saying, "Perhaps this is my lens, but I feel like classes are too quiet. The scripted response drills we've adopted to increase engagement . . . well, it's not the same. How many of you studied a foreign language in high school, aced every pattern drill, but never learned to speak?"

"I agree," said Mr. Vu, "language, words, and sentence structures don't really 'stick' until you're using them for a real purpose. This could be asking your question, sharing your thoughts, or simply requesting that your steak be 'just the right amount of pink.'" Others laughed and nodded. Ms. Drake summarized, "Do we believe that increasing the students' opportunities to talk, to truly converse, has value?" "Yes," said Mr. DeJong, "but I don't know what that would look like without losing control, or having it look to others that way. Previous principals frowned on noisy classrooms."

"Well, if that noise is students talking about what they're thinking, learning, or creating," said Ms. Drake, "I've got your back. My role is to advocate for what *we* collectively decide has the most leverage with *our* students. That will be our focus. Let's plan to meet again next week. In the meantime, write down any ideas or strategies you feel might add power, not work, to our day. This could include how to rethink a particular structure, like what happens during partner shares, or a simple prompt we all can use to cue higher level or more elaborate responses throughout the day—even in gym. Send your thoughts to Gayle. She'll compile them for discussion next week. We'll decide what is doable and how we'll know it is working. We are not ignoring 'the triangles,' but that data alone couldn't guide us to the discussion that we had today."

The meeting adjourned with 5 minutes to spare. Mrs. Ryan lagged behind. "You know, Ms. Drake, when we started today, I thought this would be a waste of time. That's what I used to feel whenever the outcome wasn't testing for special ed. We didn't know what else to do. Today we turned our resignation about student needs to a focus on how we can add traction to what we already do, instead of just spinning our wheels. Is this what you meant by 'accommodated tiers?'" "That's precisely it," Ms. Drake answered with a smile.

Grade- or subject-level problem solving may be most appropriate when many students demonstrate difficulties within an RTI/MTSS framework. Instead of negating concerns as "typical," educators are encouraged to notice themes that emerge from descriptions of actual students. This will foster more authentic and focused discussions around proactive adjustments that presume everyone's *ability* rather than *inability* to succeed. This process also helps to focus resources on gathering the information necessary to problem solve around the strengths and needs of individual students who stand out from their peers. The following process outlines the steps for group problem solving.

Group Problem Solving

Materials:

- Lists from teachers (see "Before Meeting")
- Chart paper (or documents to project)
- Markers
- Blank paper (for teachers to make notes)

Directions:

1. **Before Meeting**
   - Identify the grade or subject level with a high rate of special education or problem-solving referrals.
   - Invite teacher representatives and support personnel with insight to, and impact upoh, that group.
   - Ask teachers to bring a list of students they either referred, or feel are not benefitting from current supports.
2. **During Meeting**
   - Set up chart paper or projected document for lists that will be developed.
   - Explain time limit and purpose (i.e., to determine if themes emerge from discussion of individual needs).
   - Have teachers write down one to three concerns for each student they have come to discuss.
   - As each teacher shares, invite clarification and consensus about how that student's concern is described and/or whether it is already represented on an existing chart.
   - When all individuals have shared, invite individual reflection on any emergent themes.
   - Share thoughts. Seek consensus on one or two themes.
   - Ask participants now to reflect on current supports, routines, or practices. What adjustments might leverage greater opportunity to authentically use or develop skills?
3. **Follow-Up**
   - The facilitator, coach, or team leader consolidates ideas for follow-up discussion. Teachers determine adjustments or suggestions they feel will add power to every child's day.
   - As a group, answers are developed in response to the following questions:
     - Is professional development desired?
     - How and when will we reflect on or measure the impact?
     - Might this professional development or instructional change benefit other grades or teams?
   - Continue individualized problem solving around the more unique needs of students that also surfaced during this process.

Additional Notes:

This activity can be repeated as often as desired throughout the academic school year. For actions taken, follow-up within the first 6 to 9 weeks is needed to gauge implementation and allow for reflection.

As noted earlier, such problem-solving approaches can exist within or in addition to the standard treatment protocol to assist staff in identifying and responding to individual needs. These processes can also result in instructional insights that improve the core, thereby reducing the numbers of students who fail screeners for reasons unrelated to true ability or skill (Hamayan et al., 2014).

INDIVIDUALIZING FOR CLD STUDENTS

Within weeks of beginning 1st grade, Joaquin was referred for intensive literacy support. Teachers understood that family mobility and emotional upheavals had interfered with his participation in kindergarten, but things had stabilized and he'd become "no different than others" by midyear. Still, he failed to master all letter sounds by May and remained behind peers when school resumed. Tiered literacy interventions (e.g., scripted small-group instruction, drills) and "visuals" (i.e., marketed letter/picture charts) did not result in the rate of growth necessary to close his emerging achievement gap. Teachers began to suspect "processing" or "memory problems."

Staff at Joaquin's school had recently received training on "MTSS for Individual Students." Although designed to replace the *preassessment* process for special education (SPED), district presenters emphasized that an individualized problem-solving approach was different. It should not be considered the "road to SPED" but rather a process to determine the conditions under which the student (and teacher) experience greater success. As such, the teachers of any student, even a student already receiving special services, could benefit from this process when needed.

In the past, Joaquin's teacher would have struggled with referral. She didn't want to overidentify CLD students, but what if Joaquin had a true exceptionality? Wouldn't ignoring it be just as bad? She decided to submit his name for the problem-solving process (PSP). Prior to the meeting, one of the child study team members visited to gather details. They talked briefly about Joaquin's strengths, needs, interests, and family. How did his parent describe him? The newly created PSP form requested much more personal (biographical) information about the student. There also was a place for individual and contextualizing group screener data.

The first PSP meeting about Joaquin included several Child Study Team members, the ESOL teacher, administrator, and after-school supervisor, Mr. Aragon. He also saw Joaquin daily and had a good relationship with his mother. The PSP form was prefilled with available background information and projected on the wall. They showed Joaquin's school picture while talking about his interests and family. Mr. Aragon added that Joaquin loved having "fun homework" (e.g., coloring or counting page), but his mother had expressed worry that, speaking little English, she couldn't be of much help with his reading.

The bilingual speech language pathologist (SLP) often tried to observe students coming up for PSP discussion. Visiting class, she involved Joaquin in a short game with peers that revealed he could name far fewer pictures in English than in Spanish. This suggested that English proficiency factored in his ability to benefit from the picture accommodation assumed to cue his association of letters with sounds. These new insights inspired the PSP team to develop more refined interventions targeted specifically to Joaquin.

The first intervention involved sending home a small packet of sticky notes pre-printed with multiples of several unmastered graphemes. Parents were asked to lead Joaquin on a hunt around the house modeling the sound and placing sticky notes on objects determined to begin with that sound. They stuck a printed "p" to the door (*puerta*), a container for straws (*popotes*), and a shelf for plates (*platos*). They added "s" stickies to the chair (*silla*), couch (*sofa*), and salt (*sal*). They placed "m" stickies on the table (*mesa*), jam (*mermelada*), and even one on the sleeve (*manga*) of Mami! Joaquin found it great fun to review and add letters daily. His mother made it even more fun by hiding a candy next to "something that begins with 'ssss,' 'mmm,' or 'p.'" When this skill was probed in class 4 days later, Joaquin demonstrated 100% visual recognition and sound association for the letter/sounds worked on that week.

Joaquin's rapid learning under these conditions led the SLP to also provide parents a bilingual alphabet book to record pictures (drawn or cut out) and Spanish words beginning with the sound associated with each letter (see Figure 7.3). Pages were divided into two columns, one for home words and the other for English words. Parents were encouraged to help Joaquin discover when English letter sounds (i.e., *z*) did not exist in Spanish words. Where possible, spaces in both columns were prefilled

---

Figure 7.3   Assessment Artifact: Bilingual Alphabet Book

Templates for alphabet book pages can take many forms. Teachers can prefill with example cognates to help anchor students' and parents' understanding of the task. In this artifact, the teacher prefilled with the words "Panda" and "Piano" and provided an accompanying image for each.

Source: Maria Moran. Reprinted by permission.

with pictured cognates (*pantalones/pants*) to provide student and teacher shared referents to anchor letter-sound associations.

Use of this tool to build sound/symbol association and phonemic awareness (sound discrimination, blending, etc.) was modeled by the SLP. Telephone support was provided daily the first week.

Although given 4 weeks to complete home sections, Joaquin returned his book in two. The teacher was thrilled. She reported back to his PSP team that she and Joaquin had reviewed the letters, sounds, and corresponding Spanish words for the class. Peers loved listening for the sound in unfamiliar words and suggesting English words he could choose for the other column. Within a few short weeks of probing and responding to Joaquin's skills, it became apparent that his needs were largely situational and his assets were immense. When provided with this more targeted and authentic scaffold, Joaquin made rapid gains.

The teacher determined that *all* her students could benefit from what was originally developed to meet the almost unrecognized needs of *one*. She looked forward to adding more student-created bilingual ABC books to sit among the reference shelf materials in her classroom.

As this scenario demonstrates, educators frequently can increase the academic achievement of CLD students simply by carefully observing for, and building on, the skills and resources each already brings to class. The multitude of factors surrounding the learning of CLD students requires educators to think reflectively about the root issues of any perceived delays in learning.

As teachers explore a CLD student's history, the following questions may yield information that proves particularly relevant to the problem-solving process:

- *How is the "behavior" or perceived "delay" exhibited in the primary language or home environment?* In general, genuine behavioral, language, and some learning disabilities are also evident to family members, who note differences in this child compared with her or his siblings and peers. When parents or guardians are consulted (e.g., through home visits), they often provide wonderful insights into their child's learning patterns, knowledge bases, and background experiences. Such insights greatly enhance a teacher's capacity to check potentially inaccurate assumptions about learning and language acquisition capacities.
- *Is English achievement at an expected level given the student's stage of English acquisition?* A student's ability to participate in and benefit from instruction is invariably affected by his or her proficiency in the language of instruction, especially if accommodations are not consistently used to increase content comprehensibility.
- *Does the student's language acquisition history appear to account for strengths or weaknesses in the primary language?* If a student's opportunities to use and maintain her or his first language have diminished due to English exposure, she or he may experience some degree of first language loss before fully acquiring the second language. When such a student is assessed in both languages, neither language may appear strong, and this can be misinterpreted as an indication of an innate language delay or a learning disorder.
- *Is L1 achievement consistent with the amount and time period of L1 academic instruction?* Careful consideration of the amount and type of native language instruction is necessary to determine whether the student's current learning patterns are consistent with prior academic experiences.

- *How does the student respond to scaffolded or mediated learning?* One of the most critical sources of information is anecdotal and product evidence of how the student responds to sheltered or other forms of accommodative classroom instruction provided at a level consistent with the student's previous academic and linguistic experiences. CLD students who demonstrate grade-level or expected learning under these conditions may indeed have significant academic needs but are unlikely to have a learning disability. Many students, however, have not been given an opportunity to learn and benefit from sheltered or accommodative instruction. When such needs-based instruction has not yet been attempted, teachers and other educators must carefully guard against erroneous assumptions about the students' learning capacities.
- *Is the team that facilitates interpretation and processing of provided information, made up of or informed by diverse individuals, parents or guardians, and family and community members who understand the student's language and*

ACCOMMODATIVE ASSESSMENT PRACTICES 7.1

Throughout a child's journey through the educational system, various data are collected as a means of shedding light on his or her aptitude, progress, and potential. But what is *data* and how does it relate to what we want to know about the child? Data is simply information. It can take many forms (e.g., observation), but it often is reduced to numbers for easier management. Numbers, however, don't always tell enough of the story.

For example, how long can a person tolerate sun exposure without getting sunburned? This question presumes a lot but most adults could probably provide an answer based on experiences from their own lives. Let's say we ask 100 people this question and their responses range from 15 minutes to 4 hours. Granted, a few might say they "always" or "never" burn, but those are considered outliers; as a result, we exclude them from the study.

If the amount of time this *normative* sample can be in the sun without burning averages 90 minutes, can we be confident this is an appropriate benchmark for all? Will any be "burned" by this assumption? Might reactions also vary by time of year or geographic location? What other factors could impact an individual's response to sun?

As with skin reactions to the sun, RTI measures are best considered within an individualized context. Whenever we drill down on static indicators such as numerical data, we run the risk of missing critical interactions and insight to the big picture.

Multiple lenses are necessary to bring into focus a larger *systemic* picture, or bigger picture of any one child. If we consider the four dimensions of the learner's biography, key factors to consider include:

Sociocultural Dimension
- Internal or situational stressors
- Parental involvement in problem solving
- Classroom climate (collaborative vs. competitive)

Cognitive
- Background knowledge (home, community, and school)
- Enrichment vs. remediation
- Varied ways to show learning

Academic
- Prior education
- L1 instructional support
- Instructional approach
- Skills present in home/community contexts

Linguistic
- L1 proficiency level
- English proficiency level
- Adequacy of language accommodations
- Opportunities to access all language assets while learning ■

culture? Multiple lenses are needed to consider the student's strengths and potential challenges under differing educational conditions. The home perspective is especially critical for insights to the most authentic interpretation of factors that hinder or enable learning performance.

A well-developed problem-solving process that includes consideration of these questions may reveal that a student's current difficulties can reasonably be explained or accounted for on the basis of her or his prior opportunities to learn.

INTENSIFIED NEEDS (FEW OF THE FEW)

Although the majority of students' needs can be met within Tiers I and II, a relative *few* (3% to 5%) may require even more intensive levels of support to show gains. At this level, intervention support is delivered to even smaller groups with more frequent probes of progress. The purpose of these assessments is to ensure that the instructional methods and materials align with students' needs. Nothing is gained educationally by merely documenting interventions that don't work.

RTI models vary somewhat with regard to the most intensive tier(s) of instruction. It may be that Tier III includes both students without disabilities and those with special needs, or Tier III (or IV) may be reserved only for students with identified exceptionalities. Special education students should be assigned to the most appropriate and least restrictive tier of instruction for each curricular area based on individual need rather than on predetermined influence of (dis)ability. Although a well-designed model of RTI leads to more appropriate determination of students in need of intensive supports, RTI is, above all, a continuum of general education supports designed to *prevent* school failure in the larger population of students.

Figure 7.4 summarizes key aspects of each tier of RTI instructional support (Brown & Doolittle, 2008; Collier, 2010; Echevarria & Vogt, 2010; Fisher, Frey, & Rothenberg, 2011).

---

assessment FREEZE FRAME 7.2

Nothing is gained educationally by merely documenting interventions that don't work.

PROBLEM SOLVING VERSUS REFERRAL FOR SPED

Jaime is currently in the 7th grade. He came to the United States and entered school in the middle of last year. Teachers have become concerned that, despite occasional translation support from a Spanish-speaking paraprofessional, he is still nowhere near grade level. Jaime is not even able to work successfully with his peers on 3rd- and 4th-grade-level material used in tiered reading and ESL.

The reading teacher has expressed the concern that Jaime should be in special education, but the ESL teacher, Mrs. Jaeger, thinks that he is "bright." She has observed him during his unstructured time with other Spanish-speaking students and has noticed that Jaime usually takes the lead in organizing games. He also appears quick with responses that make his friends laugh. Tension has developed between these teachers because of their different perspectives on Jaime's inherent abilities. However, each agrees that Jaime is not able to work anywhere near grade level in either Spanish or English, so he is referred to SPED.

Figure 7.4   Key Aspects of RTI Tiers of Instruction

Tier I (All Students)

- Research-based curriculum and methods with evidence of effectiveness for the target population(s)
- English Language Development (ELD)/English to Speakers of Other Languages (ESOL) is a component of core instruction
- Culturally responsive instruction to access, assess, and build on background knowledge
- Strategies and materials appropriate for English learners
  - Sheltered, academically rich, English language instruction
  - Peer collaboration
  - Native language instruction
  - Visuals, realia
- Teaching for transfer
- Universal screening of academics
- Progress monitoring compares English learners with English learning peers
- Informed interpretation of student performance
- Explicit instruction in—and contextualized opportunities to use—phonemic awareness, phonics, fluency, vocabulary, and comprehension

Tier II (Some Students)

- 20–30 minutes in addition to core program
- Data-driven (multiple sources)
- Evidence-based curriculum and methods (e.g., sheltered English language instruction, native language instruction)
- Culturally responsive instruction to access, assess, and build on background knowledge
- Small group (three to five students)
- Systematic and explicit instruction that targets skill building, transfer, and authentic use
- Progress monitored with comparisons made to true peers; results/interpretation triangulated across settings

Tier III (Few Students)

- Appropriateness of Tier I and II evident by progress of most true peers
- 45–60 minutes in addition to core program
- Delivered by educators who can pinpoint specific needs of individual students and respond in culturally responsive ways
- Data driven (multiple sources and types)
- Culturally responsive instruction to access, assess, and build on background knowledge
- Strategies and materials appropriate for English learners (e.g., sheltered English language instruction, peer collaboration, native language instruction, visuals, realia)
- Culturally and linguistically appropriate assessments inform interpretation of need
- Special education support, as necessary, and as supported by detailed description of, and plan for, conditions under which student skills *grow*.

The school's bilingual social worker accompanies Mrs. Jaeger to Jaime's home to find out more about his family and school history. This is always an important component of the evaluation. Jaime's mother reports they had lived in a rural part of Mexico where access to education was inconsistent and offered to all children simultaneously, regardless of educational level. When asked, his mother estimates that Jaime had been in school about a total of 10 or 12 months before coming to the United States. Her answers to additional questions and the perceptions she shares of her child indicate that she does not see him as very different from other children his age that she had known in Mexico.

This information helps the evaluation team understand Jaime's case. It explains many of the perceived problems, even his difficulties with learning material in Spanish. They now know much of the prior instruction provided had not been at Jaime's learning level, regardless of language, so his lack of achievement is not conclusive evidence of an innate learning problem.

An informal probe of Spanish literacy skills reveals that Jaime does have the critical foundations of literacy in his primary language. These and other assessments indicate that Jaime is able to read and comprehend in Spanish at the early 2nd-grade level. Although consistent with his educational history, Jaime's skills are not enough for him to have benefitted from the higher-level translated texts and supports used with other newcomers. Had teachers known this information sooner, they would have better understood his inability to perform academic tasks, despite what were initially considered adequate supports.

A student interview also reveals Jaime has developed functional literacy from environmental print and is proud of his ability to write words such as *Walmart, Wendy's, open,* and *closed* without a visual model. Using an early elementary probe of English reading, teachers also discover Jaime is beginning to transfer Spanish literacy skills to his new language by phonetically spelling *naf (knife), forc (fork),* and *spun (spoon)*. Given this more detailed description of Jaime's skills, which includes statements about what he has mastered and can demonstrate, the team is able to develop much more appropriate interventions to better promote his learning and language acquisition.

Occasionally, a student—such as Jaime in this scenario—will stand out as having atypical difficulty with classroom material. Responsive teachers modify their lessons and the manner of delivery to find "keys" for opening different learning doors. Many also benefit from consultation with others. Effective teacher assistance or problem-solving teams have members with insights and expertise in pertinent areas such as English for speakers of other languages (ESOL), special education, behavior, and literacy. Family members and students themselves also provide invaluable information and insight. Without these perspectives, the ideas and recommendations provided may reflect common approaches for most students but may not be appropriately tailored to the specific needs of *this* CLD student.

In Jaime's case, what barriers or presumptions delayed attention to his needs? Would Jaime have stood out during a subject- or grade-level problem-solving process? Had the staff members participated in more individualized problem-solving discussions prior to referral for SPED (see Figure 7.5), the following proactive measures might have been taken:

- Data from Jaime's educational history would have prompted academic probes and revealed the inappropriateness of standard newcomer materials for him.
- Information about Jaime's skills and interests would have informed the development of relevant, engaging tasks that were at his learning level (e.g., Wendy's menu language and mathematics).

Figure 7.5   Informed Problem-Solving Discussions

- Use methods such as those described in Chapter 3 (e.g., records review, interview, observation) to gather preinstructional assessment information in the following areas:
  - Educational history (e.g., type, language, and consistency of instruction)
  - Primary language proficiency (e.g., developmental milestones, language use patterns within the home, current use/proficiency levels, evidence of L1 loss)
  - English proficiency (e.g., amount/type of prior exposure, current use/proficiency levels, academic performance in language-laden settings)
  - Acculturation (e.g., time in country, cultural learning norms) (refer to Chapter 4)
  - Medical history (e.g., vision, hearing, chronic mental or physical illness)
- Develop a profile of student skills based on information and evidence obtained through preinstructional assessment.
- Accommodate the delivery of instruction (e.g., first language support, sheltered English, modified instructional level) to *maximize the student's ability to participate and engage* in the curriculum.
- Monitor the student's response to comprehensible instruction provided:
  - At appropriate learning levels (regardless of age/grade)
  - With attention to differences in learning processes
  - Under individual and collaborative conditions
- Employ varied means to assess student learning in context. Identify the conditions in which the student *does* learn. Seek evidence of applied skills and learning in other contexts. Use this information to continually inform and adapt instruction so the student can experience both success and challenge with the curriculum.
- Continue effective interventions that can be supported within the accommodated tiers.
- Keep refining, adjusting, and documenting the types and intensities of supports needed in other areas until the student experiences success.
- If the amount of support exceeds what can be assured via a responsive general education program, that data is needed to help determine eligibility and need for special education.

- Bilingual paraprofessional support might have been used to bridge Jaime's prior knowledge and new concepts.
- Jaime's Spanish proficiency would have enabled him to participate orally in higher-level content discussions with heterogeneous cooperative groups that included at least one other bilingual student.
- Formative assessment to monitor Jaime's participation in, and success with, modified and accommodated instruction would have more accurately revealed his true learning capacities.

Use of RTI to support referral for special education hinges on the preinstructional and formative assessments that add critical information to presumptions of experience and static measures of universal "growth." A student like Jaime who has received limited education in his native country may be very unlikely to experience classroom success even when instructed using lower grade-level content and when provided native language support. Without an awareness of a CLD student's experiential, educational, and language acquisition history, a teacher might easily compare this student with cultural and linguistic peers who are performing well under the same conditions and mistakenly suspect the presence of a learning disability. Thus, it is extremely important to examine all aspects of a student's past and present language, learning, and social experiences for their ability to explain or nullify current assumptions about learning and language acquisition abilities.

Although previously discussed in Chapter 3 as best practice for all CLD students, *preassessment* is also a term that can be used in special education to denote the process of gathering the specific information needed to decide whether special education considerations, including evaluation, are warranted. Whereas general education preassessment strives to gather information to inform *forthcoming* instruction, special education preassessment, or prereferral, looks at similar data for its ability to shed light on *current* learning or behavioral concerns.

In the authors' view, a robust problem-solving process provides all the information and insight of typical preassessment processes, but in a more timely manner and without the presumption of disability. The goal of special education prereferral is to determine what the student knows and can do and whether knowledge and performance are consistent with what one would expect based on that student's educational and experiential history. A problem-solving process tends to go farther in helping a team determine the methods and/or adaptations that enhance success in either a general education or special education setting. Thus, we move away from the dichotomous "place" or "nonplace" decision and toward a deeper understanding of what truly helps the student learn. Discussion of assessment related to students determined to have special educational needs is further addressed in Chapter 8.

---

assessment FREEZE FRAME 7.3

Without an awareness of a CLD student's experiential, educational, and language acquisition history, a teacher might easily compare the student with cultural and linguistic peers who are performing well under the same conditions and mistakenly suspect the presence of a learning disability.

SUMMARY

Response to intervention (and similar proactive frameworks) are designed to ensure prompt attention to student needs and educational access for all. Data gathered via point-in-time probes measure student progress toward benchmarks of anticipated growth. Such data can depict the "health" of a system (school, grade, student) but may afford little insight to the nature of the needed remedy or instructional change.

As discussed in Chapter 3 and Chapter 6 determination of what students *know* and how each may *connect* with a lesson are among the most powerful tools in any teacher's instructional toolkit. This information (data) enables educators to maximize the conditions and opportunities for cognitive, social, linguistic, and academic growth. These are also the spaces in which both teacher and student discover "what works." In recent years, there has been increasing pressure to base assessment of "what

works" and consequent educational decisions, on data derived from periodic, decontextualized screeners.

Screeners do provide an important layer of information that can be monitored and charted over time. They tell us a lot about students' attainment of targeted skills under the specific condition of each probe. Data graphics provide a snapshot view of each student's, or groups' response to instruction received—or interaction with the language, technology, or cultural presumptions of the test. Although there is value to screening tools, there are limitations to broad interpretation of results. As the saying goes, "When your only tool is a hammer, every problem is a nail."

Screening data can only be *the* hammer to drive instructional decisions when all students are seen as nails from the *same* box. Fortunately, students (and teachers) come to us with varied strengths, edges, and angles, all of which can be leveraged to secure the learning fit. Problem-solving processes facilitate attention to multiple sources of data, contextualized by the student, and interpreted in light of teaching practices we can then adjust with more appropriately customized tools.

A small percentage of students might need higher levels of support. The support provided learners across RTI tiers increases to accommodate higher levels of need. For all students, equitable access to the core curriculum is essential. Students' access to culturally and linguistically responsive instruction and assessment is critical to decisions regarding placement in—and movement among—RTI tiers.

The problem-solving process enables all those who work with a student to share information that is relevant to determining actual need for specific educational supports and services. Oftentimes, the challenges a student is experiencing in a given setting are to be expected, given the biographical history of the student and the (mis)alignment of current supports to meet his or her learning needs. In all instances, a depth of knowledge surrounding the student, as well as insights into classroom factors that promote or hinder success, enable educators to make informed decisions that result in timely, effective student support.

KEY CONCEPTS

Multitiered systems of support (MTSS)

Problem-solving model

Response to intervention (RTI)

Standard treatment protocol

Tiers of instructional support

Universal screener

PROFESSIONAL CONVERSATIONS ON PRACTICE

1. Discuss the pros and cons of the standard treatment protocol (e.g., RTI) for addressing the instructional needs of CLD students.

2. Discuss potential benefits of group (grade level) and individual (student specific) problem-solving processes for CLD students.

3. Discuss what is meant by the *accommodative* core?

QUESTIONS FOR REVIEW AND REFLECTION

1. Why are RTI models considered proactive?

2. How might determination of the conditions under which a student experiences *success* lead to more proactive instructional supports?

3. Briefly describe two characteristics shared by standard treatment protocols and problem-solving models?

4. How do problem-solving models differ from standard treatment protocols?

5. What are the advantages of universal screening? Describe at least two.

6. What are some cautions to consider when interpreting screening results?

7. What sort of questions should be asked when insufficient numbers of students demonstrate growth within the core curriculum?

8. Why do the authors discourage reference to students or student groups by tier or intervention designations?

9. Why is it important to consider intervention groups "fluid"?

10. How might group and individual problem-solving processes increase the appropriateness of referrals for special education?

CHAPTER 8

SPECIAL EDUCATION ISSUES
IN THE ASSESSMENT OF CLD STUDENTS

When I moved to [a special education classroom in a new school], my class was again filled with Spanish [speaking] students. Many of them were labeled "borderline," which I soon discovered meant that they could have functioned in a regular class if [appropriate] interventions had been used. . . . I often felt my class was a dumping ground for students the teachers could not handle. More than once a teacher would remark that the student just did not "fit" in her classroom.

Shirley Wilson, Prekindergarten Teacher

Learning Outcomes

After reading this chapter, you should be able to:

- Hold informed conversations with administrators, colleagues, and parents about issues of *exceptionality* and *disproportionality* in relation to special education programs.
- Gather data to inform decisions about eligibility and need for special education as well as least restrictive environments for students.

One of the most challenging dilemmas teachers face is wondering *if* and *when* to consider special education for a culturally and linguistically diverse (CLD) student. Unless educators have substantial knowledge of—and are responsive to—the unique sociolinguistic needs of CLD students, these learners are at greater risk of being misidentified, mislabeled, and consequently miseducated in our schools. Such students may also be harmed by blanket practices that discourage referral or set an arbitrary timeline for consideration of more individualized need ("No ESL student can be referred until they've been in the country for x number of years."). Although it may seem reasonable to advise waiting until the student is proficient in English, the reality is that neither poor educational programming nor specialized need will be properly addressed by the mere passage of time. Any situation that interferes with student learning warrants a better understanding of that student and possibly adjustments to methods, materials, or mindset. When practices are in place to continually assess and respond to the majority of all students' (in all groups) needs, it becomes much easier to discuss and address the specialized needs of a very few. There is nothing inherently helpful or "special" about a program so named, unless the benefit available is specifically designed for the actual strengths and needs of the *individual* child.

WHAT IS SPECIAL EDUCATION?

Special education is the term given to a range of programs and supports that ensure each student, regardless of exceptionality, receives a free and appropriate public education (FAPE). This assurance, commonly referred to by its abbreviation, is described in Part B and Appendix C of the Individuals with Disabilities Education Act (IDEA) (Public Law 105-117, reauthorized in 2004). To be eligible for special education services, students must be identified as having one or more cognitive, linguistic, or physical exceptionalities that necessitate special instructional approaches or supports for that student to participate in *and benefit from* the curriculum. Such exceptionalities include speech or language impairments, behavioral disorders, specific learning difficulties, physical impairments (e.g., mobility, vision, hearing), or cognitive skills that are significantly higher or lower than the average range of a student's peers. In the case of students with severe cognitive impairments, academic goals may represent the general curriculum in the broader sense of helping these students develop the life skills necessary to function as independently as possible in society.

Although there is variation in the criteria required by each state to meet the definition of *exceptionality*, special education eligibility is generally understood to exclude *achievement discrepancies* that are the result of external variables such as language, experience, cultural difference, socioeconomic status, attendance, mobility, and family crises (IDEA, 1997). It also excludes the delays and skill/knowledge gaps that result from ineffective instructional programs. Because intrinsic exceptionalities can be assumed to occur in all populations at generally similar rates, we would expect all groups to be represented in special education in numbers proportional to their representation in a given population. No group would be significantly more or less likely to be placed in special education than another group (Artiles & Harry, 2004; Card & Giuliano, 2016).

For example, a school district with 35% Caucasian, 20% African American, 25% Hispanic, 10% Asian, 5% American Indian, and 5% Biracial/Other students would expect to see similar demographic patterns in all its special education programs, including those for the gifted and talented. Consider the implications for such a district that has the following special education demographics:

	American Indian	Asian	African American	Caucasian	Hispanic	Biracial/ Other
School district population	5%	10%	20%	35%	25%	5%
Gifted/talented	0%	16 %	4%	75%	4%	1%
Learning disabilities	0%	4%	27%	36%	33%	0%
Speech/language impaired	3%	14%	19%	30%	33%	1%
Behavior disorders	0%	0%	34%	28%	31%	7%
Visually impaired	6%	8%	22%	37%	24%	3%

As this table illustrates, students from different ethnic backgrounds are represented disproportionately in this district's special education programs. Although 10% of the student population is Asian, 16% of students in gifted and talented programs are Asian, and no Asian students have been identified as having behavior disorders. By contrast, African American students make up 20% of the student population, yet only 4% of students in gifted and talented programs are African American, and African Americans represent 34% of students identified as having behavior disorders.

Further examination of these data reveals "visually impaired" is the exceptionality that most closely reflects the overall representation of students in the district. Why might this be the case? For which exceptionalities might language acquisition or cultural mismatch be factors in the disproportional representation of CLD students?

Is Disproportionality Really an Issue?

Educators might wonder, "Is disproportionality really an issue?" The easy answer is, "Yes," but there is not one simple reason *why*. The variables are multilayered. Reviews of demographic data support concerns of *disproportionality*— that student representation by race, ethnicity, and language learner status frequently do not correlate with those students' representation in special education (Morgan, Farkas, Hillemeier, & Maczuga, 2017). One reason it is difficult to understand "why" is that common demographic data isn't clear when it comes to categories such as race or ethnicity or language of the home. For example, "Hispanic" can be assumed to include English learners but not all "Hispanic" or Latino/a students are English learners. If Hispanic students as a group are disproportionately represented in certain categories of special education, is that because there are English learners in this group, or is something else going on?

What further complicates consideration of English learner incidence in special education is the differing natures of those groups. Students with most types of disabilities (other than speech) will require support or continue to be so identified *throughout the educational years*. This is a fairly stable group to follow through school. By contrast, the conditions for being designated as English learner are more *situational* than innate. As such, English learners may be re-classified out of English learner status when second language (L2) competencies increase (Umansky, Thompson, & Diaz, 2017). Many such students will no longer be technically English learners by secondary school. The changing composition of this subgroup makes it difficult to derive a clear picture. Nevertheless, critical information has emerged regarding the relationship between language learning phenomena and disproportional representation in special education programs.

For example, data included in the 24th annual report to Congress on IDEA implementation in 2002 revealed that, despite the fact that the percentage of the general population who did not speak English in the home increased by only 2.5% between 1987 and 2001, there was a nearly 11% increase in special education placements for students from those homes during the same period. When this type of data is examined further, patterns emerge that remain evident today. For instance, English learners in general continue to be overrepresented in special education (Morgan et al., 2018). Additionally, there is evidence that Hispanic students remain overrepresented in special education programs for learning disabilities (although responses to highlighted discrepancies can subsequently result in *underrepresentation*) (Morgan et al., 2018). Large-scale studies reveal that this trend of *overrepresentation* may be even more apparent when those students are also English learners (Artiles, Rueda, Salazar, & Higareda, 2005; Sullivan, 2011). Other indicators of CLD student disproportionality include evidence that African American and American Indian students, especially males, are often overrepresented in programs for learning disabilities, mental retardation, and behavioral

---

assessment FREEZE FRAME 8.1

Although there is variation in the criteria required by each state to meet the definition of exceptionality, special education eligibility is generally understood to exclude achievement discrepancies that are the result of external variables such as language, experience, cultural difference, socioeconomic status, attendance, mobility, and family crises.

disorders (Chinn & Hughes, 1987; de Valenzuela, Copeland, Qi, & Park, 2006; Finn, 1982; Yates, 1998; Bal, Sullivan, & Harper, 2014). However, African American, Hispanic, and American Indian students are typically *underrepresented* in programs for the gifted and talented (Card & Giulani, 2016; Finn, 1982; Ford, 1998; Ford & Harris, 1998; de Valenzuela et al., 2006).

Researchers have identified a number of factors that appear to contribute to the disproportionate consideration of CLD students for special education. The most commonly noted themes include the following:

1. Connections to Demographic Characteristics
   * Racial and ethnic minorities are more likely to experience poverty, which is a factor in special education referrals and placements (Oswald, Coutinho, Best, & Singh, 1999; Proctor & Dalaker, 2002; Skiba et al., 2005; USDE, 2017).
   * Low-income students as a group, which includes the majority of CLD students, typically have less access to a high-quality education provided by highly qualified teachers who use techniques and materials known to be effective for diverse learners (Banks, Obiakor, & Algozzine, 2013; Biddle & Berliner, 2002; Gandara, Rumberger, Maxwell-Jolly, & Callahan, 2003).
   * Experiencing parental incarceration by age 5 has been associated with lower noncognitive school readiness as well as a greater likelihood of special education placement by age 9 (Haskins, 2014).
   * Students acquiring a L2 often exhibit academic, attention, and behavior difficulties that are similar to those of students with a learning disability (Barrera, 2006; C. Collier, 2010; Collier et al., 2007).
2. Inappropriate General Education Practices
   * Teachers may misinterpret culturally different behaviors as indicators of learning or behavioral disability (Ortiz, 2008; Salend, 2005).
   * Misinterpretation of language differences as indicators of reading and writing disability contributes to misidentification of CLD students for special education (Klingner, Artiles, & Barletta, 2004; Sullivan, 2011).
   * When CLD student needs are not recognized at the instructional level, they are unlikely to be recognized or addressed during the intervention process (Cabral, 2008; Ortiz, Wilkinson, Robertson-Courtney, & Kushner, 2006; Sanford, Brown, & Turner, 2012).
   * CLD students frequently lack opportunities to expand first language (L1) development; yet those with limited L1 and L2 proficiencies are significantly more likely to be identified as having mental retardation, learning disabilities, or speech language impairments (Artiles et al., 2005).
   * Low school achievement is found to be a significant factor in the determination of disability (Hosp & Reschly, 2004); therefore, educational practices that result in achievement gaps between CLD and dominant-culture students may contribute to the overrepresentation of CLD students in special education (Cartledge & Kourea, 2008; Fletcher & Navarrete, 2003).
3. Inappropriate Special Education Placements and Programming
   * Despite concerns regarding the influence of culture, language acquisition, and prior educational experiences, many schools continue to rely on discrepancy models that interpret achievement gaps as indicators of learning disability (Baca & Cervantes, 2004; Ortiz, 2004; Smith Bailey, 2003).

- Despite the range of considerations necessary to determine genuine educational disability, assessment teams often make decisions based on insufficient information (Huang, Clarke, Milczarski, & Raby, 2011; Overton, Fielding, & Simonsson, 2004), insensitive screeners, or use of standardized assessments that are not developed, normed, or administered appropriately for CLD students (Anaya, Peña, & Bedore, 2018; Crowley, 2011; Rhodes, Ochoa, & Ortiz, 2005; Rodríguez & Rodríguez, 2017).
- Inappropriate special education placements and actions locate achievement or behavior problems within the student population and enable the educational system to avoid taking necessary measures to identify and accommodate the general education needs of diverse students (Baca & Cervantes, 2004).
- Once identified, CLD students are more likely to be placed in more restrictive settings for longer periods of time than their non-CLD peers with similar academic or behavior concerns (Artiles et al., 2005; de Valenzuela et al., 2006).

We caution educators to remember that overreliance on data that lumps heterogeneous subgroups into broad categories can obscure within-group (e.g., gendered) patterns of over- or underreferral for special education as well as over- or underrepresentation in various tiers of intervention. With respect to the learning needs of CLD students, it is important to note that although most teachers recognize that these learners may have difficulty with skills such as vocabulary, pronunciation, and grammar, many have never considered the numerous other characteristics associated with students with learning disabilities that are also typical of students acquiring a L2 or experiencing acculturation (see Figure 8.1).

---

assessment FREEZE FRAME 8.2

Inappropriate special education placements and actions locate achievement or behavior problems within the student population and enable the educational system to avoid taking necessary measures to identify and accommodate the general education needs of diverse students.

Why Should We Be Concerned?

Disproportional representation in special education is a matter of concern for administrators, teachers, parents, and other stakeholders for several reasons. One overriding reason is the realization that disproportionality can be a strong indicator that students are not being identified for, or placed in, the most appropriate programs. By appropriate, we mean *least* restrictive. Students should be placed in the program or setting in which they can maximally participate *while also being challenged* by the curriculum.

For most students, the *least restrictive environment* is regular education. However, the nonaccommodative regular classroom may actually be very restrictive to the CLD student who is either *overwhelmed* or *underchallenged* in that setting. In this situation, it is most likely the level of instructional accommodation rather than the presence or absence of student exceptionality that should be addressed first. Careful attention to data gathered via both formal and informal means increases the teacher's ability to respond to student needs in a timely and targeted manner. As detailed in Chapter 7, the informed review of class, grade, or schoolwide data may also reveal patterns that compel systemic instructional change.

When nondisabled students are misidentified and placed in special education settings, they are disenfranchised from the broader offerings and opportunities of the grade-level classroom. For these students, the special education setting or

Figure 8.1   Typical Characteristics of Both English Speakers with a Learning Disability and Second Language Learners Without a Disability

LITERACY

Difficulty with sound–symbol association

Sounds out words but unable to blend

Poor orientation to page and text

Below grade-level reading

Struggles in content areas

Unusual spelling errors

Letter reversals

Difficulty with grammar structures

Trouble remembering
- Words/text read
- Syllable sequences
- Letters/numbers seen

SOCIAL/VOCATIONAL

Anxious or emotional

Distracted or withdrawn

Limited attention span

Frustrate or anger easily

Appear to lack motivation

Exhibits disorderly behavior

Poor-quality work

Poor social skills with peers

Oral class participation
- Limited
- Off-topic

LANGUAGE

Appear delayed compared to peers

Articulation and grammar errors

Limited vocabulary

Difficulty following directions

Forget easily
- What was just said/heard/read
- Previously learned information

Poor phonemic awareness skills
- Unable to rhyme
- Struggle with auditory sound blending

Misunderstand pragmatics—body language

Narratives lack details/sequence

Comprehension problems

SCIENCE/MATH

Overreliance on fingers or manipulatives

Poor performance on timed tests

Difficulty remembering
- Content-area vocabulary
- Processes and procedures

Poor comprehension

Difficulty with orally presented materials
- Story problem formats
- Abstract concepts

Sources: Baca and Cervantes (2004), Barrera (2006), Chu and Flores (2011), Collier et al. (2007), Fradd and McGee (1994)

classroom is a more restrictive setting that may actually constrain their learning. In contrast, the student with a genuine disability might be better able to learn specific skills when provided the type of structure and supports that would typically restrict other learners. Fortunately, many schools have begun implementing practices based on the understanding that least restrictive environments are not the same for all students. Increasing numbers are moving away from pull-out programs toward inclusive classrooms where purposeful collaboration among grade-level, ESL, and special education teachers fosters optimal learning environments for all students.

The other side of disproportional representation is underrepresentation. In some cases, truly exceptional students may be denied consideration for supports and services because their difficulties are attributed almost entirely to language. Teachers and support personnel often lack the training or experience to distinguish between language acquisition phenomena and learning disabilities (Figueroa & Newsome, 2006; Hoover, Klingner, Baca, & Patton, 2008). Whenever students are being over- or underidentified for special education services, they are being effectively disenfranchised from their maximal participation in the curriculum. In addition, more subtle consequences of disproportionality affect all students. When CLD students are more likely than others to be removed from the grade-level classroom for special programming, those left behind are denied the richness of diverse perspectives and experiences that complement their own learning.

Federal regulations require the use of nonbiased assessment measures and techniques when serving the differential needs of CLD students (U.S. Congress, 1999). Because of long-standing concerns in this area, the Individuals with Disabilities Education Improvement Act (2004) includes notable amendments and language to address issues related to CLD students. Among these amendments are the following from section 602.10-13 of the act:

(10) (A) The Federal Government must be responsive to the growing needs of an increasingly diverse society.

(11) (A) The limited English proficient population is the fastest growing in our nation, and the growth is occurring in many parts of our nation.

(B) Studies have documented apparent discrepancies in the levels of referral and placement of limited English proficient children in special education.

(C) Such discrepancies pose a special challenge for special education in the referral of, assessment of, and provision of services for our nation's students from non-English language backgrounds.

(12) (A) Greater efforts are needed to prevent the intensification of problems connected with mislabeling and high dropout rates among minority children with disabilities.

(B) More minority children continue to be served in special education than would be expected from the percentage of minority students in the general school population.

Source: Disabilities Education Improvement Act (2004) Among these amendments are the following from section 602.10-13 of the act.

These amendments strengthen the original law that stipulates a number of protections to ensure that all students, including those with limited English proficiency, receive appropriate special education evaluations. IDEA requirements state that eligible CLD students who demonstrate need are placed in least

---

assessment FREEZE FRAME 8.3

When CLD students are more likely than others to be removed from the grade-level classroom for special programming, those left behind are denied the richness of diverse perspectives and experiences that complement their own learning.

SNAPSHOT from CLASSROOM PRACTICE   8.1

Ms. Rush purposefully structures activities in which students can benefit from a variety of peer scaffolds in advance of her clarification and feedback. These include partner collaboration, L1/L2 discussion, and the opportunity to review peer models before deciding what to add or comment on for each content element. Ms. Rush finds that such techniques naturally foster all students to reach levels of individualized rigor within the accommodated core. She also uses the completed products to document students' growing conceptualizations and skills.

Essence Rush

---

restrictive learning environments that also take into account these students' unique language acquisition needs.

IMPLICATIONS FOR CLASSROOM TEACHERS

According to Brown (2004), a teacher's professional development regarding the role that language acquisition and acculturation play in student performance is "the first step in reducing the over-referral of CLD students for special education" (p. 226). Brown cites culture shock, L1 loss, inconsistent education, reduced opportunities to learn, inappropriate instructional models, low teacher expectations, and mobility among the phenomena that contribute to inappropriate referrals and placements in special education.

Chapter 7 provides a detailed explanation of the practices and processes that inform consideration of exceptionality with CLD students. Careful attention to, and accommodation for, the language, culture, and situational factors that influence a student's success and participation is required during each step. The volume of data gathered via these processes can also powerfully improve the interpretation of, and response to, early indicators of student struggle within a model of response to intervention (RTI) that does *not* presume special education need. If, however, the student's background experiences and other preassessment information (e.g., responsiveness to interventions) do not seem to account for the noted learning concerns, a full and individual evaluation of language, cognition, achievement, and social skills may be the next recommendation. Refer to Figure 8.2 for a brief overview of the process for determining whether a referral to special education might be appropriate.

Figure 8.2 Prereferral Flowchart: Questions Every Teacher Should Answer *Before* Referring a CLD Student for Special Education

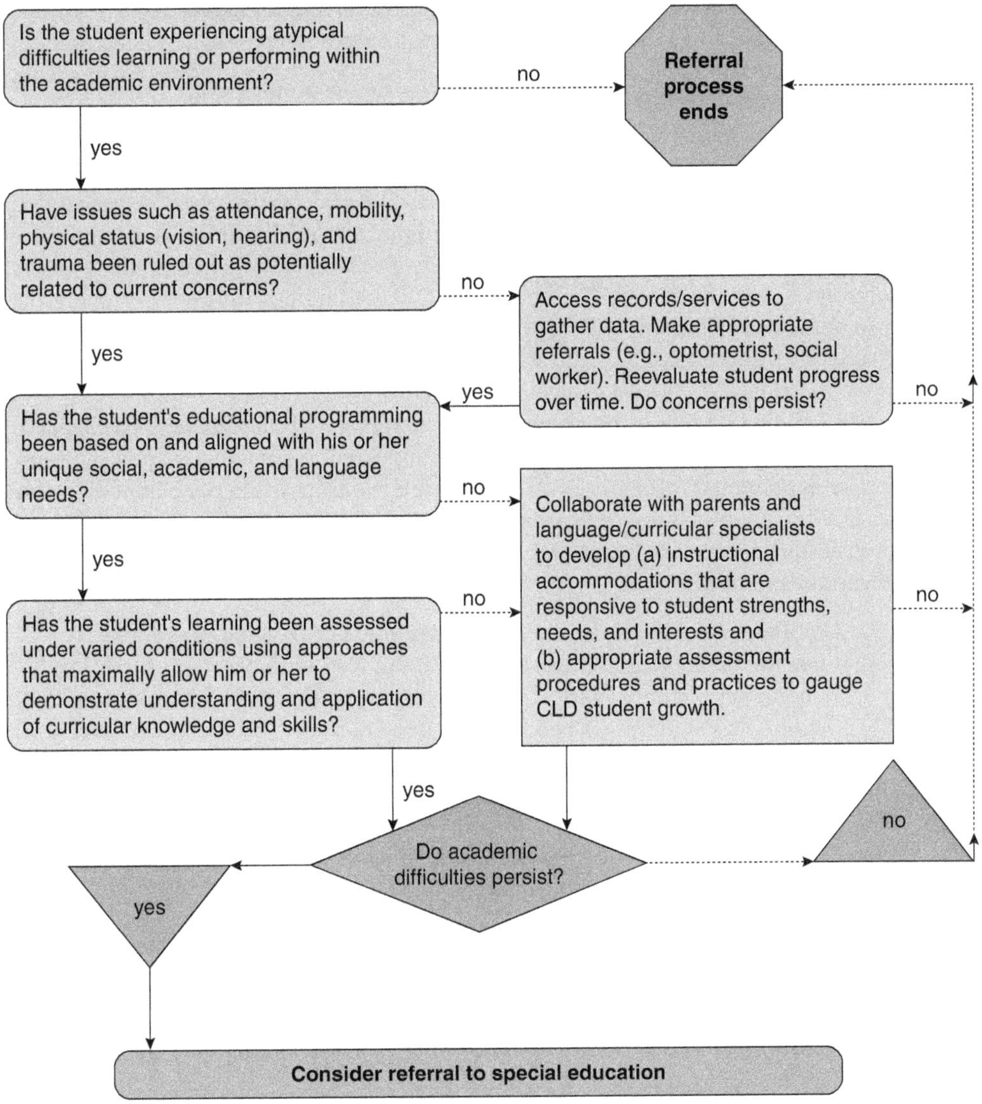

Attention to the Assessment Process

Asusena was in the 3rd grade when she was referred by her teacher to the student intervention team at her school. This team was composed of Asusena's ESL and classroom teachers; two other teachers esteemed for their knowledge and effectiveness with diverse learners; a counselor familiar with the community; a bilingual interpreter trained in special education issues and terminology; and Asusena's mother, the recognized expert on this child.

The team began by reviewing pertinent school records. According to the home language survey, Spanish was the language of the home. Asusena's mother nodded as this was reported and translated for her participation. Preassessment of L1 proficiency indicated Asusena began school with well-developed primary language skills. Asusena also demonstrated a history of consistent school attendance and ESL services. In this particular school, the majority of students were provided ESL support by classroom teachers who modified instruction in accordance with knowledge gained through an ESL endorsement or specialized training in sheltered instruction. Spanish- and Vietnamese-speaking paraprofessionals were used in the lower grades as well as with older newcomers to provide pre- and postinstructional content support in the primary language. All other instruction, including literacy development, was provided in English only.

Recent language proficiency assessments revealed that Asusena demonstrated intermediate English oral fluency. Her reading and writing skills, however, were found to be well below those of her CLD peers (even lower than those of the students who did not perform as well on oral tests). These findings were supported by the anecdotal and observational logs of Mrs. Karas, the classroom teacher. Although Asusena was able to participate well in most aspects of her accommodative classroom, writing skills were a growing concern.

In discussing Asusena's strengths, Mrs. Karas noted that Asusena participated well in class during group time and always appeared to have understood the story or lesson presented through activities or lecture. Considering her apparent ability to learn, Mrs. Karas did not understand why Asusena was unable to transfer skills and motivation to seatwork. More perplexing was Asusena's recent tendency to "act up" in certain situations.

Counselor (to Mrs. Karas): Can you describe one of these situations?

Mrs. Karas: In general, Asusena gets along well with others, but she can become very irritable with classmates during indoor recess. At first, I thought she was just having a bad day, but this has happened on several occasions and is affecting the desire of other students to let her join their play.

Counselor: Does this occur during outside recess?

Mrs. Karas: No, never. She's actually somewhat of a leader and very popular. So I've become concerned that something may be going on. It's just not like her to get so angry with friends.

As she listened to the translated comments, Asusena's mother looked puzzled. She shared that Asusena always seemed to play well at home with siblings or cousins, whether indoors or out, rain or shine.

Consulting Teacher 1 (to mother): What type of activities or games does she like to play at home?

Mother: Mostly they like to play Barbies, soccer, and jacks. She's really good at jacks. She already knows she can pick up three sets of three with one left over, and two sets of four with two left over. . . . She knows all the patterns.

Mrs. Karas: Wow, I don't see that skill in math. In fact, she rarely finishes two-digit addition pages without help. She seems to know the facts in her head but has trouble putting them on paper. Most everyone finishes before her. Lately, I've given her fewer problems, more widely spaced. This helps a little but she is still making lots of errors. One day I asked her to say everything out loud as she worked the problem. I noticed she was not only misreading some of the numbers, like 2 for 5, but she also had trouble staying in the same column while adding.

Consulting Teacher 1 (to Mrs. Karas): Despite her paperwork, I'm hearing you and Mom both say that Asusena seems to understand the facts and concepts in her head. Is that correct?

Mrs. Karas looked at Asusena's mother and nodded.

Asesena's mother (smiling): Yes.

Consulting Teacher 2: Getting back to the conflicts with peers, what type of activities are students doing during indoor recess?

Mrs. Karas: Well, I like to make everything a learning opportunity, so most of my games involve some use of reading, writing, or math skills. There are several game boards that require students to solve math problems, follow directions, or answer questions on cards.

ESL Teacher: What about your students who have yet to acquire enough English for those tasks?

Mrs. Karas: Every one of my students is aware of who may need more support, and they always offer to help read or translate so everyone can play.

Consulting Teacher 1: Do they offer to help Asusena?

Mrs. Karas: They really don't offer to help Asusena because she speaks English better than many. In fact, that can be a problem in our cooperative groups because she always wants to be the person who reports. I've heard some of the students call her a *sabelotodo* [know-it-all].

Consulting Teacher 2: What is happening in the games when Asusena gets upset?

Mrs. Karas: Now that I think of it, they complain about how she reads the cards. Some students even accuse her of cheating because she holds the cards very close, gets mad when the others ask to see them, and then decides she doesn't want to play.

Consulting Teacher 1: Tell me again—how are her reading and writing skills?

ESL Teacher: Although we know oral skills develop before reading and writing skills, Asusena is having more trouble in those areas than I would expect, given her oral English proficiency. Mrs. Karas and I have been collaborating on a few interventions, but it really doesn't appear her difficulties are related to language.

Mrs. Karas: Yes, I've allowed Asusena to buddy with a partner. Although she often contributes her share or more to the content of the discussion, she always prefers the buddy to write. At first I discouraged this, but Asusena's written work never got done or was completely indecipherable. Now I allow Asusena to copy her partner's notes of their collaborative responses, but there are still significant errors in letter recognition and orientation, even while copying.

By the time the team had met for a second and third time, all members, including Asusena's mother, had concluded that Asusena's difficulties and response to intervention could not be explained solely on the basis of her socialization, language acquisition, or prior academic experiences. Asusena was then referred to a multidisciplinary assessment team whose members were experienced professionals with keen understandings of the informal and formal approaches (as covered in Chapters 2–7) that would be least biased and most effective in the assessment of Asusena's situation. These multidimensional analyses were interpreted in light of their ability to explain or account for the volume of authentic and dynamic information that had already been compiled. In this case, multiple sources of evidence revealed that despite strong oral language, Asusena demonstrated unusual difficulties connecting discrete linguistic units with visual symbols. These problems significantly affected her ability to read, write, and learn content from text. The team determined that Asusena would not only qualify for, but (more important) *benefit from*, targeted special education support scheduled to maximize her ongoing participation in the enriched instructional core.

The scenario illustrates many of the assessment dynamics that have been discussed up to this point in the text. It also highlights appropriate ways teachers and other evaluating personnel can put into practice many of the stipulations and recommendations in the law, such as the following that address communication with parents and the language of assessment.

- Parents should be notified upon their child's initial referral to special education and their consent obtained for special education actions, including evaluation or changes to an existing placement. Although documents of notification and consent must be written in a language that is understandable to the general public, it must also be appropriately and accurately translated orally, in writing, or by other means (e.g., sign language) as necessary to ensure that CLD parents understand the content and intent of the proposed action(s).
- Students should be assessed "in the language and form most likely to yield accurate information on what the child knows and can do academically, developmentally, and functionally, unless it is not feasible to so provide or administer" (IDEIA, 2004, section 614.[a](3)[ii], p. 59).
  - In accordance with this requirement, schools should make every effort to assess students in their home or dominant language using instruments and administration procedures that are valid and reliable for that population.
  - Caution is recommended in any efforts to interpret bilingual student performance based exclusively or primarily on language or academic tests that are normed on, or compare the students with, monolingual students of either language.
  - Academic knowledge, skills, and capacities among students should be assessed in the language in which these students are receiving instruction. When this language of instruction is not the student's primary or dominant language, modifications should be employed to reduce the degree to which culture and language interferes with students' demonstration of academic knowledge, skills, and abilities.
- When reporting results, the evaluator should describe any modifications that were used to reduce the effect of potential bias in assessments. For example, the evaluator might mention "a translator was used to administer the assessment in the student's primary language" or "an interpreter translated and modified the assessment questions in a manner consistent with the student's culture and local dialect." Note that these statements are not synonymous. The second reflects much greater control for potential bias.
- If an assessment is used or administered in a manner different from the conditions under which it was standardized, it is preferable to describe student performance qualitatively and correlate that with other forms of data than to cite potentially misleading scores. Such a statement might read, "As this assessment is normed on monolingual Spanish speakers receiving consistent educational instruction in their primary language, comparison of this student to that

group is inappropriate. However, analysis of student performance reveals (e.g., mastery of the following skills . . . ; difficulties with . . .)."
* Achievement results should also be interpreted with attention to research demonstrating the impact that the instructional model (e.g., ESL pullout, bilingual transition, dual language) has on English learner achievement (Thomas & Collier, 2002, 2012).

Assessment information gathered through formal evaluation is best used to augment and illuminate rather than replace or override information gathered in more contextual and authentic situations. For this reason, references to specific diagnostic instruments are omitted in this chapter in favor of an emphasis on the knowledge bases necessary for all educators to select among, and interpret the results of, a multitude of available tools. When a detailed understanding of a student's prior life, language, and learning experiences is compared with his or her current ability to demonstrate skills in varied contexts, it is possible to make well-informed decisions about whether the student should receive special education services or more accommodative levels of sheltered instruction in the classroom.

> **assessment FREEZE FRAME 8.4**
>
> IDEA requirements state that eligible CLD students who demonstrate need are placed in least restrictive learning environments that also take into account these students' unique language acquisition needs.

The Bilingual Special Education Student

As noted in Chapter 7, special education students should be assigned to the most appropriate and least restrictive tier of instruction for each curricular need. In the case of Asusena, the team realized that she had a very specific need for some specialized instruction in reading and writing. Looking at her profile, it was also apparent that Asusena was learning well in the language-rich general classroom setting with ESL supports. She went on to participate fully in the core curriculum with accommodations for reading and writing while also receiving some direct special education support for literacy. Five years earlier, that would not have been the recommendation. Many teachers previously had thought of the dual ESL/SPED qualification as a *doubling* of need. Students like Asusena had often spent the entire language arts block away from classmates, working on remedial English skills. Because reading was required for texts, the reading disability would "require" even more pullout time—time during which students were away from core class discussions, projects, and connections that made those texts come alive.

In cases of dual ESL/SPED qualification, the multidisciplinary assessment team, including the parent(s) or guardian(s), develops a culturally and linguistically appropriate *individualized education program (IEP)* that, among other things, stipulates the languages, strategies, and settings of instruction that best minimize barriers to student achievement. Among recommended accommodations of this IEP, the multidisciplinary team is likely to incorporate a combination of accommodations that relate to the biopsychosocial and language histories of the *bilingual special education student*, as well as his or her general education needs. A sample range of potential accommodations is detailed in Figure 8.3. This figure compares and contrasts some of the pedagogical and logistical accommodations that are specific to CLD students or students in special education, as well as those that are common to both.

Figure 8.3   Comparison of CLD and SPED Accommodations

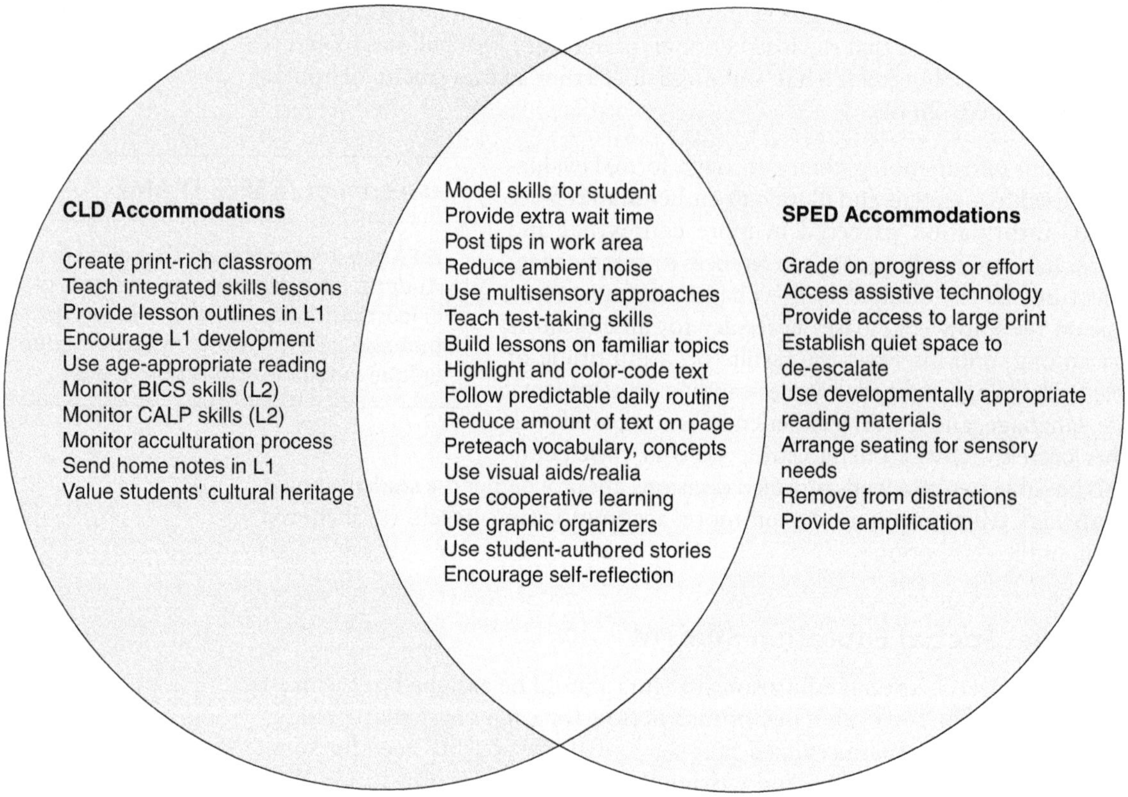

CLD Accommodations

Create print-rich classroom
Teach integrated skills lessons
Provide lesson outlines in L1
Encourage L1 development
Use age-appropriate reading
Monitor BICS skills (L2)
Monitor CALP skills (L2)
Monitor acculturation process
Send home notes in L1
Value students' cultural heritage

Model skills for student
Provide extra wait time
Post tips in work area
Reduce ambient noise
Use multisensory approaches
Teach test-taking skills
Build lessons on familiar topics
Highlight and color-code text
Follow predictable daily routine
Reduce amount of text on page
Preteach vocabulary, concepts
Use visual aids/realia
Use cooperative learning
Use graphic organizers
Use student-authored stories
Encourage self-reflection

SPED Accommodations

Grade on progress or effort
Access assistive technology
Provide access to large print
Establish quiet space to
de-escalate
Use developmentally appropriate
reading materials
Arrange seating for sensory
needs
Remove from distractions
Provide amplification

Special education is appropriate for genuinely exceptional CLD students *if it is adapted to meet unique language acquisition needs* (Baca & Cervantes, 2004; Collier, 2010; Hoover et al., 2008; Rodríguez & Rodríguez, 2017). Unfortunately, the instructional programs and recommendations for CLD students with learning disabilities are all too often the same as those recommended for their native-English-speaking peers, with little or no consideration given to their unique language needs (Chang, Lai, & Shimizu, 1995; de Valenzuela et al., 2016; Hoover et al., 2008). Whether the result of inexperience or a disinclination to spend the time and resources necessary, the tendency to simplify the needs and complexities of CLD students can compromise every stage of the education process.

Another troubling pattern is that once CLD students are determined to have a disability, they are often effectively reclassified as no longer in need of language support. This type of response derails the development of appropriate educational plans and practices for CLD students with disabilities. It is important to remember, "Under ESSA Section 3121, an LEA [local education agency] must disaggregate by English learners [ELs] with disabilities in reporting the number and percentage of ELs making progress toward English language proficiency, and in reporting the number and percentage of former ELs meeting State academic standards for each of the 4 years after they no longer receive Title III services" (USDE, 2016, p. 37).

Therefore, schools must also be accountable for the ongoing English development of CLD students with disabilities.

Misconceptions Related to CLD Students with Disabilities

The health history indicated that Jonathan was born at 30 weeks gestation and had been "a bit slower" than siblings to walk and talk. By age 1, he was also diagnosed with cerebral palsy. Nevertheless, by his fourth birthday, Jonathan was putting together four-word phrases ("Me duele el estómago" "*My stomach hurts*") and asking short questions ("¿Donde está el perro?" "*Where is the dog?*") at home. Because of Jonathan's physical needs, the pediatrician referred the family to a screening process sponsored by a local education agency. This doctor also advised Jonathan's parents to use more English at home because "children with disabilities struggle to learn any language and English will be the language of school."

Information gained via parent interview, bilingual evaluation specialists, and home observation led to Jonathan's placement in a Pre-K program for students with "developmental disabilities." The goal of this program was to provide students time and opportunity to show skills before being labeled or assigned to a more restrictive setting. During this time, Jonathan seemed to enjoy school and make new friends. His teachers praised his efforts to use English and parents confirmed they now limited use of Spanish when talking to their son. By the time of his next evaluation (2 years later), Jonathan spoke primarily one- to three-word English phrases at school. Parents also reported that he was now speaking more English than Spanish at home.

Given this information, the child study team conducted all aspects of the *reevaluation* in English. Jonathan scored particularly low on the speech pathologist's expressive and receptive language testing as well as the psychologist's measures of verbal intelligence. A home rating scale was used to gather family perceptions but parents reported that Jonathan's communication had regressed, and he was not yet independently dressing. This seemed to align with the teacher's report of fine motor and language delays. As a result, Jonathan was placed in a classroom comprised solely of students with intellectual disability. Many of these students also had language impairments and some required picture systems to communicate their wants and needs.

Jonathan is now almost age 9 and due for another reevaluation for special education. The team had only planned on updating information from the previous evaluation since he had already been tested several times. However, when Jonathan's mother met with the social worker to discuss the required consent, she voiced concerns about his progress. The translator also helped Mom convey specific worries that Jonathan was becoming less verbal and not being taught to read like others his age. The social worker tried to explain why the curriculum was somewhat different for students in Jonathan's class, but Mom said she wanted new testing by people who were bilingual "like the first time." This surprised the social worker, who questioned, "Didn't you say Jonathan speaks English at home?" Mom replied, "Oh yes, but he understands everything people around him are saying in Spanish."

Although the team did not think Jonathan's case merited a *bilingual* referral, they nevertheless contacted the personnel necessary to "cover this base." No one was more surprised than these team members when it was revealed that Jonathan had lower *average range* nonverbal intelligence. The consulting speech language pathologist was able to determine that Jonathan's combined comprehension of Spanish and

English was also in this range. Although these results indicated Jonathan may need some support, he most certainly was not intellectually disabled. Despite these positive findings, Jonathan had indeed regressed verbally and had learned fewer skills than similar peers in less restrictive settings.

The case of Jonathan demonstrates how disregard for, or inattention to, the language learning history and profile of a CLD student with disabilities can result in misinterpretation of assets/needs and placement in overly restrictive settings that impede cognitive, linguistic, and social growth. How did this go so wrong? Key insights to development occur in the early years. More careful attention to initial milestones would have revealed that Jonathan was developing Spanish at rates approximating his peers. The pediatrician's primary concern related to Jonathan's potential physical needs. Unfortunately, uninformed advice about language use contributed to changes in home dynamics that negatively affected Jonathan's ongoing language development and the ability of educators to fully recognize his many strengths.

At the heart of Jonathan's case are also misconceptions that are prevalent among educators. Three misperceptions related to CLD students with disabilities are especially common.

1. *Special education services "trump" language support services when meeting the needs of CLD students with disabilities.* This line of thinking is akin to stating that eyeglasses "trump" hearing aids. CLD students with disabilities do not cease being culturally and linguistically diverse upon placement in special education. As we have discussed in this chapter, a comprehensive picture of the individual student's social, linguistic, academic, and cognitive profile is central to the development of an appropriate IEP. Denying CLD students access to language support programs and/or accommodations within the special education setting can have damaging effects on that student's linguistic, cognitive, and social development.

2. *CLD students with disabilities should focus on learning only one language.* Unfortunately, this misconception is still being relayed by family members, teachers, and sometimes ill-informed professionals such as pediatricians, speech-pathologists, and psychologists (Marinova-Todd et al., 2016). The basis of this myth is the unsupported belief that a student with communication or cognitive challenges has "enough difficulty" learning one language. Exposure to two is thought to either confuse the child or divert critical language resources to a language not used in school. Not only is this view unfounded, but a growing body of research indicates that bilingual environments and educational approaches optimize socialization and language learning outcomes for CLD students with disabilities. Such groups include, but are not limited to, students with specific language impairment, cognitive disability, and autism spectrum disorder (Cleave, Kay-Raining Bird, Trudeau, & Sutton, 2014; Gonzalez-Barrero & Nadig, 2017; Rodríguez & Rodríguez, 2017; Thordardottir, 2010).

3. *Special education services are so specialized that they meet every need of the exceptional CLD student.* Not only is this a misconception, but special education services that disregard the CLD student's culture/language assets and needs may result in less academic and language growth than if that student had remained in more inclusive settings (Maldonado, 1994; Serpa, 2011).

Researchers have found that students with diminished or arrested L1 development, as well as those from historically marginalized economic, racial, and linguistic groups, are more likely to be assigned to more restrictive environments than their peers from the dominant culture who are identified with the same disability (Artiles et al., 2005; Artiles, Kozleski, Trent, Osher, & Ortiz, 2010). The following tips can facilitate team (parent, teacher, evaluator, counselor, etc.) conversations around the development of IEPs that better ensure maximal learning opportunity for CLD students with disabilities.

Tips for Determining Least Restrictive Environments:

- Make sure the IEP contains information describing the student's current *assets and needs* across settings.
  - Has completion of the required sections of the IEP been informed by, and did it include evidence from, the home/community environment?
- Confirm the IEP *goals* reflect the student's learning or skill levels demonstrated in different languages and/or gathered from different sources as well as performance in the targeted language.
  - For example, a student may speak in age-appropriate sentences in the L1 but use much shorter, stilted, or ungrammatical sentences in the L2. This student does not require a goal for expressive language because there is no inherent disability in that area. This student would, however, benefit from ongoing support with English language development.
- Ensure the IEP describes a coherent *plan* for meeting the student's academic, social, behavioral, or language needs that also takes into account identified need for language support, accommodations, and recommended language of instruction.
- Determine where, and with whom, the student spends the majority of his or her day.
  - How likely will it be for the student to develop friendships and authentically socialize with nondisabled peers?
  - Do the instructional approaches utilized foster *communication* and *collaboration* with nondisabled, native English-speaking peers?
- Confirm the IEP explains how the student's L1 language and academic development will be monitored along with L2 growth.

Reevaluation Considerations   Many of the CLD students featured in the scenarios in this text might easily have been referred for and placed in special education had their teachers not understood and responded to the critical information that was gathered through multiple types of assessment, most notably formative assessment of student response to high-quality, targeted, and intensive instruction in areas of individualized need. Some knowledgeable teachers providing differentiated supports and innovative assessment may find themselves questioning the status of a CLD student in their class who has already been placed in special education. It is not at all unusual to hear comments such as the following:

- "I can tell Hien is a bright student. Everything he demonstrates is what we'd expect of a CLD student with his background. Hien learns just as well as the others when given the chance to learn and show what he knows in other ways."
- "When I asked why Sonia goes to special education, I was told she has a language problem that affects learning. Then I found out she wasn't even tested in her own language."

Under IDEA, teachers and parents with concerns about the appropriateness of a student's existing placement or services can request a reevaluation at any time. During this process, the teacher will want to present evidence of current student skills that demonstrate the student's ability to learn when provided with supports known to be effective with CLD students. In some settings, a teacher with greater experience and knowledge about CLD students may need to serve as a resource to student intervention or child study teams that lack this area of expertise. This resource person may even find it necessary to advocate for best practices that are not yet familiar to diagnostic personnel. Examples of such practices include:

- Comprehensive assessment that does not rely on previous data gathered using potentially biased assessments or methods
- Inclusion of authentic assessment data and informal indicators of student achievement
- Assessment of the current instructional setting for its facilitation of learning and its differentiated responsiveness to CLD student learning
- Careful consideration of the student's achievement in light of her or his educational history (e.g., consistency of schooling, language supports)
- Inclusion of parent information regarding related skills or learning as it occurs within the context of the home and community

As illustrated throughout this chapter, the vast majority of the issues related to the over- and underreferral of CLD students to special education can be addressed through appropriate instruction and assessment in all phases of their academic, acculturation, and language acquisition processes.

VOICES *from the* FIELD 8.1

When I started the year, there was a 3rd-grade student who was on an individualized education program (IEP) for resource services in the areas of reading, math, and writing. As the year progressed, I began to wonder why she was on an IEP and receiving resource services. In my classroom, she was performing on grade level in math, and at a 2nd-grade level for reading. Her writing included a lot of run-on sentences, but that is because she wrote like she talked. Her classroom performance showed that she was able to maintain at least Cs in all areas with accommodations and modifications that the classroom teacher was able to offerred on a daily basis.

I started digging deeper and pulled old reports to see what previous information I could find. Reports showed that she didn't start speaking till after the age of 3, which caused concerns as she began basic concepts and skills. After years of interventions from speech/language and resource support, they went ahead and labeled this girl developmentally delayed (DD) and put her on an IEP.

After completing a biography card at the beginning of the year, I knew that Spanish was the primary language spoken at home. Mom spoke no English and Dad spoke limited English. The student's ELL teacher shared her IPT [Idea Proficiency Test] . . . scores (2nd grade) with me, and they showed that she was a fluent English speaker, so I thought this was the perfect opportunity to see if she was truly a student with a learning disability or whether she was simply a CLD student. I knew this would be a challenging task, but I don't believe any child should have any label if he or she doesn't have to.

So I began the testing process. I collected informal data, administered standardized testing, completed observations, and asked the ELL teacher to collect new information using the IPT. As far as her academic testing, her math scores came out in the average range, her writing scores came out in the average range, and her reading scores came out in the low average range. Based on all of these scores and knowing that she was a CLD student, I made my decision that she no longer needed special education services. If this child wasn't a CLD student, there is no way I would have qualified her for special education services; even as a CLD student, there was not enough discrepancy with her scores to qualify her for an IEP.

After all the testing was done, I called a team meeting one day after school to share these results with the staff because I wanted them to see her scores and then also make them aware of what I would be proposing to parents at her IEP meeting. By the end of the IEP meeting, we went ahead and dismissed her from an IEP because she no longer demonstrated that academic need. When determining the services a student should receive, we always have to remember to look beyond the scores to see the child from a holistic perspective.

Anonymous, Special Education Teacher

ACCOMMODATIVE ASSESSMENT PRACTICES 8.1

As discussed throughout this text, the fundamental use of assessment is to inform instruction. Practices discussed in previous chapters not only ensure the alignment between assessment and instruction but also enable classroom teachers to proactively address situations that contribute to over/underreferral of CLD students for special education. Chief among these are the necessity to:

- *Collect sufficient background information to inform appropriate CLD student placement, accommodations, and expectations.* Assumptions made about a student's prior educational experiences can lead to placement in classes that, although below grade level, are nevertheless well above the level at which the student can be expected to learn most effectively, given his or her history. Conversely, CLD students can also be placed in classes far below the level that would best support their cognitive engagement and educational growth.
- *Routinely draw upon students' existing funds of knowledge to facilitate maximal participation in and understanding of the curriculum.* The potential for gaining the most benefit from instruction is

diminished for students if their learning is limited to making connections between unfamiliar referents and the new material.

- *Differentiate between content and language performance as well as objectives.* Develop instructional strategies and routines that accommodate the language proficiency of learners with *varying* linguistic profiles. When instruction is presented through language that is not made comprehensible by scaffolding or sheltering, CLD students are unlikely to learn content-area material at expected levels.
- *Consider alternate views or perceptions related to social/interpersonal/learning behaviors observed in school settings.* Classroom instruction and assessment practices that do not account for acculturation frequently yield results that are misinterpreted. Teachers who do not understand the impact of acculturation on CLD students are more likely to misinterpret these students' difficulties as

---

ACCOMMODATIVE ASSESSMENT PRACTICES 8.1 (*Continued*)

indications of learning or behavior problems rather than as predictable reactions to the significant social, linguistic, and academic demands of their lives.

- *Proactively respond if pressured to use decontextualized drills to prepare students to take high-stakes tests.* Voice the counterperspective that presentation of new information without regard for CLD students' academic needs (e.g., ignoring identified lack of prerequisite skills) will impede student participation and effectively preclude CLD students from learning. Share alternative evidence of student learning with parents and colleagues to contextualize instructional decisions and practices.

- *Establish and practice group-level problem solving processes* (discussed in Chapter 7). Such are especially necessary when any form of data (formal assessments, screeners, teacher-made tests, curriculum-based measures, etc.) suggest that numerous students in any group are not benefitting from current instructional practices.

- *Focus individual problem solving* on determining least restrictive resolutions rather than building a case for placement or nonplacement into SPED. ■

SUMMARY

The final chapter of this text addresses CLD students and special education. As noted throughout this text, assessment practices can play a critical role in the decisions that inform—or misguide—the instruction of CLD learners. Overidentification and underidentification for special education may occur for varying reasons. However, either scenario suggests inadequate consideration of CLD students' assets and needs. Deeper examination reveals that both types of disproportionality can be prevented by developing greater awareness and capacities among educators. Instructional environments that provide students with opportunities to draw upon individual strengths and experiences permit insight into conditions that optimize learning and reduce behaviors associated with disconnection, frustration, and mental fatigue.

Careful consideration of the types of supports that foster successful participation in the general education classroom is required to determine the least restrictive environment for CLD students with exceptionalities. Discussion of least restrictive environment must also include the settings and instructional programs/practices that best support ongoing language development throughout each component of the student's instructional day. Teachers concerned about the appropriateness of a student's programming and services can request (re)evaluation of the learner's educational needs. Key to this process is the collection of data that provides historical context from the student's sociocultural, cognitive, academic, and linguistic background. Evidence of what the student is able to do and what he or she struggles with, including details about the settings and circumstances surrounding performance, is needed for informed decision making.

KEY CONCEPTS

Achievement discrepancies

Bilingual special education student

Disproportionality

Exceptionality

Individualized education program (IEP)

Least restrictive environment

Overrepresentation

Reevaluation

Underrepresentation

PROFESSIONAL CONVERSATIONS ON PRACTICE

1. CLD students are both overrepresented and underrepresented in special education. Discuss factors contributing to these types of disproportionality.
2. Explain why assessment results alone are inadequate to determine exceptionality among CLD students.
3. Discuss how general education classroom environments and practices that accommodate CLD students' needs and assets thereby reduce the possibility of overreferral.

QUESTIONS FOR REVIEW AND REFLECTION

1. How would you explain the term *exceptionality*? List three types of exceptionality that may qualify a student for special education services.
2. Eligibility requirements for special education typically exclude what types of achievement discrepancies?
3. Why would we expect demographic subgroups of students to be represented in special educations in proportions similar to which they are represented in the population at large?
4. How would you explain the term *disproportionality*?
5. CLD students whose L1 is not English sometimes exhibit academic, attention, and behavioral difficulties that teachers misinterpret as indicators of a learning disability. What are at least three examples of such difficulties?
6. Why is it important to consider the language of instruction during assessment and on the IEP of a CLD student?
7. How would you respond to the common misunderstanding that CLD students with disabilities should focus on learning one language to succeed in school?
8. What is a least restrictive environment? Explain.
9. How can too much time spent in a special education setting undermine development of a CLD student's academic, cognitive, language, and social development?
10. Why it is important to scrutinize past evaluation practices and include all sources of information when conducting a special education reevaluation for a CLD student?

APPENDIX **A**

------ ■■■■■ ------

CRITICAL STANDARDS GUIDING CHAPTER CONTENT

Teachers of English to Speakers of Other Languages (TESOL)/Commission for the Accreditation of Educator Preparation (CAEP) teacher standards (Teachers of English to Speakers of Other Languages, 2010) reflect professional consensus on standards for the quality teaching of PreK–12 culturally and linguistically diverse (CLD) students. To help educators understand how they might appropriately target and address national professional teaching standards in practice, we have designed the content of each chapter to reflect the following standards.

CHAPTER 1

Classroom Assessment Amidst Cultural and Linguistic Diversity

TESOL ESL Domain 2: Culture

Standard 2. Culture As It Affects Student Learning

2.g. Understand and apply concepts of cultural competency, particularly knowledge about how an individual's cultural identity affects their learning and academic progress and how levels of cultural identity will vary widely among students.

TESOL ESL Domain 4: Assessment

Standard 4.c. Classroom-Based Assessment for ESL

4.c.3. Use various instruments and techniques to assess content-area learning (e.g., math, science, social studies) for ESOL learners at varying levels of language and literacy development.

TESOL ESL Domain 5: Professionalism

Standard 5.b. Professional Development, Partnerships, and Advocacy

5.b.3. Work with other teachers and staff to provide comprehensive, challenging educational opportunities for ESOL students in the school.

CHAPTER 2

Authentic Assessment

TESOL ESL Domain 4: Assessment

Standard 4.c. Classroom-Based Assessment for ESL

4.c.1. Use performance-based assessment tools and tasks that measure ESOL learners' progress toward state and national standards.

4.c.3. Use various instruments and techniques to assess content-area learning (e.g., math, science, social studies) for ESOL learners at varying levels of language and literacy development.

4.c.4. Prepare ESOL students to use self- and peer-assessment techniques when appropriate.

CHAPTER 3

Preinstructional Assessment: Re-envisioning What Is Possible

TESOL ESL Domain 1: Language

Standard 1.b. Language Acquisition and Development

1.b.1. Demonstrate understanding of current and historical theories and research in language acquisition as applied to English language learners (ELLs).

1.b.2. Candidates understand theories and research that explain how first language (L1) literacy development differs from second language (L2) literacy development.

TESOL ESL Domain 3: Planning, Implementing, and Managing Instruction

Standard 3.a. Planning for Standards-Based ESL and Content Instruction

3.a.3. Plan differentiated learning experiences based on assessments of students' English and L1 proficiency, learning styles, and prior formal educational experiences and knowledge.

CHAPTER 4

Assessment of Acculturation

TESOL ESL Domain 2: Culture

Standard 2. Culture As It Affects Student Learning

2.c. Understand and apply knowledge about how an individual's cultural identity affects their ESL learning and how levels of cultural identity will vary widely among students.

2.g. Understand and apply concepts of cultural competency, particularly knowledge about how an individual's cultural identity affects their learning and academic progress and how levels of cultural identity will vary widely among students.

TESOL ESL Domain 4: Assessment

Standard 4.a. Issues of Assessment for English Language Learners

4.a.4. Demonstrate understanding of the advantages and limitations of assessment situations, including accommodations for ELLs.

CHAPTER 5

Assessment of Language Proficiency

TESOL ESL Domain 3: Planning, Implementing, and Managing Instruction

Standard 3.a. Planning for Standards-Based ESL and Content Instruction

3.a.3. Plan differentiated learning experiences based on assessments of students' English and L1 proficiency, learning styles, and prior formal educational experiences and knowledge.

TESOL ESL Domain 4: Assessment

Standard 4.b. Language Proficiency Assessment

4.b.1. Understand and implement national and state requirements for identification, reclassification, and exit of ELLs from language support programs.
4.b.2. Understand the appropriate use of norm-referenced assessments with ELLs.
4.b.3. Assess ESOL learners' language skills and communicative competence using multiple sources of information.

Standard 4.c. Classroom-Based Assessment for ESL

4.c.2. Use various instruments and techniques to assess content-area learning (e.g., math, science, social studies) for ESOL learners at varying levels of language and literacy development.

CHAPTER 6

Assessment of Content-Area Learning

TESOL ESL Domain 3: Planning, Implementing, and Managing Instruction

Standard 3.a. Planning for Standards-Based ESL and Content Instruction

3.a.3. Plan differentiated learning experiences based on assessments of students' English and L1 proficiency, learning styles, and prior formal educational experiences and knowledge.

TESOL ESL Domain 4: Assessment

Standard 4.b. Language Proficiency Assessment

4.b.1. Understand and implement national and state requirements for identification, reclassification, and exit of ESOL students from language support programs.
4.b.2. Understand the appropriate use of norm-referenced assessments with ELLs.
4.b.3. Assess ESOL learners' language skills and communicative competence using multiple sources of information.

Standard 4.c. Classroom-Based Assessment for ESL

4.c.2. Use various instruments and techniques to assess content-area learning (e.g., math, science, social studies) for ESOL learners at varying levels of language and literacy development.

CHAPTER 7

Data-Driven Problem-Solving Processes

TESOL ESL Domain 4: Assessment

Standard 4.a. Issues of Assessment for English Language Learners

4.a.5. Distinguish among ELLs' language differences, giftedness, and special education needs.

TESOL ESL Domain 5: Professionalism

Standard 5.a. ESL Research and History

5.a.3. Demonstrate ability to read and conduct classroom research.

Standard 5.b. Professional Development, Partnerships, and Advocacy

5.b.3. Work with other teachers and staff to provide comprehensive, challenging educational opportunities for ELLs in the school.
5.b.6. Support ELL families.

CHAPTER 8

Special Education Issues in the Assessment of CLD Students

TESOL ESL Domain 3: Planning, Implementing, and Managing Instruction

Standard 3.a. Planning for Standards-Based ESL and Content Instruction

3.a.3. Plan differentiated learning experiences based on assessments of students' English and L1 proficiency, learning styles, and prior formal educational experiences and knowledge.

TESOL ESL Domain 4: Assessment

Standard 4.a. Issues of Assessment for English Language Learners

4.a.5. Distinguish among ELLs' language differences, giftedness, and special education needs.

Standard 4.b. Language Proficiency Assessment

4.b.1. Understand and implement national and state requirements for identification, reclassification, and exit of ELLs from language support programs.

APPENDIX B

———■■■■■———

RESOURCE LIST

Skills Development Chart—Home Survey

Dear Parent,

Although _____ has not been in school very long, we know that some children have already been learning important academic concepts at home. Please review the types of skills listed on this page. Circle the skills that you can answer now and then post the chart on your refrigerator for a few days while you check your child's responses to a few more. This information will help us spend more time teaching new skills rather than working on those skills your child already knows.

Student's Name: _____   Grade: _____   Teacher: _____

Academic Skills Demonstrated with Clothes/Laundry

Can your child:

				Comments
Yes	No	Unsure	Sort laundry by *color?*	
Yes	No	Unsure	Locate items that *match* (e.g., socks)?	
Yes	No	Unsure	Tell you which shirt or sock is *bigger/smaller?*	

Academic Skills Demonstrated in the Kitchen

Can your child:

				Comments
Yes	No	Unsure	Sort items by *color* or *shape?*	
Yes	No	Unsure	Sort boxes or cans by *size* (e.g., large cans/small cans)?	
Yes	No	Unsure	Sort items *in order* from smallest to largest?	
Yes	No	Unsure	Show you which cup is *empty* and which is *full?*	
Yes	No	Unsure	Identify items from the same *group* (e.g., fruits, vegetables, desserts)?	
Yes	No	Unsure	Pick out foods having a particular *characteristic* (e.g., sweet, smooth)?	
Yes	No	Unsure	Tell you which bowl has *more* (e.g., ice cream, beans)?	
Yes	No	Unsure	Tell you which container has the *most* or *least* (e.g., grapes, chips)?	
Yes	No	Unsure	Tell you which foods he or she *does* or *does not* like?	
Yes	No	Unsure	Demonstrate that he or she knows *where* to find or put things in the kitchen?	
Yes	No	Unsure	Demonstrate that he or she understands that the refrigerator is *cold* and the stove is *hot?*	
Yes	No	Unsure	Select the correct *number* of spoons or napkins to help set the table for a family meal?	

Parent Signature: _____   **Date:** _____

Tabla de Destrezas para el Desarrollo–Encuesta de Hogar
(Skills Development Chart—Home Skills Survey [Spanish])

Estimado Padre,

Aunque _____ no ha atendido a la escuela mucho tiempo, sabemos que los niños aprenden conceptos importantes en casa. Repase por favor los tipos de destrezas enumeradas en esta hoja. Marque las destrezas que su hijo pueda contestar ahora. Ponga esta hoja en su refrigerador, y después de observar por algunos días, responda las preguntas faltantes. Esta información nos ayudará a tomar más tiempo en la enseñanza de nuevas destrezas y no en las que ya son conocidas por el niño.

Nombre del estudiante _____ Grado: _____ Maestra/o: _____

Destrezas académicas demostradas con la ropa   **Comentarios**

Puede su hijo/a:

Sí	No	No sé	¿Clasificar ropa por *color*?
Sí	No	No sé	¿Localizar los artículos que *emparejan*? (calcetines)
Sí	No	No sé	¿Decirle cual camisa o calcetín es *más grande* o *más chico*?

Destrezas académicas demostradas con la cocina   **Comentarios**

Puede su hijo/a:

Sí	No	No sé	¿Clasificar artículos por *color* o *forma*?
Sí	No	No sé	¿Clasificar cajas o botes por *tamaño*? (bote grande, bote chico)
Sí	No	No sé	¿Clasificar artículos *en orden* de más chico a más grande?
Sí	No	No sé	¿Enseñarle cual vaso está vacío y cual está *lleno*?
Sí	No	No sé	¿Identificar artículos del mismo *grupo*? (frutas, vegetales, postres)
Sí	No	No sé	¿Escoger comidas con *características* particulares? (dulces, lisas)
Sí	No	No sé	¿Decirle cual plato hondo tiene *más*? (helado, frijoles)
Sí	No	No sé	¿Decirle cual envase contiene *lo más* o *menos*? (uvas, papitas)
Sí	No	No sé	¿Decirle cuales comidas *le gustan* o *no le gustan*?
Sí	No	No sé	¿Sabe *donde* encontrar o poner cosas en la cocina?
Sí	No	No sé	¿Entiende que el refrigerador es *frío* y la estufa es *caliente*?
Sí	No	No sé	¿Seleccionar correctamente *el número* de cucharas y servilletas para la hora de la comida?

Firma del Padre: _____   **Fecha:** _____

Vocabulary Homework Letter to Parents

Dear Parents,

The pictures below were/will be used in class with your child. Please name the pictured word(s) or activity for your child in the home language. Then talk about something your child might associate with that word or activity at home or in the community. For example, if the picture is "cereal," you might say the word and talk about how "we put milk in cereal" or point out all the cereal boxes the next time you are in the store. Talking about your child's school words in the language he/she hears most at home really helps him/her remember what the words mean when they are heard at school in English.

Please let us know if you have any questions. You can write your comments and questions in any language.

Thank you so much!

Estimados Padres,

Las imagenes de abajo son/serán utilizadas en la clase con su niño(a). Por favor de nombre a las palabras de las imagenes o a la actividad en su idioma materno. Después hable con su hijo(a) de algo que pueda asociar con la palabra o actividad en casa o en la comunidad. Por ejemplo, si la imagen es "cereal," usted puede decir la palabra y después hablar de cómo "le ponemos leche a el cereal" o puede enseñarle todas las cajas de cereal la próxima vez que ustedes vayan a la tienda. Hablar sobre las palabras "de escuela" de su hijo(a) en el idioma que él/ella escucha mas en casa, le ayuda a recordar el significado de la palabra, cuando él/ella la escucha en inglés en la escuela.

Por favor dejenos saber si usted tiene cualquier pregunta. Puede escribir sus comentarios y preguntas en cualquier idioma.

¡Muchas Gracias!

Source: Maria Moran, Wichita, KS. Reprinted by permission.

Parent/Teacher Language Observation
(Adapted from the Student Oral Language Observation Matrix)

Student's Name: _____   Grade: _____   Date: _____

Home Language(s): _____   Completed By (signature): _____

	1	2	3	4	5
A. Comprehension	Doesn't appear to understand any conversation.	Has difficulty following everyday social conversation, even when words are spoken slowly and repeated.	Understands most of what is said at slower-than-normal speed with repetitions.	Understands nearly everything at normal speed, although occasional repetition may be necessary.	Understands everyday language and normal family conversation without difficulty.
B. Fluency	Speech is so limited that conversation is virtually impossible.	Student attempts to speak but has periods of silence due to limitations.	Speech in everyday conversation is frequently disrupted by the student's search for words.	Speech in everyday conversation is generally fluent, with occasional lapses while the student searches for the correct manner of expression.	Speech in everyday conversation is fluent and effortless.
C. Vocabulary	Vocabulary is so limited that conversation is virtually impossible.	Difficult to understand because of limited vocabulary and misuse words.	Student frequently uses wrong words: conversation somewhat limited because of inadequate vocabulary.	Occasional use of inappropriate terms and/or rephrasing of the ideas because of limited vocabulary.	Vocabulary and idioms approximately those of a native speaker.
D. Pronunciation	Pronunciation problems so severe that speech is virtually unintelligible.	Difficult to understand because of pronunciation problems; must frequently repeat in order to be understood.	Concentration required of listener; occasional misunderstandings caused by pronunciation problems.	Always intelligible (understandable), although some sounds may be in error.	Pronunciation and intonation approximately those of a native speaker.
E. Grammar	Errors in grammar and word order are so severe that speech is virtually unintelligible.	Difficult to understand because of errors in grammar and word order. Rephrases or limits speech to basic patterns.	Frequent errors in grammar and word order. Sometimes hard to understand meaning.	Occasional errors in grammar or word order. Does not interfere with meaning.	Grammar and word order are approximately those of a native speaker.

Source: Adapted SOLOM, Natasha Reyes, Wichita, KS. Reprinted by permission.

Por favor, marque una 'X' en el cuadro que mejor describa la comunicación de su hijo en cada área del idioma que se habla en su hogar.

Forma para que el Papá observe el lenguaje
(Adaptado del matriz de observación del lenguaje oral del estudiante)

Nombre del Estudiante:

Lenguaje(s) del Hogar:

Grado:

Fecha:

Completado por (firma):

	1	2	3	4	5
A. Comprensión	No parecen entender cualquier conversación.	Tiene dificultad para seguir las conversaciones sociales cotidianas, incluso cuando palabras se hablan lentamente y repetidas.	Comprende más de lo que se dice a velocidad más lenta de lo normal con repeticiones.	Entiende casi todo a velocidad normal, aunque la repetición ocasional puede ser necesaria.	Entiende el lenguaje cotidiano y normal conversación familiar sin dificultad.
B. Fluidez	Lenguaje es tan limitado que la conversación es prácticamente imposible.	Estudiante intenta hablar pero tiene periodos de silencio debido a las limitaciones.	Lenguaje en la conversación diaria es interrumpido con frecuencia, por la búsqueda de palabras del estudiante.	Lenguaje en la conversación cotidiana es generalmente fluido, con ocasionales lapsos mientras el estudiante busca la correcta manera de expresión.	Lenguaje en la conversación cotidiana es fluido y sin esfuerzo.
C. Vocabulario	Vocabulario es tan limitado que la conversación es prácticamente imposible.	Difícil de entender debido a la limitación de palabras de vocabulario y uso indebido.	Estudiante usa palabras equivocadas con frecuencia: conversación es bastante limitada debido al vocabulario inadecuado.	Uso ocasional de términos inadecuados o reformulación de las ideas por vocabulario limitado.	Vocabulario y modismos aproximadamente las de su lengua nativa.

(*Continued*)

Por favor, marque una 'X' en el cuadro que mejor describa la comunicación de su hijo en cada área del idioma que se habla en su hogar.

Forma para que el Papá observe el lenguaje
(Adaptado del matriz de observación del lenguaje oral del estudiante)

Nombre del Estudiante:		Grado:	Completado por (firma):	Fecha:
Lenguaje(s) del Hogar:				
D. Pronunciación	Problemas de pronunciación tan severos que el lenguaje es prácticamente ininteligible.	Difícil de entender debido a problemas de Pronunciación; Deben repetir con frecuencia para ser entendido.	Concentración requerida del oyente; malentendidos ocasionales causados por problemas de pronunciación.	Siempre inteligible (comprensible), aunque algunos sonidos puede estar en error.	Pronunciación y entonación aproximadamente las de su lengua nativa.
E. Gramática	Errores de gramática y orden de las palabras son tan severos que el lenguaje es prácticamente ininteligible.	Difícil de entender debido a errores de gramática y orden de las palabras. Rephrases o limita el lenguaje en los patrones básicos.	Errores frecuentes en gramática y orden de las palabras. A veces es difícil entender el significado.	Errores ocasionales de gramática u orden de las palabras. No interfiere con el significado.	Gramática y orden de las palabras son aproximadamente a su lengua nativa.

Source: Adapted SOLOM, Natasha Reyes, Wichita, KS. Reprinted by permission.

Communication Functions Checklist

Please indicate whether the following communicative behaviors are:
Observed (+)   Reported (R)   Not Observed (−)

Student Name: _____

	L1	L2
1. Student comments on actions of self or others.		
2. Student initiates conversations.		
3. Student maintains a topic in conversation.		
4. Student follows multipart directions.		
5. Student uses language to request (action/object, assistance, information, clarification, etc.).		
6. Student uses language to tell (needs, feelings, thoughts, answers to questions).		
7. Student describes experiences (retells events).		
8. Student predicts outcomes or describes solutions.		
9. Student expresses and supports opinions.		
10. Student uses language to express imaginative and creative thinking.		

Basic Interpersonal Communication Skill (BICS)

L1	L2	Listening
○	○	Understands school/classroom routines
○	○	Responds, with little hesitation, when asked to perform a nonverbal task
○	○	Follows oral directions at the end of lesson (with familiarity and modeling)
○	○	Listens to peers when process is provided
○	○	Becomes distracted when lesson is not differentiated
○	○	Distinguishes sameness or difference between English sounds

L1	L2	Speaking
○	○	Is comfortable with groups speaking English
○	○	Communicates with peers in social settings
○	○	Responds to questions in class when the question is context embedded or the teacher provides scaffolding
○	○	Is able to retell a pictured, cued, or scaffolded story
○	○	Can describe the topic of the lesson using limited vocabulary
○	○	Struggles with concept retelling when topic is not contextualized
○	○	Withdraws when group discussions go beyond known vocabulary
○	○	Is eager to participate when language demands are supported

L1	L2	Reading
○	○	Recognizes common language of school
○	○	Recognizes environmental print (e.g., signs, logos, McDonald's)
○	○	Can match or read basic sight words
○	○	Reads best when material is contextualized
○	○	Demonstrates limited use of reading strategies
○	○	Volunteers to read when material is known

L1	L2	Writing
○	○	Writes personal information (e.g., name, address, phone number)
○	○	Writes with contextual and/or instructional scaffolding
○	○	Writes with some spelling errors
○	○	Writes with many spelling errors
○	○	Writes with moderate to high levels of syntax errors

Source: Adapted from B. Bernhard & B. Loera (1992). Checklist of language skills for use with limited English proficient students. *Word of Mouth Newsletter*, 4(1). San Antonio, TX: Lauren Newton.

Cognitive Academic Language Proficiency (CALP)

L1	L2	Listening
○	○	Is able to carry out academic tasks without language support
○	○	Understands vocabulary in different content areas (e.g., *sum* in math vs. *some* in science)
○	○	Understands process/sequence across content areas
○	○	Uses selective attention when taking notes
○	○	Understands teacher idioms and humor
○	○	Understands English language functions
○	○	Comprehends teacher lecture, movies, and audiovisual presentations

L1	L2	Speaking
○	○	Asks/answers specific questions about topic of discussion
○	○	Uses temporal concepts (e.g., first, next, after) appropriately
○	○	Recognizes the need for, and seeks, clarification of academic tasks or discussion
○	○	Expresses rationale for opinion
○	○	Poses thoughtful questions
○	○	Actively participates in class activities and discussions
○	○	Volunteers to answer subject-matter questions of varying difficulty

L1	L2	Reading
○	○	Demonstrates knowledge and application of sound–symbol association
○	○	Demonstrates phonemic awareness skills such as sound blending, elision, and rhyming
○	○	Regards print with appropriate spatial skills and orientation (e.g., left to right, top to bottom)
○	○	Interprets written words and text as the print representation of speech
○	○	Understands differential use of text components (e.g., table of contents, glossary)
○	○	Reads for information and understanding
○	○	Reads independently to gather information of interest

L1	L2	Writing
○	○	Performs written tasks at levels required by the curriculum
○	○	Uses complex sentences appropriate for grade level
○	○	Writes from dictation
○	○	Writes for audience and purpose
○	○	Understands purposes and application of writing conventions
○	○	Uses writing as a tool for personal means (e.g., correspondence, notation, journaling)
○	○	Writes compellingly or creatively (e.g., editorials, poetry, lyrics, stories)

Source: Adapted from B. Bernhard & B. Loera (1992). Checklist of language skills for use with limited English proficient students. *Word of Mouth Newsletter,* 4(1). San Antonio, TX: Lauren Newton.

Continua for the Assessment of English Language Development

Student Name: _____

	Preproduction	Early Production	Speech Emergence	Intermediate Fluency	Advanced Fluency
Date					
Listening	• Cannot yet understand simple expressions or statements in English.	• Understands previously learned expressions. • Understands new vocabulary in context.	• Understands sentence-length speech. • Participates in conversation about simple information. • Understands a simple message. • Understands basic directions and instructions.	• Understands academic content. • Understands more complex directions and instructions. • Comprehends main idea. • Effectively participates in classroom discussions.	• Understands most of what is heard. • Understands and retells main idea and most details from oral presentations and conversations.
Date					
Speaking	• Is not yet able to make any statements in English.	• Uses isolated words and learned phrases. • Uses vocabulary for classroom situations. • Expresses basic courtesies. • Asks very simple questions. • Makes statements using learned materials. • Asks and answers questions about basic needs.	• Asks and answers simple questions about academic content. • Talks about familiar topics. • Responds to simple statements. • Expresses self in simple situations (e.g., ordering a meal, introducing oneself, asking directions).	• Initiates, sustains, and closes a conversation. • Effectively participates in classroom discussions. • Gives reasons for agreeing or disagreeing. • Retells a story or event. • Compares and contrasts a variety of topics.	• Communicates facts and talks casually about topics of general interest using specific vocabulary. • Participates in age-appropriate academic, technical, and social conversations using English correctly.

	Preproduction	Early Production	Speech Emergence	Intermediate Fluency	Advanced Fluency
Date					
Reading	• Is not yet able to read any words in English. • Is not yet able to identify the letters of the Roman alphabet. • Is not yet able to decode sounds of written English.	• Reads common messages, phrases, and/or expressions. • Identifies the letters of the Roman alphabet. • Decodes most sounds of written English. • Identifies learned words and phrases.	• Reads and comprehends main ideas and/or facts from simple materials.	• Understands main ideas and details from a variety of sources.	• Reads authentic text materials for comprehension. • Understands most of what is read in authentic texts.
Date					
Writing	• Is not yet able to write any words in English. • Is not yet able to write the letters of the Roman alphabet.	• Copies or transcribes familiar words or phrases. • Writes the letters from memory and/or dictation. • Writes simple expressions from memory. • Writes simple autobiographical information as well as some short phrases and simple lists. • Composes short sentences with guidance.	• Creates basic statements and questions. • Writes simple letters and messages. • Writes simple narratives.	• Writes more complex narratives. • Composes age-appropriate original materials using present, past, and future tenses. • Writes about a variety of topics for a variety of purposes.	• Write summaries. • Takes notes. • Compares and contrasts familiar topics. • Uses vivid, specific language in writing.

Source: Wichita Public Schools, Wichita, Kansas. Reprinted by permission.

Teacher Observation Checklist

Student Name	Follows directions without a model	Uses nonverbals to communicate understanding or express needs	Uses single words to answer questions or express needs	Uses simple sentence structures for social purposes	Uses simple sentence structures for curricular purposes	Other comments or observations

GLOSSARY

academic dimension of the CLD student biography the academic experiences, methods, skills, successes, and challenges influencing aspects of a learner's present educational dispositions or performance.

academic language development the building of vocabulary and language skills required for success in decontextualized, cognitively demanding, communicative situations and language-learning tasks frequently found in educational settings.

accommodation *See* mutual accommodation or assessment accommodation.

acculturation the process of adjusting to a new or non-native culture.

achievement discrepancies gaps in achievement between groups, or between the expected and actual performance of groups or individuals. When used to describe eligibility for special education, the term is often used to reference a difference in measured ability and performance or achievement in a specific area (e.g., written language) thought to be impacted by a specific learning disability.

adaptation reflects the degree to which the CLD student is capable of and comfortable participating in the norms and customary routines of different groups. Also referred to as integration. Positive adaptation does not negate the student's primary cultural and language identity.

advocacy the support of a cause that prompts a person to take action in ways that promote equitable resolutions.

affective filter related to Krashen's affective filter hypothesis, in which he argues that the amount of input reaching the CLD student is influenced by a number of affective variables, including anxiety, self-confidence, and motivation. The affective filter has been compared to a defense mechanism because, if it is raised, it may negatively influence language acquisition, academic success, and classroom behavior and action.

alternative assessment forms of assessment used to supplement, refine, or enhance prescribed formal or informal assessment(s). Alternative assessments are typically employed to provide usable information about how well students are learning what is actually being taught in class.

anecdotal logs ongoing records used by an observer to note instances or conditions of a learning, social, or language behavior.

anomie the sense of "unbelonging" that immigrants may feel as a result of the disconnection from the home culture and language that occurred before, or in absence of, positive acculturation to the new community, culture, and language.

asset perspective a mindset that adheres to locating and maximizing the cultural identity of CLD students and families and the associated assets that they offer, such as (but not limited to) cultural values and insights, familiarity with multiple cultures and ethnicities, and experience with other languages.

assessment accommodation a measure taken to ensure that the results of a student assessment reflect only measurement of the targeted skills or knowledge rather than the student's language ability, level of acculturation, or testing finesse.

assimilation a process by which the individual fully adopts the new culture as a replacement for the home culture

authentic assessment assessments that are generally developed directly from classroom instruction, group work, or related classroom activities and that provide an alternative to traditional assessments. Authentic assessments emphasize real-world problems, tasks, or applications that are relevant to the student and his or her community.

barrier games any type of activity or game that involves one person describing to another how best to create or build a targeted design. Typically, there is a barrier of some sort that impedes the message receivers' ability to view the design of the message sender. *See also* information gap activities.

basic interpersonal communication skills (BICS) the language ability needed for casual conversation. This term usually applies to the interpersonal conversation skills of English learners (e.g., playground language).

behavioral acculturation adaptation to or adoption of the language, social skills, customs, and dress of a new or host culture.

bilingual special education student refers to a CLD student from a linguistically diverse home who is determined to qualify for and demonstrate a need for special education services. Such students may be exhibit diverse patterns of language dominance (L1 and/or L2) depending on their individual histories and education.

biopsychosocial history the student's physical (bio), mental (psych), and social realities that influence his or her learning needs and assets and responses to school and classroom dynamics.

checklists a series of questions or statements that describe tasks required for activity completion or levels of product development.

cloze assessments elicit oral or written information to fill in missing words from a sentences or passage. Cloze assessments are commonly utilized to probe language comprehension, content learning, and/or aspects of grammar.

code switching the use of two or more languages in the same conversation to express oneself.

cognitive academic language proficiency (CALP) the language ability needed for learning academic skills and concepts in situations in which contextual clues are not present and an abstract use of language is required.

cognitive dimension of the CLD student biography reflects the ways a learner has come to know and understand the world as well as his or her patterns and preferences in thinking, learning, and applying.

collectivism describes overarching values, norms, and practices that promote interdependence among members of the culture to ensure group success.

commercially produced assessment a marketed test, rating scale, probe, or other such tool designed to measure student skills, achievement, or knowledge. Many such assessments include verbatim scripts, scoring protocols, and pictures predetermined to elicit the presence or absence of a given curricular or language skill.

common underlying proficiency (CUP) the conceptual knowledge that provides bilingual individuals with a foundation for building new skills. Both the L1 and L2 facilitate development of such fundamental cognitive patterns. The L1 and L2 serve as bridges, connecting new information with previously acquired knowledge.

communicative competence a language user's ability to know what to say, when to say it, to whom to say it, and under what circumstances.

constructivist perspective the idea that knowledge is constructed during learning—that students *discover* knowledge for themselves rather than *receive* knowledge from the teacher.

construct validity the extent to which the assessment tasks and items reflect the desired range of targeted knowledge bases and competencies in that area.

content objectives statements that identify what students should know and be able to do in particular subject areas, which should also support attainment of state and district standards. These objectives should be presented orally and in writing at the beginning of a lesson to provide students with learning expectations and a focus for the lesson. Teachers revisit the objectives throughout the lesson to ensure alignment of the lesson to learning goals and to assess student progress.

content validity the extent to which the assessment tasks and items represent only the domain of knowledge and skills intended to be measured. For example, a student may fail story problems designed to measure mathematical computation abilities because he or she is unable to read.

contextualization involving teacher efforts to situate instruction in ways that promote meaning and relevance for students, given their individual student biographies. As such, contextualization requires teachers to know, document, and utilize—in instructional planning and lesson implementation—the assets that each student brings to the classroom from his or her background.

cooperative group assessment the measurement or observation of skills during an intentionally planned, cooperative group endeavor.

criterion-referenced assessment measures a student's academic performance, skill acquisition, or developmental progress against explicitly defined expectations or criteria.

cultural assets knowledge bases and experiences, including manners of socialization brought from home (and home culture) that, when recognized, benefit a student's access to activities and content within the curriculum.

cultural lens an individual's way of viewing the world that is influenced by his or her own socialization.

culturally and linguistically diverse (CLD) preferred term for an individual or group of individuals whose culture or language differs from that of the dominant group.

culturally and linguistically diverse (CLD) student biography a holistic approach to characterize and provide insight on students with diverse backgrounds that includes the sociocultural, linguistic, cognitive, and academic dimensions, with emphasis on related challenges and processes,

culture "The totality of socially transmitted behavior patterns, arts, beliefs, institutions, and all other products of human work and thought typical of a population or community at a given time" (Berube et al., 2001, p. 102).

culture of the school the practices and perceptions that positively or negatively influence CLD students' experience within the school, including (dis)respect for non-English native languages, minority/majority cultures, emphasis on equality and meritocracy versus equity, as well as other challenges placed on CLD students.

culture shock commonly occurs when the novelty of the unfamiliar evolves into a frustrating reality. Students who experience culture shock may demonstrate anger, irritability, disorderly behavior, signs of depression, emotionality (e.g., crying), increased somatic complaints (e.g., headache, upset stomach), homesickness, excessive sleeping, overeating or loss of appetite, social withdrawal, or loss of interest in previously enjoyed activities.

curriculum-based measurement (CBM) a formal or informal probe designed to measure a student's incremental progress toward a curricular goal.

deculturation *See* anomie.

deficit perspective a mindset in which CLD students are viewed as liabilities, or deficits, that characterize the hopelessness of appropriate educational accommodations for the students, instead of identifying and utilizing the assets that the CLD students bring to the school and classroom.

dialogue journals an interactive format of written dialogue or conversation between the student and teacher over time. Key features of dialogue journals are the personal nature of topic development and opportunity for teachers to model spelling, grammar, or academic vocabulary in the context of authentic interaction around topics of interest.

discourse pattern the patterns characterizing the way a person expresses his or her thoughts on a subject. Speakers from other cultures often follow very different discourse patterns, in which the flow of narratives may seem circular, repetitive, or digressive to English speakers accustomed to a more linear "train of thought."

disproportionality the degree to which student representation by gender, race, ethnicity, or language learner status does not correlate with those students' representation in the educational setting. This term is often used to describe situations where students of a particular demographic are either under- or overrepresented in a category such as special education.

education history a detailed chronology of the educational opportunities and supports (or lack thereof) provided during each period of a student's educational years. *See also* academic dimension of the CLD student biography.

educational exceptionality term used to describe or designate a speech or language impairment, behavioral disorder, specific learning difficulty, physical impairment (e.g., mobility, vision, hearing), or cognitive range that is significantly higher or lower than the average range of a student's peers. True exceptionalities are generally understood to exclude achievement discrepancies that are the result of external variables such as language, experience, cultural difference, socioeconomic status, attendance, mobility, and family crises.

enculturation an individual's initial socialization to the norms, values, behaviors, language, and interaction patterns of his or her own culture or group.

English language learner (ELL) an individual who is in the process of transitioning from a home or native language to English. However, *culturally and linguistically diverse (CLD)* is the preferred term because *CLD* emphasizes both the cultural and linguistic assets a student brings to the classroom.

English submersion the sink-or-swim programmatic notion that no language services or accommodations should be provided to second language learners. Rather, students are expected to rapidly acquire the English language skills needed for full participation in the grade-level classroom, with no additional language support.

evidence factual information, not opinion. In the context of the classroom, educators provide factual descriptions of their actions, students' actions, quotations from lesson plans, classroom documentation with samples of student work, parent contact logs, and accurate professional development logs.

exceptionality *See* educational exceptionality.

familism the tendency to value family and family goals above those of the individual.

first language acquisition the process through which children learn their first language; there are multiple theories that explain how the first language is acquired.

formative assessment a tool or strategy employed by grade-level and other teachers to determine what and how their students are learning so that instruction can be modified accordingly while the instruction is still in progress.

funds of knowledge the knowledge, skills, and background experiences students and families have gained through prior socialization in a particular culture and as speakers of particular languages.

general outcome measurement purports to assess global skills from which the mastery of subskills can be inferred.

hands-on activities a common theme among variations of sheltered instruction. Such interaction is considered essential for CLD students as a means by which they can practice their emergent L2 skills, clarify concepts, and demonstrate what they have learned.

higher-order thinking skills students' ability to analyze, evaluate, synthesize, and create new knowledge, which requires application of critical thinking and judgment skills.

high-stakes test any test that has major life consequences for participants. Often this type of test yields a point-in-time data which determines whether those students, educators, or entire schools *pass* or *fail* a designated measure of success. The stakes at risk typically involve punishments or rewards that can (dis)enfranchise the subject for years to come.

home language surveys tools commonly used in school settings to gather initial information about the language(s) used in a student's home

home visit interviews discussions or dialogue related to the student that involve school personnel and the parent(s)/caregiver(s) within the context of the student's home.

individualism cultural practices and mindsets that esteem individual drive and accomplishment over group endeavor and benefit. Independence is highly valued in individualist cultures.

individualized education program (IEP) a child-specific document developed by team members (including parents/guardians) with expertise related to that student, and his or her health, socialization, language, and learning processes. All children in special education are required to have an IEP that is current and accurately reflects their strengths, needs, and manner in which they will be best supported to meet specified educational goals.

information gap activities any type of activity (e.g., barrier games) that promotes the use of descriptive language and clarifying skills under intentionally designed conditions that involve missing information.

inquiry assessment/inquiry-based learning generally occurs in tandem as student responses to guided questions provide information about their developing language skills and content knowledge. Dialogue that evolves during the inquiry-based learning process is a product of real-time formative assessment that occurs as the learning unfolds.

integration *See* adaptation.

inter-rater reliability the degree to which a student's product or performance is rated the same by different raters or evaluators.

interview-based assessment use of student-teacher interviews (casual or structured) to gather information and insights (e.g., prior knowledge, reflection on learning) needed to adapt instruction appropriately for the student's benefit.

language competence underlying cumulative knowledge about language form, structure, and use.

language history a student's personal developmental and externally influenced record of first and second (or subsequent) language acquisition.

language performance refers to language skills and capacities the student is able to demonstrate given the constraints of a given situation or task.

least restrictive environment the program or setting in which students are provided the type of supports necessary to maximally participate in, *while also being challenged* by, the curriculum.

limited English proficient (LEP) an individual in the process of acquiring English as an additional language. This term is frequently used in government documents. However, because *LEP* emphasizes inadequacies rather than abilities, *CLD* is the preferred term.

linguistic dimension of the CLD student biography the knowledge and proficiency with English, the native language, and any additional languages the learner knows, or has been exposed to during his or her life.

mastery measurement attainment to high proficiency of a distinct and specifically defined skill (e.g., addition of single digit numbers).

morphology rules and patterns for changing words to alter meaning by way of tense, person, number, and so forth. For instance, the addition of *ed* to most English verbs tells us we are referring to a past event ("I walked"), but the addition of *s* to many verbs usually indicates a present-tense action by a third person ("She walks").

multilingualism using, or having the ability to use, multiple languages, which is deemed as valuable in many cultures and countries.

multitiered system of supports (MTSS) a comprehensive, proactive system of educational supports implemented throughout a school, district, or educational cooperative. Tiers of support are developed to address academic as well as nonacademic areas (e.g., social-emotional development and behavior), or system goals (e.g., professional development, learning culture, and parent involvement) identified to have an impact on student achievement and educational climate.

mutual accommodation the process in which neither the student nor the educator expects complete accommodation; instead, both collaborate to maximize the resources each brings to the educational process and to select from among the best strategies that fit each disposition.

narrative assessment formal or informal methods of eliciting and rating targeted aspects (cohesion, sequence, syntax, vocabulary) of student narratives. Common narrative tasks involve the creation or recounting of personally relevant stories and events.

nontraditional receiving communities geographic locations that are not typically associated with high levels of student diversity due to immigrant families.

norm-referenced test a formal assessment that yields static information (e.g., a score) comparing one student's performance with the group of students who originally comprised the "norm" at the time the test was developed.

observation assessment formal or informal means by which insights are gained through the intentional observation of student skills or approaches to a task.

opportunity to learn the degree to which potential barriers to learning are addressed so that all students have equitable access to the curriculum. Conditions that may affect a student's opportunity to learn include the (in)appropriateness of curricula, instructional strategies, materials, and facilities, as well as the skills and commitment of educational personnel (e.g., teachers, school administrators, superintendents) to ensure the academic success of all students.

overrepresentation occurs when students from an identifiable group (based on race, gender, language profile, etc.) are placed in a specific academic program or designation in numbers that exceed what would be expected given the demographic makeup of the school or larger group. This term is often used when describing (dis)proportionality of student groups in programs such as special education and gifted, but may also apply to recipients of punitive actions (e.g., demerits, failing grades, suspension).

peer assessment a process by which students evaluate the accuracy or quality of other students' work in accordance with criteria set forth or guided by the teacher.

performance-based assessment (PBA) an assessment in which students are rated on their ability to execute a project or perform a task rather than on their response to decontextualized questions or prompts related to the target material.

phonemic awareness the ability to recognize, discriminate, and manipulate the sounds or sound units of spoken language.

phonology the sounds and patterns of sounds in a language that we use to form words.

play-based assessment the intentional use of play settings and scenarios to elicit and observe behaviors (e.g., language, motor, social, or cognitive skills) to inform understandings related to children's developmental and/or academic assets and needs.

point-in-time assessments quizzes or tests that a teacher employs to gather immediate quantitative feedback about student learning.

portfolio a systematic collection of documents/artifacts that exemplify socioemotional, linguistic, and academic growth. Common portfolio types may include examples of skill development, written expression, art, content applications, and audiotaped speech samples,

pragmatics refers to ways in which social context and experience influence the interpretation of language. Such influences depend on the speaker, listener, setting, and intent rather than on just the static meaning of the spoken words.

preassessment assessment that occurs *before* instruction. Preassessment can take many forms, from mass marketed group screeners to informal 1:1 interviews. The primary role of preassessment is to gain insights that inform instructional decisions. In general, the more personalized the preassessment, the more information will be revealed about the conditions and supports that foster an individual student's growth.

problem-solving model a guiding structure that enables teams of child experts (e.g., teachers, parents, counselors, ESL support) to more fully describe a child's assets, needs, and learning behaviors to develop the instructional refinements necessary to determine the conditions in which that student experiences *success*.

psychological acculturation adaptation to or adoption of the values, belief systems, attitudes, and so forth of a new or host culture.

rebus cue the use of a rebus picture to aid in the generation or interpretation of text. *See also* rebus picture.

rebus picture a picture or symbol used to represent a syllable or word in text or puzzles.

redesignation also referred to as reclassification, this term describes the process of determining the transitional need of a student for additional or continuing participation in language services.

reductionist curricula courses of study that inordinately focus on basic skills, redundant workbooks, drill-and-practice approaches to instruction, rote memorization of decontextualized facts and declarative knowledge, isolated practice of computations, and repetitive routines that target the retention of basic test-taking strategies.

reevaluation any evaluation taking place subsequent to an evaluation in which baseline skills, assets, needs, or dispositions were described. Students identified as having a special education need must be reevaluated at least every three years to ensure appropriateness of educational decisions and placement.

rejection the conscious choice an individual makes to shun either the host or the home culture.

relevance level of significance attached to information that arises from the learner's cultural lens, which filters incoming information according to schemata established by long-standing socialization in that culture.

reliability the power of an assessment to gather consistent evidence of skills, regardless of the examiner, time, place, or other variables related to its administration.

response to intervention (RTI) a protocol of actions in which schools use data to identify students at risk for poor learning outcomes, monitor student progress or "response," and provide evidence-based interventions to adjust the nature and intensity of supports.

rubric a scoring guide used to evaluate a student product along multiple quantitative and/or explicitly defined qualitative criteria.

scaffolded essays writing tasks that incorporate the structural support students need to compose a classroom essay. Scaffolds can take many forms, such as fill-in-the-blank (with or without word bank) and guided development of connection statements to form key ideas.

scaffolding instructional and contextual support provided in the early stages of learning, followed by a gradual withdrawal of such support as the student's performance suggests independence.

schema a memory framework that enables one to store declarative knowledge as interrelated concepts and ideas that can be recalled as isolated facts or as structured associations (pl. schemata).

self-assessment the process by which students (or teachers) reflect upon learning and/or performance to identify areas of strength, growth, or need. Self-assessment in classroom settings often involves the use of tools such as rubrics, lists, charts, and other depictions of the skills or components required to meet criteria for the targeted skill, performance, or product.

semantics the meanings of words, phrases, and sentences. Semantics can be expressed by our choice of words, their endings or prefixes, and the order in which the words are arranged.

separate underlying proficiency (SUP) a perspective that assumes two languages operate independently; therefore, no transfer occurs between them.

silent period the first stage of the second language acquisition process, also known as the preproduction stage, in which the student may not communicate except in nonverbal ways. During this period, the CLD student is primarily listening to the new or target language and trying to understand its patterns and rules before attempting production in that language.

socialization the process by which humans (from infancy) acquire different behaviors, knowledge, biases, and assumptions based on family and cultural contexts and influences. These behaviors and assumptions are oftentimes so ingrained that we cannot always articulate why they exist.

sociocultural dimension of the CLD student biography the complex social and cultural factors that influence the learner's acculturation and academic success; includes affective influences such as self-concept, self-esteem, social identity, cultural identity, and motivation.

stages of second language acquisition the various linguistic stages that one encounters when acquiring a language, including preproduction, early production, speech emergence, intermediate fluency, and advanced fluency. These stages fall in line with Krashen's natural order hypothesis, meaning that language is essentially acquired in a natural order—a predictable sequence of progression.

standard treatment protocol provision of the same research-based treatment to all students within a given level of a tiered system (*See* tiers of instructional support). Progress is measured against set indicators ("cut scores") or benchmarks of achievement. Students who do not meet these criteria receive an additional predetermined treatment of more intensive supports.

story-telling assessment *See* narrative assessment.

student-centered a focus on the holistic interests of the learners, rather than those of the individuals who are involved in guiding the educational process, such as teachers and administrators.

style shifting occurs when an individual consciously or unconsciously adjusts vocabulary, syntax, intonation, and grammar to fit the discourse style necessary for that particular setting or purpose.

summative assessment a tool or strategy employed by grade-level and other teachers to measure the knowledge or skills of students upon the completion of an instructional lesson, theme, or unit.

syntax refers to language-appropriate word order. Errors with word order or completeness can impact not only the perception of proficiency but also one's ability to correctly understand the message (e.g., "The orange in under the chair." "The orange cat is under the chair." "The cat is under the orange chair.").

teacher-made test any type of assessment or assessment task created by the teacher to probe student acquisition of content-related understandings or skills.

technology-supported assessment any type of assessment that involves use of a technology device or platform. Applications range from mass-marketed computer programs to a single individual's creative use of technology supported stimuli (sound, pictures, lights) to elicit, reinforce, or measure student response.

tiers of instructional support a hierarchy of levels corresponding to student academic need with intensity of instructional support. In most tiered models, the largest or *core* level represents the effective educational practices provided to *all* students. A well-implemented instructional core successfully meets the needs of 70% to 80% of students across settings and populations. Under this model, 15% to 20% of students may require additional supports at some time, and a relative *few* (3% to 5%) may need more intensive levels of support to show gains.

U-curve hypothesis the hypothesis that there are four stages of the acculturation process that occur over time: the honeymoon phase, the hostility phase, the humor phase, and the home phase.

underrepresentation occurs when students from an identifiable group (based on race, gender, language profile, etc.) are placed in a specific academic program or designation in fewer numbers than would be expected given the demographic makeup of the school or larger group.

universal screener a quick probe of student skill(s) administered to all learners in a defined group to differentiate between students who are "on track" to make expected academic or language gains and those who may require additional support. Screener results do not typically provide insight to the nature of issues impacting any individual student's performance on a static task.

validity the ability of an assessment to measure the knowledge or skills it is intended to measure.

visuals a common theme among variations of sheltered instruction. This type of learning support includes pictures, graphics, charts, movies, video clips, or any other material with images that supplements the concepts being taught in the classroom.

working memory the brain's capacity for temporarily holding and manipulating information for a brief period during the performance of an array of cognitive tasks including, but not limited to, comprehension, learning, and reasoning. Working memory is characterized by limited storage capacity and rapid turnover, as differentiated from the larger capacity and archival system of long-term memory.

zone of proximal development (ZPD) a theoretical construct developed by Vygotsky to describe the area between a learner's level of independent performance and the level of performance possible with assistance. Vygotsky argues that learning occurs when new information and skills fall within the space, or the zone between what the learner already knows and what he or she can do with the help of an expert. The ZPD shifts as the individual learns more complex concepts and skills and becomes capable of independently achieving the tasks that once required the assistance of another.

REFERENCES

Abedi, J. (2001, Summer). *Assessment and accommodations for English language learners: Issues, concerns, and recommendations.* National Center for Research on Evaluation, Standards, and Student Testing (CRESST) Policy Brief, 4.

Abedi, J. (2004). The No Child Left Behind Act and English language learners: Assessment and accountability issues. *Educational Researcher, 33*(1), 4–14.

Abedi, J. (2006). Psychometric issues in the ELL assessment and special education eligibility. *Teachers College Record, 108*(11), 2282–2303.

Abedi, J. (2009). *Assessments of English language learners: The race to the top assessment program.* Retrieved from www.cse.ucla.edu/products /overheads/OTHER/abedi_rttt2.ppt

Abedi, J., & Dietel, R. (2004). Challenges in the No Child Left Behind Act for English-language learners. *Phi Delta Kappan, 85*(10), 782–785.

Abedi, J., Lord, C., & Hoffstetter, C. (1998). *Impact of selected background variables on students' NAEP math performance* (CSE Tech. Rep. No. 478). Los Angeles: University of California, National Center for Research on Evaluation, Standards, and Student Testing.

Amrein, A. L., & Berliner, D. C. (2002). High-stakes testing, uncertainty, and student learning. *Education Policy Analysis Archives, 10*(18). Available from http://epaa.asu.edu/epaa/v10n18

Anaya, J. B., Peña, E. D., & Bedore, L. M. (2018). Conceptual scoring and classification accuracy of vocabulary testing in bilingual children. *Language, Speech, and Hearing Services in Schools, 49*(1), 85–97. doi:10.1044/2017_LSHSS-16-0081

Anderson, J., Moeschberger, M., Chen, M. S., Jr., Kunn, P., Wewers, M. E., & Guthrie, R. (1993). An acculturation scale for Southeast Asians. *Social Psychiatry and Psychiatric Epidemiology, 28*, 134–141.

Anderson, S. (2017). *The contributions of the children of immigrants to science in America.* Arlington, VA: National Foundation for American Policy. Retrieved July 26, 2017, from http://nfap.com/wp-content /uploads/2017/03/Children-of-Immigrants-in-Science .NFAP-Policy-Brief.March-2017.pdf

Arbeit, C. A., Staklis, S., & Horn, L. (2016). *New American undergraduates: Enrollment trends and age at arrival of immigrant and second-generation students.* Washington, DC: U.S. Department of Education, Institute of Education Sciences, National Center for Education Statistics. Retrieved August 4, 2017, from https://nces.ed.gov/pubs2017/2017414.pdf

Arnold, J. (2009). Affect in L2 learning and teaching. *Estudios de Lingüística Inglesa Aplicada, 9*, 145–151.

Artiles, A. J., & Harry, B. (2004). *Addressing culturally and linguistically diverse student overrepresentation in special education: Guidelines for parents.* Practitioner Brief Series. Denver, CO: National Center for Culturally Responsive Educational Systems.

Artiles, A. J., Kozleski, E. B., Trent, S. C., Osher, D., & Ortiz, A. (2010). Justifying and explaining disproportionality, 1968–2008: A critique of underlying views of culture. *Exceptional Children, 76*(3), 279–299. doi:10.1177/001440291007600303.

Artiles, A. J., Rueda, R., Salazar, J., & Higareda, I. (2005). Within-group diversity in minority disproportionate representation: English language learners in urban school districts. *Exceptional Children, 71*, 283–300.

Aud, S., Fox, M., & KewalRamani, A. (2010). *Status and trends in the education of racial and ethnic groups* (NCES 2010-015). Washington, DC: U.S. Department of Education, National Center for Education Statistics. Retrieved August 4, 2017, from https://nces.ed.gov/pubs2010/2010015.pdf

Aud, S., Hussar, W., Kena, G., Bianco, K., Frohlich, L., Kemp, J., & Tahan, K. (2011). *The condition of education 2011* (NCES 2011-033). Washington, DC: U.S. Department of Education, National Center for Education Statistics, U.S. Government Printing Office.

August, D., & Hakuta, K. (Eds.). (1997). *Improving schooling for language-minority children: A research agenda.* Washington, DC: National Academy Press.

August, D., & Shanahan, T. (Eds.). (2006). *Developing literacy in second-language learners.* Mahwah, NJ: Lawrence Erlbaum.

Baca, L. M., & Cervantes, H. T. (2004). *The bilingual special education interface* (4th ed.). Upper Saddle River, NJ: Prentice Hall.

Baca, L., & Cervantes, H. (1998). *The bilingual special education interface*. Upper Saddle River, NJ: Merrill.

Bal, A., Sullivan, A. L., & Harper, J. (2014). A situated analysis of special education disproportionality for systemic transformation in an urban school district. *Remedial and Special Education, 35*(1), 3–14. doi:10.1177/0741932513507754.

Ballard & Tighe. (2004). *IDEA Proficiency Test (IPT)*. Brea, CA: Author.

Balu, R., Zhu, P., Doolittle, F., Schiller, E., Jenkins, J., & Gersten, R. (2015). Evaluation of response to intervention practices for elementary school reading (NCEE 2016-4000). Washington, DC: National Center for Education Evaluation and Regional Assistance, Institute of Education Sciences, U.S. Department of Education.

Banks, T., Obiakor, F., & Algozzine, B. (2013). Preparing teachers for urban students who have been labeled as having special needs. *Multicultural Learning and Teaching, 8*(1), 155–170.

Barrera, M. (2006). Roles of definitional and assessment models in the identification of new or second language learners of English for special education. *Journal of Learning Disabilities, 39*(2), 142–156. doi 10.1177/00222194060390020301.

Batalova, J., & Zong, J. (2016). *Language diversity and English proficiency in the United States*. Washington, DC: Migration Policy Institute. Retrieved August 2, 2017, from www.migrationpolicy.org/article/language-diversity-and-english-proficiency-united-states

Bender, W. N., & Shores, C. F. (Eds.). (2007). *Response to intervention: A practical guide for every teacher*. Thousand Oaks, CA: Corwin Press.

Berkowitz, A. J., Desmarais, K. H., Hogan, K., & Moorcroft, T. A. (2000). Authentic assessment in the informal setting: How it can work for you. *Journal of Environmental Education, 31*(3), 20–24.

Berry, J. W. (1992). Cross-cultural psychology: Research and applications. New York: Cambridge University Press.

Berube, M. S., et al. (2001). *Webster's II new college dictionary*. Boston: Houghton Mifflin.

Biddle, B. J., & Berliner, D.C. (2002). Unequal school funding in the United States. *Educational Leadership, 59*(8), 48–59.

Bloom, L., & Lahey, M. (1978). *Language development and language disorders*. New York: Wiley.

Bluestone, K. (2009). Acculturation, interpersonal networks, and the learner's sense of self: The effects of social relationships on second-language learning. *Working Papers in TESOL and Applied Linguistics, 9*(2), 135–164.

Boehm, A. E. (1973). Criterion-referenced assessment for the teacher. *Teachers College Record, 75*(1), 117–126.

Bond, L. A. (1996). Norm- and criterion-referenced testing. *Practical Assessment, Research & Evaluation, 5*(2). Retrieved January 10, 2012, from http://PAREonline.net/getvn.asp?v=5&n=2

Bond, N. (2008). Questioning strategies that minimize behaviour problems. *Education Digest, 73*(6), 41–45.

Bondie, R., & Zusho, A. (2017). Racing against yourself: High stakes for adolescent English language learners with disabilities. *Teachers College Record, 119*(9). Available at www.tcrecord.org.

Bransford, J., Brown, A., & Cocking, R. (Eds.). (2000). *How people learn: Brain, mind experience, and school*. Washington, DC: National Academy Press.

Branum-Martin, L., Tao, S., Garnaat, S., Bunta, F., & Francis, D. J. (2012). Meta-analysis of bilingual phonological awareness: Language, age, and psycholinguistic grain size. *Journal of Educational Psychology, 104*(4), 932–944. doi:10.1037/a0027755

Briceno, M. (2008). *Success story—Title I's targeted funding formula*. Retrieved on January 10, 2012, from www.schoolfunding.info/news/federal/1-10-08TitleI.php3

Brown, C. L. (2004). Reducing the over-referral of culturally and linguistically diverse students (CLD) for language disabilities. *NABE Journal of Research and Practice, 2*(1), 225–234.

Brown, G. T. L., & Harris, L. R. (2014). The future of self-assessment in classroom practice: Reframing self-assessment as a core competency. *Frontline Learning Research, 2*(1). Retrieved from http://dx.doi.org/10.14786/flr.v2i1.24

Brown, J. (2013, Winter/Spring). Considerations for including English language learners in a response to intervention system. *Impact, 26*(1), 14–15, 35. Retrieved from https://ici.umn.edu/products/impact/261/261.pdf

Brown, J. D. (2014). Questions and answers about language testing statistics: Differences in how norm-referenced and criterion-referenced tests are developed and validated. *Shiken, 18*(1), 29–33. Retrieved from http://teval.jalt.org/sites/teval.jalt.org/files/18-1-29%20Brown%20Statistics%20Corner.pdf

Brown, J. E., & Doolittle, J. (2008). A cultural, linguistic, and ecological framework for response to intervention with English language learners. *Teaching Exceptional Children, 40*(5), 67–72.

Brownell, R. (Ed.). (2000a). *Expressive One-Word Picture Vocabulary Test.* Novato, CA: Academic Therapy Publications.

Brownell, R. (Ed.). (2000b). *Receptive One-Word Picture Vocabulary Test.* Novato, CA: Academic Therapy Publications.

Burger, J. M., & Krueger, M. (2003). A balanced approach to high-stakes achievement testing: An analysis of the literature with policy implications. *International Electronic Journal for Leadership in Learning, 7*(4). Retrieved January 10, 2012, from www.ucalgary.ca/iejll/burger_krueger

Burkam, D. T., & Lee, V. E. (2002). *Inequality at the starting gate: Social background differences in achievement as children begin school.* Washington, DC: Economic Policy Institute.

Buzan, T. (1983). *Use both sides of your brain: New techniques to help you read efficiently, study effectively, solve problems, remember more, think clearly.* New York: E. P. Dutton.

Byram, M., Holmes, P., & Savvides, N. (2013). Intercultural communicative competence in foreign language education: Questions of theory, practice and research. *The Language Learning Journal, 41*(3), 251–253. doi:10.1080/09571736.2013 .836343

Cárdenas-Hagan, E., Carlson, C. D., & Pollard-Durodola, S. D. (2007). The cross-linguistic transfer of early literacy skills: The role of initial L1 and L2 skills and language of instruction. *Language Speech and Hearing Services in Schools, 38*(3), 249. doi:10.1044/0161-1461(2007/026)

Cabral, R. M. (2008). *Student learning behaviors and intervention practices cited among Midwestern teachers referring bilingual CLD students for special education evaluation.* Unpublished doctoral dissertation, Kansas State University, Manhattan.

Caldwell, L. D., & Siwatu, K. O. (2003). Promoting academic persistence in African American and Latino high school students: The educational navigation skills seminar in an Upward Bound program. *High School Journal, 87*(1), 30–38.

California Department of Education. (n.d.[a]). *Student oral language observation matrix* (SOLOM). Unpublished instrument. Sacramento: Author.

California Department of Education. (n.d.[b]). *Student written language observation matrix* (SWLOM). Unpublished instrument. Sacramento: Author.

Capps, R., Fix, M., & Zong, J. (2016). *A profile of U.S. children with unauthorized immigrant parents.* Washington, DC: Migration Policy Institute.

Retrieved August 2, 2017, from www.migrationpolicy .org/research/profile-us-children-unauthorized -immigrant-parents

Card, D., & Giuliano, L. (2016). Universal screening increases the representation of low-income and minority students in gifted education. *Proceedings of the National Academy of Sciences of the United States of America (PNAS), 113*(48), 13678–13683. doi: 10.1073/pnas.1605043113

Cartledge, G., & Kourea, L. (2008). Culturally responsive classrooms for culturally diverse students with and at risk for disabilities. *Exceptional Children, 74*(3), 351–371.

Chang, J. M., Lai, A., & Shimizu, W. (1995). LEP, LD, poor, and missed learning opportunities: A case of inner-city Chinese American children. In L. L. Cheng (Ed.), *Integrating language and learning for inclusion: An Asian/Pacific focus* (pp. 265–290). San Diego, CA: Singular Publishing Group.

Chappuis, S., & Stiggins, R. J. (2002). Classroom assessment for learning. *Educational Leadership, 60*(1), 40–43.

Chen S. X., Benet-Martínez, V., & Bond, M. H. (2008). Bicultural identity, bilingualism, and psychological adjustment in multicultural societies: Immigration-based and globalization-based acculturation. *Journal of Personality, 76*(4), 803–838. doi:10.1111/ j.1467-6494.2008.00505.

Chien, S., Wu, H., & Hsu, Y. (2014). An investigation of teachers' beliefs and their use of technology-based assessments. *Computers in Human Behavior, 31,* 198–210. Retrieved from https://doi.org/10.1016/j .chb.2013.10.037

Chinn, P., & Hughes, S. (1987). Representation of minority students in special education classes. *Remedial and Special Education, 4,* 41–46.

Chomsky, N. (1968). *Language and mind.* New York: Harcourt, Brace & World.

Christ, T. J., White, M. J., Ardoin, S. P., & Eckert, T. L. (2013). Curriculum based measurement of reading: Consistency and validity across best, fastest, and question reading conditions. *School Psychology Review, 42*(4), 415–436.

Chu, S.-Y., & Flores, S. (2011). Assessment of English language learners with learning disabilities. *The Clearing House: A Journal of Educational Strategies, Issues and Ideas, 84*(6), 244–248. doi:10.1080/0009 8655.2011.590550.

Cleave, P. L., Kay-Raining Bird, E., Trudeau, N., & Sutton, A. (2014). Syntactic bootstrapping in children with down syndrome: The impact of bilingualism. *Journal of Communication Disorders, 49*, 42–54. doi:10.1016/j.jcomdis.2014.02.006.

Coerr, E. (1986). *The Josefina story quilt.* New York: HarperCollins.

Coleman, R., & Goldenberg, C. (2010). What does research say about effective practices for English learners? *Kappa Delta Pi Record, 46*(2), 60–65. doi: 10.1080/00228958.2010.10516695

Collier, C. (2015). Separating difference from disability workbook. Ferndale, WA: CrossCultural Developmental Education Services.

Collier, C. (2010). *RTI for diverse learners: More than 200 instructional interventions.* Thousand Oaks, CA: Corwin Press.

Collier, C. (2016). *Acculturation Quick Screen (AQS III) administration manual & screening form* (3rd ed). Ferndale, WA: CrossCultural Developmental Education Services. Retrieved January 16, 2018, from www.k12.wa.us/MigrantBilingual/pubdocs/AQSIII2016.pdf

Collier, C. (2016). *Acculturation Quick Screen (AQS III) administration manual & screening form* (3rd ed.). Ferndale, WA: CrossCultural Developmental Education Services. Retrieved from www.k12.wa.us/MigrantBilingual/pubdocs/AQSIII2016.pdf

Collier, C., Brice, A. E., Oades-Sese, G. V. (2007). Assessment of acculturation. In G. B. Esquivel, E. C. Lopez, & S. Nahari, (Eds.), *Handbook of multicultural school psychology: An interdisciplinary perspective.* Mahwah NJ: Lawrence Erlbaum.

Collier, V. P., & Thomas, W. P. (2004). The astounding effectiveness of dual language education for all. *NABE Journal of Research and Practice, 2*(1), 1–20.

Collier, V. P., & Thomas, W. P. (2009). *Educating English learners for a transformed world.* Albuquerque, NM: Fuente Press.

Cooper, T. (1999). *Portfolio assessment: A guide for lecturers, teachers, and course designers.* Perth, WA: Praxis Education.

Core, C., Hoff, E., Rumiche, R., & Señor, M. (2013). Total and conceptual vocabulary in Spanish-English bilinguals from 22 to 30 months: Implications for assessment. *Journal of Speech, Language, and Hearing Research, 56*, 1637–1649. doi:10.1044/1092-4388(2013/11-0044)

Cosentino de Cohen, C., & Clewell, B. C. (2007). *Putting English language learners on the educational map: The No Child Left Behind Act implemented.* Washington, DC: Urban Institute. Retrieved January 17, 2012, from www.urban.org/url.cfm?ID=311468

Costa, D., Cooper, D., & Shierholz, H. (2014). *Facts about immigration and the U.S. economy: Answers to frequently asked questions.* Washington, DC: Economic Policy Institute. Retrieved July 25, 2017, from www.epi.org/files/2014/EPI-Immigration-Facts-08-12-2014.pdf

Cramer, E. D., & Bennett, K. D. (2015). Implementing culturally responsive positive behavior interventions and supports in middle school classrooms. *Middle School Journal, 46*(3), 18–24. doi:10.1080/00940771.2015.11461911

Crawford, J. (2004). *No Child Left Behind: Misguided approach to school accountability for English language learners.* Session presented at the annual meeting of the National Association for Bilingual Education, San Antonio, TX.

Crawford, J., & Impara, J. C. (2001). Critical issues, current trends, and possible futures in quantitative methods. In V. Richardson (Ed.), *Handbook of research on teaching* (4th ed., pp. 133–173). Washington, DC: American Educational Research Association.

Critchlow, D. E. (1996). *Dos Amigos verbal language scales.* Novato, CA: Academic Therapy Publications.

Crowley, C. J. (2011, July). *Acquiring the skills needed to distinguish disability from difference.* Presentation at the Bilingual Therapies Spanish Speech-Language Pathology Symposium, San Juan, Puerto Rico.

Cuéllar, I., Arnold, B., & Maldonado, R. (1995). Acculturation Rating Scale for Mexican Americans—II: A revision of the original ARSMA scale. *Hispanic Journal of Behavioral Sciences, 17*(3), 275–304.

Cummins, J. (1981). The role of primary language development in promoting educational success for language minority students. In C. F. Leyba (Ed.), *Schooling and language minority students: A theoretical framework* (pp. 3–49). Los Angeles: Evaluation, Dissemination and Assessment Center, CSULA.

Cummins, J. (1984). *Bilingualism and special education: Issues in assessment and pedagogy.* Clevedon, UK: Multilingual Matters.

Cummins, J. (1996). *Negotiating identities: Education for empowerment in a diverse society.* Los Angeles: California Association for Bilingual Education.

Cummins, J. (2001). *Language, power, and pedagogy: Bilingual children in the crossfire.* Philadelphia: Multicultural Matters.

Cushner, K., McClelland, A., & Safford, P. (2012). *Human diversity in education: An intercultural approach* (7th ed.). New York: McGraw-Hill.

Custodio, B., & O'Loughlin, J. B. (2017). *Students with interrupted formal education: Bridging where they are and what they need.* Thousand Oaks, CA: Corwin.

Datnow, A., Choi, B., Park, V. & St. John, E. (2018). Teacher talk about student ability and achievement in the era of data-driven decision making. *Teachers College Record, 120*(4).

Davis, M. H., & Ponnamperuma, G. G. (2005). Portfolio assessment. *Journal of Veterinary Medical Education, 32*(3), 279–284. doi: 10.3138/jvme.32.3.279

de Valenzuela, J. S., Bird, E. K., Parkington, K., Mirenda, P., Cain, K., MacLeod, A. A., & Segers, E. (2016). Access to opportunities for bilingualism for individuals with developmental disabilities: Key informant interviews. *Journal of Communication Disorders, 63*, 32–46. doi:10.1016/j.jcomdis.2016.05.005.

De Valenzuela, J. S., Copeland, S. R., Qi, C. H., & Park, M. (2006). Examining educational equity: Revisiting the disproportionate representation of minority students in special education. *Exceptional Children, 72*(4), 425–441.

Dearnley, C. A., & Meddings, F. S. (2007). Student self-assessment and its impact on learning—A pilot study. *Nurse Education Today, 27*(4), 333–340. doi:10.1016/j.nedt.2006.05.014

Denne-Bolton, S. (2013). The dialogue journal: A tool for building better writers. *English Teaching Forum, 51*(2), 2–11. Retrieved from http://search.ebscohost.com/login.aspx?direct=true&db=eft&AN=123510082&site=ehost-live

Diaz-Rico, L. T., & Weed, K. Z. (2006). *The cross-cultural, language, and academic development handbook: A complete K–12 reference guide* (3rd ed.). Boston: Allyn and Bacon.

Dixon Rayle, A., & Myers, J. E. (2004). Wellness in adolescence: The roles of ethnic identity, acculturation, and mattering. *Professional School Counseling, 8*, 81–90.

Duncan, S. E., & DeAvila, E. A. (1990). *Language Assessment Scales.* Monterey, CA: CTB/ McGraw-Hill.

Duncan, S. E., & DeAvila, E. A. (1998). *Pre-Language Assessment Scale 2000.* Monterey, CA: CTB/ McGraw-Hill.

Durgunoglu, A. Y., Nagy, W. E., & Hancin-Bhatt, B. J. (1993). Cross-language transfer of phonological awareness. *Journal of Educational Psychology, 85*(3), 453–465.

Durkheim, E. (1951). *Suicide* (J. A. Spaulding & G. Simpson, Trans.). New York: Free Press. (Original work published 1897)

Echevarria, J., & Hasbrouck, J. (2009). *Response to intervention and English learners.* Center for Research on the Educational Achievement and Teaching of English Language Learners (CREATE) Brief. Retrieved January 17, 2012, from www.cal.org/create/resources/pubs/responsetointerv.html

Echevarria, J., & Vogt, M. (2010). *Response to intervention (RTI) and English learners: Making it happen.* Boston: Allyn and Bacon.

Echevarria, J., Vogt, M., & Short, D. J. (2004). *Making content comprehensible for English language learners: The SIOP model* (2nd ed.). Boston: Allyn and Bacon.

Educational Testing Service (ETS). (2003). *Linking classroom assessment with student learning.* Princeton, NJ: Author.

Edwards, R., & Ortega, F. (2016). *The economic impacts of removing unauthorized immigrant workers: An industry- and state-level analysis.* Washington, DC: Center for American Progress. Available at www.americanprogress.org

Engel, G. (1977). The need for a new medical model: A challenge to biomedicine. *Science, 196*(4286), 129–136.

Escamilla, K. (1999). The false dichotomy between ESL and transitional bilingual education programs: Issues that challenge all of us. *Educational Considerations, 26*(2), 1–6.

Esparza, P., & Sánchez, B. (2008). The role of attitudinal familism in academic outcomes: A study of urban, Latino high school seniors. *Cultural Diversity and Ethnic Minority Psychology, 14*(3), 193–200. doi:10.1037/1099-9809.14.3.193

Fenk-Oczlon, G., & Fenk, A. (2014). Complexity trade-offs do not prove the equal complexity hypothesis. *Poznan Studies in Contemporary Linguistics, 50*(2). doi:10.1515/psicl-2014-0010

Figueroa, R., & Newsome, J. (2006). The diagnosis of LD in English learners: Is it nondiscriminatory? *Journal of Learning Disabilities, 39*, 206–214.

Finn, J. D. (1982). Patterns in special education placement as revealed by the OCR surveys. In K. A. Heller, W. H. Holtzman, & S. Messick (Eds.), *Placing children in special education: A strategy for equity* (pp. 322–381). Washington, DC: National Academy Press.

Fix, M., Passel, J. S., & Ruiz-de-Velasco, J. (2004). *School reform: The demographic imperative and challenge.* Paper presented at the IZA/Urban Institute Workshop on Migration, Washington, DC. Retrieved January 10, 2012, from www.iza.org/conference_files/iza_ui_2004/fix.pdf

Fletcher, J. M., & Vaughn, S. (2009). Response to intervention: Preventing and remediating academic difficulties. *Child Development Perspectives, 3*(1), 30–37.

Fletcher, T. V., & Navarrete, L. A. (2003, Fall). Learning disabilities or difference: A critical look at issues associated with the misidentification and placement of Hispanic students in special education programs. *Rural Special Education Quarterly, 22*(4): 37–46.

Ford, D. Y. (1998). The underrepresentation of minority students in gifted education: Problems and promises in recruitment and retention. *Journal of Special Education, 32*(1), 4–14.

Ford, D. Y., & Harris, J. J., III. (1998). *Multicultural gifted education.* New York: Teachers College Press.

Freeman, D. E., & Freeman, Y. S. (2014). *Essential linguistics: What teachers need to know to teach.* Portsmouth, NH: Heinemann.

Fuchs, D., & Deshler, D. D. (2007). What we need to know about responsiveness to intervention (and shouldn't be afraid to ask). *Learning Disabilities Research & Practice, 22*(2), 129–136.

Fuchs, D., Mock, D., Morgan, P. L., & Young, C. (2003). Responsiveness to intervention: Definitions, evidence, and implications for the learning disabilities construct. *Learning Disabilities Research and Practice, 18*(3), 157–171.

Fuchs, L. S. (2004). The past, present, and future of curriculum-based measurement research. *School Psychology Review, 33*(2), 188–192.

Gámez, P. B., & González, D. (2017). A comparison of narrative skill in Spanish-English bilinguals and their functionally monolingual Spanish-speaking and English-only peers. *International Journal of Bilingualism.* doi:10.1177/1367006917728391

Gándara, P., Rumberger, R. W., Maxwell-Jolly, J., & Callahan, R. (2003). English learners in California schools: Unequal resources, unequal outcomes. *Educational Policy Analysis Archives, 11.* Available at http://epaa.asu.edu/epaa/v11n36/

García, O., Ibarra Johnson, S., & Seltzer, K. (2017). *The translanguaging classroom: Leveraging student bilingualism for learning.* Philadelphia, PA: Caslon.

Garriott, P. O., Raque-Bogdan, T. L., Zoma, L., Mackie-Hernandez, D., & Lavin, K. (2016). Social cognitive predictors of Mexican American high school students' math/science career goals. *Journal of Career Development, 44*(1), 77–90. doi:10.1177/0894845316633860

Gates, M. L. & Hutchinson, K. (2005, April). *Cultural competence education and the need to reject cultural neutrality: The importance of what we teach and do not teach about culture.* Paper presented at the College of Education, Criminal Justice, and Human Services (CECH) Spring Research Conference, University of Cincinnati, OH.

Germán, M., Gonzales, N. A., & Dumka, L. (2009). Familism values as a protective factor for Mexican-origin adolescents exposed to deviant peers. *Journal of Early Adolescence, 29*(1), 16–42.

Gim Chung, R. H., Kim, B. S., & Abreu, J. M. (2004). Asian American Multidimensional Acculturation Scale: Development, factor analysis, reliability, and validity. *Cultural Diversity and Ethnic Minority Psychology, 10*(1), 66–80. doi:10.1037/1099-9809.10.1.66

Glaser, R. & Silver, E. (1994). Assessment, testing, and instruction: Retrospect and prospect. In L. Darling-Hammond (Ed.), *Review of research in education* (Vol. 20, pp. 393–419), p. 22.

Goffreda, C. T., & DiPerna, J. C. (2010). An empirical review of psychometric evidence for the Dynamic Indicators of Basic Early Literacy Skills. *School Psychology Review, 39*(3), 463–483. Retrieved June 11, 2018, from http://rachaelrobinsonedsi.wiki.westg

Goldenberg, C. (2008, Summer). Teaching English language learners: What the research does—and does not—say. *American Educator, 32*(2) 8–44.

Goldenberg, C., & Wagner, K. (2015, Fall). Bilingual education: Reviving an American tradition. *American Educator, 39*(3), 28–32, 44.

Gonzalez, R., Pagan, M., Wendell, L., & Love, C. (2011). *Supporting ELL/culturally and linguistically diverse students for academic achievement.* New York: International Center for Leadership in Education.

Good, R. H., & Kaminski, R. A. (Eds.). (2002). *Dynamic Indicators of Basic Early Literacy Skills* (6th ed.). Eugene, OR: Institute for Development of Educational Achievement.

Goodnough, A. (1999, December 9). New York City teachers nabbed in school-test cheating scandal. *National Post,* p. B1.

Goodyear, R. K., Newcomb, M. D., & Locke, T. F. (2002). Pregnant Latina teenagers: Psychosocial and developmental determinants of how they select and perceive the men who father their children. *Journal of Counseling Psychology, 49*(2), 187–201.

Gutierrez-Clellan, V. F., & Quinn, R. (1993). Assessing narratives of children from diverse cultural/linguistic groups. *Language, Speech, and Hearing Services in Schools, 24*(1), 2–9.

Hakuta, K. (1987). Degree of bilingualism and cognitive ability in mainland Puerto Rican children. *Child Development, 58,* 1372–1388.

Hale, J., Alfonso, V., Berninger, V., Bracken, B., Christo, C., Clark, E., . . . Yalof, J. (2010). Critical issues in response-to-intervention, comprehensive evaluation, and specific learning disabilities identification and intervention: An expert white paper consensus. *Learning Disability Quarterly, 33*(3), 223–236.

Hamayan, E. V., & Damico, J. S. (Eds.). (1991). *Limiting bias in the assessment of bilingual students.* Austin, TX: PRO-ED.

Hamayan, E., Marler, B., Sánchez-López, C., & Damico, J. (2014). *Special education considerations for English language learners: Delivering a continuum of services* (2nd ed.). Philadelphia, PA: Caslon.

Hancock, C. R. (1994). Alternative assessment and second language study: What and why? *ERIC Digest.* Retrieved January 11, 2012, from www.cal.org/resources/digest/hancoc01.html

Harcourt Assessment. (2003). *Stanford English Language Proficiency (SELP) Test.* San Antonio, TX: Author.

Harper-Young, K. (2018). *The impact of progress monitoring structures on student achievement* (Unpublished doctoral dissertation). National Louis University, Chicago. Retrieved from https://digital-commons.nl.edu/diss/301

Hart, B., & Risley, T. R. (2005). The early catastrophe: The 30 million word gap. *American Educator, 27*(1), 4–9.

Headden, S. (2014). *Beginners in the classroom: What the changing demographics of teaching mean for schools, students, and society.* Stanford, CA: Carnegie Foundation for the Advancement of Teaching.

Hendershot, C. S., MacPherson, L., Myers, M. G., Carr, L. G., & Wall, T. L. (2005). Psychosocial, cultural and genetic influences on alcohol use in Asian American youth. *Journal of Studies on Alcohol, 66*(2), 185–195.

Herrera, S. (2001). *Classroom strategies for the English language learner: A practical guide for accelerating language and literacy development.* Manhattan, KS: The MASTER Teacher.

Herrera, S. (2010). *Biography-driven culturally responsive teaching* (2nd ed). New York: Teachers College Press.

Herrera, S. G. (2016). *Biography-driven culturally responsive teaching* (2nd ed.). New York: Teachers College Press.

Herrera, S. G., Kavimandan, S. K., & Holmes, M. A. (2011). *Crossing the vocabulary bridge: Differentiated strategies for diverse secondary classrooms.* New York: Teachers College Press.

Herrera, S. G., Kavimandan, S. K., Perez, D. R., & Wessels, S. (2017). *Accelerating literacy for diverse learners: Classroom strategies that integrate social/emotional engagement and academic achievement, K–8.* New York: Teachers College Press.

Herrera, S., & Murry, K. (2006). *Accountability by assumption: Implications of reform agendas for teacher preparation. Journal of Latinos and Education, 5*(3), 189–207.

Herrera, S. G., & Murry, K. (2016). *Mastering ESL/EFL methods: Differentiated instruction for culturally and linguistically diverse students* (3rd ed.). Boston: Pearson.

Heubert, J. (2009). *High-stakes testing: Opportunities and risks for students of color, English-language learners, and students with disabilities* (Policy Issues Report 00-02). Baltimore, MD: Sar Levitan Center for Social Policy Studies.

Hiebert, E. H., Stewart, J. D., & Uzicanin, M. (2010, July). *A comparison of word features affecting word recognition of at-risk beginning readers and their peers.* Paper presented at the annual meeting of the Society for the Scientific Study of Reading, Berlin.

Hopkins, M., Lowenhaupt, R., & Sweet, T. M. (2015). Organizing English learner instruction in new immigrant destinations: District infrastructure and subject-specific school practice. *American Educational Research Journal, 52*(3), 408–439.

Hosp, J. L., & Reschly, D. J. (2004). Disproportionate representation of minority students in special education: Academic, demographic, and economic predictors. *Exceptional Children, 70*(2), 185–199.

Hosp, M. K., & Hosp, J. (2003). Curriculum-based measurement for reading, spelling, and math: How to do it and why. *Preventing School Failure, 48*(1), 10–17.

Hosp, M. K., Hosp, J. L., & Howell, K. W. (2016). CBM for assessment and problem solving. In *The ABCs of CBM: A practical guide to curriculum-based measurement* (2nd ed.). New York: Guilford Press.

Huang, J., Clarke, K., Milczarski, E., & Raby, C. (2011). The assessment of English language learners with learning disabilities: Issues, concerns, and implications. *Education, 131*(4), 732–739. Retrieved from https://tep-547-548-wrodgers-fall1-2011.wikispaces.com/file/view/6s8.pdf

Immordino-Yang, M. H., & Faeth, M. (2010). The role of emotion and skilled intuition in learning. In D. A. Sousa (Ed.), *Mind, brain, and education: Neuroscience implications for the classroom* (pp. 69–83). Bloomington, IN: Solution Tree Press.

Indiana Department of Education. (2005). *Best practices: The use of native language during instructional & non-instructional time.* Retrieved August 26, 2005, from www.doe.state.in.us/lmmp/pdf/ native_language_use.pdf

Individuals with Disabilities Act (IDEA) Amendments of 1997. (1997).

Individuals with Disabilities Education Improvement Act of 2004, Pub. L. No. 108–446, §101. Retrieved on January 11, 2012, from www.copyright.gov /legislation/pl108-446.pdf

Jarrett, K. M. (2011). *The influences of acculturation, marianismo and ethnic identity on sexual activity among Latina adolescents* (Doctoral dissertation, Marquette University. Retrieved January 29, 2018, from http://epublications.marquette.edu /dissertations_mu/93

Jensen, E. (2000). *Brain-based learning* (Rev. ed.). San Diego: The Brain Store.

Jensen, E., & Nickelsen, L. (2008). *Deeper learning: 7 powerful strategies for in-depth and longer-lasting learning*. Thousand Oaks, CA: Corwin Press.

Jensen, L. A., Arnett, J. J., & McKenzie J. (2011). Globalization and cultural identity. In S. J. Schwartz, K. Luyckx, & V. L. Vignoles (Eds.), *Handbook of identity theory and research* (pp. 285–301). New York NY: Springer. doi:10.1007/978-1-4419-7988-9_13

Jiang, Y. (2014). Exploring questioning as a formative assessment strategy. *RELC Journal, 45*(3), 287–304. doi:10.1177/0033688214546962

Johnston, P., & Afflerbach, P. (2015, September 17). Formative assessment used to its greatest advantage. *Literacy Daily*. Retrieved from https://www.literacy worldwide.org/blog/literacy-daily/2015/09/17/ formative-assessment-used-to-its-greatest-advantage

Juffer, K. A. (1983). Culture shock: A theoretical framework for understanding adaptation. In J. Bransford (Ed.), *BUENO Center for Multicultural Education Monograph Series* (Vol. 4, No. 1). Boulder: University of Colorado.

Kameenui, E., & Carnine, D. (1998). *Effective teaching strategies that accommodate diverse learners*. Upper Saddle River, NJ: Prentice Hall.

Kaplan, R. (2005). Contrastive rhetoric. In E. Hinkel (Ed.), *Handbook of research in second language teaching and learning* (pp. 375–391). Mahwah, NJ: Lawrence Erlbaum.

Kaur, H., & Hashim, C. N. (2014). The use of wait-time in questioning during reading comprehension lessons by secondary school teachers in Selangor. *International Journal of Education and Social Science, 1*(3), 70–76. Retrieved from http://www .ijessnet.com/wp-content/uploads/2014/10/8.pdf

Kayser, H. (1998) Educating Latino Preschool Children, San Diego: Plural

Kayser, H. (2008). *Educating Latino preschool children*. San Diego: Plural Publishing.

Kingsley, T., & Tancock, S. (2014). Internet inquiry. *Reading Teacher, 67*(5), 389–399. doi:10.1002/trtr.1223

Klingner, J. K., Artiles, A. J., & Barletta, L. M. (2004, November). *English language learners who struggle with reading: Language acquisition or learning disabilities*. Paper presented at NCCREST's national research conference, English Language Learners Struggling to Learn: Emergent Research on Linguistic Differences and Learning Disabilities, Scottsdale, AZ.

Klingner, J., Hoover, J., & Baca, L. (2008). *Why do English language learners struggle with reading? Distinguishing language acquisition from learning disabilities*. Thousand Oaks, CA: Corwin Press.

Krashen, S. (1982). *Principles and practice in second language acquisition*. Oxford, UK: Pergamon Press.

Krashen, S. (1996). *Under attack: The case against bilingual education*. Culver City, CA: Language Education Associates.

Krashen, S. (2000). *Has whole language failed?* University of Southern California Rossier School of Education. Retrieved on January 11, 2012, from www .usc.edu/dept/education/CMMR/text/Krashen_ WholeLang.html

Krashen, S. D. (1984/2005). Bilingual education and second language acquisition theory. In C. F. Leyba, *Schooling and language minority students: A theoretico-practical framework* (3rd ed., pp. 47–75). Los Angeles: Legal Books. (Original work published 1984)

Krashen, S. D., & Terrell, T. (1983). *The natural approach: Language acquisition in the classroom*. Oxford, UK: Pergamon.

Kulis, S., Napoli, M., & Marsiglia, F. F. (2002). Ethnic pride, biculturalism, and drug use norms of urban American Indian adolescents. *Social Work Research, 26*(2), 101–112.

Kuo, L., Uchikoshi, Y., Kim, T., & Yang, X. (2016). Bilingualism and phonological awareness: Re-examining theories of cross-language transfer and structural sensitivity. *Contemporary Educational Psychology, 46*, 1–9. doi:10.1016/j.cedpsych.2016.03.002

Landale, N., Thomas, K., & Van Hook, J. (2011). The living arrangements of children of immigrants. *The Future of Children, 21*(1), 44–70.

Landrine, H., & Klonoff, E. A. (1994). The African American Acculturation Scale: Development, reliability, and validity. *Journal of Black Psychology, 20*(2), 104–127.

Lara, J., & August, D. (1996). *Systemic reform and limited English proficient students*. Washington, DC: Council of Chief State School Officers, and Stanford, CA: Stanford Working Group.

Learning and Teaching Coordinators Network. (2016). *Personalising feedback to support student research and enquiry across the disciplines*. Retrieved from https://nanopdf.com/download/personalising-feedback-to-support-student-research-and-enquiry_pdf

Lewis, L., & Gray, L. (2016). *Programs and services for high school English learners in public school districts: 2015–16* (NCES 2016-150). Washington, DC: National Center for Education Statistics. Retrieved August 4, 2017, from https://nces.ed.gov/pubs2016/2016150.pdf

Lewis, T. J., & Jungman, R. E. (Eds.). (1986). *On being foreign: Culture shock in short fiction, an international anthology.* Yarmouth, ME: Intercultural Press.

Linn, R. L., & Miller, M. D. (2005). *Measurement and assessment in teaching* (9th ed.). Upper Saddle River, NJ: Prentice Hall.

Loretan, S., & Lenica, J. (1993). *Bob the snowman.* New York: Scholastic.

Lovett, M. C. (2013). Making exams worth more than the grade. In M. Kaplan, N. Silver, D. LaVaque-Manty, & D. Meizlish (Eds.), *Using reflection and metacognition to improve student learning: Across the disciplines, across the academy* (pp. 18–48). Sterling, VA: Stylus.

Luo, Y. C. (2014). Concurrent and longitudinal cross-linguistic transfer of phonological awareness and morphological awareness in Chinese-English bilingual children. *Written Language and Literacy, 17*(1), 89–115. doi:10.1075/wll.17.1.05luo

Lurie, N. O. (1991). The American Indian: Historical background. In N. R. Yetman (Ed.), *Majority and minority: The dynamics of race and ethnicity in American life* (pp. 132–145). Boston: Allyn & Bacon.

MacSwan, J., Rolstad, K., & Glass, G. V. (2002). Do some school-age children have no language? Some problems of construct validity in the Pre-LAS Español. *Bilingual Research Journal, 26*(2), 213–238.

Maldonado, J. A. (1994). Bilingual special education: Specific learning disabilities in language and reading. *Journal of Educational Issues of Language Minority Students, 14,* 127–147.

Marin, G., & Gamba, R. J. (1996). A new measurement of acculturation for Hispanics: The bidimensional acculturation scale for Hispanics (BAS). *Hispanic Journal of Behavioral Sciences, 18*(3), 297–316.

Marinova-Todd, S. H., Colozzo, P., Mirenda, P., Stahl, H., Kay-Raining Bird, E., Parkington, K., . . . Genesee, F. (2016). Professional practices and opinions about services available to bilingual children with developmental disabilities: An international study. *Journal of Communication Disorders, 63,* 47–62. doi:10.1016/j.jcomdis.2016.05.004.

Martin, P. C. (2016). Text-based education for students with disabilities and English language learners: The impact of assessment pressures on educational planning. *Teachers College Record, 118*(14).

Marzano, R. J. (2004). *Building background knowledge for academic achievement: Research on what works in schools.* Alexandria, VA: Association for Supervision and Curriculum Development.

Maslow, A. H. (1943). A theory of human motivation. *Psychological Review, 50*(4), 370–396.

Maslow, A. H. (1970). *Motivation and personality.* New York: Harper & Row.

Masters, G. N. (2013). Reforming educational assessment: Imperatives, principles and challenges. In S. Mellor (Series Ed.). *Australian Education Review, 57.* Melbourne, Australia: ACER Press. Retrieved from https://research.acer.edu.au/cgi/viewcontent.cgi?article=1021&context=aer

Mather, M. (2009). *Children in immigrant families chart new path.* Washington, DC: Population Reference Bureau.

Mattes, L. J., & Nguyen, L. (1996). *Bilingual Language Proficiency Questionnaire: English/Vietnamese edition.* Oceanside, CA: Academic Communication Associates.

Mattes, L. J., & Santiago, G. (1985). *Bilingual Language Proficiency Questionnaire: English/Spanish edition.* Oceanside, CA: Academic Communication Associates.

Matthews, T., & Kostelis, K. (2009). *Prevalence and perceived impact of authentic assessment.* Retrieved from aahperd.confex.com/aahperd/2009/.../Kostelis_Matthews.pdf

Maxwell, L. A. (2014, August 19). U.S. school enrollment hits majority-minority milestone. *Education Week.* Retrieved August 3, 2017, from www.edweek.org/ew/articles/2014/08/20/01demographics.h34.html

McGlinchey, M. T., & Hixson, M. D. (2004). Using curriculum-based measurement to predict performance on state assessments in reading. *School Psychology Review, 33,* 193–203.

Millard, M. (2015). *State funding mechanisms for English language learners.* Denver, CO: Education Commission of the States. Retrieved August 3, 2017, from www.ecs.org/clearinghouse/01/16/94/11694.pdf

Millis, B. J. (2016). *Using metacognition to promote learning.* IDEA Paper #63. Manhattan, KS: IDEA. Retrieved from https://www.ideaedu.org/Portals/0/Uploads/Documents/IDEA%20Papers/IDEA%20Papers/PaperIDEA_63.pdf

Missouri National Education Association. (2011). *Teacher-made tests.* Retrieved from https://www.mnea.org/Missouri/TeachingTips1/4.aspx

Mitchell, C. (2016, December 7). Majority of English-learner students are born in the United States, analysis finds. *Education Week*, Learning the Language blog. Retrieved August 4, 2017, from http://blogs.edweek.org/edweek/learning-the-language/2016/12/majority_of_english-learner_students_are_born_in_the_united_states.html

Molix, L., & Bettencourt, B. A. (2010). Predicting well-being among ethnic minorities: Psychological empowerment and group identity. *Journal of Applied Social Psychology, 40*(3), 513-533. doi: 10.1111/j.1559-1816.2010.00585

Moll, L. C., Armanti, C., Neff, D., & Gonzalez, N. (1992). Funds of knowledge for teaching: Using a qualitative approach to connect homes and classrooms. *Theory into Practice, 31*(2), 132–141.

Mondy, S. (2007). *The acculturation model: A look into socio/psycho perspectives of SLA*. Retrieved January 17, 2018, from http://www.osk-ymca-intl.ed.jp/users/smondy/The%20Acculturation%20Model%20A%20look%20into%20Socio:Psycho%20perspectives%20of%20SLA.pdf

Morgan, P. L., Farkas, G., Cook, M., Strassfeld, N. M., Hillemeier, M. M., Pun, W. H., . . . Schussler, D. L. (2018). Are Hispanic, Asian, Native American, or language-minority children overrepresented in special education? *Exceptional Children, 84*(3), 261–279. doi:10.1177/0014402917748303.

Morgan, P. L., Farkas, G., Hillemeier, M. M., & Maczuga, S. (2017). Replicated evidence of racial and ethnic disparities in disability identification in U.S. schools. *Educational Researcher, 46*(6), 305–322. doi:10.3102/0013189x17726282.

Mossaad, N. (2016). *Refugees and asylees: 2015*. Washington, DC: Office of Immigration Statistics. Retrieved August 3, 2017, from www.dhs.gov/sites/default/files/publications/Refugees_Asylees_2015.pdf

Muñoz-Sandoval, A. F., Cummins, J., Alvaredo, C. G., Ruef, M., & Schrank, F. A. (2005). *Bilingual Verbal Ability Tests Normative Update (BVAT-NU)*. Itasca, IL: Riverside.

Mueller, J. (2011). *Assessing critical skills*. Santa Barbara, CA: Linworth.

Murry, K., Herrera, S., Miller, S., Fanning, C., Kavimandan, S., & Holmes, M. (2015). Effect of transnational standards on U.S. teacher education. *Forum for International Research in Education, 1*(3), 41–63.

Musu-Gillette, L., Robinson, J., McFarland, J., KewalRamani, A., Zhang, A., & Wilkinson-Flicker, S. (2016). *Status and trends in the education of racial and ethnic groups 2016* (NCES 2016-007). Washington, DC: U.S. Department of Education, National Center for Education Statistics. Retrieved August 4, 2017, from https://nces.ed.gov/pubs2016/2016007.pdf

National Academies of Sciences, Engineering, and Medicine. (2017). *The economic and fiscal consequences of immigration*. Washington, DC: The National Academies Press. doi: https://doi.org/10.17226/23550

National Center for Education Evaluation and Regional Assistance. (2014). *Building teacher capacity to support English language learners in schools receiving school improvement grants*. Washington, DC: Institute of Education Sciences.

National Center for Education Statistics (2016). *The condition of education 2016* (NCES 2016-144). Washington, DC: U.S. Department of Education.

National Center for Education Statistics. (2015). National Assessment of Educational Progress (NAEP), 2015 Mathematics and Reading Assessments. Washington, DC: U.S. Department of Education, Institute of Education Sciences.

National Center on Response to Intervention. (2010, March). *Essential components of RTI—A closer look at response to intervention*. Washington, DC: U.S. Department of Education, Office of Special Education Programs, Author.

National Education Association. (n.d.). *Understanding the gaps: Who are we leaving behind—and how far?* Washington, DC: Author. Retrieved August 4, 2017, from www.nea.org/assets/docs/18021-Closing_Achve_Gap_backgrndr_7-FINAL.pdf

National Staff Development Council (NSDC). (2009). *Professional learning in the learning profession: A status report on teacher development in the United States and abroad*. Dallas, TX: Author. Retrieved on January 11, 2012, from www.learningforward.org/news/NSDCstudy2009.pdf

Neil, S. (2010). A child is not a test score: Assessment as a civil rights issue. *Root and Branch, II*(2), 29–35.

Neuenschwander, R., Röthlisberger, M., Cimeli, P., & Roebers, C. M. (2012). How do different aspects of self-regulation predict successful adaptation to school? *Journal of Experimental Child Psychology, 113*(3), 353–371. Retrieved from https://doi.org/10.1016/j.jecp.2012.07.004

New American Economy. (2017). *Not lost in translation: The growing importance of foreign language skills in the U.S. job market*. New York: Author. Retrieved

July 25, 2017, from http://www.newamericaneconomy.org/wp-content/uploads/2017/03/NAE_Bilingual_V9.pdf

New York State Education Department. (2002). *Key issues in bilingual special education work paper #5.* Retrieved November 12, 2002, from www. vesid.nysed.gov/lsn/bilingual/trainingmodules 05rr.pdf

Nicolaidou, I. (2013). E-portfolios supporting primary students' writing performance and peer feedback. *Computers & Education, 68,* 404–415. doi:10.1016/j.compedu.2013.06.004

Numeroff, L. (1985). *If you give a mouse a cookie.* New York: HarperCollins Children's Books.

Office of English Language Acquisition (2015). *English learners (ELS) and NAEP* (OLEA Fast Facts). Washington, DC: Author. Retrieved from https://www2.ed.gov/about/offices/list/oela/fast-facts/elnaep.pdf

Ojalvo, H. (2010). *Teacher Q: How has NCLB affected your teaching?* Retrieved from http://learning.blogs.nytimes.com/2010/02/05/teacher-q-how-would-you-reform-nclb/

Olah, L. N. (n.d.). *Every teacher a language teacher* (Penn GSE: Review of Research). Retrieved on January 11, 2012, from www.gse.upenn.edu/node/575

Ortiz, A. A. (2004 September). *Language acquisition and assessment: Distinguishing differences from disabilities for English language learners.* Session presented at Getting It Right: Improving Education for English Language Learners with Special Needs Workshop, Emporia State University, Emporia, Kansas.

Ortiz, A., Wilkinson, C., Robertson-Courtney, P., & Kushner, M. (2006). Considerations in implementing intervention assistance teams to support English language learners. *Remedial and Special Education, 27*(1), 53–63.

Ortiz, S. O. (2008). Best practices in nondiscriminatory assessment. In A. Thomas & J. Grimes (Eds.), *Best practices in school psychology V* (pp. 666–678). Bethesda, MD: National Association of School Psychologists.

Oswald, D. P., Coutinho, M. J., Best, A. M., & Singh, N. N. (1999). Ethnic representation in special education: The influence of school-related economic and demographic variables. *Journal of Special Education, 32*(3), 194–206.

Ovando, C. J., & Combs, M. C. (2018). *Bilingual and ESL classrooms: Teaching in multicultural contexts* (6th ed.). Lanham, MD: Rowman & Littlefield.

Overton, T., Fielding, C., & Simonsson, M. (2004). Decision making in determining eligibility of culturally and linguistically diverse learners: Reasons given by assessment personnel. *Journal of Learning Disabilities, 37*(4), 319–330.

Passel, J. S. (2011). Demography of immigrant youth: Past, present, and future. *The Future of Children, 21*(1), 19–41.

Paul, A. M. (2015, August 1). Researchers find that frequent tests can boost learning. *Scientific American.* Retrieved from https://www.scientificamerican.com/article/researchers-find-that-frequent-tests-can-boost-learning/

Pew Charitable Trusts. (2014). *Changing patterns in U.S. immigration and population: Immigrants slow population decline in many counties.* Philadelphia, PA: Author.

Pew Research Center. (2017). Key findings about U.S. immigrants. Washington, DC: Author. Retrieved July 31, 2017, from www.pewresearch.org/fact-tank/2017/05/03/key-findings-about-u-s-immigrants/

Proctor, B. D., & Dalaker, J. (2002). *Poverty in the United States: 2001* (Current Population Reports P60-219). Washington, DC: US Census Bureau. Retrieved on January 11, 2012, from www.census.gov/prod/2002pubs/p60-219.pdf

Ramírez, J. D., Yuen, S. D., Ramey, D. R., & Pasta, D. J. (1991). *Final report: Longitudinal study of structured English immersion strategy, early-exit and late-exit transitional bilingual education programs for language-minority children* (Vols. I and II). San Mateo, CA: Aguirre International.

Rangel, R., & Bansberg, B. (1999). *Snapshot Assessment System: An informal tool for classroom teachers for migrant, language-minority, and mobile students. Grades 1–3, 4–6, 7–8.* Aurora, CO: McREL Institute.

Ratcliffe, C., & McKernan, S. (2012). *Child poverty and its lasting consequence.* Washington, DC: Urban Institute. Retrieved August 4, 2017, from www.urban.org/research/publication/child-poverty-and-its-lasting-consequence/view/full_report

Research for Better Teaching (2016). *Using data and formative assessment to drive instruction.* Acton, MA: Author. Retrieved from https://www.siprep.org/uploaded/ProfessionalDevelopment/Minutes/Using_Data_Formative_Assessment_St.Ignatius_MAHS_Oct2016.pdf

Reyes, S., & Vallone, T. (2007). *Constructivist strategies for teaching English language learners.* Thousand Oaks, CA: Corwin Press.

Reynolds, C. R., & Shaywitz, S. E. (2009). Response to intervention: Ready or not? Or, from wait-to-fail to watch-them-fail. *School Psychology Quarterly, 24*(2), 130–145.

Rhodes, R. L., Ochoa, S. H., & Ortiz, S. O. (2005). *Assessing culturally and linguistically diverse students: A practical guide*. Practical Intervention in the Schools Series. New York: Guilford Press.

Rodríguez, A., & Rodríguez, D. (2017). English learners with learning disabilities: What is the current state? *Insights Into Learning Disabilities, 14*(1), 97–112.

Rogers-Sirin, L., Ryce, P., Sirin, S. R. (2014). Acculturation, acculturative stress, and cultural mismatch and their influences on immigrant children and adolescents' well-being. In R. Dimitrova, M. Bender, & F. van de Vijver (Eds.), *Global perspectives on well-being in immigrant families: Advances in immigrant family research* (Vol. 1, pp. 11–30). New York: Springer. doi: 10.1007/978-1-4614-9129-3_2

Rogoff, B. (2014). Learning by observing and pitching in to family and community endeavors: An orientation. *Human Development, 57*(2–3), 69–81.

Romero, A. J., Robinson, T. N., Haydel, K. F., Mendoza, F., & Killen, J. D. (2004). Associations among familism, language preference, and education in Mexican-American mothers and their children. *Journal of Developmental & Behavioral Pediatrics, 25*(1), 34–40.

Roskos, K. A., & Christie, J. F. (2002). "Knowing in the doing": Observing literacy learning in play. *Young Children, 57*(2), 46–54.

Rosner, J. (1993). Helping children overcome learning difficulties (3rd ed). New York: Walker and Company.

Rueda, R., & Windmueller, M. P. (2006). English language learners, LD, and overrepresentation: A multiple-level analysis. *Journal of Learning Disabilities, 39*, 99–107.

Ruiz Soto, A. G., Hooker, S., & Batalova, J. (2015). *Top languages spoken by English language learners nationally and by state*. Washington, DC: Migration Policy Institute. Retrieved August 4, 2017, from www.migrationpolicy.org/research/top-languages-spoken-english-language-learners-nationally-and-state

Ruiz-de-Velasco, J., & Fix, M. (with Clewell, B.). (2000). *Overlooked and underserved: Immigrant students in U.S. secondary schools*. Washington, DC: Urban Institute Press.

Ryder, A. G., Alden, L. E., & Paulhus, D. L. (2000). Is acculturation unidimensional or bidimensional? A head-to-head comparison in the prediction of personality, self-identity, and adjustment. *Journal of Personality and Social Psychology, 79*(1), 49–65. doi:10.1037/0022-3514.79.1.49

Sabatier, C. (2008). Ethnic and national identity among second-generation immigrant adolescents in France: The role of social context and family. *Journal of Adolescence, 31*(2), 185–205.

Sajedi, R. (2014). Self-assessment and portfolio production of Iranian EFL learners. *Social and Behavioral Sciences, 98*, 1641–1649. doi:10.1016/j.sbspro.2014.03.588

Saleebey, D. (2001). *Human behavior and social environments: A biopsychosocial approach*. New York: Columbia University Press.

Salend, S. J. (2005). *Creating inclusive classrooms: Effective and reflective practices for all students* (5th ed.). Upper Saddle River, NJ: Prentice Hall.

Salend, S. J. (2009a). *Classroom testing and assessment for ALL students: Beyond standardization*. Thousand Oaks, CA: Sage.

Salend, S. J. (2009b). Technology-based classroom assessments. *Teaching Exceptional Children, 41*(6), 48–58.

Sanchez, C. (2017). *English language learners: How your state is doing*. New York: NPR. Retrieved August 3, 2017, from www.npr.org/sections/ed/2017/02/23/512451228/5-million-english-language-learners-a-vast-pool-of-talent-at-risk?utm_source=facebook.com&utm_medium=social&utm_campaign=npr&utm_term=nprnews&utm_content=20170223

Sanford, A. K., Brown, J. E., & Turner, M. (2012). Enhancing instruction for English learners in response to intervention systems: The PLUSS model. *Multiple Voices for Ethnically Diverse Exceptional Learners, 13*(1), 56–70.

Schumann, J. H. (1978). *The Pidgination process: A model for second language acquisition*. Rowley, MA: Newbury House.

Searle, W., & Ward, C. (1990). The prediction of psychological and socio-cultural adjustment during cross-cultural transitions. *International Journal of Intercultural Relations, 14*, 449–464.

Serpa, M. d. L. B. (2011). *An imperative for change: Bridging special and language learning education to ensure a free and appropriate education in the least restrictive environment for ELLs with disabilities in Massachusetts* (Paper 152). Boston: Gastón Institute Publications, University of Massachusetts. Retrieved from http://scholarworks.umb.edu/gaston_pubs/152

Shrake, E. K., & Rhee, S. (2004). Ethnic identity as a predictor of problem behaviors among Korean American adolescents. *Adolescence, 39*, 601–632.

Skiba, R. J., Poloni-Staudinger, L., Simmons, A. B., Feggins-Azziz, L. R., & Chung, C. G. (2005). Unproven links: Can poverty explain ethnic disproportionality in special education? *Journal of Special Education, 39*(3), 130–144.

Skinner, C., Wight, V. R., Aratani, Y., Cooper, J. L., & Thampi, K. (2010). *English language proficiency, family economic security, and child development* (Research Report No. 948). New York: National Center for Children in Poverty.

Smith Bailey, D. (2003). Who is learning disabled? Psychologists and educators debate over how to identify students with learning disabilities. *Monitor on Psychology, 34*(8), 58.

Smyth, T. S. (2008). Who is No Child Left Behind leaving behind? *The Clearing House, 81*(3), 133–137.

Soltero-Gonzalez, L., Escamilla, K., & Hopewell, S. (2012). Changing teachers' perceptions about the writing abilities of emerging bilingual students: Towards a holistic bilingual perspective on writing assessment. *International Journal of Bilingual Education and Bilingualism, 15*(1), 71–94.

Sousa, D. A. (2017). *How the brain learns* (5th ed.). Thousand Oaks, CA: Corwin Press.

Sporleder, J., & Forbes, H. T. (2016). *The trauma-informed school: A step-by-step implementation guide for administrators and school personnel.* Boulder, CO: Beyond Consequences Institute.

Stiggins, R. J. (2002). Assessment crisis: The absence of assessment FOR learning. *Phi Delta Kappan, 83*(10), 758–765. Available at www.kappanmagazine.org /content/83/10/758.abstract

Stiggins, R., & Chappuis, J. (2017). *An introduction to student-involved assessment for learning* (7th ed.). Upper Saddle River, NJ: Pearson-Merrill Prentice Hall.

Stillman, J., Anderson, L., & Struthers, K. (2014). Returning to reciprocity: Using dialogue journals to teach and learn. *Language Arts, 91*(3), 146–160.

Sue, D. W., & Sue, D. (2015). *Counseling the culturally diverse: Theory and practice* (7th ed.). Hoboken, NJ: John Wiley & Sons.

Suinn, R. M., Richard-Figueroa, K., Lew, S., & Vigil, P. (1987). The Suinn-Lew Asian Self-Identity Acculturation Scale: An initial report. *Educational & Psychological Measurement, 47*(2), 401–407.

Sullivan, A. L. (2011). Disproportionality in special education identification and placement of English language learners. *Exceptional Children, 77*(3), 317–334. doi:10.1177/001440291107700304.

Sun, Z. (2012). An empirical study on new teacher-student relationship and questioning strategies in ESL classroom. *English Language Teaching, 5*(7), 175–183. Retrieved from http://dx.doi.org/10.5539/ elt.v5n7p175

Sun-Alperin, M. K., & Wang, M. (2009). Cross-language transfer of phonological and orthographic processing skills from Spanish L1 to English L2. *Reading and Writing, 24*(5), 591–614. doi:10.1007/ s11145-009-9221-7

Szapocznik, J., & Kurtines, W. (1980). Acculturation, biculturism, and adjustment among Cuban Americans. In A. Padilla (Ed.), *Acculturation, theory, models, and new findings* (pp. 139–159). Boulder, CO: Westview Press.

Thomas, W. P., & Collier, V. P. (2002). *A national study of school effectiveness for language minority students' long-term academic achievement.* Santa Cruz, CA: Center for Research on Education, Diversity & Excellence, University California-Santa Cruz.

Thomas, W. P., & Collier, V. P. (2012). *Dual language education for a transformed world.* Albuquerque, NM: Fuente Press.

Thordardottir, E. (2010). Towards evidence-based practice in language intervention for bilingual children. *Journal of Communication Disorders, 43*(6), 523–537. doi: 10.1016/j.jcomdis.2010. 06.001.

Tong, X., He, X., & Deacon, S. H. (2017). Tone matters for Cantonese-English bilingual children's English word reading development: A unified model of phonological transfer. *Memory & Cognition, 45*(2), 320–333. doi:10.3758/s13421-016-0657-0

Trifonovitch, G. (1977). Culture learning—culture teaching. *Educational Perspectives, 16*(4), 18–22.

Turkan, S., & Oliveri, M. E. (2014). Considerations for providing test translation accommodations to English language learners on Common Core Standards-based assessments. *ETS Research Report Series, 2014*(1), 1–13. Retrieved from https://doi .org/10.1002/ets2.12003

U.S. Congress. (1999, March 12). IDEA: Rules and regulations. *Federal Register, 64*(8). Washington, DC: Author.

U.S. Department of Education (USDE). (2016). *Nonregulatory guidance: English learners and Title III of the Elementary and Secondary Education Act (ESEA), as amended by the Every Student Succeeds Act (ESSA).*

U.S. Department of Education (USDE). (2017). *IDEA Part B regulations: Significant disproportionality (Equity in IDEA): Essential questions and answers.* Washington, DC: Office of Special Education Programs, Office of Special Education and Rehabilitative Services. Retrieved from https://sites.ed.gov /idea/files/significant-disproportionality-qa-03-08-17-1.pdf

Umaña-Taylor, A. J. (2011). Ethnic identity. In S. J. Schwartz, K. Luyckx, & V. L. Vignoles (Eds.), *Handbook of identity theory and research* (pp. 791–810). New York: Springer.

Umaña-Taylor, A. J., Wong, J. J., Gonzales, N. A., & Dumka, L. E. (2012). Ethnic identity and gender as moderators of the association between discrimination and academic adjustment among Mexican-origin adolescents. *Journal of Adolescence, 35*(4), 773–786.

Umansky, I. M., Thompson, K. D., & Díaz, G. (2017). Using an ever–English learner framework to examine disproportionality in special education. *Exceptional Children, 84*(1), 76–96. doi:10.1177/ 0014402917707470.

Unger, J. B., Gallaher, P., Shakib, S., Ritt-Olson, A., Palmer, P. H., & Johnson, C. A. (2002). The AHIMSA Acculturation Scale: A new measure of acculturation for adolescents in a multicultural society. *The Journal of Early Adolescence, 22*(3), 225–251. doi:10.1177/02731602022003001

Van Horn, R. (2003). Technology: Computer adaptive tests and computer-based tests. *Phi Delta Kappan, 84*(8), 567, 630.

Vanderheyden, A. M. (2005). Intervention-driven assessment practices in early childhood/early intervention: Measuring what is possible rather than what is present. *Journal of Early Intervention, 28*(1), 28–33. doi:10.1177/105381510502800104

Volante, L. (2004). Teaching to the test: What every educator and policy-maker should know. *Canadian Journal of Educational Administration and Policy, 35.* Retrieved on January 12, 2012, from www.umanitoba.ca/publications/cjeap/articles /volante.html

Vygotsky, L. (1978). *Mind in society.* Cambridge, MA: Harvard University Press.

Walqui, A. W., & Heritage, M. (2012). Instruction for diverse groups of English language learners.

Weisleder, A., & Fernald, A. (2013). Talking to children matters: Early language experience strengthens processing and builds vocabulary. *Psychological Science, 24*(11), 2143–2152. Retrieved from https: //web.stanford.edu/group/langlearninglab/cgi-bin/ publications/WeislederFernald2013.pdf

Wells, A. S., Fox, L., & Cordova-Cobo, D. (2016). *How racially diverse schools and classrooms can benefit all students.* New York: Century Foundation. Retrieved August 3, 2017, from: https://tcf.org /content/report/how-racially-diverse-schools-and-classrooms-can-benefit-all-students/

Wiliam, D. (2004). Working inside the black box: Assessment for learning in the classroom. *Phi Delta Kappan, 86*(1), 8–21.

Wolf, M. K., Herman, J. L., & Dietel, R. (2010). *Improving the validity of English language learner assessment systems* (Policy Brief 10). Los Angeles: National Center for Research on Evaluation, Standards, and Student Testing.

Woodcock, R. W., McGrew, K. S., & Mather, N. (2001). *Woodcock-Johnson III Tests of Achievement.* Itasca, IL: Riverside.

Woodcock, R., Muñoz-Sandoval, A. F., Ruef, M., & Alvaredo, C. G. (2005). *Woodcock-Muñoz Language Survey Revised (WMLS-R).* Itasca, IL: Riverside.

Wright, J. A., & Kersner, M. (2015). *Supporting children with communication problems: Sharing the workload* (4th ed.). New York: Routledge.

Wright, M. O., & Littleford, L. N. (2002). Experiences and beliefs as predictors of ethnic identity and intergroup relations. *Journal of Multicultural Counseling and Development, 30*, 2–20.

Yates, J. R. (1998, April). *The state of practice in the education of CLD students.* Presentation at the annual meeting of the Council for Exceptional Children, Minneapolis, MN.

Yesil-Dagli, U. (2011). Predicting ELL students' beginning first grade English oral reading fluency from initial kindergarten vocabulary, letter naming, and phonological awareness skills. *Early Childhood Research Quarterly, 26*(1), 15–29. doi:10.1016 /j.ecresq.2010.06.001

Yeung, S. S., & Chan, C. K. (2012). Phonological awareness and oral language proficiency in learning to read English among Chinese kindergarten children in Hong Kong. *British Journal of Educational Psychology, 83*(4), 550-568. doi:10.1111/j.2044-8279.2012.02082.x

Yoon, K. S., Duncan T., Lee, S. W.-Y., Scarloss, B., & Shapley, K. L. (2007). *Reviewing the evidence on how teacher professional development affects student achievement.* (Issues & Answers Report, REL 2007–No. 033). Washington, DC: National Center for Education Evaluation and Regional Assistance, Regional Education Laboratory Southwest. Retrieved on January 12, 2012, from http://ies.ed.gov/ncee/edlabs/regions/southwest/pdf/REL_2007033.pdf

Zaker, A. (2016). The acculturation model of second language acquisition: Inspecting weaknesses and strengths. *Indonesian EFL Journal, 2*(2), 80–87.

Zong, J., & Batalova, J. (2017). *Frequently requested statistics on immigrants and immigration in the United States.* Washington, DC: Migration Policy Institute. Retrieved July 31, 2017, from www.migrationpolicy.org/article/frequently-requested-statistics-immigrants-and-immigration-united-states#CurrentHistoricalNumbers

Zubrzycki, J. (2015). Students 'self-assess' their way to learning: Can students learn more by assessing their progress? *Education Week, 35*(12), s12. Retrieved from https://www.edweek.org/ew/articles/2015/11/11/students-self-assess-their-way-to-learning.html

INDEX